The Rise of Oriental Travel

Also by Gerald MacLean

TIME'S WITNESS: Historical Representation in English Poetry, 1603–1660

MATERIALIST FEMINISMS (*with Donna Landry*)

THE RETURN OF THE KING: An Anthology of English Poems Commemorating the Stuart Restoration, 1660 (*editor*)

CULTURE AND SOCIETY IN THE STUART RESTORATION: Literature, Drama, History (*editor*)

THE SPIVAK READER (*co-editor with Donna Landry*)

THE COUNTRY AND THE CITY REVISITED: England and the Politics of Culture, c. 1550–1850 (*co-editor with Donna Landry and Joseph Ward*)

The Rise of Oriental Travel

English Visitors to the Ottoman Empire,
1580–1720

Gerald M. MacLean

First published in hardback 2004
First published in paperback 2006 by
PALGRAVE MACMILLAN
Houndmills, Basingstoke, Hampshire RG21 6XS and
175 Fifth Avenue, New York, N.Y. 10010
Companies and representatives throughout the world

PALGRAVE MACMILLAN is the global academic imprint of the Palgrave
Macmillan division of St. Martin's Press, LLC and of Palgrave Macmillan Ltd.
Macmillan® is a registered trademark in the United States, United Kingdom
and other countries. Palgrave is a registered trademark in the European
Union and other countries.

ISBN-13: 978–0–333–97364–6 hardback
ISBN-10: 0–333–97364–X hardback
ISBN-13: 978–0–230–00326–2 paperback
ISBN-10: 0–230–00326–5 paperback

This book is printed on paper suitable for recycling and made from fully
managed and sustained forest sources.

A catalogue record for this book is available from the British Library.

Library of Congress Cataloging-in-Publication Data
MacLean, Gerald M., 1952–
   The rise of oriental travel : English visitors to the Ottoman Empire,
   1580–1720 / Gerald M. MacLean.
      p.   cm.
   Includes bibliographical references (p.) and index.
   ISBN 0–333–97364–X — 0–230–00326–5 (pbk.)
   1. Turkey—Description and travel.   2. Turkey—Social life and customs.
   I. Title.
DR429.4.M333 2004
915.604′15—dc22   2003063051

10   9   8   7   6   5   4   3   2   1
15   14   13   12   11   10   09   08   07   06

Printed and bound in Great Britain by
Antony Rowe Ltd, Chippenham and Eastbourne

In memory of Bridget and Christopher Hill

Contents

List of Illustrations ix

Prologue xi

The Argument xiii

Preface xv

Note on Texts and Transcriptions xix

Acknowledgements xx

Part I   Dallam's Organ: By Sea to Istanbul, 1599   **1**

1.   Thomas Dallam (c.1575–c.1630) 3
2.   On First Setting Out 7
3.   Mediterranean Encounters 17
4.   Istanbul 33

Part II   Biddulph's Ministry: Travels around
Aleppo, 1600–12   **49**

5.   William Biddulph's Anxiety of Authorship 51
6.   Preacher among the Diplomats 56
7.   Troublesome Travelling Churchmen 66
8.   Journey to Aleppo 78
9.   Biddulph's Lessons from Aleppo 84
10.   Journey to Jerusalem 100

Part III   Blount's *Voyage*: The Ottoman Levant, 1634–36   **115**

11.   Sir Henry Blount, 15 December 1602–9 October 1682 117
12.   On Becoming a Passenger 123
13.   The Sinews of Empire: Venice to Istanbul 142
14.   Ottoman Egypt: African Empire in Ruins 157

Part IV   'T.S.' in Captivity: North African Slavery, 1648–70   **177**

15.   The *Adventures* of 'Mr. T.S.' and Restoration England 179
16.   Captive Agency 183

17. For the Vainglory of Being a 'Traveller'   187
18. Slavery in Algiers   194
19. On Tour with the Ottoman Army   200
20. Tlemcen: Life in a Desert City   212

Epilogue: What About the Women, Then?   221

Notes   226

References   245

Index   254

List of Illustrations

Colour plates

1.   Samson Rowlie, aka Assan Aga. From a German traveller's picture book, c. 1588. Courtesy of The Bodleian Library, University of Oxford (Ms. Bodl. Or. 430, f. 47).

2. & 3.   Portraits of European men by the Ottoman artist known as Levni, c.1720. By courtesy of the Department of Oriental Antiquities, British Museum (BM 1960–11–12–01 and 1960–11–12–02).

4.   Murad III (1574–95), from Lokman's *Kiyafet ül-insaniye fi semail il-osmaniye*. By permission of the British Library (Add Ms 7880, f. 63v).

5.   Mehmed III (1595–1603) added to the *Kiyafet ül-insaniye fi semail il-osmaniye*. By permission of the British Library (Add Ms 7880, f. 67v).

6.   Ahmed I (1603–17). By permission of the British Library (OR Ms 41291, f. 5v).

7.   A Women of Chios, from a rare German edition of Nicholas de Nicolay's *Navigations* published in 1572 with hand-coloured plates by Georg Mack, entitled *Der Erst Theil. Von der Schiffart und Raisz in die Turckey und gegen Orient beschriben durch H. N. Nicolay*. By permission of the British Library (c.55.i.4).

8.   A Delly Warrior; hand-coloured engraving by Georg Mack, as above. By permission of the British Library (from BL c.55.i.4).

9. & 10.   A Zulphaline Christian and his wife, from a seventeenth-century costume book. By permission of the British Library (BL Add Ms 5255, ff. 5 and 8).

11. & 12.   Henry and Hester Blount, artist unknown. By courtesy of John Bonnington, Tittenhanger House, Herts.

13.   Henry Blount by Jacob Huysmans. By courtesy of John Bonnington, Tittenhanger House, Herts.

14.   The Sinan Pasha Mosque, An'nabk, Syria.

15.   Mount Scopos, Zante, Greece.

Black and white plates

16. A 'Curious Musical Instrument', *Illustrated London News* (20 October 1860), p. 380. By permission of the British Library (7611).
17. A Woman of Malta, from the first French edition of Nicolay's *Navigations* (1568). By permission of the British Library (455.e.5).
18. A Calendar, from Nicolay as above. By permission of the British Library (455.e.5).
19. Upstairs corridor, the Khan al-Gümrük, Aleppo souk, Syria.
20. The lower courtyard, Khan al-Gümrük, Aleppo.
21. The Sinan Pasha Khan, An'nabk, Syria.
22. The Murad Pasha Khan, Ma'arret en Nu'man, Syria.
23. The 'Khan of the Bridegroom', Qutaifah, Syria.
24. Remains of the 'Old Castle', Hisyah, Syria.
25. The Khan Haramain, Damascus souk, Syria.
26. Quneitrah, Syria.
27. The House of Ananias, Bab Sharqi area, Damascus.
28. A nineteenth-century engraving of Tittenhanger House, drawn by J.P. Neale and engraved by H. Hobson. By permission of the British Library (BL Add Ms 32350, f. 210).
29. Henry Blount, an engraved portrait 'Published Nov 1st. 1801 by Wm. Richardson York House, 32 Strand'. By permission of the British Library (Add Ms 32350, f. 209).
30. Tittenhanger House from the south-west in 1832, by the topographical artist John Buckler (1770–1851). By permission of the British Library (Add Ms 36367, f. 18).
31. A map of Henry Blount's journey, from *Zee-En Land Voyagie Van den Ridder Hendrik Blunt, Na da Levant*, 1737 edition. By permission of the British Library (BL 566.1.7).
32. Istanbul from the Dardanelles, from *Zee-En Land* as above, by permission of the British Library (BL 566.1.7).
33. A Plan of Rhodes, from *Zee-En Land* as above, by permission of the British Library (BL 566.1.7).
34. A Map of T.S.'s journey, from *De Ongelukkiege Voyagie van Mr. T. S. Engels Koopman, Gedaan in den Jaare 1648*, 1737 edition. By permission of the British Library (BL 566.1.7).
35. The slave market in Algiers, from *De Ongelukkiege Voyagie* as above, by permission of the British Library (BL 566.1.7).
36. Torture in Tlemcen, from *De Ongelukkiege Voyagie* as above, by permission of the British Library (BL 566.1.7).

Photo credits, Donna Landry and the author, and with Jo Laundon at Tittenhanger.

Prologue

Anecdote. Now, in the age of the sublime dynasty and the period of the present exalted reign, the following tale was told by Mustapha Agha, the chief Black Eunuch of the Abode of Felicity, glory of courtiers and backbone of the trustworthy, who has made the pilgrimage to the two holy cities and visited the illustrious places, and of whom a full account will be given as and when appropriate.

During the sultanate of Murad,[1] the grandfather of the present Padishah, the ruler of the Lutheran kingdom among the Franks took of old the road of submission to the Padishah of the House of Osman and at that time was, it is said, a woman, Queen of a sizeable kingdom. This person, in order to approach the Abode of Majesty and the shadow of its protection, sent as a gift a masterpiece of craftsmanship, a clock. It was three cubits in width and depth, and more than the height of a man. On it were pictures and diverse figures, some of them stringed instruments, some flutes, some layers of six-stringed lutes, some drums, some drummers. It showed various kinds of stringed instrument apart from these. At the turn of every hour, from each picture and figure came some sort of movement and some kind of admonitory gesture. The instruments in their hands or mouths gave out wondrous notes and marvellous sounds and voices, such that the mind wondered how to describe them, and men of intelligence were too perplexed to define them. To sum up, the aforementioned Queen expended boundless wealth and unlimited treasure, while the experts who built the clock laboured for many years, toiling and preserving, to complete and perfect it. It became a work of art, studded with jewels. The Queen had ordered that it be dispatched with great care and arrive safely at the Threshold of Felicity.

The divine wisdom and will of God intervening, however, by the time it arrived the bird that was the ever victorious soul of Sultan Murad, whose dwelling is in Paradise, had flown to its shining nest, and his benevolent successor, the late Sultan Mehmed[2] whose dwelling is the lote-tree, sat on the throne of majesty. The matchless gift was presented to that glorious sovereign and was placed in one of the lofty palaces in the private garden. He visited it and favoured it with his presence. He examined and scrutinized that unique wonder and listened, astonished, to the voices and sounds of those persons and likenesses, and for each he marvelled at what mankind is capable of.

When the throne of the sultanate of the Padishah and seat of the caliphate of the King of Kings passed to his successor, the period became the present period and the age became the age of Ahmed Khan[3] and all the regions of the world were full of the Sultan's reputation and fame, the Padishah of the world, the chosen one among the children of Adam, went round the groves and the rose-garden and viewed the clock and saw the persons and likenesses and heard the sounds and unholy voices they gave forth. 'O God!' he said, 'What are things coming to? What a senseless innovation this is!' His honest heart and upright nature loathed disorder and that meaningless thing. He said that in the capital of the sultanate and majesty, the site of the Throne of Felicity and, above all, a place where the Supreme Lord was worshipped, the existence of pictures and likenesses and an assembly of such entities was against the sacred law and reason, and reviled by God and man; it could not be accepted. Exceedingly valuable and precious though the clock was, as has been described, he showed it no respect but took a heavy battleaxe into his hand that routed the enemy, and in accordance with the Words of Truth 'he smashed them into fragments,'[4] like Ibrahim the Friend of God[5] he destroyed that assembly and razed those idolatrous images to the ground. To the men of the Bostancis[6] he then gave an order as irrevocable as a decree of God, and they burnt them as in the Words of Truth: 'we shall burn it, then reduce it to dust and scatter it into the sea.'[7]

Mustapha bin Ibrahim Safi, *Zubdetu't-tevarih* (Beyazit Devlet Library, Veliyyüddin Efendi Yazmalari, nr. 2428, ff. 32–4), kindly transcribed by Dr Idris Bostan and translated by Professor Geoffrey Lewis.

The Argument

The Rise of Oriental Travel retells the stories of four journeys into the Ottoman Mediterranean undertaken by Englishmen during the century before there was a British Empire. It is a study of English people encountering Islamic cultures, and so it is also necessarily an enquiry into the global formations of English- ness itself. The men in question, though all native to England, could hardly have differed more, yet each of them represents Englishness in the making. Thomas Dallam from Lancashire was a skilled artisan who travelled to Istanbul in 1599. A man of minimum prejudice, Dallam was amazed by everything he saw. In this he was quite unlike William Biddulph, a clergyman whose pre- judices were legion. While chaplain in Aleppo, Biddulph travelled to Jerusalem using the Bible as his guidebook and disbelieved anything he saw that was not confirmed by it. To expose just such prejudicial attitudes towards the East, Henry Blount travelled to the Levant in 1634 to see for himself and test received opinion by careful observation. The fourth journey retold here is that of T.S., whose narrative of captivity in Ottoman Algeria was published in 1670. If not entirely fictitious, this work is most likely a concatenation of facts and fantasies, and shows how firmly the imaginations of English readers had become gripped by stories of encounters inside the Ottoman Mediterranean towards the century's end, even as their own empire in the East was coming into being.

In retelling these journeys, I pursue three general and interlocking argu- ments. The first is that English attitudes towards the Ottoman Empire in the early modern period were not as uniformly hostile or as fearful as we have often been led to believe by followers of the school of Richard Knolles who, in 1603, declared the Ottomans to be 'the present terrour of the world'. In various forms, this is a war cry that continues to haunt us today. By linking crusading rhetoric with millennial literalism, a powerful tradition of Protestant thought has perpetuated the belief that there can be, and indeed must be, only conflict with Islam. All too often, a selective use of history has generated stories that make hostility between Christian and Muslim nations appear to be the way things have always been and therefore must remain. The New York journalist Stephen Kinzer opens *Turkey Between Two Worlds* (2002), his highly praised reflections on four years in Istanbul during the 1990s, by recalling how Othello is called from his marriage bed to take up arms against 'the Turk'. Kinzer emphatically assures us that in Shakespeare's day, and for later generations, 'nearly all' Europeans considered the 'Turk' to be 'the scourge of civilization', and believed Islam to be 'a satanic affront to everything a Christian held sacred'.[8] Simply repeating the prejudiced opinions of the past in this way can make a partial truth sound like the whole and only truth, especially when no alternatives are offered.

In this book I have tried to show that, in Shakespeare's time especially, Kinzer's claim is far enough away from the much more complicated historical truth to be not simply misleading, but potentially dangerous.[9] When Knolles and Shakespeare were writing, there was also enormous admiration and great envy of the magnificent courtliness, immense wealth and exquisite splendour of Ottoman culture. And there was widespread fascination with the far-reaching military authority of a mighty Ottoman army that hardly threatened the English, and indeed never shows up in *Othello*. For the Elizabethans, theological differences with Islam and the Ottomans were important, but nothing like the whole story. Trading agreements brought wealth to London merchants, employed hundreds in the silk industry alone and entailed diplomatic and cultural exchanges that tell a different story from one of inevitable conflict.

The second and related general argument of this book has already forcefully been made by Nabil Matar, but cannot be emphasized often enough: that for many English people at the time, life within the Islamic Mediterranean offered an enormously attractive alternative to life in the British Isles. Many went and stayed. Those who visited, returned and wrote accounts bring me to my third general argument: that, for those who came back, the experience of going had changed what it meant to be English.

Preface

Research for this book began in 1993 in Oxford's Bodleian Library where I sat reading poems praising Charles II for restoring monarchy to England in 1660. I was struck by the way several poets expected readers would understand allusions and references to the Ottoman Empire that were sometimes quite obscure, and so I asked the computerized catalogue to supply a list of English books about the Ottomans printed before 1660. I was already something of a Turcophile. Ever since first visiting Istanbul for New Year 1976, I had regularly returned to see an ever-expanding group of Turkish and expatriate friends. With my partner, Donna Landry, I had climbed in the Lycian hills, ridden horses in Cappadoccia, taken buses into the East and visited Urfa, Harran, Diyarbakir and Van. I sat astonished watching the Bodleian printer spill out page after page listing titles of books and pamphlets, sermons and poems that could have been read, in English, about the Turks and the Ottoman Empire before 1660. *The Rise of Oriental Travel* came into focus some years later.

Early Anglo-Ottoman relations had received little attention since Samuel Chew surveyed the literary materials in the 1930s. Even as the 1990s drew to a close and I began thinking of a new general study that would engage continuing debates over Edward Said's *Orientalism* (1978), important new research into Ottoman and Islamic influences on the Shakespearean theatre started appearing from scholars such as Daniel Vitkus, Richmond Barbour and Jonathan Burton. Nabil Matar's books on Islam in early modern Britain and relations among Turks, Moors and the English appeared in rapid succession, while at the same time Lisa Jardine and Jerry Brotton were busily deconstructing the Renaissance from its Eurocentrism.

Once I started writing about Thomas Dallam and what I now think of as his 'wretched' organ, I realized that an historical focus on early travel writers would both open and add nuance to the continuing Orientalism debate. Dallam's fascinating account of travelling to Istanbul to present a clockwork organ to Sultan Mehmed III as a gift from Queen Elizabeth provided excellent material for showing how the earliest visitors both did and did not conform to the attitudes and prejudices of later Orientalists. Even as I was thinking and writing about Dallam, Kenneth Parker's anthology of early modern travels to the Orient appeared and cleared much of the ground, showing how the Orientalist paradigms need to be revised to account for the experiences of those who went at a time when the Ottomans were a powerful empire and the English insular and insignificant.

Meanwhile, trips to Turkey had become more regular, urgent and full of purpose. We revisited the harem of the Topkapi Palace with renewed interests. Where in the palace did Dallam set up his organ? Into which of the lofty palaces in the private garden was it moved and later destroyed by Sultan Ahmed's fury? Wandering around the Topkapi gardens wondering why Dallam could not be tempted to stay made it clearer to me that his account really was the best place to start, and then the rest of the book planned itself. William Biddulph's *Travels* (1609), describing life in Aleppo and a journey to Jerusalem, made obvious sense to include next, since Dallam's relatively unschooled, intrepid and rather open approach to foreign encounters differed so dramatically from the ways the clergyman's learned and pious posing controlled his experience and understanding of the East. Here were two distinct ways of being English among the Ottomans and writing about that experience.

Henry Blount's *Travels* (1636) through the Balkans and onward to Ottoman Cairo provided a third way, the secular and sceptical approach of a legally trained wit who was probably also a spy. Blount's itinerary neatly continues the journey around the Ottoman Mediterranean started by Dallam's voyage to Istanbul and followed by Biddulph in Aleppo, Damascus and Jerusalem. The *Adventures* (1670) of T.S., a captivity narrative set in Algeria on the westernmost edge of the Ottoman Empire, completes the geographical survey and, in its outlandish claims and racy style, shows travel writing developing narrative features that would influence early novels by Aphra Behn and Daniel Defoe.

In *The Rise of Oriental Travel*, then, I try to recapture something of how these different Englishmen felt about their experiences and encounters in the Ottoman Mediterranean, travelling and living among peoples that religion had long branded enemies. By the late sixteenth century, English merchants and diplomats were as eager to deal directly with the Ottomans as the Ottomans themselves were keen to ally themselves with the English against the Spanish, and formal hostilities were mostly set aside. However, the journey itself, either by land or sea, could prove only the start of dangers and exciting adventures in parts of the world where formal agreements between Istanbul and London counted for very little: robbery, kidnapping, captivity, being taken for a spy were all very real dangers threatening travellers. By the end of the seventeenth century, such stories of journeys into the Ottoman Empire had entered the cultural fabric of a nation seeking its own empire in the East.

The scene of this book lies between the first agreements established by Queen Elizabeth and Sultan Murad III in the 1580s, and the early decades of the eighteenth century, when the great Ottoman artist Abdelcelil Çelebi, known as Levni, first portrayed European visitors strolling the streets of Istanbul, and Lady Mary Wortley Montagu was writing her celebrated letters. This is the fullest account of the earliest first-person records of what it was like to be an Englishman in the Ottoman Empire before the Grand Tourists arrived. I consider the contemporary historical setting of these visits as seen from the Ottoman side and use previously unpublished manuscript sources that reveal both comic and scandalous details of expatriate life.

In seeking to recover past experience from written materials, I follow the journeys as they are described in each of the narratives. In adopting a narrative approach, my aim has been to recreate, as far as possible, the sense that travel writers themselves seek to create of discovering things as they go. Along the way, I comment on the places they visit from accounts in contemporary and other sources that help us read between the lines. While a more analytical approach, organizing material by themes and topics, would no doubt provide a neater argument than retelling the journeys, I decided it would lose the important sense in which narratives of travel invite being read as stories about journeys and the ways they unfold. The narrative rhythms by which travellers report finding things out along the way seem worth preserving. By journeying and finding out as we go, perhaps we can begin to grasp these documents from the early modern past both as testimony to extraordinary personal experience and as cultural elements of a powerful discourse that rendered Oriental travel both imaginable and desirable for later generations.

Over the years, Donna and I, sometimes in company with friends, have wandered deliberately into and across the footsteps of these four travellers. We have yet to sail across the Bay of Biscay, and when we did spend twenty-two days under sail crossing the Atlantic on the topsail schooner *The Sir Robert*, we enjoyed modern facilities and the company of an amazingly skilful, witty and well-read crew. At least nobody complained when, usually on night watch, I would chatter incessantly about what life aboard the *Hector* in 1599 must have been like for Dallam and the three hundred others, with no running water or refrigeration. None of the authors treated here sailed the Atlantic, but that is as close as we have come to finding out what life at sea might have been like for them. We have also ridden horses among the Pyramids, eaten Nile perch and been shown mummies in sand graves, much as Henry Blount reported in 1634. We have been to Lancashire and visited the prosperous town of Flixton where Dallam may have been born, and wandered through the industrial park built on the site where the hamlet of Dallam stood in his day. And we have photographed the depressed 1940s housing estate near Warrington now called Dallam. We have entered Zante harbour by ferry and watched for the first glimpse of Mount Scopos, that bit of high green that so attracted Dallam's attention. The next day we climbed it to visit the site of his adventures: despite earthquakes, ruins of the church Dallam visited are still evident and the place just as magical. Thanks to the courtesy of the current owner, John Bonnington, we have also visited the house that Henry Blount built for himself after returning from the Levant, and discovered there portraits of Henry and his wife Hester. In May 2003 we visited Tlemcen and Algiers, and retraced Biddulph's journey from Aleppo as far as Quneitrah.

In these wanderings I think of myself not simply as a literary biographer investigating authors, but also in some sense as a biographer of the books themselves. I have found out as much as I can about the authors, their families and the people they knew, but make no claims to have conducted original genealogical research. While seeking to recapture how they experienced and wrote about the East, I regard with caution all claims to know what an historically remote person actually felt. However, the books they wrote survive and, in some sense, so too do the places they visited; and without the inspiration of those places, the books themselves could not have been written. So, when revisiting specific locations and imagining that I am writing the biographies of travel books, I have found myself looking for, or sometimes directly at, the places where these books came into being.

Until the 1720s and Lady Mary Wortley Montagu's letters describing her life in Istanbul, records by and about English women travelling into the Ottoman Empire are regrettably revealingly thin. For a short final chapter, I have reserved the story of Anne, Lady Glover, and how it came to be that, having died on 2 November 1608 in Istanbul, her funeral did not take place until 14 April 1612, her body having been preserved in bran for nearly four years.

I have written *The Rise of Oriental Travel* in the hope that a variety of readers will want to read it, not only students, but everyone interested in reading about English history and England's encounters with the Islamic Mediterranean. I hope that nobody will be put off reading passages quoted in their original spelling. For those interested in methodological questions, my thinking owes a great deal to studying and teaching the work of Raymond Williams, Edward Said, Gayatri Chakravorty Spivak and Homi Bhabha, with whom I share a critical outlook informed variously by historicism, feminism and Marx's 'Eighteenth Brumaire'. From them I have learned ways of thinking that I can no longer distinguish from my own. In that sense this book makes no claims to advance cultural theory as such. But I do hope to have brought certain ways of thinking to bear upon some unfamiliar archival materials revealing how the English became fascinated with the Ottoman Mediterranean.

Note on Texts and Transcriptions

Printed texts in English are quoted as they appear in the editions cited. For older works I have retained original spelling and punctuation with a few exceptions: s for long s, w for vv, and so on. I have silently corrected obvious errors.

Except when quoting sources, the names of persons and places have generally been modernized (Izmir for Smyrna), romanized (Quneitrah) and, in the case of the Barbarossa brothers, given in the modern Turkish forms Oruç and Hayreddin rather than Aroudj and Kheir Al-din.

Acknowledgements

I would like to thank Dr Walter Edwards of the Humanities Center, the Dean of Liberal Arts, the Dean of Graduate Studies, and several Chairs of the Department of English at Wayne State University for financial assistance and time off from teaching. I would especially like to thank the Charles Gershenson Foundation for electing me Distinguished Fellow for 1998–2000. For other forms of institutional support I would like to thank: Dr Abdeljelil Temimi of the Fondation Temimi, Tunisia; Dr Vassily Christides of the Institute for Graeco-Oriental and African Studies, Athens; Dr Oya Başak and Dr Sibel Irzik of the Department of Western Languages and Literatures, Bosphorus University, Istanbul; Dr Tim Niblock and Dr Mohammed-Salah Omri of the Mediterranean Studies Programme and the Institute for Arab and Islamic Studies, University of Exeter; Abdellah Abdi of the Bibliothèque de l'Université d'Alger, Algeria; Abdelkader Belhorma of the Bibliothèque Centrale, Université Abou Bakr Belkaid, Tlemcen, Algeria; Kim Duistermaat, Director of the Netherlands Institute for Academic Studies, Damascus, Syria; and Dr Tony Greenwood, Director of the American Research Institute in Turkey, Istanbul.

My thanks to the staff in the Bodleian Library, University of Oxford, and the Manuscripts and Rare Books rooms of the British Library for their patience and efficiency over the years; special thanks to Mohammed Isa Walley, and M.C. Breay of the British Library. Commercial booksellers who have kindly assisted and deserve special thanks include: The Old Bookroom in Canberra (Australia), Bernard Shapero (London), Nadeem Elissa (Joppa Books) and Barry Swabey (Plymouth).

I also owe innumerable thanks to the following friends, students and colleagues:

In Algeria - Amine Belmekki, Rachid Benkhenafou, Zoubir Dendane, Fayssal Fatmi, Rafia Ghalmi, Abdelhamid Hadjiat, Mohammed sidi Negadi, and staff of the Hotel Safir for taking excellent care of us during the earthquake of 21 May 2003.

In Egypt – David Blanks.

In Greece – N.G. Moschonas, George Tsoutsos and Evangelos Angelakos, Mayor of Oinoussai, for extending extraordinary hospitality.

In Israel – Tal Shuval.

In Syria – Mahran Shalil, Michel Tannous, Nassib Tomeh, and Lucin Soghikian of the Hotel Baron, Aleppo.

In Turkey – Idris Bostan, Selim Deringil, Caroline Finkel, Yonca Karakilic, Mahmut Mutman, Salih Ozbaran, M. Halim Spatar, Tolga Temuge, Meyda

Yeğenoğlu, students at Bosphorus University, the staff of the Halı Hotel, Cemberlitas, and friends in Adrasan, Diyarbekir, Şanlıurfa and Van.

In the UK – Matthew Birchwood, John Bonnington, Edmund Bosworth, Jerry Brotton, Mat Dimmock, Kate Fleet, Pauline Grant, Colin Heywood, Rosemary Hooley, Christopher LeBrun, Geoffrey and Raphaela Lewis, Philip Mansel, Rhoads Murphey, David Norbrook, Ken Parker, Angela Tawn, Paul Tindall and Graham Whitehouse.

In the USA – Mark Aune, Richmond Barbour, Bob Burgoyne, Jonathan Burton, Jennie Evenson, Dan Goffman, David Loewenstein, Arthur Marotti, Nabil Matar, Bridget Orr, Dan Vitkus, Jyotsna Singh, Gayatri Chakravorty Spivak, Joan Taylor, James Grantham Turner, Harold Weber, Steve Zwicker and students at Wayne State.

Some material in Parts II and IV appeared in different form in previous publications: 'Ottomanism before Orientalism: Bishop Henry King Praises Henry Blount, Passenger in the Levant', in Ivo Kamps and Jyotsna Singh, eds., *Travel Knowledge*; and 'Performing East: English Captives in the Ottoman Maghreb', in *Actes du Ier Congrès International sur: Le Grande Bretagne et le Maghreb*, ed. Abdeljelil Temimi.

At Palgrave Macmillan, I owe enormous thanks to Josie Dixon for taking the book on at an early stage, and more recently to Luciana O'Flaherty, Jen Nelson, Dan Bunyard, Ruth Willats and the production team, as well as the anonymous readers of the typescript.

Special thanks to those who have made extraordinary efforts to make this a better book than it would otherwise have been: Caroline Finkel has tried to keep me straight on Ottoman history and historiography; Idris Bostan went out of his way to transcribe what looks to me like a tricky piece of Ottoman prose; Geoffrey Lewis produced a splendid translation at very short notice; Nabil Matar has been an inspiring source of cheerful diligence and calm thought; without Ali Tablit, we would never have made it to Algeria. And thanks to Donna Landry for being there, every step of the way.

Part I

Dallam's Organ: By Sea to Istanbul, 1599

A great and curious present is going to the Grand Turk, which will scandalize other nations, especially the Germans.

John Chamberlain to Dudley Carleton, 31 January 1599[1]

1
Thomas Dallam (c.1575–c.1630)

In February 1599, Thomas Dallam set sail from Gravesend aboard the newly commissioned 300-ton *Hector*, pride of Queen Elizabeth's fleet. His voyage would take him around the Iberian peninsula, eastward through the Mediterranean and into the very heart of the Ottoman Empire (the seraglio of Sultan Mehmed III in Istanbul). This was not his first journey from home – he had left his native Lancashire some years before to join the swelling numbers of men and women moving to metropolitan London – but he could hardly have imagined that his travels would take him so far.

Uncertainty surrounds his early years. Thomas was probably born in 1575, either in Flixton or the nearby hamlet of Dallam, near Warrington. Whether his family took their name from the place or the place from the family remains unclear.[2] In London he entered the Blacksmiths' Guild and was already a Freeman of that Company when he sailed. As a skilled musician, Dallam specialized in manufacturing organ pipes. His great chance came when Queen Elizabeth learned of an ingenious clockwork musical organ he had built. He performed on this instrument for her at Whitehall and so dazzled the Queen that she shrewdly recognized that it would make an ideal gift with which to flatter the new Sultan, Mehmed III. In league with the Levant Company, Elizabeth also arranged to send a coach as present for the Valide Sultan Safiye, the Sultan's mother, with whom the Queen had established a friendly correspondence.[3] For Thomas Dallam invention, trade and diplomacy converged into the career opportunity of a lifetime. Despite a moment of stage fright, his performance on his organ in September not only brought him into personal contact with Mehmed himself, but was so successful that the Sultan offered him two wives from the harem 'of the beste I Could Chuse my selfe' if he would stay on at the Ottoman court. Mehmed was so keen to keep Dallam in Istanbul that for a time the young musician and metalworker became the most important Englishman at the Ottoman court. For several crucial weeks, Dallam was of more consequence than Elizabeth's new ambassador, Henry Lello. Yet

Dallam resisted the tempting offer of fame, influence and Ottoman luxury. Pretending to have a wife and children at home, he made his excuses and returned to England later the same year.

Today, 'one looks in vain for Dallam's organ'.[4] Shortly before leaving Istanbul, Dallam reassembled it in a seraglio garden where, some years later, it was destroyed by Mehmed's son, Ahmed I, intent on proving himself 'to be more scrupulous about the Islamic interdiction of images' than his father.[5] But Dallam's more enduring legacy is his manuscript journal titled 'A brefe Relation of my Travell from The Royall Cittie of London towardes The Straite of mariemediteranum and what hapened by the waye'. Unnoticed in its own day and not edited until 1893,[6] this account has occasionally inspired subsequent writers who, for the most part, have focused exclusively on the organ. Orhan Pamuk's novel *My Name Is Red* (1998)[7] is a most notable recent instance. Pamuk picks up the tale at the point when Ahmed seizes a battleaxe and smashes it 'into fragments'. Safi called the 'senseless innovation' a 'clock', using the Turkish term 'saat' having no more appropriate word, though some of the pneumatic devices evidently continued to work after Dallam's final servicing. The story of Dallam's organ has proved so fascinating that it has generated a whole host of interesting errors,[8] but apart from Stanley Mayes' 1956 historical biography, *An Organ for the Sultan*, the greater part of Dallam's narrative of his voyage aboard the *Hector* has been ignored and, I believe, it has sometimes been misunderstood by Mayes.[9]

The enigma of Dallam's manuscript

Compared with travellers from other Western European nations, relatively few written accounts by Englishmen of journeys into the Ottoman Empire during the fifteenth and sixteenth centuries have come down to us. Stephane Yerasimos has shown how it was only during the very final decades of the sixteenth century, once direct trade between England and Ottoman ports had become well established, that English visitors in any number began writing, and sometimes publishing, reports of visiting the lands of the Ottomans.[10] Nearly all the first English travel writers were, unlike Dallam, directly engaged in commerce.[11] If we regard Dallam as a member of those Yerasimos calls 'les classes moyennes', he appears even more unusual since he clearly did not write in the hope of producing a 'bestseller', as did the Hungarian Georgievits Bartholemew, whose account of thirteen years' slavery among the Ottomans had been translated and reprinted no fewer than 88 times between its first publication in 1544 and 1600, the year when Dallam arrived home.[12]

Dallam's decision not to publish is all the more remarkable since he was writing at a time of tremendous interest in tales by Englishmen who had travelled to Eastern and Islamic countries.[13] The success of Richard Hakluyt's multi-volume

The Principal Navigations, Voyages, and Discoveries of the English Nation (1589) had inspired Samuel Purchas to plan his supplemental collections *Hakluytus Posthumus* (1625). The first two decades of the new century, moreover, witnessed a new development among English book production: the professionalization of Oriental travel writing by English writers who went East precisely in order to write about it. Thomas Coryate, William Lithgow, Fynes Moryson and Sir George Sandys all composed and published celebrated travels during the first decades of the new century, an era that opened with the publication of several important English works on the Ottomans. In 1603 alone, there appeared Richard Knolles' great compilation *The Generall Historie of the Turkes*, Alexander Hartwell's translation of Lazaro Soranzo's *Ottomano* and Henry Timberlake's *A True and Strange Discourse of the Travailes of two English Pilgrimes*. At such a time, it really does seem odd that Dallam chose to keep his journal to himself. Surely Purchas knew of Dallam and would have sought out his account?[14] Perhaps, as a student once suggested to me, he wrote it exclusively for his immediate family. One consequence of his reticence was that his adventurous journey to Istanbul would be forgotten for nearly three centuries.

The manuscript was unknown until 11 November 1848, when the British Museum bought it from the collector Henry Rhodes.[15] Experts have assured me that 'there is no reason to suspect' that the manuscript is a forgery,[16] but even so its sudden reappearance is strange. 1848 was a year of revolutionary insurgency across Europe. The appearance of this 'account of an Organ carried to the Grand Seignor and Other Curious Matters' was entirely ignored by scholars for decades. Twelve years later, following scenes of the Garibaldi uprising and British forces arriving in China, a short article in the *Illustrated London News* (20 October 1860) reproduced a pictorial account of 'a nameless instrument of the Elizabethan era' not unlike the one Dallam describes. The anonymous authors of the article knew nothing about Thomas Dallam's journey or manuscript. They claimed, rather, to have discovered this 'remarkable drawing on parchment' attached to a contractual agreement between Randolph Bull, a London goldsmith, and Richard Stapers, governor of the Levant Company. The contract details the commission and construction of a clockwork organ. Costing the not inconsiderable sum of £550 in materials alone, the instrument was apparently intended for Queen Elizabeth, but the authors conclude there was 'no record to show how this singular instrument sped, or how the Queen was pleased to dispose of it, if, indeed, it ever came to her disposal'.[17] The instrument described differs from Dallam's, and the illustrated parchment and contract papers unfortunately disappeared, never again to be seen by anyone other than the anonymous authors.

If the *Illustrated London News* article sparked any interest at the time, it soon faded. Only four years later, Edward Rimbault wrote in his history of the English organ that he had discovered a 'Mr. Dallam' who had built an organ for King's

College, Cambridge between June 1605 and August 1606: Rimbault had no idea that Thomas Dallam had been to Istanbul.[18] Two decades later, Dallam's manuscript and Rimbault's book were both unknown to William Barclay Squires when he composed his *Dictionary of National Biography* entry for Thomas Dallam in 1888. Neither Squires nor any of his helpers knew that 'the eldest member of the great family of English organ-builders' began his career bearing a royal gift to Istanbul. Although Squires found documents enabling him to detail Dallam's achievements after returning from Istanbul, he clearly had no idea of Dallam's involvement with Elizabeth's gift to Mehmed. Not until Theodore Bent edited the manuscript for the Hakluyt Society in 1893 did anyone link Dallam with the organ sent to Mehmed III.

And that may have been just what Thomas Dallam wanted – for his part in the episode to be forgotten. He may have wanted to avoid further involvement in disputes among the merchants by keeping quiet about what he thought of Henry Lello, the English ambassador. But we will probably never know why he kept the journal to himself. The experience of writing down his adventures without thought of publication must have been enough. On his successful return from Istanbul, Dallam's reputation as an organ builder won him important commissions to build pipe-organs for King's College Cambridge (1605) and Worcester Cathedral (1613).[19] Like the organ he took to Istanbul, these too were destroyed in the name of religious piety; only this time by Christian zealots in the 1640s.

References to quotations from Dallam's journal are given parenthetically to Theodore J. Bent's edition in *Early Voyages and Travels in the Levant*. Of Dallam's account in Bent's edition, G.F. Abbott observed in 1906: 'a valuable work, wretchedly edited. The Introduction to it is by far the wildest piece of historical writing ever executed outside a lunatic asylum – a veritable nightmare of gross inaccuracies and grotesque anachronisms.'[20] This is needlessly vindictive, but Bent's introduction is speculative and unreliable, while his edition is sometimes careless; he omits, for example, all of Dallam's marginal additions. I have collated all passages quoted with the original manuscript in the British Library (BL Add. Ms 17480), always indicating whenever substantial changes to Bent's text have been made.

2
On First Setting Out

Thomas Dallam was unlike any Englishman who had ever written about visiting the Ottoman Empire before. He had little advance notice and packed in a hurry. Dallam's very lack of preparation for the journey makes what he has to say peculiarly interesting. Since he was not a classically educated gentleman engaged on diplomatic service or a biblically knowledgeable clergyman in service to the Levant Company, and because he lacked the experiential knowledge of a canny private merchant, a mariner or even a professional soldier of fortune, Dallam's report of the journey through the Mediterranean tells us much we would not otherwise have known.

There is little reason to think that Dallam ever imagined himself going to the East, or that he had ever thought much about the Ottomans before learning he would be meeting them. His commission to go came suddenly and was unexpected. On arrival at the Ottoman court, he instantly found himself embroiled in diplomatic disputes from which he stood to gain nothing. For Dallam, the real delights of travelling came from the company of fellow travellers and having adventures in exotic places along the way. Attracted as he was by many aspects of life in Istanbul, Dallam had no desire to stay there. The very success of his performance aroused envy in the new ambassador, Henry Lello, and Dallam feared he would be forced to stay, betrayed by a fellow countryman 'into the Turkes hands' ever more to 'Live a slavish Life, and never companie againe with Christians' (p. 76). Anxieties that he might never again 'companie' with Christians – as we will see, his use of 'company' as a verb here tells us something – proved strong enough to outweigh the considerable wealth, sexual opportunities and influential status that would be his if he remained at Sultan Mehmed's court.

Keeping account

Dallam was certainly not indifferent to the possessions money could buy, and he must have found the opportunities for accumulating wealth that life at the

Ottoman court provided very attractive. His concern with money and personal belongings appears right from the start when he lists all the 'Necessaries for my voyege into Turkie, which I bought upon a verrie short warninge', and includes the cost of each item (p. 1). He listed the bedding, clothing and other items he took aboard the *Hector*, noted the prices and detailed some further expenses incurred along the way.

In Dallam's currency, total expenses for the trip came to £18 15s 5d, a considerable outlay that would have taken a skilled artisan of the time earning one shilling a day more than a year to earn, never mind save.[1] Dallam must have had sponsors to have raised so much in a short time. His most expensive purchases, items costing more than one pound each, are several pieces of clothing and 'a pare of virginals'. He also took a considerable quantity of bulk tin to be used for currency: 'one grose of tin spounes, the which coste me nyne shillinges; and thirtie pounde of tin in bares, which coste me 18s.' (p. 4). Nine shillings – the cost of the spoons or half the cost of the tin bullion – proved a useful unit of exchange, since the thin gilded coin, the *zecchino* or chequin, which he later encounters and calls 'chickenes' or 'chickers', were worth roughly nine shillings each at the time (a little less than half an English pound, with 20 shillings to the pound).[2] Dallam's list also indicates a certain amount of re-exportation going on: to supplement his diet, he took several items previously imported to England, such as oil, prunes, sun-dried raisins, cloves, sugar, mace, pepper and nutmegs. Regardless of their mixed origins, all these items went aboard at a total cost of 10s 1d.

Having detailed his expenses, Dallam never indicates how he defrayed his costs or how he expected to be paid. While in Istanbul, he twice received gifts of cash worth a total of £35, rather more than his initial outgoings. Both were public occasions when he was free to boast of the amount received, a matter of some importance since there was considerable rivalry among Englishmen over gifts received from the Ottomans. Certainly, a great deal of gossip circulated about the generosity of the gifts given to the English artisans who accompanied the coach which Elizabeth had sent to Mehmed's mother, Safiye. John Sanderson, treasurer to the Levant Company, wrote to a friend in London how 'She sent the cotchman 50 ducats gould, and a grop [bunch] of 3 or 400 to the rest'.[3] Amidst such jealously observed scenes of gift exchange, Dallam never reports whether he shared his gifts with his fellow workmen or whether he received any further gifts during his stay, other than a promised set of livery.

A further curiosity is that Dallam never describes the circumstances under which he was sent. Once his 'chiste' was packed, he was off. Beyond a brief aside, he recalls nothing about performing before Queen Elizabeth at Whitehall, and he seems not to have known any of the Levant Company representatives aboard the *Hector*, men who might have been instrumental in his journey.

Nor does he ever seem to have understood the fraught political situation into which he was sailing.

For several years, the officers of the Levant Company had been badgering Elizabeth to send a suitable present that would encourage Mehmed to reissue the capitulations permitting the English Levant Company to continue direct trade with Ottoman ports.[4] Lello, the new ambassador, would not be officially recognized by Mehmed until a present was received. Lello meanwhile faced the ominous challenge of attempting to create between himself and Mehmed the close relation that had existed between the previous ambassador, Edward Barton, and the previous sultan, Murad III. When Murad died in 1595, Barton wrote immediately to Queen Elizabeth pressing her to send a present as quickly as possible. By the time of Barton's own death two years later, no gift had arrived and Anglo-Ottoman relations were in jeopardy. Elizabeth and ambassador-elect Lello wanted Mehmed to grant the English consular control over Dutch ships in Ottoman ports. The French desired this privilege too. With a new sultan, Barton dead and a new and untried ambassador in place, Elizabeth and her merchants were keen to stimulate trade in defiance of the French, while continuing the diplomatic negotiations regarding a combined Anglo-Ottoman naval effort against Spain.

Dallam remained oblivious to the political importance of his journey except when it pressed on his freedom to return to England. Instead, he wrote about the people he met and whether or not he liked them.

The desire of company

Dallam cast himself as organized, intrepid and bold, prone to adventure, patriotic but interested in foreigners and their strange cultural habits. He combined a delicate sense of propriety with an eye for reading the local scene. He had an instinct for understanding and communicating by gestures and signs when there was no common language, a skill that made him a welcome guest even in potentially hostile predicaments. These characteristics made him a natural traveller, bold but seldom reckless, enthusiastic in his wanderings, but instinctively able to stay out of danger.

Dallam was keen on company. For him company was not a thing, a noun, but a verb, an activity involving other people, a set of relationships. During his months at sea, he frequently reveals how the excitement of travel was all about being in company; both the Company you travel to represent and the company you keep on the journey. Unlike the accountant John Sanderson, who was also aboard the *Hector*, Dallam was by no means a 'Company man'; indeed, he never mentions the Levant Company. Yet Dallam reports with evident fascination and revealing detail on his encounters with a wide range of other people. And there are several we know he must have met, but about whom he says nothing.

He is especially excited when describing his earliest dealings with exotic foreigners, who turn out to be two fellow passengers on board the *Hector*, 'an ould Jue That was a passinger in our ship', who tells him of an aeolian statue on Crete, and a 'Greke' seeking passage home to 'Siprus', who comes on board in Zante (pp. 26, 27). But Dallam was even more interested in the other Englishmen on board, and proves acutely sensitive to divisions of rank and regional origin among them. Living in cramped quarters for months at sea appears to have done little to level social distinctions, and Dallam never once mentions several fellow passengers, such as Sanderson, or the merchant John Mildenhall.[5] But when referring to those whom he liked or could not avoid, Dallam comments indirectly on matters of personality and character in the way he uses names and titles.

Dallam names fellow travellers

As we might expect from a highly skilled Northern lad made good in metropolitan London, Dallam displays a strong-willed confidence combined with a healthy disrespect for formal authority. But there is no reason to think of him as 'little', the unfounded epithet favoured by his biographer, Stanley Mayes. Bearing the name of a hamlet in Lancashire, Dallam understood the importance of names, places and titles. Naming and not-naming his fellow travellers prove important to his narrative technique and to the way he represents himself as a discerning judge of character. Of the forty or so Englishmen Dallam mentions meeting, many remain unnamed yet, with minor exceptions, only the names of Englishmen are recorded. In the case of two important Englishmen whose authority he did not respect, Dallam uses only titles. He never tells us that Richard Parsons was the captain of the *Hector*, calling him simply 'Mr' (meaning 'Master'), or 'Captain'.[6] Nor does he mention Henry Lello by name, calling him instead 'the ambassador' and later 'my Lord'. He never names the Sultan or any other Turk with whom he has personal dealings, except English dragomen (interpreters).

For Dallam, the journey into Ottoman lands proved socially enabling. His friends on the outward journey were mostly skilled artisans like himself. When he returned, he was on first-name terms with courtiers and diplomats. Dallam names his co-workers on the way out – John Harvie the engineer, Rowland Buckett the painter[7] and 'Myghell' Watson the carpenter. He also introduces Edward Hale, sent to drive the coach for Safiye, who becomes the proverbial donkey 'Ned' whenever Dallam finds him acting foolishly. Together, these craftsmen attending on the royal gifts shared adventures while often keeping themselves separate from others on board. On the return trip, Dallam reports mostly keeping company with important men he had met in Istanbul: Thomas Glover, a career diplomat who would be knighted and appointed ambassador after Lello in 1606; Paul Pindar, who would be knighted in 1611 and follow Glover as ambassador; and Humphrey Conisby, gentleman-treasurer to Queen Elizabeth.[8] Dallam reports first meeting Glover on the outward voyage when the *Hector* arrived at Gallipoli, and doubtless had Glover in mind when noting his delight at finding 'that thar was good Company reddie to com for Inglande, such as in 2 or 3 years I could not have had the lik, if I had stayed behinde them, and they weare all desierus to have my company' (p. 81). Mutual desire for company was, for Dallam, what being an Englishman abroad was all about.

Two English 'Turks'

But Dallam was no simple snob. Another Englishman he memorializes in reporting the return journey from Istanbul was 'our drugaman, or Intarpreater...an Inglishe man, borne in Chorlaye in Lancashier; his name Finche. He was also in religion a perfit Turke, but he was our trustie frende' (p. 84). An equivocal figure, Finch accompanied Dallam's party as far as the Ottoman border of western Greece, saving them from conspiratorial brigands and natural hazards several times along the way. Dallam regularly calls Finch, who no longer had a first or Christian name, 'our Turke', but liked him well enough to name him not once but twice, the second time in a very moving valediction: 'Heare, at the sea sid, we parted from our drugaman, or the Turke that was our gidd from Constantinople. Thoughe he was a Turke, his righte name was Finche, borne at Chorlaye in Longcashier' (p. 89). The poignancy of the moment is powerful as Dallam took his leave, forever, of the company of a fellow Lancastrian with whom he had shared adventures in foreign parts. Without passing judgement, Dallam evidently felt that a native-born Englishman might become a 'perfit' Turk and yet remain a trusty friend since what counted in the end was his 'righte name' and place of birth. Left behind on an Ottoman-occupied shore, this Englishman turned Turk passed, patronymic intact, into the idiomatic past tense of an epitaph.

Finch earned his name by proving a 'trustie frende', unlike another English dragoman who was assigned to him during his time in the seraglio. Despite their weeks together, Dallam's first interpreter proved unreliable, abandoning him to be chased in fear of his life:

I caled to my drugaman and asked him the cause of theire runinge awaye; than he saide the Grand Sinyor and his Conquebines weare cominge, we muste be gone in paine of deathe; but they run all away and lefte me behinde, and before I gott oute of the house they were run over the grene quit out at the gate, and I runn as faste as my leggss would carrie me aftere, and 4 neageres or blackamoors cam runinge towardes me with their semetaries drawne;

yf they could have catchte me theye would have hewed me all in peecis with there semeteris. (p. 79)

Having escaped, Dallam took evident delight in reporting that the negligent interpreter was sacked from Lello's employment.

Asoune as my drugaman came home, my Lord [Lello] made him beleve that he would hange him for leaving me in that dainger; but at laste granted him his Life, but forbid him to com to his any more. He was a Turke, but a Cornishe man borne. (p. 79)

So much for the careless Cornishman, who disappears from the account, sacked from Lello's service, minus a name.

Dangers at sea: storms and pirates

I think the Seamans life fitt for None but such dull souls, as thinck themselves happy... No time is so pleasant to me as when the wind blows fresh, & I see 24. or 25 Men stand cursing themselves And damning others, just as if the divel himself and his comrades were come to show tricks: then I get me to a corner, where I am sure to be out of the way, & sit me downe pleased with observing, till a new & contrary motion of the vessel, raises to a tempest in my gutts, and then to lighten the ship, I heav overboard all I eat last, and have enough to doe to keep back entrails, heart, & all, & then I lay me down again.

Sir Dudley North, c.1683[9]

Unlike Dudley North and other Englishmen who made lengthy voyages by sea and hated every moment of it, Dallam enjoyed his journey to Istanbul. Of the details of life aboard the *Hector*, however, we hear nothing. His narrative of the six-month passage keeps before us the excitement rather than the tedium of the voyage. He describes overcoming dangers in remarkably secular terms, attributing success to human agency more often than to providential intervention.

The thrills and dangers began immediately the *Hector* left London. Only slowly do events become marked by seafaring jargon of the sort later to be parodied by Defoe and satirized by Swift. After being delayed for several days, 'a contrarye wynde' (p. 5) carries them off course and into the Atlantic. Swept dangerously close to fog-bound rocks along the Devon coast, 'it pleased almyghtie God so to defend us from harme that we weare juste before the harbur at Dartmouthe' (p. 6). This will be the only time Dallam attributes any form of agency to a divine or supernatural force, this moment of otherwise unaccountably perilous weather in British waters. Once initial dangers at sea were overcome, God seldom had very much to do with the way Dallam saw the world working. Repairs complete, they set off again from Plymouth and it was no time at all before human perfidy struck in the form of seven pirate ships, Dunkirkers. The predators soon turned tail and tried to run before the greater speed and ordinance of the mighty *Hector*. By now, Dallam has picked up the vocabulary of the sea:

> Than our captain bid the Mr. goner give them a chace peece shout at the amberall, but hitt him not, so the Mr. goner gave him a shott cloce by his fore bowe...Than our Mr. bid the goner shoute throughe the amberall his maynsayle, and so he did verrie near her drablinge. (pp. 8–9)

Their 'amberall' immobilized, her mainsail shot to ribbons 'verrie near her drablinge',[10] the other pirate ships heave to. Three pirates come aboard the *Hector* and bribe the captain to let them go,

> which greved the sayeleres and the Reste of our company verrie moche. Yf he had done, as he myghte verrie well have done, broughte these seven sayle as a prise into Inglande, it would have been the braveste sarvis that ever an Inglishe marchante shipe did, and tharby have Reaped greate credit as any ever did. (p. 10)

Dallam was clearly scandalized that the captain took 'the prise in his cabbin', rather than take the Dunkirkers 'a prise into Inglande'. Dallam frequently criticizes Parsons for allowing his personal greed and parsimony to determine how he conducted business while at sea. Nationalist pride – 'a prise into Inglande' – provided Dallam with a language suitable for condemning the captain, while also expressing his personal disappointment at not sharing the 'greate cridit' that he considered was due to the 'company' aboard the *Hector* for 'the braveste sarvis'.

Dallam never once condemns or even criticizes piracy as such, except when the loss was to England, and displays a remarkably confident understanding of how such matters deserved to be negotiated. After armed conflict at sea, the victors expected to take prizes proportionate to the wealth and importance of the vanquished. Outraged that the captain's 'prise' was England's loss, Dallam later noted in the margins of his manuscript how the seven Dunkirkers subsequently 'had taken and Robed upon the seae, betwyxt London and New Castell, thre score sayle of Inglishe and other countrie ships' (p. 11). Dallam's view of the world and how it works was nationalist, but almost entirely secular.

The dangers of Dunkirk pirates behind, he sights dolphins off Portugal without praising or pondering their creator – '2 or 3 greate monstrus fishis or whales, the which did spoute water up into the eayere' (p. 11). On entering the Mediterranean, Dallam was immediately struck by the climate and seasonal advance over England's green and pleasant land:

> We set oute from Plimouthe the 16th of Marche, havinge than verrie could wether, and no sine of any grene thinge on trees or hedgis; and the 27, at the entringe of the straites [of Gibraltar], the wether was exsedinge hoote, and we myghte se the feeldes on both sides verrie grene, and the tres full blowne...a verrie greate wonder. (p. 12)

A keen observer of the natural world both for what it produced and what it looked like, Dallam also showed interest in how strange towns defended themselves and managed local resources, and was fascinated by local clothing. He was concerned for what there was to drink and eat, and whether it could be bought, begged, wheedled as a gift, dug up, picked or shot.

Between Algiers and Istanbul, Dallam related some dangerous adventures searching for provisions on unknown shores, on islands and on hills amidst strange peoples. He had a good eye for a bit of country, and he had more than a passing interest in exotic flora and fauna, edible and otherwise. Natural risks became more and more strange and exotic, but only began to prove deadly to the English as they began to sail closer and closer to Istanbul and the seat of the sultan.

First foreign soil: Algiers

Once the *Hector* began docking in Ottoman-controlled ports and the English started going ashore, Dallam emerges as a natural traveller with a sharp and often comical instinct for handling the unexpected. Stepping on foreign soil, he presumed the Englishman's right to wander over any part of the world he cared to venture into, at once inquisitive, acquisitive and perhaps a little imperious, yet bold and friendly. Having made the journey from rural Lancashire to metropolitan London, Dallam knew about negotiating with the unfamiliar codes of strangers who could cause trouble – or provide assistance.

Once ashore in Algiers, Dallam noted the strange houses, admired the water supplies and then set off 'to gather som harbs and Routes' in company with the ship's surgeon, Chancie.

> This dai being the Laste Day of Marche, it was a wonder to us to se how forwarde the springe was: trees and hedgis wear full blowne, corne, wheate, and barly shott, yong oringis and apples upon the trees. (pp. 13–14)

Dallam wanders about Ottoman Africa looking with an English country-man's eye for a productive bit of land. But he could hear the cries of the city too and was quick to grasp the foreign sound of danger. Back in town 'we mett Mores and other people drivinge assis laden with grene beanes' who called out 'balocke, balocke, that is to saye, bewarr, or take heede' (p. 14). He notes what is for sale in the markets where food of all sorts was to be found, marvelling at the cheapness of partridge and quail, 'less than one pennye', and admires the 'cooke's housis, that dress meate verrie well' (pp. 14, 15). Dallam frequently noticed the food available in new places: I think we can presume there was fine dining among the English travellers that night moored off Algiers.

Dallam's first time ashore must greatly have boosted his confidence. He recalls the danger from the 'greate number of Turks that be but Renied cristians of all nations' who 'proule about the costes of other contries, with all the skill and pollacie thei can, to betraye cristians, which they sell unto the Moors and other marchantes of Barbarie for slaves' (pp. 14–15). Since Dallam never encountered any such villains, he must have been repeating hearsay picked up on board. This is the kind of scare-story likely to seem credible to an Englishman of the time, who had been brought up to believe that the renegade was, as Nabil Matar puts it, 'a type representing the new villain in England's conflict with the anti-Christ' (p. 51) – especially if he was originally from a Catholic country such as Spain or Italy. Dallam encountered no predatory renegades in Algiers, but he did record personal success in his first dealings with foreign authorities.

While the *Hector* was moored in Algiers, 'the kinge sent worde to our captaine that he should come unto him and bringe with hime the presente which he had to carrie unto the Grand Sinyor'. The captain duly explained that the present had been dismantled and could not be disturbed, but 'the kinge . . . would give no cridite unto his wordes, but kepte him as a prisner, and caused me and my mate to be sente for'. Once Dallam and Harvie had confirmed 'the same tale . . . than was our captane Released and we discharged, and the kinge sente our captaine for a presente a borde our shipe tow buls and thre sheepe, the which weare verrie leane, for they do thinke the worste thinges they have is tow good for cristians' (p. 15). After this adventure, Dallam started offering general maxims from personal observation. With all the authority of an old Turkey hand, he declared 'the Turkes Drinke nothinge but water', and are 'all in generall verrie covitus' (pp. 13, 15).

It was in Algiers that he first sighted veiled Muslim women, happily repeating and commenting on what was evidently hearsay:

The Turkishe, and Morishe, weomen, do goo all wayes in the streetes with there facis covered, and the common reporte goethe thare that they beleve, or thinke that the weomen have no souls. And I doe thinke, that it weare well for them if they had none, for they never goo to churche, or other prayers, as the men dothe. (pp. 15–16)

Soon he would be generalizing even further on the topic of foreign women.

3
Mediterranean Encounters

Sex tours to Zante? Dallam meets Hero's sisters

> On the other side of the harbor, upon the top of the Promontory, they have another [church] far lesse; with a Chappel dedicated to the Virgin *Mary*, called *Madonna del Scopo*, reputed effectresse of miracles, and much invocated by sea-faring men.
>
> Sir George Sandys, 1615[1]

Once the *Hector* had left Algiers, Dallam swiftly compiled a catalogue of what he had just seen. Emboldened by his first experiences on foreign soil, he then set to work planning his next foray. For Dallam, life at sea was proving to be both exciting and empowering. He seems to have learned more during the journey itself than from any reading he might have done beforehand. After all, Dallam was at sea with a number of well-read and highly educated men, so there is every likelihood that ideas about what to expect were available from a wide range of rumour, previous experience and written report. And there is every reason to imagine that, being men at sea, they regularly talked about women.

Four hundred years ago, before Zante was annually visited by sun-seeking English holidaymakers, Dallam conceived and led what may well have been the first English group tour onto the island. Zante at the time had peculiarly strong commercial links with England. By 1609, the Scotsman William Lithgow could scoff at how the English were so addicted to the currants of Zante that the islanders had grown rich and lazy because 'some Liquourous lips...can hardly digest...without these curraunts'. 'There is,' he declared, 'no other Nation save this, thus addicted to that miserable Ile.'[2] When Dallam arrived, Zante was governed by a Providore who served 'under the Ducke of Venis', who in turn but 'houldes it under the great Turke' (p. 19). Nevertheless, ships from ports 'whear Turks do live' were held in quarantine before being allowed to land, and the *Hector* was coming from Algiers, where it had picked up some Turkish passengers.

There and then, anchored for days outside Zante harbour, being held in virtual bondage, the Englishman in Dallam emerged, yearning for the freedom to go for a walk in the country, to wander amidst the green and see what was there. Dallam's eye for a prospect surely bespeaks a childhood spent walking in the dales:

> Whyleste we lay thus for six dayes upon the seae before the towne, I touke great notis of a little mountayne, the which, as I thought, did ly close to the seae, and semed to be a verrie pleasante place to take a vew of the whole iland and the seae before it. It showed to be verrie greene and playen ground on the tope of it, and a whyte thinge lyke a rocke in the mydle tharof. I touke suche pleasour in behouldinge this hill that I made a kinde of vow or promise to my selfe that assowne as I sett foute on shore I would nether eate nor Drinke untill I had bene on the tope tharof; and in the meane time did labur with tow of my companyons, and perswaded them to beare me company. (pp. 19–20)

This desire to command the new landscape from a high place, to behold a prospect view, combines with a desire to gain proximity to the green plain he can glimpse on the mountain top. And he wants to discover what landmark or monument marks the spot, that 'whyte thinge lyke a rock'. Once allowed ashore, Dallam sets off to climb that hill – Mount Scopos – taking Michael Watson and Edward Hale in tow. As it happens, Dallam's 'pleasour' in viewing the hill and fancying himself on top of it, taking in 'a vew of the whole iland', proves wholly anticipatory, a pleasure of the imagination that is soon displaced by the strange and unexpected.

Dallam's adventures on Zante make a remarkable contribution to that subspecies within the genre of travel writing, the moment when the traveller offers advice to future travellers by exemplifying how to deal with the local population. Since local folk probably have something you want and will most likely be friendly if you are courteous towards them, it will pay to be friendly and make yourself a welcomed guest while wandering in foreign parts. Regardless of language or presumptive class or religious barriers, Dallam seems to know instinctively when it is safe to brazen it out and when better to turn and run. Unlike his friend Watson, he can tell the difference between a Zantean goatherd wearing a stag's pelt and carrying a big stick, and a threatening 'savidge' ogre.

> So, assendinge the hill aboute halfe a myle, and loukinge up, we sawe upon a storie of the hill above us a man goinge with a great staffe on his shoulder,

havinge a clubed end, and on his heade a cape which seemed to hus to have five horns standinge outyghte, and a greate heard of gootes and shepe folloed him.

My frende Myghell Watson, when he saw this, he seemed to be verrie fearfull, and would have perswaded us to go no farther, tellinge us that surly those that did inhabite thare weare savidge men, and myghte easalye wronge us, we havinge no sordes or dageres, nether any more Company; but I tould him that yf thei were divers, I would, with Godes help, be as good as my worde. (p. 20)

A substitute for more 'Company', God makes one of his infrequent appearances, but the expression is more a part of that self-reliant and intrepid rhetoric that has got Dallam where he is than evidence of piety. Leaving Watson behind to cower in a bush, he leads Hale further up the hill, where they meet a local man who, 'having nothinge in his handes', is evidently unarmed. Dallam takes charge before the coachman can become fearful:

Cothe I to my fellow: Nede, we shall see by this man what people they be that inhabit heare. When this man came unto us he lay his hand upon his breste, and boued his head and bodye with smylinge countinance, makinge us a sine to go up still. (p. 21)

Reading gestures and 'sines' and knowing when to trust them seem to come naturally. While Ned proves timorous, Dallam urges him along until they reach the top:

Cominge to the top thare was a prittie fair grene, and on one sid of it a whyte house bulte of lyme, and some square, the whyche had bene the house of an ancoriste, who, as I harde after wardes, Died but a litle before our cominge thether, and that she had lived five hundrethe years. (p. 21)

Dallam records the anecdote without surprise or comment. A tale about a 500-year-old anchorite who once inhabited the magical 'whyte thinge lyke a rocke' did not seem so very remarkable. By the time he came to write of his tour of Zante, he had learned a great deal and might well have been prepared to believe almost anything. In fulfilling the promise he made to himself while quarantined, however, Dallam discovered more than he expected.

Perhaps the reason Dallam never recorded his much anticipated view over the harbour from the hill is that, on Zante, he encountered some women very like Christopher Marlowe's Hero – indeed, who might have been her sisters. Untrained in the classics, Dallam was unaware of the tale of Venus and her temple Vestals. Having climbed to the 'greene and playen ground on the tope', Dallam recalled the rest of his bargain to himself:

> Than saide I to Ned Hale: I will go to yender house to gitt som drinke, for I have greate neede. The wether was verrie hote, and I was fastinge. But Ned Hale told me that I had no reason to drinke at there handes, nether to go any nearer them. Yeate I wente bouldly to the sid of the house, whear I saw another man drinke, and made a sine to him within that I woulde drinke. (p. 21)

Dallam had water in mind, and clearly figured that since it was what the locals drank, it must be safe. Yet his evident success in appearing both harmless and friendly gets him rather more than he asked for; carpets were spread and 'six bottels full of verrie good wyne' produced. Raising his cup 'full of a redeishe wyne, which they do cale Rebola', Dallam proposed a 'carrouse to all our frendes in Inglande', much to the horror of his fellow Englishman. Timorous Ned kept true to his trepidations about ingesting foreign substances and refused to drink or eat anything. But Dallam made bold: 'When I had give God thankes for it, I drank it of, and it was the beste that ever I dranke' (p. 22). Refreshed, Dallam wanted to give his host a gift; 'mony' in the form of a Spanish silver half-dollar was summarily refused, but the offer of a small knife provoked boisterous excitement:

> When he had taken it oute of the sheathe and louked upon it, he caled with a loude voyce: Sisto, Sisto! Than another man Came runninge, unto whom he showed but only the hafte of it, and than they began to wrastell for the knife. (p. 22)

Presuming 'Sisto' to be the fellow's name (perhaps 'Christos'?), Dallam here names the one and only foreigner he would ever identify. He it was who, the wrestling over, took our hero 'into a Chappell, whear we found a preste at mass and wex candls burninge'. His guide conducted Dallam to a 'pue' from which 'I satt and saw the behaveour of the people, for thare weare about 20 men, but not a woman emongste them; for the wemen weare in a lower chapell by them selves' (p. 23). Having hung back, poor 'Ned Hale cam after' and unknowingly stumbled into the midst of the women's quarters, where 'tow wemmen put oute there heades and laughed at him – as indeed they myghte, for he behaved himself very foolishly. Nether he nor I had ever sene any parte of a mass before, nether weare we thinge the wyser for that' (p. 23).

Dallam's first detailed observation of women in the Ottoman Empire occurs during this appropriately farcical episode inside an Orthodox church occasioned by the foolish mistake of Ned living up to his name and donkeying about among the women. Claiming that he remained uncontaminated by the

Orthodox liturgy because he could not understood what was going on, Dallam soon became involved in a further series of events that he also, at first, failed to understand. With no small instinct for narrative decorum, Dallam was cagey in reporting what happened next, carefully preserving his original impressions with only a tantalizing hint of hindsight.

> Sarvis beinge ended, we Departed out of the chapell; but presently one cam after us, who did seme verrie kindly to intreat me to goo backe againe, and he leed us throughe the chappell into the cloyster, wheare we found standing eyghte verrie fayre wemen, and rychly apparled, som in reed satten, som whyte, and som in watchell Damaske, there heads verrie finly attiered, cheanes of pearle and juels in there eares, 7 of them verrie yonge wemen, the eighte was Anchante, and all in blacke. I thoughte they hade bene nones, but presently after I kenewe they wear not. Than weare we brought into that house wheare before I had dranke. (p. 23)

Ned reluctantly accepted some water, but Dallam 'did eate one egge, bread and chese, and I dranke tow boules of wyne' (p. 24). With the heat, exercise and wine, he must have been fairly intoxicated by now, and was soon having all sorts of uncertain ideas about those 'eyghte verrie fayre wemen' outside in the cloister. When these finely dressed young women who 'wear not' nuns came in, Dallam hoped they were going to join in the merry-making:

> Whyleste we satt there, the Jentelwemen came in, and thre of them came verrie neare us, and louked earnestly upon us. I offered one of them the cup to drinke, but she would not. Than I offered to give him that tended upon us my halfe Dollor, but he would not take any monye. These wemen standing all to gether before us, I thoughte they had bene Dwelleres there, because no mony would be taken. (p. 24)

Dallam clearly recognized that something was going on, but simply could not figure out how the system operated; cash must somehow be involved, but his half-dollar of Spanish silver was again refused. Covering perplexity in fine sententious style – 'I thoughte they had bene Dwelleres there, because no mony would be taken' – Dallam offered his 'other knyfe, of 2s. price' to the 'ould Jentlewoman'. It almost worked: the young women 'wondered muche at' the knife and then 'they came altogether towarde me and bowed there bodies, to show ther thankfulnes. So Ned Hale and I Touke our leves and wente awaye verrie merrily' (p. 24). Merrily they went, but further merriment would follow.

By the time they had collected Michael Watson from behind the bush and rejoined the ship's company, Dallam and his companions had been so long away that the English passengers were angry at having been made to wait. But Dallam took charge of the murmuring party by narrating his adventures. The immediate result was that several of the 'gentlemen' demanded to be taken to the church. A member of the local community seized the opportunity of showing them the way:

> I bid them hould ther peace, and lett me tell them my adventurs. When I had toulde them all the storie, they wondered at my bouldnes, and some Grekes that weare thare sayde that they never hard that any Inglishe man was ever thare before. It was than aboute 12 of the clocke, and nyne of these Jentlmen would needes go presently thether to se That which I had done, and because I would not go againe, beinge wearie, for it was 4 myles thether, they hiered a gide, and yeate, when they came to the mountaine, they myste of the Ryghte way, and did climbe upon the Rockes, so that som of them gott fales and broke there shins; but at laste they got thether, and the waye for them, by me, beinge preparede, thei were bid verrie welcom; but there gide hade Instrucktede them with that which I never thought on, the which was, that at ther firste cominge they should go Into the chappell, and thar offer som mony, as litle as they would, and than they should have all kinde entertainmente. So, verrie late in the evininge, they Returned safly againe, and gave me thankes for that which theye had sene.
>
> The 30th day I wente with 3 more, havinge a Greke to show us the way into the Castle. (p. 25)

'All kinde entertainment' indeed. Still no doubt flushed from the wine and the climbing after being kept so long at sea, and from the erotic excitement of finding more than simply a hilltop spot with a view, Dallam paused to stake his claim to being an original, the first Englishman up there, even if the other nine 'gentlemen' were the first to be clued in to local custom. Dallam's desire for a prospect view precipitated a series of further tours by Englishmen to the hilltop. The nine unnamed gentlemen were certainly keen to try their luck and 'the waye for them by me beinge preparde', they received 'all kinde entertainmente'. Dallam himself, of course, claimed that he returned only for a guided visit to the castle, yet was again back in town the next day. May day on Zante in 1599 turns out to have been a day of competitive horsemanship among 'all the able men of the Greeks' (p. 25), no doubt pumping up their springtime energies for a walk up Mount Scopos later on.

The top of Mount Scopos is still a magical place, despite the radio and television towers. The anchorite's tomb has gone, but the view of Zante harbour remains magnificent. The church and outbuildings Dallam visited have been ruined by earthquakes, but a small chapel has been built within the rubble. It is surrounded by wild oats.

Casual piracy

The *Hector* left Zante on 2 May. For the next two weeks Dallam remained on board as they sailed east on the standard merchant's route, calling at Iskenderun for the Aleppo trade before turning back west for Istanbul.[3] Ever since the episode with the Dunkirk pirates, Dallam had been growing increasingly critical of the captain of the *Hector* and the way he began predating upon any and all non-British vessels smaller than the *Hector* once she entered the Mediterranean. At 300 tons, with 27 guns under the control of a highly skilled master gunner and a crew of 100 men, the *Hector* was a spectacular and intimidating presence at sea.[4] She was big enough, and loaded with enough sail and firepower, to outgun and out-sail most sea-borne predators.[5]

Piracy of the casual sort Dallam describes was common in the Mediterranean. Indeed, Dallam did not criticize the practice itself – he seems to have found nothing wrong in attacking and demanding 'prizes' and 'presents' from any and every smaller ship that happened not to be flying a British flag. What did draw his anger was the way that Parsons negotiated privately with the captains of captured ships and accepted personal bribes, refusing to share the ransoms gained with the other members of the crew, and not honouring his duties as a servant of the English Crown.

Dallam first reports casual piracy off Malta in May, when the *Hector* chased and intimidated the captain of a smaller vessel into paying up without having to fire a shot. In such cases, Dallam writes of 'presents' rather than 'prizes' being demanded. He described the incident clinically, commenting only on the massive difference in size and power between the two ships, noting especially the symbolic power of the *Hector*'s flag:

A litle before we cam so farr as Malta, we gave chace to a shipe, being the 15th daye. After the mayster of that shipp parsaved by our flage whate we weare, and did se that thre suche as him selfe was not able to contende with us, he caste out his boote and came a borde us, and broughte with him for a presente diverse Comodities: som turkie carpites, some quiltede Coveringes of watchat silke, and tow or thre great peecis of salte fishe that wear 7 or 8 foute longe and one foute square. It was strainge fishe unto us. (p. 17)

Such fish would remain strange to Dallam and his fellow passengers and crew. Once again, Dallam grumbled on behalf of the crew who were 'muche greved' because Parsons, 'having recaved som secrite bribe', returned the presents and demanded no further ransom despite the fact that everyone on board knew there were ten thousand dollars' worth of Spanish goods aboard the suppliant ship (p. 18). Rather than condemning the activity itself, Dallam felt that, united under 'our flage', the *Hector*'s entire company shared presumptive rights to negotiate and accept the 'presente' from any wealthy, smaller, foreign vessel they came upon. Without further comment, Dallam notes blandly how two days later 'we gave chace to another shipp of Massillia, and borded here, but had litle or nothinge from her' (p. 18).

While at sea, Dallam grew familiar with and complicit in this world where the biggest and most powerful expect to take presents from smaller ships. As the *Hector* entered Ottoman waters, however, her position was equivocal: after all, her mission was to bear gifts from England's Queen to the Ottoman Sultan, not to demand presents from Ottoman ships. International diplomacy put an end to the *Hector*'s predatory activities: casual piracy was replaced by new types of informal exchange in which the captain of the *Hector* had to give rather than take. Later in the journey, while moored off Troy, Dallam is duly impressed by his first sighting of an Ottoman fleet which 'to our thinkinge, was a marvalus show' (p. 48). Captain Parsons dutifully ordered 'the gonors to give them thre peecis' in salutation, but 'the which was meserably done; yeate, beinge so neare the wales of Troy, the ecko was suche that everie peece semed to be five by the reporte'. Unimpressed, the Ottoman admiral 'sente a gallie to us to demande his presente, and also to aske whye we did salute him no better'. Reluctantly, Parsons eventually sent 'two holland chestis' to the Ottoman admiral, and 'som tobacko and tobacko-pipes' to the captain of the galley who conveyed the demand (pp. 48–9).

On this occasion, when the powerful Ottomans were making inflated demands for presents from the *Hector*, Dallam evidently felt personally entitled, as a representative of his nation, to take a trophy back home from Ottoman soil in exchange for the affront. The very next morning he went ashore, 'boughte som breade and hens' from some Greek villagers, and set off to the ruins: 'and from thence I broughte a peece of a whyte marble piller, the which I broke with my owne handes, havinge a good hamer, which my mate Harvie did carrie a shore for the same purpose; and I broughte this peece of marble to London' (pp. 49–50). Dallam can hardly be thought to have been driven by archaeological interests. His desire, rather, involved bringing a souvenir of ancient Troy back to London.

It is hardly surprising that, while they were happy to pay the Greeks for the groceries, Dallam and his mate went ashore near where they thought Troy had been, fully prepared to steal antiquities from Ottoman shores. For weeks they had been living where the presumptive right of those with power to take whatever they wished had been the name of the game. Dallam had learned about casual piracy, about taking what you can, and was one of the first, but by no means last, British tourist to assume the right to engage in amateur archaeology and souvenir gathering.

Beasts, bugs and death

Like tourists today, Dallam was often preoccupied by clothing, food and strange sights. But he also had something of the natural historian about him that led him to notice and describe some of the exotic creatures he had seen. Whenever he set foot ashore, usually to search for fresh food or wash his clothes, Dallam seemed to stumble upon some new and often frightening creature. By the time he arrived in Istanbul, his trepidations had by no means overwhelmed his confidence, but he had become increasingly anxious that, having entered the Ottoman Empire, he might never see home again.

At sea, Dallam's recorded desires mostly involve the possibilities of fresh food. Passing Cyprus, he noticed 'great store of wylde swyne; but, out of all question it is a verrie fruitful contrie' (p. 28), and was clearly not alone in having fresh comestibles – especially flesh – on his mind. Once the *Hector* had anchored 'in the Roode before Scanderoune', Dallam set off with 'our Mr. Guner, tow of his mates, Mr. Chancie, our surgin, one of our Trumpeteres', as well as 'my maete, John Harvie, every one of us havinge a muskett' (p. 28), with a view to a kill. Hoping to bag 'som wylde foule', they returned without a shot being fired. Once on shore, the hunting party began worrying about tearing their clothing in the undergrowth and very soon noticed that the woods contained 'a man called a mountaineard, lyinge in a bushe' and armed (p. 29). After wandering for some miles, they spotted some 'buffelawes, beastes biger then our great oxen', but soone turned and ran when 'aboute 40, of the afore sayde mountayneares' began closing in on the Englishmen, no doubt anxious to protect their livestock. Abandoning hopes of a bag, the English hunters made off: 'Runninge at a ventur throughe thicke and thine, thorns and bryeres, tearinge our close, at the laste we recovered a fayer playne, wheare we myghte se our shipe' (p. 29).

The next day Dallam and Harvie went ashore again, but only to 'washe our lininge', no doubt filthy after two weeks at sea and the previous day's adventures. They stayed close to the shore, and Dallam noticed how these parts were infested with all manner of wildlife:

> We did se thare, upon the wales of an oulde house, verrie strainge varmentes Runing up and downe at great pace, som of them biger than a great toude, and of the same collore, but they had longe tayles lyk a Ratt. (p. 30)

Dallam's nineteenth-century editor annotated the sentence 'Lizards'.

While their linen dried, they collected some unnamed fruit and 'espied a great Ader that was in the tre upon the bowes, at least 12 or 14 foute from the grounde. He was even Reddie to leape upon one of us' (p. 31). Dallam again sensibly backed off, but he clearly cannot be trusted if he imagined that adders hang out in trees, even in southern Anatolia.

Moored off Iskenderun, Dallam saw the Ottoman army for the first time, 'souldieres of Damascus, a parte of the greate Turkes armye, that were goinge to the warres', and was rather more fascinated by the spectacle than threatened by these enemies of Christendom. Their proximity, however, held the *Hector* at anchor for two weeks since 'our marchantes durste not adventure to unlode any goods' lest the soldiers seized them.[6] The delay gave Dallam plenty of opportunity for admiring their activities. 'Everie daye,' he reported, 'thar would com Ridinge to the seae side, a great company of brave horsmen, with their lancis. Som hade their neagors to carrie their Lancis and other weapins' (p. 31). Dallam wanted to talk with them, or at least learn their number, but was frustrated 'because I could not be conversante with them, or any that did know' the 'number of brave Jenesaries' (p. 32). Instead, he joined a food-buying trip to Tarsus, pausing on the way back to gather samphire from the very shore where Jonah was 'caste out of the whales bellie, as the Turkes and Greekes tould us' (p. 32).

Beasts biblical, real, misnamed or entirely imagined appear as the *Hector* approached ever closer and closer to Istanbul. Most worrying of all, Englishmen started dying. On 4 June, while still anchored off the coast near Iskenderun, 'died one Edwarde Hayes we did carrie out of Ingland to be couke for our marchants at alippo'.[7] Once they left Iskenderun, even more English passengers fell sick. On 17 June, after a week at sea, Thomas Cable, 'who was under 20 yearis of age, and son to one of the owneres of our shipe', died (p. 34). Exactly two weeks later, on 8 July, 'Died one John Knill, sarvante to Mr. Wyseman, marchante, who was also one of the owneres of our shipp' (p. 41). Thirteen days later, on 21 July, 'Died a boye Caled John Felton, who was borne at Yarmouthe' (p. 47). That is all Dallam reported, offering neither description nor speculative account of why these English passengers, two youths and two domestic servants, died. Surely someone on board must have mentioned that Iskenderun was notoriously 'the bane of Franks' because of the bad air and filthy water – that is why it was better to sleep on board than spend any time ashore, according to William Biddulph and others.[8] Superstitious rather than pious, Dallam simply recorded the names and dates of deaths among English passengers. Unlike many at the time, he did not think in astrological terms, neither seeking to find some meaning in the dates, nor even addressing how these first deaths occurred with an uncanny regularity every two weeks.

Island interludes: Rhodes and Chios

Among the qualities that made Dallam so attractive to the Ottomans was his musical talent. He not only designed and built organs, but also played them, and had brought from London 'a pare of virginals' costing £1 15s (p. 2). On board ship in Rhodes harbour the night after young Thomas Cable died, Dallam gave a performance that would later save him from prison. Since 'the Captaine basha, governer of the towne' was away, the highest ranking official was a deputy:

[T]he Chia his Debitie, who for the time was Captaine, he, with the chefeest men of the towne, came abord our ship, and she was trimed up in as handsom maner as we could for the time. Our gonroume was one of the fayereste Roumes in the ship, and pleasant to com into. In the gonroume I had a pare of virginals, the which our Mr. goner, to make the better showe, desired me to sett them open. When the Turkes and Jues came in and saw them, they wondered what it should be; but when I played on them, than they wondered more. Diveres of them would take me in there armes and kis me, and wyshe that I would dwell with them. (p. 35)

Dallam's first reported musical performance was a major success, eliciting the first of many invitations he would receive to stay and 'dwell'. The Ottomans and the Jews, it seems, were hospitable to Englishmen, their instruments and their skills. Being made welcome evidently increased Dallam's confidence among strangers. Only later would he register trepidation at being physically embraced by foreigners.

The day following his onboard performance, he went sightseeing with Harvie and 'the stuerde of our ship and his men' (p. 34). Dallam and friends evidently knew how to conduct themselves safely under the eye of a potentially hostile authority. Marvelling at the fortifications and ordinance, 'bothe of brass and Iron, the which was made by Christians' (p. 35), the English group 'paste Rounde aboute the towne with oute any contradicktion', pausing only to drink some very cheap wine (p. 36). Problems arrived on the boat that came to take them back to the *Hector* in the form of two fellow travellers, the Reverend Mr Maye, 'our preatcher', and 'one that was appoynted to be our Imbaseders under butler'. These two cajoled Dallam's party to wait while the inquisitive Maye examined an inscription over the city gate.

When we weare thare, he saw a farr of a fountaine of water, made lyke to one of our Conducktes, with a fayre, brighte Dishe of steele hanginge in a cheane, for the Turkes drinke nothinge but water. I praye you, cothe Mr. Maye, goe with me to yonder fountaine. (p. 36)

Dallam had already insisted that he was eager to get back on board the *Hector*, being 'verrie hungrie and wearrie with travel' (p. 36), and one can almost feel his reluctant deference to the preacher – 'So we wente all with him to the fountaine, and everie one of us did drinke a dishe of water' (p. 36). Maye, despite having lived in Aleppo for some years, almost immediately caused trouble by talking with the locals.[9] His eagerness to speak Italian with 'tow stout Turkes' led him into difficulties because he lacked that combination of canniness and charm that had been protecting our hero Dallam:

Soe, as theye weare a talkinge, I louked aboute me, and a Turke, settinge upon his stale, who did know me – for he had hard me play on my virginals and kissed me aborde our shipe – he beckened me to com unto him; and when I came som what neare him, in kindnes and som love he bore unto me, made a sine to be gone; and poynted to the gate, and bid me make haste. So to the gate went I as faste as I coulde Truge, and my mate Harvie and the Reste of my Company followed after as faste as theye could; leavinge Mr. Maye and the under butler talkinge with the Turkes, for theye tow could speake Ittallian a litle, and so could none of us. (pp. 36–7)

For all their linguistic virtuosity, Maye and the 'under butler' landed up in prison, held for ransom by the very 'Chia' for whom Dallam had performed the night before. Back on board the *Hector*, Dallam argued once again with Captain Parsons, who tried to pin responsibility on Dallam by accusing him of having caused some previous offence. But after much wrangling, the Chia's demand vindicated our author, pointing the finger once again at Parson's parsimony and 'the base and covetous condition of these Rude and barbarus doged Turkes' (p. 39).

The Answer of the Chial was this:
Yeaster Day I was abord your Shipp presentinge my Captayn's person in his absence; you gave me not suche entertainmente as my place Did Requier; you made me no good cheare, nether Did you give me a presente for my Captaine. (p. 38)

Once the Chia had been presented with a gift for himself, 'as muche brode Clothe' as will make a 'Vest', the captives were released, enabling Dallam once again to fault Parsons while restating his maxims that the Turks were covetous and 'how litle they do Regard Christians' (p. 39). He might have noted also how evidently happy they were to receive gifts of English broadcloth.

Following his personal dealings with the 'Chia' on Rhodes, Dallam must have felt rather pleased with himself. Ignoring a warning from the captain, he welcomed an invitation from three gentlemen 'pasingeres' to accompany them ashore at Chios to buy 'freshe vittals'. This shopping trip caused such excitement that when the party went to pay their respects to the Consul, children broke down the wall of the Consul's garden. Leaving the 'Consull verrie angrie' at this vandalism, Dallam's party discovered that they were the best – indeed the only – show in town:

Goinge Downe the ladder from the scaffould, upon bothe sides of the ladder did stand the chefeste wemen in the towne, in degrees one above Another, to se us at our goinge awaye; they stoode in suche order as we myghte se theire facis and bristes nakede, yeate weare they verrie richly appareled, with cheanes aboute theyre neckes, and juels in them and in there eares, theire heades verrie comly dressed with rebbininge of diverse collores; but that which made us moste admiere them was their beautie and cleare complecktion. I thinke that no part of the worlde can compare with the wemen in That contrie for beautie. (pp. 45–6)

On the subject of women, Dallam felt suddenly authorized to generalize globally. Is this simply the effect of too much time spent in the all-male society aboard the *Hector*? The women of Chios certainly were renowned for their beauty at the time. Dallam might have learned about them on board either from experienced sailors or from someone familiar with Nicholas Nicolay's claim that 'in all the East partes' there are no women 'more acomplished in beautie and good grace, & amarous courtesie' than those of Chios.[10] On the other hand, he may simply have been reporting what he saw for himself.

Travels with Thomas Glover: Gallipoli to Istanbul

When the *Hector* entered the Dardanelles, Dallam took his first opportunity to leave the ship for better company. Together with the others 'that weare for the presente', he left the *Hector* becalmed off Gallipoli, and set off 'two hundrethe and fiftie myle' for Istanbul in three smaller boats, in company with a group from the embassy who had arrived to meet them. Others who joined the shore party included Maye, the 'preatcher, and other Jentlmen that wente to sarve the Imbassader', who feared 'that one of our sailores was infeckted with the plague' (p. 51). The perils encountered by this group, 'in all, 16, with Mr. Glover and Mr. Baylye' – embassy officials from Istanbul – were of a suitably comic kind, in which the dangers were very small, entirely imagined or caused by the rowdy behaviour of the travellers themselves.

The English party soon ran into trouble 'at a greate Towne Called Relezea' [Marmara Ereglisi] where, despite plenty of available 'wyne and breade . . . some of our Company' broke into a vineyard to steal grapes (p. 51). Dallam was happy to name the culprits and heroes. After 'beinge pursued by the Greekes that owned the vinyard', the vandals were 'not only in Dainger of receavinge som hurte, but also of lousing theire garmentes. Cuthberte Bull had loste his Cloake, and one that wente to be the Imbassaderes Couke was pinyonede, his girdle and knyfes taken awaye; but Mr. Gonzale, a verrie stoute man, redemed these thinges againe' (pp. 51–2).

The incident was not yet over, however. The 'pore Greeks' whose vineyards had been robbed complained to the governor who, to make the situation even more tense, 'was than in our company, and had broughte us a sheepe for a presente'. In light of the governor's hospitality, the thieving behaviour of the Englishmen must have seemed particularly odious. Thomas Glover quickly took command of the situation. Unlike the parsimonious Parsons, Glover knew how to take care of local difficulties and potential embarrassments. He quickly earned Dallam's respect for being 'verrie willinge to make the Greekes restetution for the hurte was Done them...The nexte morninge, our captaine, Mr. Glover, gave unto this governor or captaine, 2 or 3 peecis of goold caled chickenes' (p. 52), those thin coins worth roughly nine shillings each.

Dallam was delighted to travel in the company of a man like Glover, who was not simply an experienced traveller, but a professional expatriate. He knew when and how to take control, and the importance of having deep pockets and ready cash. When they met, Glover, Istanbul bred, was already a wealthy merchant who spoke several languages fluently. Here was someone Dallam could admire and trust to sort out local difficulties. They proceeded the next day a further 'ten myles' to a town Dallam calls 'Hora', where they left the boats for a trip inland, stopping in 'a towne caled Cannosea' where 'our captaine, Mr. Glover,' rented a house for the night (p. 53).[11]

Dallam's sense of narrative anticipation can be remarkably Chaucerian. Since leaving the ship 'we never put off our clothis', and finding that there were no beds, only wooden platforms, the Englishmen were reluctant to turn in for the night. After a 'shorte diner', Dallam and friends strolled by the shore, spotting 'diverse sortes of varmen, which we have not the like in Inglande'. Stumbling upon 'a thicke softe weed, that growed by the wood sid', they eagerly gathered up armfuls of the stuff 'to laye under our heades, when we should sleepe' (p. 54). Such details about dirty linen and alien 'varmen' feed directly into the Englishmen's fears when eventually they do bed down for the night, and find fulfilment in a comic catastrophe that we might have seen coming:

> Everie man had his Sorde reddie Drawne lyinge by his side; tow of our com-
> pany had musketes. When we had layne about halfe an houre, we that had
> our weeden pillowes weare sodonly wonderfully tormented with a varmen
> that was in our pillowes, the which did bite farr worss than fleaes, so that we
> weare glad to throw awaye our pillowes, and swepe the house cleane; but we
> could not clense our selves so sowne. (p. 54)

We will not dwell on the condition of Dallam's underclothing and what it was probably carrying before this new foreign infestation appeared. With several of the party writhing on the floor, moaning and scratching as the new species of louse, tick or sandfly enjoyed the novel flavour of English blood, Glover again took charge, regaling the new arrivals with scary tales:

Thus as we lay wakinge in a Darke uncomfortable house, Mr. Glover tould us what strainge varmen and beastes he had sene in that contrie, for he had lived longe thare. He spoake verrie muche of Aderes, snaykes, and sarpentes, the defferance and the bignes of som which he had sene. (p. 54)

Whatever Glover may have conveyed about the differences between 'Aderes, snaykes, and sarpentes', he could not have accounted for the kind about to appear once they had all finally settled down. While some managed to sleep, those that could 'not sleepe laye still and sayd nothinge for disquietinge of the reste, all being whyste'. At this moment, 'Mr. Bayly had occasion to goe to the dore to make water':

My Baylle, when he lay downe to sleepe, had untied his garters a litle, so that when he came into the gallarie, the wynde blew his garter, that was louse and trayled after him, rounde aboute the other legge; it was a greate silke garter, and by the force of the wynde it fettered his legges bothe faste together. Our talke a litle before, of Aders, snakes, and sarpentes, was yeat in his rememberance, and the place was neare wheare muche varmen was. He thoughte they had swarmed aboute him, but about his legges he Thought he was sur of a sarpente, so that soddonly he cried oute with all the voyce he hade: A sarpente! a sarpente! a sarpente! and was so frighted that he could not finde the doore to gitt in, but made a great bustlinge and noyse in the gallarie. On the other side, we that weare in the house, did thinke that he had saide: Assalted! assalted! for before nyghte we doubted that some tritcherie would hapen unto us in that towne. (p. 55)

In the panic, swords are drawn, shelves upturned and 'pitchers and plateres' sent crashing to the floor. One of the group tried to hide in the chimney and was injured by falling masonry. Glover quickly stepped in to sort out the confusion over Baylye's shout, calling 'everie man by his name, to se yf any man weare slayne or wounded' (p. 56). Since Dallam himself had already shown a remarkable ability to hear the sounds of warning when shouted in a foreign language, how ironic it seems that the fracas occurred over a misheard English word. Awash in the strange sounds of other tongues, the English seem to have lost the ability to recognize their own language.

Exhausted from the night's adventures, Sharpe, Lambert 'and tow jentlmen more, hiered mules' and took off next morning overland for the three days' further journey to Istanbul (p. 57). But Dallam stayed with Glover and his party and returned the *Hector*, which finally anchored two miles off the seraglio on the 16 August 'and the nexte daye she begane to be new payntede' (p. 58).

Another death, further doubts

On 28 August, the very day that the *Hector* 'made hire salutation to the Great Turke' (pp. 58–9), death struck again. Anchored 'on the northe side of the Surralya, the Grande Sinyor beinge in his Cuske', the refurbished *Hector* fired a volley:

> This salutation was verrie strange and wonderfull in the sighte of the Grand Turke and all other Turkes. She was, as I have saide before, new paynted (upon everie topp an anshante, viz., mayne top, fore top, myseen top, sprid saile top, and at everie yardes arme a silk penante). (p. 59)

Dallam's nautical vocabulary has come a long way. Pausing to commend the skilful timing of the ordinance, 'eighte score great shotte' interspersed with vollies of 'smale shott', Dallam, the inventor of clockwork musical instruments, could not help noticing that 'it was done with verrie good decorume and true time'. However, he also could not help worrying about what it meant.

> But one thinge I noteed, which perswaded my simple consaite that this great triumpte and charge was verrie evile bestowed, beinge done unto an infidell. Thare was one man sicke in the ship, who was the ship carpinder, and wyth the reporte of the firste greate peece that was discharged he died.
>
> Lyke wyse at the verrie end of this sarvis an other man, who was one of the stouteste saileres in the shipp, and all this whyle had plyed a great peece in the beake heade of the shipe, as he was raminge in his cartridge of pouder, som fier being lefte in the bretche of the peece, the pouder touke fire and blew that man quite awaye in the smoke; about 3 dayes after all his lower parte, from his waste downward, was founde tow myle from that place, and his heade in an other place. (pp. 59–60)

This is the closest Dallam ever comes to anything resembling supernaturalism, providentialism or even metaphysical speculation. At the time, Dallam was anxiously repairing his organ to make it ready for performance before the 'Grand Sinyor'. Was he simply too preoccupied to learn the names of the dead carpenter and gunner? Or did he imagine that naming these victims of England's tribute to an infidel would somehow compound the evil? These last deaths bring reports of dying among the English on the *Hector* to an end, and in so doing mark a crucial shift in Dallam's account. From now on, and for the rest of his stay in Istanbul, he lived amidst increasing fears, not so much of dying, but of being forced to live out the rest of his life there.

4
Istanbul

Istanbul [is] in the forme of a Triangle in circule 15 myles, seated upon seaven hills, and therefore some would have it the seate of the Anti-christe.

'Mr Stamp', 1609. 'Mr Stamp's Observations in his Voyage to Constantinople', BL Ms Stowe 180, f. 28

Dallam had yet to deal with two of the greatest challenges of his voyage: presenting his organ to Mehmed III and dealing with Henry Lello, the agent of the Levant Company who was nervously waiting to be appointed 'Imbassader'. Lello had not been formally invited to kiss the Sultan's hand because no present had been sent by Elizabeth. From Lello's point of view, Dallam and his organ were both crucial for rather fraught negotiations with the Sultan for a renewal of capitulations in defiance of French claims that would include diplomatic control over Dutch shipping in Ottoman ports. This was not simply a lucrative matter of collecting duty from Dutch merchants, but an issue of national prestige. So, from Lello's point of view, his entire career depended on the success of Dallam and the gifts. Dallam remained oblivious to this potential crisis in Anglo-Ottoman diplomacy, yet increasingly resented Lello's attitude towards him once he found himself unavoidably caught in a diplomatic triangle between the ambassador and Sultan. Significantly, he never once mentions Lello by name, but refers to him as either the 'Imbassader' or, sometimes with irony, 'my Lord'. Indeed, Dallam was soon as anxious about the way Lello lorded it over him as he was threatened by foreign dangers.

Tensions among the English community in Istanbul when the *Hector* arrived were close to breaking point. Anxieties over Elizabeth's present went back four years to the days of Edward Barton when Mehmed first came to the throne, and had dominated the mission of the English expatriate community ever since. As early as 20 September 1595, Barton had written to the Queen renewing his plea that she must act fast before Anglo-Ottoman trading relations suffered serious damage. His specific instructions regarding what form the present should take reveal how well he understood the Ottoman sensibility:

> Hitherto Mr Barton hath excused the sending of her Maties present; but the merchants not satisfyed, have wrongfully complayned of him; he hath now no further excuse for delay; it is needful therefore, it be presently provided & sent; for the longer it is delayed, the lesse affection it will represent, as it hath bene objected to others & will be to our selves. For the particularitie of the present, it is to be regarded, that it be correspondent to her Majesties fame & reputation; & that her Majestie doe bestow some particular bounti-fulness on the Grand Signor, as the Clocke in forme of a Cocke; and doe also send some token to the old Empresse; thirdly that a Principal tall ship of her Majesties owne be sent with the present, for increasing her Majesties reputa-tion. Fourthly that her Majesties portrature at lardg be sent; as wel to comfort her subjects there, as to shew to the Turk. Finally he requesteth some bounty from her Majestie to himself for the better furnishing his charge & enter-taynment of Embassadors, in this so great a Solempnitie.[1]

Barton himself died before the *Hector* arrived, but he would have been pleased at the form of the gift. Dallam's organ was certainly far more prestigious than a clockwork cockerel, while the carriage sent to Safiye greatly exceeded Barton's request for a token. Even the appearance in the Bosphorus of the *Hector* proved a great wonder to the Turks. Sanderson noted how, in expectation of her arrival, 'the Gran Signor hath appointed to be by the watersid at his place of pleasur, of purpose to see her'.[2] The Venetian bailo Girolamo Capello grudgingly reported how the *Hector* 'is much admired by crowds of Turks; and indeed I understand she deserves to be visited, as she is wonderfully well found in all that is required for fighting, as well as being beautifully decorated and very commodious'.[3] So excited was she by news of the carriage she was about to receive, that Safiye peremptorily sent 'two horses, out of hir owne stable, to drawe the same'. Lello was irritated at having to stable and feed them while the carriage was being repaired and repainted.[4]

After four years' delay, the arrival of the *Hector* with the English gifts had Capello worried that a new era of Anglo-Ottoman relations would destroy Venetian trade.[5] Worse yet, he wrote, 'English vanity in showing off this ship, its artillery, and ammunition, which they allow anyone who goes on board to see, will do a damage to Christendom, and will open the eyes of the Turks to things they do not know.'[6]

Dallam meets Lello

However things appeared to the Venetian bailo, all was not well among the English. Dallam quarrelled with Lello at their first meeting. On Friday, 17 August, he took the chests containing the organ to 'the imbassaders house in the Cittie of Gallata', where a special room had been set up 'that it myghte there be made perfitt before it should be carried to the surralia'. When, on the following Monday, he returned to 'louke into our worke', it seemed that his entire mission would prove a disaster. Jolted inside its packing chests, the organ had literally come unstuck:

> when we opened our chistes we founde that all glewinge worke was clene Decayed, by reason that it hade layne above sixe monthes in the hould of our ship, whicte was but newly bulte, so that the extremetie of the heete in the hould of the shipe, with the workinge of the sea and the hootnes of the cuntrie, was the cause that all glewinge fayled; lyke wyse divers of my mettle pipes were brused and broken. (p. 58)

Making matters worse, the ambassadorial party were haughtily contemptuous at their first sight of Dallam's workmanship, turning up their noses at its worthlessness in cash terms. Lello must have felt especially desperate, knowing that a great deal of the cloth sent as gifts aboard the *Hector* had been ruined in the passage.[7] But Dallam rose to the challenge and answered back in terms he preferred not to record:

> When our Imbassader, Mr. Wyllyam Aldridge, and other jentlmen, se in what case it was in, theye weare all amayzed, and sayde that it was not worthe ii*d*. My answeare unto our Imbassader and to Mr. Aldridge, at this time I will omitt; but when Mr. Alderidge harde what I sayede, he tould me that yf I did make it perfitt he would give me, of his owne purss, 15*li*., so aboute my worke I wente. (p. 58)

Dallam had not come all this way to allow his organ to be snubbed, and certainly not without vigorously speaking up on his own behalf, fully confident he could set things right. He also knew a good deal when he heard one: £15 would nearly pay off his travelling expenses of £18 5s 5d.

For the next ten days, Dallam and his mates set about rebuilding the organ. Dallam quickly acquired a certain status among those jockeying for position within the international community, recording that on the 23rd the King of Fez 'cam to se my worke, and he satt by me halfe a daye', clearly so fascinated by Dallam and his organ that he appeared again four days later (p. 58). During the first week of September, Ottoman interest in the English, their ship and Dallam's organ provoked a series of visits. Sultan Mehmed sailed round the *Hector* for a closer look, while important court officials – the Kapıcı and Bostancı Basha – visited Lello's house in order to see the celebrated organ for themselves (p. 60). Capello's outrage at the audacity of the English continued to grow once he learned of Lello's plans to establish a Protestant church in Pera. The Venetian insisted that he would 'make every effort in order to thwart this excessive and arrogant pretension of the English, who would endeavour to sow even here the perversity and impiety of Calvin to the ruin of these poor Christian Perots'.[8] Meanwhile, Dallam got on with the task before him. Confident of his craftsmanship and still, perhaps, encouraged by the success of his performance on the virginals before the Chia of Rhodes, Dallam dismantled the newly restored organ and transferred it from Pera for reassembly within the seraglio.

Inside the seraglio

Dallam's description of entering the seraglio offers a very clear sense of how Ottoman society operated horizontally, a system that measured status, privilege and rank in terms of how close to the centre one was permitted to get. At the centre was the Great Turk himself. Dallam entered the old city through one of the twelve gates in the city walls, before arriving at the first of the seraglio entrances that led deeper and deeper into the courtyards of the Topkapi palace: 'Beinge entered within the firste gate, thare was placed righte againste the gate five greate peecis of brass, with Christians armes upon them...Than we passed throughe verrie Delitfull walkes and garthins' (p. 61). The ellipsis is authorial and marks how Dallam himself paused to confront the symbolic threat of those captured arms before moving on to witness the delights ahead of him as he penetrated deeper and deeper, moved closer and closer to the centre of Ottoman power. At the gate into the second court, Dallam first met that unnamed Cornishman, 'my Intarpreter', who called out to 'tow jemeglans' to open up (pp. 61–2). Here Dallam paused to comment on the gardens, noting that he had seen 'none so well kept in the world' as those within the first courtyard. Within the second court he reported that there were 'no gardens, but statly buildinges; many courtes paved with marble and suche lyke stone' (p. 62). Dallam was already entering places into which the merchant turned diplomat Lello had never been admitted.

Once inside, Dallam's thoughts turned to food. He was amazed that 'in November, as I satt at diner, I se them gather grapes upon the vines, and theye broughte them to me to eat' (p. 62). He was thrilled to report how for 'the space of a monthe I Dined everie day in the Surralia, and we had everie day grapes after our meate', that he almost repeated himself word for word four paragraphs later: '[I] dinede Thare almoste everie Daye for the space of a monthe; which no Christian ever did in there memorie that wente awaye a Christian' (p. 64).

Although he took only four days to re-erect his organ in the appointed room, Dallam managed to dine in the seraglio for a month. He expressed something of his excitement at being inside the palace all this time by a series of pointed antitheses that describe the place and its functions:

> Cominge into the house whear I was appoynted to sett up the presente or instramente; it semed to be rether a churche than a dwellinge house; to say the truthe, it was no dwellinge house, but a house of pleasur, and lyke wyse a house of slaughter; for in that house was bulte one litle house, verrie curius bothe within and witheout; for carvinge, gildinge, good Collors and vernishe, I have not sene the lyke. In this litle house, that emperor that rained when I was thare, had nyntene brotheres put to deathe in it, and it was bulte for no other use but for the stranglinge of everie emperors bretherin. (pp. 62–3)

Having recently restored his own 'instramente', Dallam had his eye in for a decent paint and varnish job, and went on to list the sumptuous hangings, silk carpets, marble pillars, brass and gold fixtures adorning this 'house of pleasur' that was 'lyke wyse a house of slaughter'. In this palace of luxurious attractions and implicit dangers, Dallam soon began to sense that his own liberty was at risk, the threat taking the form of foreign men who hugged and kissed him after a performance:

> The 18 daye (stayinge somethinge longe before I wente), the Coppagawe who is the Grand Sinyor's secritarie, sente for me that one of his frendes myghte heare the instramente. Before I wente awaye, the tow jemaglanes, who is keepers of that house, touke me in theire armes and Kised me, and used many perswations to have me staye with the Grand Sinyor, and sarve him. (p. 64)

It is a shame that we hear nothing further of those 'many perswations', but Dallam perhaps noticed only the intention to make him stay without any detailed sense of what he was being offered.

Performance anxieties: Lello's advice

With his organ successfully repaired, Dallam turned swiftly to his next challenge, his strained relations with Lello. The night before he was scheduled to perform before Mehmed, Dallam was summoned to the ambassadorial chamber and given, not encouragement, but such stern advice that he felt impelled to write it down, word for word. He even gave Lello's speech a little title in his manuscript. 'The Imbassadores spetche unto me in Love after he had given me my charge' is the only extended passage of reported speech in the entire account. The term 'Love' here is emphatically diplomatically ironic since, in context, the speech served as a declaration of the terms of an unequal class struggle going on between Dallam and Lello.[9] Almost every detail of Lello's stern advice cues a moment in Dallam's subsequent description of how his own performance achieved a victory for the craftsman over his 'lord'.

Lello began pompously, presuming on the title of the Queen to make sure that Dallam understood his place amongst the various court players. 'Yow are,' Lello commenced, 'com hether wythe a presente from our gratious Quene, not to an ordinarie prince or kinge, but to a myghtie monarke of the worlde,' from whom, it seems, Dallam was to expect no reward. 'It was,' Lello continued:

> never knowne that upon the receaving of any presente he gave any rewarde unto any Christian, and tharfore you muste louke for nothinge at his handes. Yow would thinke that for yor longe and wearriesom voyege, with dainger of lyfe, that yow weare worthy to have a litle sighte of him; but that yow muste not loake for nether. (p. 65)

In reporting how Lello instructed him to be humble and to expect nothing, not even a sighting of the Sultan, Dallam ratchets up the tension. Lello's pomposity increased while he elaborated on the dangers of proximity to the Sultan, describing how even a great ambassador must act humbly and how he himself would only ever be led into the presence under physical restraint. Anticipating his own meeting with Mehmed, Lello expansively rehearsed the adherence to protocol that would be required of him:

> We cale it kisinge of the Grand Sinyor's hande; bute when I com to his gates I shalbe taken of my horse and seartcht, and lede betwyxte tow men holdinge my handes downe close to my sides, and so lede into the presence of the Grand Sinyor, and I muste kiss his kne or his hanginge sleve. Havinge deliverede my letteres unto the Coppagawe, I shalbe presently ledd awaye, goinge backwardes as longe as I can se him, and in payne of my heade I muste not turne my backe upon him, and therefore you muste not louke to have a sighte of him. (p. 65)

Retrospectively, Dallam must have relished this self-conjured image of Lello's obsequious behaviour, especially the possibility of mortal danger were Lello to adopt an improper attitude while leaving. But at the time of delivering his speech, Lello was attempting to impress and frighten Dallam with multiple threats and minimal hope of reward. With supreme condescension, he continued waving a big stick while offering only tiny future carrots.

Lello, it seems, had already come to resent not only Dallam's skilled confidence, but also the fact of his own reliance on the craftsman's success. If tomorrow's performance did not please the Sultan, he warned, Dallam would face more than Ottoman diffidence:

> I thoughte good to tell yow this, because yow shall not hereafter blame me, or say that I myghte have tould yow so muche; lett not your worke be anythinge the more carlesly louked unto, and at your cominge home our martchantes shall give yow thankes, yf it give the Grand Sinyor contente this one daye. I car not yf it be non after the nexte, yf it doo not please him at the firste sighte, and performe not those thinges which it is Toulde him that it can Dow, he will cause it to be puled downe that he may trample it under his feete. And than shall we have no sute grantede, but all our charge will be loste. (pp. 65–6)

At this point Dallam termed Lello 'my Lorde' for the first time in a moment of what is clearly ironic excess: 'After I had given my Lorde thankes for this frindly spetche . . . ' For the rest of his stay in Istanbul, he would use the term with varying degrees of sarcasm and contempt. Since none of Lello's dire warnings materialized, Dallam's use of reported speech was clearly aimed at setting up the details of his triumph over this haughty superior.

Personal rivalry between ambassador and craftsman frames Dallam's report of his performance in the seraglio. Dallam sought to avoid any obligation to Lello by insisting how his own position was by no means constrained by the ambassador's authority. In a spirited response to Lello's speech, Dallam invoked the figure of Queen Elizabeth for the first and only time, thereby allying himself and his mission with an authority higher than Lello's:

> After I had given my Lorde thankes for this frindly spetche, thoughe smale comforte in it, I tould him that thus muche I understoode by our martchantes before my cominge oute of London, and that he needed not to Doubte that thare should be any faulte either in me or my worke, for he hade sene the trial of my care and skill in makinge that perfickte and good which was thoughte to be uncurable, and in somthinges better than it was when Her Maiestie sawe it in the banketinge house at Whyte Hale. (p. 66)

Amidst this jockeying for place and position, Dallam's mention of the great day when he had performed at Whitehall boldly placed him closer to royal authority than Lello.

On the morning of 25 September, Dallam, Harvie, Buckett and Watson were already in the seraglio when Lello, who 'did ride lyuke unto a kinge, onlye tht he wanted a crowne', arrived:

> Thare roode with him 22 jentlmen and martchantes, all in clothe of goulde; ye jentlemen weare these: Mr. Humfrye Cunisbye, Mr. Baylie of Salsburie,

> Mr. Paule Pinder, Mr. Wyllyam Alderidg, Mr. Jonas Aldridge, and Mr. Thomas Glover. The other six weare martchantes; these did ride in vestes of clothe of goulde, made after the cuntrie fation; thare wente on foute 28 more in blew gounes made after the Turkie fation, and everie man a silke grogren cape, after the Ittallian fation. My livery was a faire clooke of a Franche greene, etc. (pp. 66–7)

Like other Englishman of his age, Dallam understood ceremonial pomp and how processions were about whether one rode or walked, one's position relative to others in the parade and what clothes one wore. The Venetian bailo was understandably concerned that the ostentatious costliness of Lello's entourage on this occasion would greatly contribute to England's prestige with the Sultan.[10] Lello was being set up, like a king without a crown, waiting to be invited in to kiss the Sultan's hand, but inevitably delayed.

Command performance: Dallam meets Mehmed

> In the Turkishe Empire now raignethe Mahomet the thirde of that name: a Prince by Nature of Witt and Courage: but by Accident, dull, timorous, and very effeminate; as hath appeared by divers proofes, bothe bifore he came to the crowne and sithens.
>
> Humphrey Conisby, c.1600[11]

The character given to Mehmed III by contemporary European reports is that of a gross and unpleasant sensualist who enjoyed killing people and torturing women in particular. Dallam knew that the man he was about to meet had had nineteen of his brothers strangled upon acceding to the throne. Other rumours of Mehmed's activities would have proved equally unprepossessing. Lazaro Soranzo's *Ottomano* of 1598 tells how, in his youth, Mehmed enjoying burning women with red-hot instruments, and how, upon hearing that a scholar in Konya had spoken ill of him, had peremptorily ordered 2,000 students to be executed. Abraham Hartwell's English translation of Soranzo's account would not be printed until 1603, but Dallam might easily have heard these stories from Humphrey Conisby, a fellow passenger on the *Hector*, who made his own translation of Soranzo's portrait of Mehmed, now among the manuscripts in the British Library.[12]

Whatever his views regarding Mehmed might have been, Dallam's performance was a great success and a considerable personal victory over Lello. Dallam set the scene by noting that, while the diplomatic party were left to wait in an outer court, 'I and my company' (p. 67) were formally escorted without delay into the seraglio, and led further and further inside through a series of doors, until Dallam could hear yet another door opening into an adjacent room 'and upon a sodon a wonderfull noyes of people' broke upon them:

> for a litle space it should seme that at the Grand Sinyore's coming into the house the dore which I hard opene did sett at libertie four hundrethe persons which weare locked up all the time of the Grand Sinyore's absence, and juste at his cominge in theye weare sett at libertie, and at the first sighte of the presente, with great admyration did make a wonderinge noyes.(p. 67)

Left in the corridor and unable to see anything, Dallam could still hear the gasps of wonder and amazement. He heard too when the 'Grand Sinyor, beinge seated in his Chaire of estate', commanded silence. Unlike an obsequious ambassador, constrained by guards, Dallam had a machine to do his grovelling for him:

> All beinge quiett, and no noyes at all, the presente began to salute the Grand Sinyor; for when I lefte it I did alow a quarter of an houre for his cominge thether. First the clocke strouke 22; than The chime of 16 bels went of, and played a songe of 4 partes. That beinge done, tow personagis which stood upon to corners of the seconde storie, houldinge tow silver trumpetes in there handes, did lift them to theire heades, and sounded a tantarra. Than the muzicke went of, and the orgon played a song of 5 partes twyse over. In the tope of the orgon, being 16 foute hie, did stande a holly bushe full of blacke birds and thrushis, which at the end of the muscik did singe and shake theire wynges. Divers other motions thare was which the Grand Sinyor wondered at. (pp. 67–8)

At the very moment when 'the presente began to salute the Grand Sinyor', Ottoman desires for skilled English craftsmanship were assured. Far from wishing to trample this mechanical instrument under foot as Lello had imagined, Mehmed requested an encore. Dallam instructed the 'Coppagaw' (Kapıcı) how to reset the clockwork mechanism, 'and it did the lyke as it did before. Than the Grand Sinyor sayed it was good', and called for Dallam himself to perform personally on the organ's keyboard (p. 68).

Dallam's meeting with Mehmed can rightly claim to be the first and most intimate direct encounter between an ordinary Englishman and an Ottoman emperor. When the 'Coppagaw' opened a door and took him 'by the hande', Dallam checked with his 'drugaman' before allowing himself to be led through:

> When I came within the Dore, That which I did se was verrie wonderfull unto me. I cam in direcktly upon the Grand Sinyore's ryghte hande, som 16 of my passis from him, but he would not turne his head to louke upon me.

He satt in greate state, yeat the sighte of him was nothinge in Comparrison of the traine that stood behinde him, the sighte whearof did make me almoste to thinke that I was in another worlde. (p. 69)

Peopled by two hundred 'padgis...all verrie proper men, and Christians borne', a hundred 'Dum men' and a hundred 'dwarffs, big bodied men, but verrie low of stature' (pp. 69–71), all of them dressed in exotic costumes, the other world into which Dallam had now entered pulled him further and further into itself by means of a symbolic disrobing:

Than the Coppagaw cam unto me, and touke my cloake from aboute me, and laye it Doune upon the Carpites, and bid me go and play on the organ; but I refused to do so, because the Grand Sinyor satt so neare the place wheare I should playe that I could not com at it, but I muste needes turne my backe Towardes him and touche his Kne with my britchis, which no man, in paine of deathe, myghte dow, savinge only the Coppagaw. So he smyled, and lett me stande a litle. Than the Grand Sinyor spoake againe, and the Coppagaw, with a merrie countenance, bid me go with a good curridge, and thruste me on. (p. 70)

To approach the keyboard, Dallam had to get so close that he was able to observe 'a ringe with a diamon in it halfe an inche square' on Mehmed's thumb, and found himself practically sitting on the Sultan's knee. With Lello's warnings about how getting too close could prove fatal, Dallam remained anxious:

He satt so righte behinde me that he could not se what I did; therefore he stood up, and his Coppagaw removed his Chaire to one side, where he myghte se my handes; but, in his risinge from his chaire, he gave me a thruste forwardes, which he could not otherwyse dow, he satt so neare me; but I thought he had bene drawinge his sorde to cut of my heade.(p. 71)

Despite his trepidation, Dallam 'stood thar playinge suche thinge as I coulde' until the clock 'strouke', when he stopped playing on the keyboard and carefully backed away with his head bowed to retrieve his cloak. But his performance in the seraglio was far from over. The Kapıcı ordered him to leave his cloak and return to the keyboard:

then I wente Close to the Grand Sinyor againe, and bowed myselfe, and then I wente backewardes to my Cloake. When the Company saw me do so theye semed to be glad, and laughed. Than I saw the Grand Sinyor put his hande behinde him full of goulde, which the Coppagaw Receved, and broughte unto me fortie and five peecis of gould called chickers, and than was I put out againe wheare I came in, beinge not a little joyfull of my good suckses. (p. 71)

Forty-five 'chickers' were worth £20 5s – considerably more than he had spent on his luggage; but to Dallam the value of the gold lay also in the fact that it was a gift signalling his personal success with the Sultan.

Dallam must have taken peculiar delight in recording how the effects of his performance served to deflate Lello's self-importance. For while Dallam had been entertaining and being entertained inside the seraglio, not simply seeing and touching the Sultan, but receiving a valuable gift from his hand, Lello had been kept waiting outside, standing 'all these tow houres' (p. 71). Dallam had been so long closely closeted with Mehmed, however, that the diplomatic hand-kissing was postponed and Lello thoroughly snubbed. Stanley Mayes sees this incident as the trigger of Lello's impatience and double-dealing with Dallam.[13] But if we have been paying close attention to Dallam's language, the way he uses names and titles, then we have surely been alerted to the nuances of irony and sarcasm of which the organ-maker was both fond and capable.

In the event, everything had gone exactly as Lello had said that it would not. By delighting Mehmed, Dallam became temporarily the most important Englishman in Istanbul. Upstaged by the organ-maker, Lello tried to save face. Later that evening, after receiving a detailed report of Dallam's performance, Lello grudgingly confessed that if someone had warned him, 'he would have bestowed 30 or 40*li*. in apparell for' Dallam (p. 73). Dallam did not record whether he ever received the clothes or their value in kind.

Rewards, promises, betrayal and return

His triumphal recital gave Dallam personal prestige, but greatly complicated his position. Having found unimaginable favour with Mehmed, Dallam now found himself caught between two powerful and jealous masters. He had become such a crucial player that both the Ottomans and his master wanted to prevent him from returning home. For the rest of his stay in Istanbul, Dallam shrewdly navigated between Lello's demands and Ottoman promises. Enormously empowered by his journey thus far, Dallam nevertheless could not help recognizing that there were very real limits to what he could do without Lello's support.

Within days of the performance, Dallam was 'sente for againe to the surralia' where 'those two jemoglans which kepte that house made me verrie kindly welcom, and asked me that I would be contented to stay with them always, and I should not wante anythinge, but have all the contentt that I could desier' (p. 73). Somewhere along the way, Dallam may have picked up the notion that it was legitimate to tell lies to the ungodly Ottomans and quickly invented a wife and children in England to whom he must return: 'Thoughe in deede I had nether wyfe nor childrin, yeat to excuse my selfe I made them that Answeare' (p. 73). Since Dallam was then thought to be a family man interested in women, the enticements being offered him to stay only increased: 'Than they toulde me that yf I would staye, the Grand Sinyor would give tow wyfes, ether tow of his Concubines of els tow virgins of the beste I could Chuse my selfe, in Cittie or contrie' (p. 73). Since Dallam had already seen the most beautiful women in the world on Chios, we must presume that female beauty alone could not tempt him. All too aware of the delights being offered if he were to stay – attentive audiences for his musical and mechanical performances, wonderful weather, grapes after every meal, prestige, wealth, and his choice of women – Dallam had also to struggle to avoid becoming enmeshed in the machinations of international diplomacy. He simply did not want to become a foreign agent working for a master such as Lello.

Lello continually attempted to impose controls that Dallam wished to avoid. Lello instructed him never to say no 'flatly' to any offer made by an important Ottoman, and to 'tell them that yf it did please my Lorde that I should stay, I should be the better contented to staye; by that meanes they will not go about to staye you by force, and yow may finde a time the better to goo awaye when you please' (p. 73). Lello's advice fitted the conventional wisdom of the time: the Ottomans themselves 'slavishly' respected authority and would consequently understand how a man of Dallam's rank could not be entirely free of the will of his 'Lorde'. None the less, Dallam clearly felt very anxious about even rhetorically acknowledging Lello's control over him in such a way, and he did not record whether he took the advice. If he did, it proved very ineffective, since Dallam's friends at court simply intensified their enticements. One took him to see secret treasures of the seraglio, including the Sultan's 'privie Chamberes' where he even allowed Dallam to sit in one of the thrones and 'to draw that sord out of the sheathe with the which the Grand Sinyor doth croune his kinge' (p. 74).

For a moment, Dallam found himself impersonating a sultan, yet he strangely said very little about how it felt to sit, even if momentarily, and hold the sword with which, god-like, sultans crowned kings. His indifference might be explained by the fact that this pleasure proved to be merely a prelude to the visual delights that were offered next.

> When he had showed me many other thinges which I wondered at, than crossinge throughe a litle squar courte paved with marble, he poynted me to goo to a graite in a wale, but made a sine that he myghte not goo thether him selfe. When I came to the grait the wale was verrie thicke, and graited on bothe the sides with iron verrie strongly; but through that graite I did se thirtie of the Grand Siyor's Concobines that weare playinge with a bale in

another courte. At the first sighte of them I thoughte they had bene yonge men, but when I saw the hare of their heades hange doone on their backes, platted together with a tasle of smale pearle hanginge in the lower end of it, and by other plaine tokens, I did know them to be women, and verrie prettie ones in deede. (p. 74)

Overcoming initial confusion and bewilderment, Dallam soon developed an eye for what was going, cataloguing jewels and costumes with a practised eye and obvious pleasure: 'they wore britchis of scamatie, a fine clothe made of coton woll, as whyte as snow and as fine as lane; for I could desarne the skin of their thies throughe it' (p. 74). Caught up in the eroticism of the gaze, Dallam stayed rather too long and his tour guide 'stamped with his foute to make me give over looking; the which I was verrie lothe to dow, for that sighte did please me wondrous well' (p. 75). As well it might, for apart from its immediate gratifications, its glimpses of such jewels and thighs, Dallam must have known he was probably the first Englishman ever to see any women of the harem.[14]

Being able to make these claims of eye-witness experience, to have been so deeply inside the 'privie' places of the seraglio, to have been entertained and fed on grapes every day, to have sat upon the throne, to have seen some of the harem women – even if clothed and playing a ball game rather than naked in a bath-house – and to have been offered these privileges as enticements to stay on and perform his music, proved sufficient in themselves. None of these pleasing prospects persuaded Dallam to stay. The *Hector* was leaving the next day, and he wanted to be on board. Here is English subjectivity in the making, a process that brings a man from Lancashire right into the very heart of the Ottoman Empire, then makes him want to go home and write about it rather than stay on and become some sort of double-agent, living at the sultan's pleasure while also subject to the authority of a control such as Lello. What Dallam took back to England with him was a transformed sense of what it meant to be English, a sense transformed by his crossing over into the exotic and global registers of imperial power.

During his stay in Istanbul, Dallam made himself wanted: the Ottomans wanted him to stay and play his instrument; the English ambassador wanted him to stay because they did. The morning after his glimpse inside the harem, and after a stern warning from his interpreter not to mention what he had seen to anyone on pain of death, Dallam was unpacking his 'beed' and 'Chiste' back aboard the *Hector*, when word came that Mehmed would not let the ship leave with him on board: 'yf the workman that sett up the presente in the surralia would not be perswaded to stay behind the shipe, the ship muste staye untill he had removed the presente unto another place' (p. 76). Dallam was furious when Lello insisted that he obey. He now literally had a price on his head, and he projected his anger in the form of grudging sarcasm directed at Lello. In a lengthy sentence that already expostulated at 'my Lorde' no fewer than three times, Dallam wrung that particular irony for all it was worth:

> but when my lord tould me that I muste be contented to staye and Lette the ship goo, than was I in a wonderfull perplixatie, and in my furie I tould my lorde that that was now come to pass which I ever feared, and that was that he in the end would betray me, and turne me over into the Turkes hands, whear I should Live a slavish Life, and never companie againe with Christians, with many other suche-like words. (p. 76)

Since Dallam was not particularly prone to outbursts of religiosity, we may presume that his use here of 'Christians' offers a rather flexible category designed to leave Ottomans out of the frame. Dallam was so concerned with friendship and community, with what for him constituted the fabric of life, that once again 'companie' was a verb, a doing, an activity to which he felt himself entitled. Dallam remained true to his well-practised understanding that keeping good company was more important than just about anything else; certainly more important than money and the most beautiful women in the world. Despite his eagerness to leave for home, and because he could not prevent the ship from going without him, Dallam finally, in his own phrase, 'lets go' by taking out his 'furie' on Lello. Unfortunately, he did not record what he said. Perhaps understandably. Under these new circumstances, the relation between organ-maker and ambassador changed once again.

As a result of his protracted stay in Istanbul, Dallam came to revise his attitude towards Lello, accepting that he might not have been conspiring to keep Dallam against his will and that he might, this time if not before, have understood how things worked. Dallam never quite allowed himself to admire Lello, but was soon referring again to 'my Lorde' almost with respect. Lello might have been wrong about how Dallam would be received by the Sultan, but he eventually managed to persuade Dallam to be less anxious about missing the ship. The *Hector*, after all, must return via Iskenderun – and in Iskenderun there was always the threat of plague.

> My Lorde did speake this so frindly and nobly to unto me, that upon a sodon he had altered my mynde, and I tould him that I would yeld my selfe into Godes hand and his. (p. 77)

Surely cash must have been exchanged, or at least the promise of compensation for expenses. In the event, Dallam was fortunate in his timing. Having travelled overland across Greece, he waited 46 days on the island of Zante for a ship to take him home to England 'but the firste that came war the Heckter, in the which I wente out of Inglande...When I saw her I was somwhat sorie, for I had a great desier to have gone to Venis; but yeat I was glad againe, because I knew that in her was a sur passidge, and emongste men that did know me' (p. 90). The desire to see Venice, to take in a few more sights, soon gave way to the more important consideration of travelling among familiar company, on a familiar ship manned by familiar faces: companying with Christians. But of his former travelling companions, Rowland Buckett, Michael Watson and Ned Hale, Dallam made no mention. Although his 'mate' John Harvie appears on the final page of the manuscript, stepping ashore in May at Dover, one cannot help but suspect that Thomas Dallam felt he had moved up in the world.

Part II

Biddulph's Ministry: Travels around Aleppo, 1600–12

The *Turke* permitteth Christs Gospel to be preached; the Pope condemneth it to the racke and inquisition; who is the better man?

William Forde, sermon at the funeral of Anne, Lady Glover in Istanbul, 14 April 1612[1]

5
Biddulph's Anxiety of Authorship

William Biddulph was an English clergyman who arrived in the Levant at the same time as Dallam, but stayed on for eight more years. During this time he served as Protestant chaplain in Aleppo, travelled overland to Jerusalem and meddled in the diplomatic life of Istanbul. Published in 1609, Biddulph's *Travels* was reissued in 1612, but his name appears on neither title-page. Selections were reprinted by Samuel Purchas, so, unlike Dallam, Biddulph was by no means entirely shy of publishing.[2] None the less Biddulph proves an illusive fellow. The elaborate preface to *The Travels* obscures matters. Of Biddulph's life before and after his appearance in the East I have found little evidence. He cannot have been a member of the 'ancient family' of Biddulphs 'originally of Staffordshire [and] denominated from Biddulph, a village in the north parts of the county' since there are no Williams in the family of suitable age.[3] He may have been the 'William Biddle' listed as a member of Brasenose College, Oxford, who received his MA in July 1590, but there is no proof.[4]

Throughout, I have quoted from the first edition: 'The Travels of *certaine Englishmen into* Africa, Asia, Troy, Bythnia, Thracia, *and to the Blacke Sea.* And into Syria, Cilicia, Pisidia, Mesopotamia, Damascus, Canaan, Galile, Samaria, Judea, Palestina, Jerusalem, Jericho and to the Red Sea, and to sundry other places. Begunne in the yeere of Jubile 1600 and by some of them finished this yeere 1608. The others not yet returned. Very profitable for the helpe of Travellers, and no lesse delightfull to all persons who take pleasure to heare of the Manners, Government, Religion, and Customes of Forraine and Heathen Countries. London. Printed by Th. Haveland, for W. Sepley, and are to been sold at his shop in Paules Church yard, at the signe of the Parrot. 1609.' Biddulph's companions were Edward Abbott, John Elkin, Jasper Tyon and Jeffrey Kirbie.

Biddulph was the first English chaplain to publish an account of life in the Ottoman Empire. He showed considerable interest in meeting the Christian communities there, visiting biblical sites and judging peoples and places by their biblical past. Insisting that he was not himself a pilgrim, Biddulph remained highly conscious that, by representing the Church of England, his duty was to remain steadfast, unchanged by his experience. He often notes how his clerical appearance earned him particular respect. 'At *Jerusalem*,' he comments, 'many strangers of sundry Nations understanding I was an English Preacher, came and kissed my hand, and called me the English Patriarch.' Later he noted, 'if a man have a faire long beard, they reverence him' (pp. 62, 99). Of his own beard, more later.

Biddulph clearly intended to publish, yet took considerable pains to disclaim any personal responsibility for the book, and for good reason. In part, he confronted the challenge facing all clergymen; since travel writers were presumed guilty of exaggeration, mendacity and immorality, such work ranked among the lowest and least respectable kinds of writing. More to the point, however, *The Travels* contains thinly veiled accusations aimed at living Englishmen, material that would cause offence and must have been included from personal motives. To avoid accusations of frivolous impiety on the one hand, and of scandalmongering on the other, Biddulph claimed that he had objected to publication while also outlining a rationale for going public that was intellectually respectable, seemingly pious and a means of pursuing personal grudges.

'Theophilus Lavender' defends travel writing

Biddulph's solution was to adopt a stratagem that Pope, Swift and the Scriblerians would have applauded. By assuming an editorial persona named 'Theophilus Lavender', he explained how the book was published against his wishes. Consisting of four letters, as if the familiar epistolary form confirmed that publication was never intended, *The Travels* recounts Biddulph's journeys and describes many of the sites he visited on trips into biblical lands. Facing the title-page, in large bold print and framed within an ornate border, the very first words of the book command 'Good Reader read the Preface, or else reade nothing'. Dutiful readers here learn that Lavender compiled these composite epistles by editing several letters sent from abroad by both William Biddulph and his brother, Peter. Since any contribution Peter might have made is entirely erased by the editing – all four are signed by William himself – this pretence of dual authorship can be nothing more than a further strategy for obscuring authorial responsibility.

Lavender reports that William objected to the publication of the letters because he was 'not ignorant of the incredulitie of others in such cases' and did not wish to be considered a mendacious travel writer (sig. A). Although previous scholars have accepted this claim at face value, there is ample reason for considering it no more than a fiction signalled by the fanciful name, 'Friend of God' Lavender.[5]

In a spirited defence of travel writing, Lavender overrules modest reservations by insisting that 'publike good is to be preferred before a private' (sig. Av) and arguing that publishing these letters will cause 'good' to 'redounde unto others, by reading of this discourse'. Lavender admits compressing several letters into four and rearranging material into a geographical order. 'I have,' Lavender reports, 'thought good to write of those places first, which lie neerest unto *England*, and so to proceed unto every place *ordine quaeque suo*, as they stand in order, that they which read it, may the better profit by it' (sig. A3). The itinerary described in *The Travels* is rhetorical rather than factual, aimed at creating the sense of how moving further into foreign and ungodly places brings increasing dangers that test the resolution of the Protestant soul.

Lavender's case for publishing is both pious and nationalist: 'For hereby all men may see how God hath blessed our Countrie above others, and be stirred up to thankefulnesse' (sig. A2). The English in general, Lavender insists, will learn to appreciate having a 'good and gratious King' as well as exemplary, loving church ministers; women will learn 'to love their husbands, when they shal read in what slavery women live in other Contries'; servants will learn duty to their benevolent masters; the rich will learn how free they are to accumulate and enjoy their wealth; the poor will learn that their conditions could be much worse; while those who travel in England will learn 'what a benefit it is to have the refuge of Innes in their travel' (sigs. A2–A2v). What readers will not find is an accurate, day-by-day itinerary of Biddulph's travels, but rather a carefully plotted sense of the increasing dangers from exposure to false beliefs and wicked practices the further from England one travelled.

Setting the record straight

Lavender's preface introduces an additional motive for publishing against the author's wishes. Claiming to have assembled the letters without intentions of publishing, Lavender simply 'yeelded' to the 'importunities of others' in order that 'the truth may be the better knowen' (sig. A3v). Having argued that exposure to foreign cultures corrupts, he warns against the dangers of reading writers who were contaminated by travel. In particular, publishing Biddulph's letters enable him to correct errors circulated by Henry Timberlake's *A True and Strange Discourse . . . of two English Pilgrims*, first published in 1603 and reprinted as recently as 1608. Lavender writes:

> The voyage of Master *Tymberley* was imprinted (as I understand) without his consent, and before his comming into England, by a Copy which hee sent to his friend, wherein they [*sic*] have done him wrong; for (as many men of learning and judgement report, whereof some have seene, and some read

of those Countries) many things in that pamphlet (put foorth in his name) are false, and say it is a shame it should come in print. (sigs. A3v–A4)

By hiding behind Theophilus Lavender, Biddulph could pretend that he was not accusing Timberlake the man, but rather deploring the practice of introducing errors by publishing books without the authors' consent. Having distinguished the man from the unauthorized publication of his writings, Lavender enthusiastically corrects several errors in Timberlake's pamphlet where, 'against the expresse word of God', the geography of the Holy Land has been misrepresented. Not only the Bible itself, but also other travellers who have visited the Holy Land agree, for example, that Mounts Tabor and Hermon are not 'nere together' and consequently 'Master *Tymberley* hath not beene neere either of them by forty miles' (sig. A4). More personally, Lavender claims that Timberlake's book makes its author appear so credulous as to believe everything he has been told: 'that Pamphlet setteth downe all things for truth which were told unto the Author, whereas many of them are most false and ridiculous', since they were told to him by infidels and, what is much worse, Catholics.

By publishing Biddulph's letters, Lavender hopes to protect readers from such contaminating lies, for 'it is a foule shame that any Christian, brought up in so blessed a Common-Wealth as England, should be so simple to beleeve such Untruths as the superstitious Friers of *Rome* (which sojourne at *Jerusalem*) doe demonstrate or declare unto them' (sig. A4v). Having thus accused the text, not the author, of *A True and Strange Discourse* for repeating dangerous Catholic lies, Lavender backs off and protests rather too loudly that Timberlake himself could not possibly have been taken in since 'all men speake well of Master *Tymberley*'. Moreover, no pious Englishman would have consented to the title of this work, 'calling them *English Pilgrims*: for Pilgrims goe with a superstitious devotion to worship Reliques at *Jerusalem*; but master *Tymberley* and his companions went thither onely as travelers to see the Holy Land' (sigs. A4v–B). A nice distinction, and one that prepares for the fully venomous insinuation with which Lavender next insists how Timberlake, 'being both wise and Religious...would never bee so simple to publish of his owne disgrace in Printe, in going to Masse, and observing many other ceremonies as are mentioned in that booke which goeth foorth under his name' (sig. B).

Lavender never mentions that Biddulph and Timberlake met in Jerusalem, and one cannot help suspecting that, beneath the editorial posturing, Biddulph clearly harboured a grudge against Timberlake and was using the opportunity to accuse him of crypto-Catholicism without seeming to do so. The carefully guarded insinuations strongly suggest that Timberlake had been contaminated by exposure to Catholic ceremonial, but without making Biddulph personally responsible for bringing the accusation. For his part, so to speak, Lavender seeks nothing more or less than to promote the cause of Protestant reform by clearing away some superstitious errors of the Roman Church perpetuated by Timberlake's book in order to warn how even the godly can be duped. Meanwhile, no one could accuse Biddulph himself of pursuing personal goals, though envy at the republication of Timberlake's book might well have spurred him on. If Biddulph entertained ambitions of producing a bestseller, the success of Timberlake's book must have galled him, since it was reprinted twelve times during the seventeenth century, 'a performance unequaled by any travel book in English until that time'.[6]

Whatever undisclosed motives and secret aspirations might lurk beneath Lavender's rhetoric, the Preface illustrates how debates concerning the nature, status and purpose of travel and travel writing were symptomatic of growing popular interest in foreign parts. One of the most theoretically sophisticated accounts at the time was expounded in 1606 by Sir Thomas Palmer, who presumed that not only travel writing but also travel itself needed defending. He did so in secular, commercial and nationalistic terms, arguing that 'the people of great *Britaine*', being 'of all other famous and glorious Nations separated from the maine Continent of the world', are necessarily therefore 'by so much the more interessed to become Travaillers, by how much the necessitie of everie severall estate of men doth require that, for their better advancement'.[7] And travellers needed accurate information before setting out. Nevertheless, pious writers condemned travel writing for being frivolous and morally subversive. In *Quo Vadis? A Just Censure of Travel* (1617), Bishop Joseph Hall insisted that books could provide everything one needed to know about foreign parts, while travel itself entailed needlessly exposing oneself to dangers, both physical and spiritual.

With such debates currently in the air, Biddulph needed to justify himself since publishing in his own name would invariably invite accusations of ungodly self-promotion: Theophilus Lavender, that sweet-smelling lover of god, provided an excellent strategy for avoiding suspicion. Even so, Biddulph had other, more immediate reasons for taking so much trouble to conceal his responsibility for publishing. Before his book even appeared, at least one reader was ready and expecting to find Biddulph spreading malice against members of the English community trading in the Levant.

6
Preacher among the Diplomats

> ...you will contyneue and proceade in yor charge both in the instruction
> of our people in knowledg of Religyon and in reproving and rebuking
> whatsoever you shall ether see or be dewly informed of to deserve
> reproof or admonition.
>
> Sir Thomas Smith, Governor of the Levant and East India
> Companies, to William Biddulph, March 1600[1]

When *The Travels* appeared in print, Biddulph's editorial hedging about his role
in publication was carefully scrutinized by none other than the gossipmonger
John Sanderson, now back in London but regularly writing to friends in
Aleppo and Istanbul. Thanks to Sanderson and his overseas correspondents,
we know a good deal about the publication of Biddulph's book and details
of several incidents that Biddulph deliberately omitted. Through Sanderson
we glimpse something of the nervous excitement generated by the book
among members of the Levant Company in both England and the Levant,
and why it was that Biddulph went to such lengths to hide himself behind
a sham editor.

Istanbul intrigues

Early in 1608, Henry Lello, the officious and anxiety-prone diplomat familiarly
known as 'Fog' by the English community in Istanbul, returned to England and
was knighted for his services as ambassador. He had been succeeded by his
former secretary, Dallam's travelling companion, Thomas Glover, who had
already been knighted and appointed to replace Lello on 16 August 1606.[2] The
fact that Glover received his knighthood before taking up the appointment
clearly irritated Lello, who had to wait until retirement for his, and added fuel
to a longstanding rivalry between the two men, which continued across the
distance separating London from Istanbul. In the acrimonious quarrelling,

Sanderson and friends took Glover's side, while Biddulph proved to be one of Lello's staunchest supporters.

In November 1608, some months before the publication of Biddulph's *Travels*, Sanderson wrote to Glover that Lello, now back in London, had recently informed him that Biddulph had visited Richard Bancroft, Archbishop of Canterbury, and complained about Glover. Biddulph had produced 'two letters which you [Glover] had writt against him [Biddulph]; but My Lords Grace graced him nevertheless. And said he redd to him all the lines of your letters and that they weare ridiculus.' What the contents of these letters might have been is not reported. Sanderson does, however, note how, at Lello's 'request', Biddulph had recently been able to purchase 'an adviouson of six score pounds per yeare' with the help of John Eldred, an influential merchant who had served in Aleppo as Consul and as Treasurer to the Levant Company, and was now a London Alderman.[3] But why was Biddulph, now back in England, campaigning against the new ambassador, Sir Thomas Glover?

A month later, just weeks before Biddulph's *Travels* appeared in print, Sanderson again wrote to Glover, this time reporting that 'Mr Biddle is putting to print all his travailes; and,' he adds ominously, 'one Stracie is making a booke against you; which yf it should be so, it peradventure may cost him both his ears.'[4] William Strachey, the man in danger of losing his ears – and this was no idle threat – was a secretary that Glover had taken with him from London, but quickly dismissed. Strachey's book never appeared.[5] But Biddulph's did. Why should the publication of Biddulph's *Travels* have caused Sanderson such anxiety on Glover's behalf?

For more than a year before Biddulph's book appeared, Sanderson had been hearing disturbing rumours circulating in London about Glover's behaviour since he had become ambassador. Yet despite his network of friends in Istanbul and Aleppo, Sanderson did not know everything. Unknown to him, hostilities between Lello and Glover had begun before the new ambassador arrived. With his new wife, Anne *née* Lamb, the recently knighted Sir Thomas returned by sea during the autumn of 1606 to take up his appointment. In November, during a stopover on Chios, he wrote ahead to Lello instructing him to vacate the Company house in Pera, and leave behind 'all the household stuffe whatsover, as Plate, pewter, lynene, carpetts, kitchin stuffe as all thynges belonginge unto that house'.[6] Lello, however, dragged his heels and stayed on, largely, it seems, in order to gather as much money as possible before returning to England. But he also wanted to interfere with Glover's assumption of office by spreading malicious gossip, and in this task he was greatly assisted by William Biddulph.

Glover becomes ambassador

According to Ottaviano Bon, the Venetian bailo, Glover entered Istanbul on 9 January 1607 'in honourable style, and in a few days he will be presented to the Sultan'.[7] Soon after arriving, Glover wrote to Robert Cecil, King James's Secretary of State, complaining that Lello was refusing to acknowledge his authority. Glover's complaint, however, was not simply that Lello was maligning him personally, but that these attacks were jeopardizing the credibility of the English diplomatic and mercantile community in Istanbul. Glover accused Lello of conspiring with the French ambassador, Gontaut-Biron, baron de Salignac, and of spreading word that his appointment had not been authorized by the King, but only by the English merchants – 'yet God whoe is stronger then an envious man or the Divell hath furthered my just cause'.[8] That was on 18 March. On 1 April, Glover wrote again to Cecil that he had obtained '3000 crowns' for Lello as arrears of his allowance, and was evidently hoping that Lello would now take the money and leave.[9] Yet two days later he was writing to Cecil once again, this time reporting that he had formally ordered Lello to return to England.[10]

The breakdown of civil relations between Lello and Glover was hot gossip in London. On the last day of April, Sanderson wrote to Glover that he was 'sory to heare' the two diplomats 'agree no better', for rumours had already started to spread 'and men censure at thier pleasure'.[11]

Biddulph spreads scandal: The Coxden affair

The English merchants in Istanbul became personally involved in the open dispute between Glover and Lello. With a breach splitting the English enclave, the Venetian bailo Ottaviano Bon seized the opportunity to interfere, and Biddulph girded himself to take part. On 16 April, Glover wrote to Cecil, adding a postscript:

> The Baylo of Venice sent me worde mervelynge that our Englishe merchants here resident, as in perticuler Anthonie Abdie, William Pearche, John Markham, and my Preacher by name William Bidolphe (whom the Turques here calle my Muftie, as in deede he is more factious then Muftie, or the devill himselfe) were all my secret ennemies and that they were devoted freinds to my Predicessor: and that the Frenche Ambassador alsoe was a plotinge adjunct with them againste me; whereunto I could hardlie give credit, that the above sayed Merchants should offer me that wronge, without any cause on my behalfe ever to my knowledge given them.[12]

Glover did not entirely trust Bon, but was determined to investigate the possibility that Biddulph and others were conspiring against him.

For his part, Lello wrote to Cecil the very next day, 17 April, accusing Glover of refusing to pay him the '2000 dollers' supplied by the Company for his return journey to England.[13] The same day, Lello's supporters petitioned Cecil again, attacking Glover in the most vituperative terms. The first to sign the petition was 'William Biddulph preacher of the gospell'.[14] Besides indicating the extent of hostilities between the two camps, the petition firmly places Biddulph in Istanbul during the spring of 1607 when Glover was taking office from Lello. He had presumably been there long enough to have become familiar with the circumstances and persons involved in the change of regime.

As Glover had suspected, rumours that Lello and the French ambassador de Salignac were plotting his death came to nothing. Lello finally left Istanbul on 24 May 1607,[15] but took his time travelling back to England – by September he had only reached Venice where he addressed the Doge and Senate:[16] 'Nowe that foule foggie cloude beinge vanished, the wether is cleare at the vines of Pera,' opined Sanderson.[17] Once 'Fog' Lello had departed, Glover accused him of financial double-dealing,[18] while the fractious preacher Biddulph, as we shall see, continued to stir up trouble for the new ambassador.

Meanwhile, back in England, gossip concerning quite a different side to the diplomatic rivalry had started circulating. In February 1608, Sanderson wrote to John Kitely, the Company physician in Istanbul, commenting that Lello had received his knighthood (on 21 January 1608), while others in England continued to slander his successor:

> Of divers formerlie, and nowe of late, I have heard bad reports of the ambasiators crueltie; as that he should geve one of his servants many bastinadoes one the feet and then imprison him, and upoon the blowes he died. God forbid ther should be any such matter; Inglishmen ar tender footed. (p. 247)

Having himself once pistol-whipped one Edward Bushell, a 'vild makebate' or mischief-maker, until he was 'brused on the head, wounded in the necke, and his eare torne in the middest' (p. 11), Sanderson understood how expatriate life could sometimes erupt into what seemed to him to be justifiable physical violence. Perhaps that is why he was prepared to make so light of a servant's reported death.

But who was spreading these tales about Glover's behaviour and why? Did Sanderson know that, in July 1607, none other than Biddulph had written a letter describing this very incident, going so far as to claim that Glover himself had beaten George Coxden, the unfortunate servant with tender feet?[19] Coxden's crimes, according to a list of charges signed by the merchant Nathaniell Percivall, involved spreading dangerous slanders against Glover that were designed to ruin his influence at the Ottoman court. According to Percivall, Coxden had publicly proclaimed several times 'that my Lord was the vilest man that ever came out of England, for none was ever good, that did contynue to longe in this contrye', and that he had even attempted to prostitute his new wife 'to the greate Turke or som other'.[20]

Glover's secretary, William Strachey, had thrown in his hand on behalf of the anti-Glover group and prepared a document claiming that Coxden's subsequent death in prison was the result of poison administered by Sanderson's friend, the physician Kitely. In defiance of Strachey's charges, Glover produced a document, signed by Coxden himself, to the effect that the victim was still very much alive.[21] It was doubtless this incident that caused Glover to dismiss Strachey, though he had earlier complained to Cecil that, 'allmost everie night, when I and all my people were abeade', Strachey had, 'by stelthe', been spending time with the French ambassador, taking with him important letters and showing them to 'a notorious Papist one Hugh Holland whom I have stayed upoon a suspition'.[22]

What remains unclear about the Coxden affair is whether there was a conspiracy afoot among Biddulph and other Lello's supporters to dishonour Glover by circulating exaggerated claims or a full-scale cover-up underway among Glover and his friends. Either way, once Lello had returned to England and had been knighted, Sanderson found reason to be concerned for Glover's personal and professional reputation. In his view, Biddulph's book was designed to add fuel to the conflagration, and Sanderson wanted Glover to know what was being said behind his back in London. Whether or not he knew that Biddulph was among those accusing Glover of beating Coxden, he had every reason to fear that the appearance of Biddulph's book would provide further ammunition for the Lello camp.

Between the lines: Reading Biddulph

By December 1608, just weeks before Biddulph's *Travels* appeared, Sanderson was confident that Biddulph himself was behind its publication, and suspected that its contents would prove mightily offensive and dangerous to Glover. In January, once the book was in print, Sanderson tore out several pages and sent them to Kitely, this time with orders to make sure that his own letters should not be circulated:

> For my letters, I praye you very hartly that you will reserve them safely, and I earnestly intreat His Lordship to do the like, for you see we ar all mortall; and many (as by experience of Lillo) most malitious and in thier foolishe humours triomphes uppon papers and letters of others and spares not to put in printt matters of wournout newes and ould date, with malitiouse additions and faulse flatteries, as by the inclosed you may perceave; which I tore out of a booke sett out to the wourld, nominated the Travails of Divers Inglishmen into Africa etc., by one Theophilus Lavender; a sweet and virtiouse name, and yet the booke stinkes of lies and foolerye...to avoyd further imagination of ill, I have sent you all spoken both of reproch and faulse praises: a matter

but a fewe dayes prattle and too slight to be regarded of the wisest and best... Let him [Sir Thomas Glover] not abase his mind but scorne the relation, laugh at malitious folly, and lett it passe for foolery.[23]

The book 'stinkes of lies and foolerye', 'malitiouse additions and faulse flatteries': these are strong terms. Yet at this distance of time, it is difficult to find anything very sensational by way of malice in Biddulph's pages. Which were the offending pages that Sanderson tore out and sent overseas?

Sanderson must have torn out Theophilus Lavender's preface, since it ends by calling Christ 'our Pilot and Jenisary to conduct us' to the heavenly Jerusalem, a comparison which Sanderson notes finding offensive, but characteristic of the author: 'No other abhominable asse would be (I thinke) so senselesse to liken our Saviour, Jesus Christ... to a janizary, a Christians most opposite.'[24] Having received the offending pages, Kitely replied to Sanderson employing a series of excruciating puns that satirize Biddulph for being something worse than a two-faced, bearded hypocrite. 'I would take some pains with my penne,' he wrote,

> to perfume Theophilus Lavender, but you knowe the nature of the stuffe is rancke and not to be stird in, what maie be done besid in other places wilbe knowne... In the meanewhile I smell his kinsman, Theologus Spickenard (which is another kind of Lavender), to scent of a foole (as hott as oyle of spike) in his similitude of our Savioure Christ to the Janisary; and ever hath shewed more beard than witt or religion in all his 10 yeares travils.[25]

Both Kitely and Sanderson thought Biddulph himself responsible for the preface, though Sanderson, ever cynical concerning what people believed, sarcastically noted that some in England had been persuaded to think he had taken no hand in the publication: 'some affirme that they weare in print without his knowledge and consent; and so may be verely thought' (p. 260). Whatever others might think, Sanderson and Kitely were certain that Biddulph himself was responsible for the content of the book; and this is where the accusations of flattery and malice come in.

Flattery is not hard to find. In the third letter Biddulph fulsomely praises both Barton and Lello, Glover's predecessors, but ignores Glover entirely. Biddulph calls Barton, whom he never met, 'the mirror of all Ambassadours that ever came to *Constantinople*' and commemorates Barton's 'immortal fame', by reporting how Heybeliada, the island off the Asian coast of Istanbul on which Barton had been buried, has been renamed '*Bartons* Iland' to this day.[26] These are very high standards for subsequent ambassadors to equal, and might be considered an attempt to put Glover in his place. But this is hardly malice towards the living via flattery of the dead. Of Lello, whom he knew, Biddulph was even more effusive in his praise:

> Master *Henry Lello* (as learned, wise, and religious English gentleman, some-time student in *Oxford*, and afterwards at the Innes of the Court) suceeded Master Barton in his place, and in many things exceeded him, especially in his religious carriage and unspotted life: and had not the times beene more troublesome in his regiment, than in the time of his predecessor Master Barton; he would every way have gone beyond him. He first of all reformed his family, and afterwards so ordered himselfe in his whole carriage, that he credited our Countrey, and after ten yeeres government of the English Nation there, he returned into his Countrey with the teares of many, and with generall good report of all Nations there dwelling or sojourning. (pp. 40–1)

This passage is the only unqualified praise of Lello left by anyone who had personal dealings with him during his embassy to Istanbul. Sanderson comments on the 'mallice' that the English 'in generall had to the ambassiator' (p. 18).

By 1609, Sanderson and friends would have found Biddulph's account of Lello's career to be 'faulse flatteries' of the most egregious kind. A decade earlier, soon after Dallam had left Istanbul, many of the English merchants refused to follow his orders and were shipped home.[27] Someone – most probably Glover himself – compiled a set of manuscripts and titled them 'A Register of such lies as are written by the Honorable Henry Lello established his Majesties Ambassador with the Gran Signior in Constantinople; to the Levant Companie, beggininge the 21st of June Anno Domini 1600'.[28] Sanderson formally complained to the Company of Lello's unsuitablility for office as early as 1603 (p. 252), and was complaining of Biddulph's 'liing extolling of Sir Lillo' in May, several months after his book had appeared. 'Uppon Sonday last in Poules Bidle passed by me and gave me a conjoye [a bow],' he writes to Kitely on the 18th, 'but my hart rosse at his gotes beard, that I had no power to speake to him' (p. 265).

In addition to Lavender's preface, then, Sanderson no doubt also tore out these pages flattering Barton and 'Fog' Lello as being of interest to friends in Istanbul. But what of the imputed malice directed at Sir Thomas Glover, the man Dallam had so much admired during their journey from Gallipoli to Istanbul? There would appear to be nothing about Glover anywhere in Biddulph's pages, not a word about bastinadoed or poisoned servants. Nevertheless, Sanderson evidently found something in Biddulph's book that bore directly on Glover's reputation since he advises the ambassador to 'scorne the relation, laugh at malitious folly, and lett it passe for foolery'. The answer, perhaps rather predictably, involved sexual conduct.

Biddulph spreads more scandal: Glover's first wife

Biddulph tells the story of 'a most famous (or rather infamous) Greeke whore called *Charatza Sophia*, that is, *Mistresse Sophia*'. Finding herself dissatisfied with

her Greek husband 'because he kept her not fine enough', she complained to
the Orthodox Patriarch and received a divorce. Then, according to Biddulph's
report, she

> presently thereupon tooke another man, who was a Christian in name,
> but no Greeke, but one who was (as is reported of him) borne in no land in
> the world, but by sea, and brought up in *Polonia* untill he were thirteene or
> fourteene yeeres of age, and then came to Constantinople, and served many
> masters there, at the first in the basest services, both in the stable, and in the
> kitchin, and afterwards in better services than he deserved, being both
> unlearned and irreligious.
>
> This man had many children by this infamous woman *Sophia*; yet after
> many yeeres (arising to higher fortunes) turned her away, and married
> another woman: And (to dawbe by the matter somewhat smoothly) procured
> a Greeke Taylor to marry with this *Sophia* and gave many hundred Dolers
> with her to her marriage. But this *Charatza* could not content her selfe long
> with this Greeke Taylor, but admitted dayly other men into her companie,
> whereupon the poore Taylor ran away with his money, and left this light
> huswife to the mercie of her former lovers, having three husbands living,
> yet shee her selfe living with none of them. This is common in every mans
> mouth thereabouts, and talked of many thousand miles off, to the disgrace
> of his Countrie and slander of Christianitie. (pp. 80–1)

The story may be a 'disgrace', but to whose 'Countrie' exactly? Not to that of
the Greek tailor surely, but to the nation of the second husband who, 'borne in
no land', sold her off.

Biddulph continued:

> both at *Constantinople, Aleppo*, and other places of Turkey where there is
> trafficking and trading of Merchants, it is no rare matter for popish
> Christians of sundery other Countries to *Cut Cabine* (as they call it) that is:
> to take any woman of that contrie where they sojourne, (Turkish women
> onely excepted, for it is death for a Christian to meddle with them) and
> when they have bought them, and enroled them in the *Cadies* booke, to use
> them as wives so long as they soujourne in that countrie, and maintaine
> them gallantly, to the consuming of their wealth, diminishing of their
> health, and endangering of their owne soules. And when they depart out of
> that Country, they shake off these their sweet-hearts, & leave them to shift
> for themselves and their children. And this they account no sinne, or at
> least wise such a sinne as may be washed away with a litle holy water.
>
> And these are the vertues which many Christians learne by sojourning
> long in Heathen Countries: which is not to be marvelled at; for if *Joseph*

(a good man) living in *Pharoah* his Court, had learned to sweare by the life of *Pharoah*; and *Peter* (a great Apostle) being in the high Priests hall but once, denied Christ thrice; we may well thinke that they which dwell long in wicked Countries, and converse with wicked men, are somewhat tainted with their sinnes, if not altogether sowzed with the leaven of their ungodliness. (p. 81)

Although unnamed, Glover must have felt 'sowzed' with the leaven of his own ungodliness after reading these pages from Sanderson's mutilated copy of *The Travels*. For Sanderson and friends, there would have been no doubt that the finger pointed directly at Glover.

By naming and praising both Barton and Lello, but not naming Glover, Biddulph left readers free to draw their own inferences from his account of cutting cabin; after all only those who knew about Glover's first wife would find anything more than a pious tirade against what Catholics were up to. And surely nobody was insinuating that Glover, nephew of a celebrated Protestant martyr, could be a 'popish' Christian.[29] Yet Glover is certainly the unnamed target of Biddulph's account.

Years after *The Travels* appeared, William Lithgow wrote praising Glover for relieving more 'slaves from the Galleys' and for keeping 'a better house, than any Ambassadour did'. As if in answer to Biddulph's oblique portrait, he provides biographical information: 'His mother was a Pollonian, who, comming from Dansicke to London, was delivered of him upon the Sea: Afterward he was brought up at Constantinople from a boy, and spoke, and wrot the Slavonian Tongue perfectly.'[30]

Gossip about Glover's irregular sexual life had been circulating since at least November 1607. In a vigorous defence of his virtues as ambassador, John Kitely wrote to Sanderson in response to rumours that Glover was guilty of 'bigami'. But rather than deny the accusation, he described instead what he presumed Sanderson would agree was an acceptable practice:

I dare be sworne [he] had never any such thought [as 'bigami'], for he hath shewed thes evident arguments of godliness and chastitie. As sone as he could convenientlie find a husband, he maried the woman; and by the first fittinge oportunitie he sent the boy into Germany, and the girl is dead. So that she, beinge thus freed and welbestowed, is warned never to come nere the house; and hearin, I hope, he hath geven the wourld satisfaction. (p. 242)

In expatriate idiom, 'godliness and chastitie' clearly permitted local marriage arrangements. How fortunate for Glover that the daughter should have died. Once the boy had been packed off to Germany and the woman well bestowed in marriage, what else was there to say? At the same time, Kitely's account of the arrangements for Glover's other family sounds rather like the sort of thing that might have happened when the son of a good family back home in England became too involved with an unsuitable woman.

Other pages that Sanderson tore from Biddulph's *Travels* and sent to Istanbul must have been those describing and deploring 'cutting cabin', the system of ad hoc divorce Glover adopted. Thanks to Biddulph's moral indignation and personal animosity towards Glover, we learn that the unfortunate Mistress Sophia, the first Mrs Glover, proved to have been rather more resilient than we would otherwise have known.

7
Troublesome Travelling Churchmen

> I assuer you heare [in Istanbul] ar a jolly sett of divers devells, fooles, maddmen, antiques, monsters, beasts, whoremongers. And a whore should have bine at [supper] in mans apparrell, but was sent out of the rome because a cuckould of this damned crue could not brooke her company.
>
> John Sanderson, 1600[1]

The appointment of chaplains to the English communities living in Ottoman lands proved to be a tricky business.[2] They enjoyed only uncertain authority, a problem compounded by the delay in receiving orders of dubious enforceability from the Company in London, and by the unlicensed and riotous habits of the European community. Indeed, their greatest challenge was resistance from the expatriates themselves. For many English merchants, the attractions of living in foreign cities included not only the opportunity to make a great deal of money, but also the chance to behave in ways that might have come under prohibitive scrutiny in London. The attentions of a church official would hardly be welcome to those Sanderson considered devils, madmen and whoremongers.

The chaplains themselves were very much a mixed bunch. Some no doubt had been unable to find clerical employment in England, while others later became eminent scholars and churchmen. Several wrote important books based on their travels, while others took up college and church offices on their return. Edward Pocock, Fellow of Corpus Christi and the greatest English Arabist of his generation, for example, served as chaplain in Aleppo between 1630 and 1635.[3] Thomas Smith (Istanbul, 1668–70), John Covel (Istanbul, 1670–76), Henry Maundrell (Aleppo, 1695–1701) and Edmund Chishull (Izmir, 1689–1701) all wrote notable accounts based on their chaplaincies.[4] Robert Frampton (Aleppo, 1655–66) later became Bishop of Gloucester, while the collection of oriental manuscripts gathered by Robert Huntington (Aleppo, 1670–81) helped form the basis of the Bodleian collection. Unfortunately, very little can be known of the very earliest appointments, since the Company records concerning the appointment of chaplains for Istanbul began only in 1611, those for Aleppo in 1624, and those for Izmir not until 1634.[5]

But chaplains were arriving well before these dates and were quickly making themselves unpopular with the community of expatriates, who had grown accustomed to behaving without interference from godly ministers. In Istanbul, at least, Ottoman policy had long permitted the Orthodox, Jewish and Catholic communities freedom to practise their own religions in their own churches, but for the recently arrived Protestant English, there were obvious problems with this arrangement: all the Christian buildings had already been occupied by Greece and Rome. In October 1599, the Venetian bailo, Girolamo Capello, indignantly wrote to the Doge that Lello had plans to establish the Church of England in Galata: 'He goes working away at various chimerical schemes, principally the idea of asking the Grand Signor to give him one of the churches in Galata for the use of a preaching minister whom he has brought with him.' But Capello was reassuring that, together with the French ambassador, he had gained enough support at the Ottoman court to 'thwart this excessive and arrogant pretension of the English, who would endeavour to sow even here the perversity and impiety of Calvin to the ruin of these poor Christian Perots who have applied for our advice and assistance'.[6] Capello does not name the 'preaching minister' in question, but he must have been mistaken about the fact of his arriving with Lello, since the latter had been permanently resident in Istanbul for some years. By October, when Capello was writing, Biddulph had been in Aleppo for at least three months, as we will see. Who, then, might this preaching minister have been?

Was Biddulph aboard the *Hector*?

In August, when the *Hector* arrived in Istanbul with Dallam's organ, she also brought one Reverend Mr Maye, the 'preacher' who got himself in trouble speaking Italian with the locals and who had to be ransomed to secure his release from prison on Rhodes. It can only have been Maye to whom Capello referred. Dallam does not mention it, but Maye evidently joined the ship in Iskenderun, having served as chaplain in Aleppo from August 1596.[7] Maye must have come aboard between late May and early June while the *Hector* was moored off Iskenderun, the period when Dallam admired the Ottoman troops and went ashore to shoot game. Also on board the *Hector* at the time was Sanderson, who would later call Maye 'that factiouse man and pevish humorest'.[8] Sanderson kept himself characteristically busy with Company business by writing letters including one to Richard Colthurst, the English Consul in Aleppo, warning him not to contravene Company orders by encouraging Biddulph to agree to replace Maye in the chaplaincy at Aleppo.

So where was Biddulph at the time unless he too was aboard the *Hector*? How else could he have contacted Sanderson concerning this matter of whether to accept an offer to replace Maye in Aleppo?

Biddulph himself never says whether he had initially set out for Aleppo or Istanbul, and the evidence is entirely ambiguous. On 23 May 1599, Sanderson wrote to Colthurst from Iskenderun: 'this Mr Biddall the minister sent to the Ambassador did require me to writt you in his excuse for not resolving to com to Alepo but I refused telling him playnely that I would not impach my selfe in ther matters for I se nothing but disturb & disquietment therein for they them selves are as humorouse & covetious & contintious.'[9] From this account, Biddulph had been sent 'to the Ambassador' in Istanbul, possibly to help Lello establish the first Protestant church there. Sanderson's letter to Colthurst continues: 'I tell you, in the faith of a frend, the Company wilbe offended with you if he [Biddulph] go to Alepo, and with him for contrarying ther order. For the other [Maye] I am suer the Company will not (for so they said) be at chardg to mantayne him ther any longer, nor any other before they be out of debt' (pp. 175–6). The 'other' in this case can be none other than Maye, who had made such a nuisance of himself in Aleppo that he was dismissed by Colthurst and struck off the Company payroll. But Sanderson left no hint as to Biddulph's whereabouts when he requested Sanderson's help.

To complicate matters further, there is also contrary evidence suggesting that Biddulph had been sent to Aleppo to replace Maye. For his part, Maye clearly possessed a remarkable capacity for being kept on at Company expense despite an equally remarkable tendency to make himself unpopular. Once in Istanbul, to Sanderson's grudging surprise, 'Master Maye likwise pleaseth here greatly' (p. 177), yet he did not survive long and was back in Aleppo by December supposedly *en route* to England. 'I am sorry,' Colthurst sarcastically wrote to Sanderson on 1 December, 'for Master Maye his retourne; who, if he remayne hear, will sett us all together by the ears' (p. 187). Three months later, however, it was still a topic of doubt whether Maye really had left for England. 'That troublesom May is departed is well; but I fear,' Sanderson writes,

if the ship tutche at Sant [Zante], from thence he will com hether againe to troble Isaraell. For suer I thinke he dare scarse goe for Ingland. In Constantinople he was permitted to dispute in the chefest sinagog; was derided and confuted (as they say) by a Jewe that had ben a Christian; and that his disputation (as som Jewes say) rather confermed then revoked them from ther Jueismie. (p. 198)

Sanderson evidently hoped that Maye had finally departed by March 1600, but whether it was via Zante or not, Maye was back in Istanbul by September. In that month Sir Thomas Smith, governor of both the Levant and newly founded

East India Companies, wrote to Maye in terms that complicate matters, since he implies that Biddulph had been sent to replace Maye right from the start:

'To Mr May at Constantynople'

Sir,

   After my very harty commendacions. Whereas you were enterteyned by the company to goe for Aleppo and ther to preache the worde and minister the sacraments to our nation there resident in which ministery ther toke not soe good effecte as I for my part and the residewe of the company could have wished it had. Soe as by the discontentement and disagreement betwene our factors and you wee were occasioned to sende mr Beddle to minister at Aleppo to supply your place entendinge that you shuld have come directly for England not withstanding contrary to our expectation and order you have gone up to Constantynople, and ther remained ever since. the company still expecting your returne for England which at lengeth they perceaving you entended not hath moved them at a Generall court to geave order for your coming home.[10]

How Maye had managed to remain in, or return to, Istanbul remains uncertain, yet he clearly had an extraordinary capacity for staying on despite his unpopularity. No doubt his disputatiousness – and, if we can trust Sanderson's highly biased account, weakness as a defender of Christianity – as well as his evident inability to obey the commands of Company superiors were qualities that had made him unsuited for appointment to a church living in England in the first place.

Maye disappears from the record until 1608, shortly before Biddulph's book appeared. In July that year Sanderson wrote to Glover that 'newes it is for me to heare that you should writt for Master May, that factiouse man and pevish humorest' (p. 252), and again six weeks later that he was still 'greatly mervailinge how you were incensed to writt for him' (p. 254). Could it be that Maye, after some years back in England and still in need of employment, had been resorting to the persuasive powers of blackmail?

In May 1599 while Maye was being dismissed from Aleppo and shipped to Istanbul on the *Hector*, where was Biddulph? The most obvious answer is that Biddulph too was on board the *Hector*, having travelled out from England. If not, how could he have asked Sanderson, the ranking Company agent aboard ship, to write to Colthurst on his behalf concerning a change in plans? Moreover, in a letter dated 22 October 1601, Biddulph himself wrote to Sanderson: 'I have been sundry times sorrie that ever I came out of England, or that I had not gone with you to Constantinople.'[11] We know Biddulph was in Istanbul early in 1607, perhaps a little sooner. What he wrote to Sanderson in 1601 is that he wished he had gone there 'with you'.

From such indirect evidence it seems likely that Biddulph, with an initial commission to go to Istanbul, left England aboard the *Hector* in February, arriving in Iskenderun that May. He was in Aleppo by late July, since on the 26th Colthurst wrote to Sanderson that 'Master Biddell hath been extreamly sick, but now (thanks be to God) is well recovered'. If he had arrived after the *Hector* left Iskenderun for Istanbul, he would have been in Aleppo for some weeks before taking sick, and this fits with other epistolary evidence. Colthurst confirms that Biddulph had been there long enough to impress the English who had sacked Maye, writing, 'His cariadg geveth great content to the hole nation, and to mysealf' (p. 176). The next month, when reporting on the arrival of the *Hector*, Sanderson commented that, despite earlier orders, the new arrangement of Biddulph in Aleppo and Maye in Istanbul seemed to be working out, but 'had ben better' if those involved 'had followed order first' (p. 177).

Since Sanderson is generally reliable in such matters, it seems most likely that Biddulph was initially sent to Istanbul when the *Hector* sailed. Sir Thomas Smith's letter to Maye of September 1600 appears to register a strategic change in plans following Maye's dismissal by Colthurst shortly before the *Hector* arrived off Iskenderun, when Maye came aboard and Biddulph went ashore for Aleppo. The account of Biddulph's journey from England to Istanbul offered in *The Travels* does not correspond at any point with the voyage of the *Hector*. Produced as a result of Lavender's editorializing, the book never once mentions the name of the ship and offers an idealized journey, organized according to a specific design rather than as an accurate itinerary.

Biddulph's transfer to Aleppo was later formally confirmed, making his the earliest recorded official appointment to the chaplaincy there.[12] In a letter dated March 1600, Sir Thomas Smith addressed himself to 'my very lovinge frend Mr Byddell preacher at Aleppo' and outlined his terms of employment, including details of salary and duties. Smith's letter also tells us that Biddulph had been in Company service as early as Michaelmas 1598, since that is the date from which his pay was to begin. Nothing is said, however, about plans to take over a church building in Istanbul to serve the Protestant community. On arrival, however, Biddulph was expected to act as the English enclave's moral conscience.[13] Without commenting on the circumstances involving the switching of Biddulph's job to the chaplaincy at Aleppo, Smith outlines clearly how Company ministers were expected to police English expatriates. 'You will,' he instructs Biddulph, 'contyneue and proceade in yor charge both in the instruction of our people in knowledg of Religyon and in reproving and rebuking whatsoever you shall ether see or be dewly informed of to deserve reproof or admonition.'[14]

Given the numerous glimpses we have had of the constant drunkenness, violence and irregular sexual practices among English expatriates, it is easy to see how chaplains would have been considered a great nuisance if they had attempted to set things in order. Biddulph himself reflected on his own treatment by the expatriate community:

> Yea in all my ten yeeres travels, I never received, neither was offered wrong by any Nation but mine own Countrimen, and by them chiefly whom it chiefly concerned to protect me from wrongs; yet have I found them most forward to offer me wrong only for doing my duty, and following the order of our Church of England. (p. 62)

Changing the air, staying the same

By late July 1599, Biddulph was ill and living in Aleppo. He missed the ceremonial arrival of the *Hector* in Istanbul, events he must have heard about but never once mentions. In *The Travels*, he never mentions Glover, Sanderson or Maye by name, or anything about plans for an English church in Istanbul, nor does he even hint at the confusion over his appointment. Despite occasional accusations against the English expatriates, he does not devote very much space to reports of life among the merchants. Of himself he reveals very little. Unlike Dallam, he seldom appears in his own book except in the depersonalized figure of the narrating traveller set apart from the immediate surroundings being described. Whereas Dallam wrote from within the experience of his immediate circumstances, Biddulph's narrative position remains detached, a disengagement that strives for a longer historical view.

At the core of *The Travels*, nevertheless, is Biddulph's performing being a Protestant minister among the heathens. He associated himself with great travellers of the past, justifying his own travels by recalling how Pythagoras, Plato, Appolonius, Jerome and Jacob all travelled for love of wisdom and learning (sig. ¶3v). The Preface goes so far as to claim that Biddulph exceeded the achievements of former travellers: 'By land, he hath traveled further then *Jacob* ... By Sea, farther then *S. Paul*, then *Aeneas*, or *Ulysses* have done, and all the whole way that they all have traveled, and further' (sig. A4v).

In one exceptional moment of self-awareness, Biddulph steps forth from his account. After months living in the lands of the infidel, Biddulph turns to himself and reports finding that he is just the same as when he left home, having changed only the air he breathes. In a moment worthy of Descartes, he locates himself, finds his enduring identity, in what he calls his mind. In the third letter of the series, purporting to have been written after two years in Aleppo, Biddulph observes:

> although I am now many thousand miles distant from you, yet I have changed but the aire, I remaine still the same man, and of the same minde, according to that old verse, though spoken in another sense,

> *Coelum, non animos mutant qui trans mare currunt.*
>
> That is,
>
> They that over the sea from place to place doe passe,
>
> Change but the aire, their minde is as it was. (pp. 31–2)

The assertion is important since Biddulph promoted the not uncommon notion that simply being in a foreign environment, most especially witnessing Catholic ceremonies, was to risk spiritual contamination. Insisting that he remained the same, having changed only the air he breathed, Biddulph admitted, 'I am weary of this uncomfortable Country, and did thinke to have repaired towards my native country long before this time' (p. 32).

Doubtless Biddulph was feeling homesick after two years away, but here, as throughout *The Travels*, internal chronology follows rhetorical design, not historical accuracy. Biddulph had been two years in Aleppo by the summer of 1601, yet in this third letter he describes how news of Queen Elizabeth's death in 1603 was received in this ancient Syrian city:

> at the hearing whereof not onely I and our English Nation mourned, but many other Christians who were never in Christendome, but borne and brought up in Heathen countries, wept to heare of her death, and said she was the most famous Queene that ever they heard or read of since the world began. (sig. G)[15]

None of this could have happened before 1603, and the chronological discrepancy serves to remind us how the editorial labours of Theophilus Lavender commonly altered events from their sequence.

At the death of Queen Elizabeth and accession of King James, Biddulph registered himself as a loyal agent of the Crown by engaging in pious and patriotic flattery. Representing the Church of England, Biddulph dutifully took charge and 'appointed one day to be kept holy' for mourning Elizabeth's death. At such historical and political moments, the clergy must naturally take charge. The day of mourning over, Biddulph took it upon himself to rouse the English community into

> thanksgiving unto God for the happy advancement of so noble, wise, learned, and religious a King over us. And in signe of joy, wee feasted and triumphed in such sort, that the very Heathen people were partakers with us of our joy. And I beseech God continue such joyfull daies unto our Land so long as the Sunne and Moone endureth. *Amen.* (sig. G)

In that final brief allusion to Psalm 72, Biddulph not only confirmed his patriotism, but also linked himself with another true believer who dwelt among heathens: King David.

Perhaps it had nothing to do with the time spent in biblical lands, but Biddulph could not help imagining himself performing within the timeless present of scriptural history. He regularly represents himself in the company of biblical travellers, taking comfort from the belief that the God who looked after the chosen people would take care of him too, and return him soon to England's Zion:

> a poore Christian, living amongst Heathen men, doe comfort my selfe with this confidence, that he which broght Jacob from *Padan Aram* in *Mesopotamia* to his owne countrey in safety, after twenty yeeres service; and *Naomi* after ten yeers sojourning in idolatrous *Moab*, to *Bethlehem Ephrata* her own Countrye; the same God, in his good time, will bring mee from this Heathenish *Babylon*, to *Israel* his people, and English *Sion*, where, with the true *Israelites*, the remembrance of *Babylon* will make me sing more sweetly in *Sion*. (p. 32)

Despite claims of being unchanged, Biddulph could not possibly have felt quite this longing for England's Sion before he left it. Rather more than the air must have changed during his sojourn, whether it was apparent to Biddulph or not.

This emphatic testimony that he has remained unchanged apart from feeling some plangent nostalgia for home is as close as Biddulph ever comes to recording his travels as personal experience. While Dallam wrote about himself and his experiences, for Biddulph writing was all about setting the record straight. Frequently, the information he records about places and peoples and their past had little or nothing to do with his having travelled and directly witnessed these scenes. Much of Biddulph's text is directly citational in the sense that it repeats, confirms or qualifies what was already known or suspected. Indeed, his report of Istanbul is taken word for word from Thomas Washington's 1585 translation of Nicolas de Nicolay's *Navigations*, while further sections of *The Travels* are transcribed from other printed sources. What today would be considered plagiarism can more usefully be described as an extreme instance of citationality, a not uncommon convention in travel writing and, according to Edward Said, a key feature of Orientalism.[16]

But many aspects of Biddulph's account are nevertheless evidence of personal testimony, such as his clergyman's eye for religious buildings and his interest in the conduct and administration of foreign churches. Reporting on clerical culture was high on his list of priorities. Although his account of his voyage to Istanbul shows remarkably little interest in the ship or other passengers, his descriptions of places are often illustrated with anecdotes suggesting personal experience. Biddulph adopts a documentary style much favoured by later travel writers: he arrives somewhere, describes the geographical and physical features of the place, reports on the history of its peoples from the published accounts of classical and modern historians, and then, having established the place in terms of its situation and past, comments on how it appeared to him. It is worth recalling how Lavender editorialized by putting 'those places first, which lie neerest unto *England*, and so to proceed unto every place *ordine queque suo*, as they stand in order, that they which read it may better profit by it' (sig. A3).

The first letter recounts a voyage from Tenerife to Istanbul via Venice. Along the way Biddulph recorded sightings of sea creatures and various islands and ports, stopovers in Algiers, Malta, Zante, Venice, and Chios, with suitable reflections on church history and the status of the clergy. On Malta, he reflected on St Paul's visit and briefly identifies with the apostle. Before describing Zante castle and the currant trade, he complained about the boredom of being in quarantine.

While most of Biddulph's reports could easily have been compiled from available sources, moments of personal testimony sometimes demand our attention: '*Zante* is very much subject to earthquakes…especially in the moneths of September and October, in which moneths I have knowen two or three earthquakes in one weeke' (p. 6). How he came to be so long on Zante at that time of year remains unexplained, but the claim seems authentic. At other times, details seem more like editorial conveniences:

> The Citie *Venice* standeth in the *Adriaticke* sea, not far from the countrey of *Venice*. We stayed in *Venice* 17. daies, and having ended our businesse there, wee returned to Zante, where after we had staied three daies, we set saile for *Constantinople*. (p. 9)

The journey reported in the first letter consists of elements from several journeys. We know that Biddulph eventually arrived in Istanbul by sea, but only after he had spent time in Aleppo. We know that he returned to England via Zante, and so may well have travelled to Venice on that trip. As described by Lavender's prefatory comments, the published account is not so much an accurate chronicle of a particular voyage, but rather a carefully designed moral journey aimed at the 'better profit' of 'they which read it'.

The further from England, the greater the danger of falling in with local custom and superstition. Fear of the increasing danger of spiritual contagion the further from England one finds oneself animates Biddulph's account. *En route* to Venice, he mockingly relates how an Italian captain promised the blessed Virgin 'a candle as bigge as the maine maste of my ship' for assistance in a storm. When challenged, the captain remarked that 'I will make her content with a candle of seven or eight in the pound' if he survived (p. 8). By indicating the impious folly of a religion that allowed bargaining with the mother of Christ, the anecdote serves as a sort of apotropaic gesture, aimed at warding off the dangers of imminent arrival in a city run by Catholics. Venice itself left Biddulph unimpressed.

1. Samson Rowlie, aka Assan Aga, was Treasurer to Uluç Hassan, Ottoman Beylerbey of Algiers. As the illustration coyly suggests, he was also a eunuch. He was nevertheless wealthier and more powerful than he could have become in his native England. From a German traveller's picture book, *c.* 1588.

2. Portrait of a European man, Levni, c. 1720.

3. Portrait of a European man, Levni, *c.* 1720.

4. Murad III (1574–95), the sultan who
signed the first trading agreement with
England.

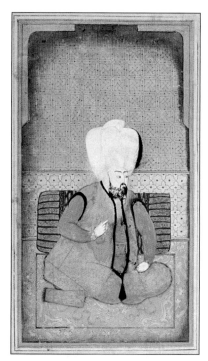

5. Mehmed III (1595–1603), the sultan
who took pleasure from seeing and
hearing Thomas Dallam's organ.

6. Ahmed I (1603–17), the sultan who
piously destroyed Dallam's organ, but
nevertheless allowed this portrait of
himself to adorn a collection of poems.

7. The women of Chios were renowned for their beauty. From a rare German edition of Nicolay's *Navigations*, published in 1572 with hand-coloured plates by Georg Mack.

8. A Delly warrior, such as Blount might have seen on the march outside Belgrade. Hand-coloured engraving by Georg Mack.

9. and 10. (right) A Zulphaline Christian and his wife, members of an Eastern sect that took its name from their habit of wearing their hair in long braids. From a seventeenth-century costume book.

11. and 12. (right) Companion portraits of Sir Henry and Lady Hester Blount, likely to have been painted after their wedding in 1647, still hang together on the staircase at Tittenhanger House. Henry's motto, 'Radicem Pete' (Seek the Root) was in keeping with his radical ideas. Artist unknown.

13. In this later portrait by Jacob Huysmans, Sir Henry Blount adopted the style of wig fashionable after the Restoration.

14. The Sinan Pasha Mosque, An'nabk, Syria.

15. The top of Mount Scopos, Zante, where Thomas Dallam was kindly welcomed.

Sailing to Istanbul, he remarked on a sect of hermits, regretted the ruination of temples on Crete, Milos and Delos, speculated on whether Homer was indeed born on Chios, and noted passing through the Hellespont and pausing briefly at Gallipoli before arriving in the city of the world's desire:

> After our Ship had saluted the Port, we went over to the other side, and anchored at *Fundaclee*, and went on shore at *Gallata*, to salute the honourable Sir *Henrie Lello*, Lord Ambassadour for Queene *Elizabeth* of famous memorie, and to visit our English Merchants resident there. (p. 16)

Biddulph may have arrived in Istanbul at any time between October 1601, the date of his letter to Sanderson, and early 1607, by which time he is among those conspiring against Glover.

Memorializing English travellers

Biddulph's first letter ends with a general view of a city 'most pleasant to behold, being like unto a City in a wood, or a wood in a city, having firr tress, Cyprus trees, and other pleasant trees in gardens adjoining to their houses' (p. 15). Biddulph might well have seen and thought these things at some point in his travels. His second letter begins by claiming that he will provide an eye witness description:

> Since the writing of my former letters, I having often beene at Constantinople, and thorowly viewed the same, according to promise, I have thought good to write somthing unto you thereof. (p. 17)

What follows is a lightly abridged transcription of Thomas Washington's 1585 translation of Nicolas de Nicolay's chapters on the city. At times, Biddulph follows Washington precisely:

> This citie (according to the saying of many ancient Authors) was first builded by the Lacedemonians under the conduct of their Captaine *Pausanias* ... (Biddulph, p. 17)

> This city, according to the saying of many ancient authors, was first builded by the Lacedemonians under the conduct of theyr Duke Pausane ... (Nicolay, p. 47)

Biddulph even repeated, almost verbatim, Nicolay's account of the sacking of ancient Byzantium by Mehmed II in 1453, evidently relishing certain prurient details that serve to revile the Islamic invaders:

And afterwards *Mahomet* not contenting himselfe with the violating and deflouring of the Emperours wife, daughters, and other Ladies of honour, by a savage cruelty, caused them in his presence to be dismembred and cut in peeces. During the time of the sacking (which continued three daies) there was no kinde of fornication, Sodometry, sacrilege, nor cruelty, by them left unexecuted.

They spoiled the incomparable Temple of *S. Sophia* (which was built by the Emperour *Justinian*) of all ornaments and hallowed vessels, and made thereof a stable, and a brodell for bugerers and whores. (p. 22; see Nicolay p. 48)

Biddulph's most interesting contribution to this description is the additional syllable creating the coinage 'bugerers', though even this might have been the printer's creation. In the name of Theophilus Lavender, it will be recalled, Biddulph stoutly denounced the tendency of travellers to believe everything they have been told, but here he seems willing to take things entirely on trust if they have previously appeared in print and confirmed his dislike of the Turks.

The description of Istanbul, once a Christian city 'being chiefe of the Orientall Empire' (p. 22), closely follows Nicolay's organization: a brief account of her founding by Constantine, including changes under the Ottomans, details of great fires and earthquakes, a survey of antiquities and description of the great tower at Yedi Kale. Throughout, Biddulph's text follows Nicolay (book 2, chapters 13–17) with unerring devotion, yet it also introduces occasional comments and asides. Of Constantine's mother, St Helena, we are additionally informed that 'some report [her] to have beene an Englishwoman borne at *Cholchester*'. Biddulph wistfully inserts how 'the Turks have a Prophecie, that as the Empire was gotten by *Mahomet*, so by another of that name Mahomet it shall be lost againe' (p. 23), and compares Yedi Kale with the Tower of London (p. 28).

Where Nicolay describes the seraglio and harem, however, Biddulph turns aside to record what he has himself seen; once again the emphases are on matters learned and of English interest. Not for the last time, Biddulph reports on an activity that seems already to have become a favourite with English sightseers. 'At the Blacke sea we saw *Pompeis* Piller of marble,' he writes.

whereon some of our company wrote their names, *viz.* master *Robert Yong*, Gentleman (who also there wrote the name of our noble Prince *Henry*)
> *Nathaniel Persivall*
> *John Milward*
> *Thomas Marston*, and others. (p. 28)

But Biddulph's real interest lay in correcting vulgar errors, such as the belief that the waters of the Black Sea are black: not so, he pronounced, 'but from the dangerous currents, because in blacke and darke nights many ships are cast away' (p. 28). Similarly, the Red Sea is not so named because its waters are 'redder than others' having been turned to blood after Moses 'wrought miracles before *Pharaoh*', but 'because of the red gravell and red bull-rushes which still grow in great abundance' (p. 28). Since he never visited the Red Sea, Biddulph really was happy enough to rely on hearsay whenever it suited his purposes.

His second letter ends on a personal note suited to the epistolary mode. Although none of these composite letters is personally addressed, here Biddulph reports on his brother's activities as if writing to a family friend. His brother Peter, he writes, was currently in Italy making money by cutting '*Diamonds, Rubies, Saphiers, Emrods*, and all other sorts of precious stones' (p. 29). Aptly named for a dealer in stones, Peter emerges as an emblem of how an adventurous Englishman may profitably engage in travelling and trading abroad:

> his purpose was to follow the trade of a *Lapidarie*, and buying and selling precious stones, which he buyeth rough and rouged: and when he hath smoothed them and curiously wrought them, then he selleth them againe ... I understand he hath a purpose to travel to *Spahan* in *Persia*, and to other of the chiefest Cities there to buy precious stones, which are brought thither from *India* and other places. (p. 29)

Peter's story becomes part of the greater family history of the English, one of industriously making an honest profit by bringing and applying the superior technical skills of the West to the undiscovered riches of the East.

The second letter ends within the epistolary fiction by directing the imaginary addressee: 'if you write hereafter unto mee, direct your letters to *Aleppo* in *Syria*, for there I hope to bee before your letters can come' (p. 30), as if Biddulph really had been in Istanbul all the time he was copying out lengthy passages from Nicolay.

8
Journey to Aleppo

While composing *The Travels* for the press, a further matter that Biddulph must often have considered was how the epistolary form was Pauline in inspiration. He needed to make it apparent to his readers that, like Paul, his object had been to meet other Christians, to teach and thereby to set the record straight on matters of crucial concern. His third letter, purporting to be written after two years in Aleppo, records his doubts and his strategies for overcoming them. It concludes: 'And that is the best lesson which I have learned in my travels, *Mundi contemptum*, that is, *The contempt of the world*. And S. *Pauls* lesson, Phil. 4.11: *In whatsoever state I am, therwith to be content*' (p. 84).

The third letter mostly recounts his journey to, and travels from, Aleppo. Biddulph focuses on meetings, places and sites where the past and present of the Christian religion come together. Although travelling in company, Biddulph most often conveys the sense that he is alone. He does mention travelling companions, sometimes by name, but tells us no more of them than circumstances require. With his Bible ever at hand, Biddulph casts himself among the great Old Testament travellers, thinking of Jacob whenever desert travel requires him to find a rock to use for his pillow.

Meetings with remarkable Christians

For Biddulph, one of the great pleasures of Levantine travel was meeting communities of other Christians. Setting sail from Istanbul, Biddulph traces a rather circuitous route. His ship pauses briefly for customs duties in the Hellespont before visiting Chios and then crossing through the Sporades and Cyclades sails to Rhodes and on to Cyprus. Here an unnamed 'French Gentleman' disembarked 'with a purpose to goe to Jerusalem', only two days distant, by changing ships. But Biddulph's unnamed ship 'went to Tripoly in Syria', where she stayed long enough for passengers to visit the cedars on Mount Lebanon at a place 'by the Christians there dwelling...called *Eden* [modern Ehden], not the garden of *Eden*, (which place is unknowen unto this day) but because it is a pleasant place, resembling in some sort the garden of *Eden*' (sig. G2).[1]

Here Biddulph enjoys the hospitality of the community of Syrian-speaking Christians, '*Nostranes* quasi *Nazaritans*', who, he explains, are usually 'called Maronites, but this name is common to them with others' (sig. G4). Their 'Bishop was born in the same parish, but brought up at Rome; his name was *Franciscus Amyra*' (sig. G2v). Out of respect for his host, perhaps, Biddulph withholds further comment while telling us that the Pope, in an attempt to persuade the Maronites to 'yeeld themselves to the Church of *Rome*', eventually agreed that they might retain 'liberty to use their owne Liturgie, and Ceremonies, and Lents (for they strictly observe foure Lents in the yeere) and other customes' (sig. G2v). Scorning such ecumenical latitude, he notes that the Maronites are credulous, being 'very simple and ignorant people' (sig. G2v).

While touring Mount Lebanon, Biddulph regularly found himself a welcome guest among local Christian communities. Disappointed at counting only 24 cedars growing on the mountain, Biddulph travelled on to 'a village of the *Maroniticall Christians*, called *Hatcheeth*' (modern Hadchit) where, he writes,

> all the men, women, and children, came out of their houses to behold us: And when we were yet farre off riding towards them, they gave a joyfull shout all together jointly, to expresse their joy for our comming . . . their women with chaffing dishes of coales burnt incense in our way, and their *Caffeeses*, that is, their Churchmen (with blew shashes about their heads) made crosses with their fingers towards us (as their manner is in signe of welcome) and blessed us, giving God thankes that he had brought Christian Frankes (that is, freemen) of such farre countries as they understood we were of, to come to visit them.(sig. G3)

Full of patriotic fervour, Biddulph and companions are feasted by the 'chiefe *Sheh*, with all the rest of their ancientest men', seated on sumptuous carpets spread with 'many bottles or ingesters of exceeding good wine, with olives, sallets, egges, and such like things, as on the sudden they had ready' (sig. G3).

Turning down offers to stay the night and continue feasting on 'hens, kids, and other good cheere', Biddulph moved on to 'Sharry' (modern Bsharri), a village three miles away, because the local patriarch had sent word that he was waiting there to welcome the itinerant English clergyman. Once again, carpets were spread and refreshments served while the Patriarch

> conferred with us of our countrey, and many other matters, saving matters of Religion, for the poore man had no Latine, and little learning in any other Language; only he had the Syriac (which was his naturall language) with the Turkish and Arabian tongue. (sig. G3)

Without telling us what language they did use, Biddulph spent an hour in conversation and then, equally without explanation, left the Patriarch

> with his neighbours at *Sharry*, where wee found him, for hee could not conveniently come from them: for their manner is, when they feast, to sit from midday untill midnight, and sometimes all night, never all together rising from their good cheere, but now and then one by intercourses, as occasion requireth, returning againe speedily. Yet he sent with us three men to bring us to his own house. (sigs. G3–G3v)

Why didn't Biddulph remain and feast with the patriarch? What urgency drove him onward? Was it the need to spend the night inside a house? Was it social diffidence born of cultural difference that caused him to feel he might be outstaying his welcome? Or was he simply not invited? Biddulph does not say. Instead, he offers a short language lesson, telling us that the patriarch's house in the village of 'Boloza, but vulgarly *Blouza* [modern Blaouza]' is 'called *Kanobeen kadischa Mir-iam* in the Syriac tongue, but in Latine, *Coenobium sanctae Mariae*; that is, *The Monasterie of Saint Mary*' (sig. G3v).

Biddulph was greatly interested in how other Christians lived, especially members of the upper clergy, and was fascinated by the magnificent situation and design of the patriarch's house. Like houses in the village, the monastery was 'hewed out of the lively rocke' in order to resist invasion. The house of 'Emeer Useph', for example, had been so contrived that 'the passage descending unto it [is] so narrow and dangerous, that it is counted invincible, which maketh him to hold out against the Turke, and to domineere in this mountaine, will he, nill he' (sig. G3v). Well fortified against invasion from the infidel, this outpost of Christianity also guarded a sublime location. Below the monastery,

> the water runneth downe into a deepe valley...and in the fall, the water maketh an exceeding great noise...There is also an extraordinary *Eccho* thereabout...It is a most intricate mountaine with hilles and valleyes, woods and rivers, and fruitfull pastures, olives, vines, and figtrees, goates, sheepe, and other cattle. It is also exceeding high, having snow on the top all the yeere long. (sig. G3v)

Biddulph's rapture over this *locus amoenus* allowed him to notice that the scene was also a fertile landscape, producing not only sublime awe in the beholder, but also plenty of fresh fruit and meat.

Biddulph's attitude towards the Maronites differs noticeably from his obsessive hostility toward Roman Catholicism. Obviously a few hundred Syrian-speaking Christians living on Mount Lebanon, however splendid their rural isolation, were in no respect a threat to the Church of England, unlike the

Church of Rome. Yet his account sounds more envious than condescending. Having excoriated Henry Timberlake's book for recording his attendance at Catholic mass, Biddulph blithely relates being at services while over-nighting at St Mary's.

At this Monastery of S. *Mary* (which is the Patriarches house) we lodged all night, and both on Saterday at Evening Praier, and on Sunday at morning Praier, we both heard and sawe the manner of their Service in the *Syriac* tongue, both read and sung very reverently, with Confessions, Praiers, Thanksgivings, the Psalmes of *David* sung, and Chapters both out of the old Testament and the new distinctly read. It rejoyced me greatly to see their order: and I observed in these ancient Christians called *Nazarites*, the antiquitie of using set formes of Praiers in Churches, and also the necessitie thereof, that the people might have something to say Amen unto, being read in their mother tongue, that they may learne to pray privately by those Praiers which they daily heare read publikely. (sigs. G3v–G4)

Like Dallam claiming that his attendance at an Orthodox liturgy did not compromise his faith because he did not understand what was being said, Biddulph evidently thought that understanding the language made all the difference. Clearly, he could tell what was going on at any given time, and doubtless he greatly enjoyed hearing the Psalms sung in this ancient tongue. Yet the very backwardness of these 'ancient Christians' praying daily in their 'mother tongue' provided an object lesson furthering the cause of Protestant reform against the residual tokens of Rome still to be found in the Church of England. Far from coming to harm from observing services in Syriac, a godly English clergyman such as Biddulph could not help but observe how the antiquity and necessity of set forms of vernacular prayer enabled congregations in their private prayers. 'This,' he concluded, 'is too much neglected in *England*, God grant reformation thereof' (sig. G4). It is perhaps worth recalling that the King James Bible did not appear until 1611, two years after *The Travels* appeared.

Biddulph also found lessons for the English among his observations of other local communities. He noted that nearby lived a 'kind of Christians called Drusies' who had forgotten all Christian belief 'yet used still Baptisme, and retained still the name of Christians' (sig. G4). Former Christians were not much to his taste, while from the social order of pastoral Muslim nomads – whom he calls 'Turcomanni' – Biddulph found instruction for folks at home in England:

the women keepe their tents, and spend their time in spinning, or carding, or knitting, or some houshold huswifery, not spending their time in gossipping and gadding abroad from place to place, and from house to house, from ale-house to wine-taverne, as many idle huswives in *England* doe. (sig. G4v)

Returning to Tripoli, Biddulph found his ship not ready to depart, so he took the opportunity for more sightseeing, this time visiting 'the tombe of Zabulon the soune of Jacob' in Sidon, Tyre and 'Sarepta', the site 'where the Prophet Elias raised the Widdowes sonne from death to life' (p. 37). Encountering no notable instances of hospitality, he returned to his ship and soon arrived in Iskenderun.

Overland from Iskenderun: Graves, Kurds, pigeons and watermelon

Iskenderun was Biddulph's final stop before striking off overland to Aleppo. Like Dallam, he sensed the myriad dangers of the place, the unhealthy air, the vermin, the dangerous beasts. Quickly assuming the wisdom and jargon of experienced travellers, he advises: 'It is far more healthfull to sleepe aboard then on the shoare' (p. 37). While waiting for cargo to be unloaded, he 'tooke boat' and spent several days in Tarsus where the air was cleaner (p. 38). Here he noticed the abundant silkworms which 'at first bee but little graines like unto Mustardseed' until they are warmed 'in womens bosomes...whereby they come to life, and so prove wormes'. From here too he reported on the nightly howlings of 'ravenous beasts' called '*Jackalles*, engendered (as they say) of a Fox and a Woolfe' who dig up graves, 'pull up the corps and eat it' (p. 38). On returning to Iskenderun, Biddulph must have been greatly relieved to find that Edward Rose, 'our Factor marine', had arrived with horses to take them on to Aleppo with an armed guard consisting of a Janissary 'called *Paravan Bashaw* with two Jimmoglans' (pp. 38–9). Barely had they left that 'pestiferous place *Scanderone*' behind, 'which one very well called, *The bane of Franks*', when Biddulph had the opportunity to prove the point while recording a national monument in the mountain village of Belen:

> about eight miles from Scanderone, we came to a towne called Bylan, where there lieth an English Gentleman, named Henry Morison, who died there comming downe from Aleppo in companie with his brother master Phines Morison, who left his Armes in that countrie with these verses under written.
>
> > To thee deare HENRY MORISON
> > Thy brother PHINES here left alone:
> > Hath left this fading memorie,
> > For monuments, and all must die. (p. 39)

Biddulph does not tell us that Henry Morison had died of dysentery, the 'flux',[2] most likely preferring not to think of such matters while he remained queasily within reach of that particular danger. In Belen today, a restored bell tower still marks the spot where Christians were once buried, but the gravestones have gone and the tower lacks a bell.

For the rest of his journey to Aleppo, Biddulph continued his interest in Christian communities, identifying himself whenever possible with biblical travellers. Arriving in Antioch (modern Antakya), he noted that here 'the Disciples were first called Christians' (p. 39), but seems not to have known of the cave in the cliffs to the north of the city – a consecrated church to this day – where this naming is reported to have taken place.[3] Instead, he comments on how the Orthodox patriarch at Antioch, like those of Jerusalem and Alexandria, was ruled by the patriarch of Istanbul. This point of information provides occasion for recording how, recently, an Englishman in Istanbul, the ambassador Edward Barton, had the honour of playing a leading role in the appointment of 'one Milesius' to this supreme position (p. 40). Praising Barton led, as we have seen, to praising Lello, whom Biddulph knew.

On the road again, Biddulph tells of the 'Coords' living in the 'Mountaines betwixt *Scanderone* and *Aleppo* ... who worship the Devill, and allege for their reason in so doing, that God is a good man, and will doe no man harme, but that the Devill is bad, and must be pleased lest he hurt them'. He further noted that among 'our Carriers was one ... *Abdell Phat*, who was said to be of that Race and Religion' (p. 41). This is perhaps the earliest report in English of the Yezidis, worshippers of the Peacock Angel, a sect of Kurds still persecuted by Sunni Muslims and Christians alike.[4] After spending a night in the desert, 'a stone to our pillow (as *Jacob* in his travel had)', Biddulph comes to the village of 'Hanadan' (modern Anadane) where, he reports, 'are many pigion houses, whereof the poore people make much profit, bringing them to *Aleppo* to sell. At this village,' he continues without noting the connection, 'we dined with Musmelons' (p. 42).

Had he looked about a little more carefully, he would most likely have noticed a familiar arrangement for watermelon farming, whereby pigeon houses are built at one end of an irrigated field so that the birds, flying out, fertilize the crop naturally. What made the melons of Hanadan so notable was the incomparable and characteristic sweetness thus achieved. Throughout central Anatolia to this day, farmers continue to keep, and jealously guard, pigeons for their manure, not for their flesh. In Aleppo too, the market in pigeons was not about food as Biddulph discovered on arrival. He reported how trade passing through from the great eastern emporia of Mosul and Baghdad was greatly facilitated by an efficient pigeon post (p. 43).

9
Biddulph's Lessons from Aleppo

[Aleppo] is the greatest place of traffique for a dry towne that is in all those parts: for hither resort Jewes, Tartarians, Persians, Armenians, Egyptians, Indians, and many sorts of Christians, and injoy freedome of their consciences, and bring thither many kinds of rich marchandises.

John Eldred (1583)[1]

Captured from the Mamelukes by Sultan Selim I in 1516, Aleppo at the start of the seventeenth century was the largest and most important centre of eastern trade within the Ottoman Empire, rivalled only by Cairo. When William Barrett, the first English vice-consul, arrived in 1583, the Ottomans had 'more than doubled the commercial core' to include 'fifty-six separate markets and fifty-three caravansaries'. Three years later, Aleppo replaced Damascus as the principal centre of the Levant Company in Syria.[2] Fynes Moryson, visiting in 1596, noted how 'the Trafficke in this place is exceeding great' since 'the goods of all Asia and the Easterne Ilands are brought hither, or to Cayro in Egypt'.[3] He also noted how 'the aire was so hot, as me thought I supped hot broth, when I drew it in; but it is very subtile, so as the Christians comming hither from Scanderona . . . continually fall sicke, and often die'.[4]

Despite the unhealthy air, English merchants settled in Aleppo since it was here they bought the raw materials required by the massively expanding domestic silk industry: 'In London alone, it was estimated that the number of people employed in the manufacture of silk cloth rose from three hundred in 1600 to over ten thousand in 1640.'[5] Aleppo was so well known by 1594 that Richard Wragg could pass through merely commenting, 'the state and trade of which place, because it is so well knowen to most of our nation I omitte to write of'.[6] Biddulph, however, took time to note that the city was 'inhabited by *Turkes, Moores, Arabians, Jewes, Greekes, Armenians, Chelfalines, Nostranes*,[7] and people of sundry other Nations' (p. 45). Adding to this international assembly, the

84

English community in Aleppo shortly before Biddulph's arrival numbered over fifteen merchants, in addition to the consul, Richard Colthurst.[8]

Living inside Islam

When Biddulph arrived, the English merchants, together with the French and Dutch, lived in a splendid Ottoman khan, a two-storey building with stabling and warehousing arranged around a central courtyard. Today, the Khan al-Gümrük ('Customs House') is still the finest of the khans in the Aleppo souk and is used for storage by textile merchants.

To keep himself unaffected by all the commercial wealth, luxury, backbiting, bad air and foreign influences while in Aleppo, Biddulph turned at once to his Bible, using it to set the record straight on Syrian history. He identifies Aleppo itself with '*Aram Sobah*' of which 'I finde mention made, 2 *Sam.* 8.3.4.5 And also in the title of the sixty Psalme where mention is made of the salt valley' (p. 45). With scriptural evidence before him, he corrects local errors: 'Some *Jewes* there dwelling, doe also say, that *Aleppo* was the City *Sepheruiam*: but I thinke it to be a latter City' (p. 45). He could have written his ensuing account of Syrian peoples and their history without leaving England.

For Biddulph, the Bible was more than a comprehensive guide for living among heathens; it also enabled him to conceive that his mission fell firmly within the grander schemes of Christian apocalyptic history. The rest of the third epistle offers an entirely citational account of Islam and the differences between Turks, Jews and Arabs that belongs to a tradition of Protestant eschatological commentary on the books of Daniel and Revelations, broken up by occasional firsthand observations and illustrative anecdotes. The epistle ends with final observations on the Christian communities of Maronites, Greeks and other 'Franks', and a suitable moral: 'Oh how happie are you in England if you knew your own happinesse!' (p. 85). Biddulph frequently derives lessons for English readers and future travellers from personal experience, but his version of the life of the Prophet and the rise of Islam owes less to direct observation than adherence to a Protestant tradition of anti-Islamic propaganda initiated by Martin Luther and Englished by George Foxe.

Dealing with Islam

In describing this tradition, Nabil Matar has shown how Reformation theology in England and Scotland turned to the millennarian prophecies of Daniel and Revelations in order to cope with the twin threats of Ottoman sea power and the Counter-Reformation, while explaining the failure of the Christian crusaders to recapture the sacred lands of the Near East.[9] Daniel's prophecy was used to understand the emergence of Islam as part of a divinely ordained apocalyptic scheme of history. Protestant reformers such as Biddulph reviled Muslims not only in dogmatic terms, but also for being racially different. Thus, in Matar's terms, arose the 'demonization of the Muslims – both the Turks and the Arab "Saracens" who had given rise to Islam' (pp. 154–5). By using race to distinguish Arabs from Saracens, Protestant eschatologists separated the achievements of medieval Arab civilization from the militarized dissemination of (Saracen) Islam. Although scholarly Arabists of the time such as William Bedwell knew this to be nonsense, the distinction endured, supported by etymological and ethnographic myths of origin: the Saracens were variously held to be the sons of Sarah, or Hagar or, as in Biddulph's version of a story largely invented by Luther, simply a group of unpaid soldiers whose leader, Muhammad, founded a new religion grounded in aggressive military expansion.

Expositors of Daniel had little difficulty treating the Saracens as the 'Kings of the South' who drove Christianity from the East; a process they believed was simply continued by the Ottoman Turks.[10] Having thus reduced the history of Arabic civilization to military conquest, Protestant writers claimed that Muhammad himself had prophesied that Islam would last only 1,000 years, a period that was about to end. As Matar puts it: 'Muslim eschatology secured the victory of Christ over Mohammad' (p. 161). Implicit in this historical scheme, Matar points out, is an emergent ideology of progress in which the story of the past merely confirmed Anglo-Protestants in the sense of their own godly superiority: pro-Israelite but anti-Jewish, pro-Arab but anti-Saracen, pro-Roman but anti-Catholic.

Biddulph's contribution to anti-Islamic propaganda belongs firmly within this tradition of bigoted disinformation. He felt no need to distinguish Arabs from Saracens since he had nothing good to say about Arabic or Islamic civilization. For him Islam was simply a hybridized 'Turkish' belief, the religion of Ottoman imperial power, and so he begins with 'the first Author thereof, which was (no doubt) the Devill, who used that false Prophet *Mahomet* as his instrument to broach it abroad' (p. 46). Biddulph framed the rest of his account within the eschatological tradition, turning directly to the prophecy of Daniel which tells how the fall of the empire of the fourth beast (Rome) will be followed by a king who 'shall subdue three Kings, and shall speak words against the most high' (p. 47).

Once again, Biddulph relied on printed sources. In order to denigrate Muhammad's social origins and moral character, Biddulph copied out, word for word, a brief life of the Prophet from *The Policy of the Turkish Empire* (1597).[11] In this account, Muhammad's parents differed in both race and religion – his mother *'Cadige'* was 'a Jew both by birth and profession' – and were of such 'meane and base' condition that only the young boy's 'subtill and crafty nature and disposition' enabled him to overcome the 'baseness and obscurity of his birth' (p. 47). Having acquired money and status by marrying his dead master's wealthy widow, he sought 'to rise in honour and estimation' by coining 'a new kinde of Doctrine and Religion' that would appeal to the ignorant masses. Assisted by '*Sergius* a fugitive Monke' of the '*Arrian* Sect', the ambitious young man 'patched up a particular doctrine' by 'depraving' elements of Christianity, Judaism and Arianism into 'a monstrous and most divellish Religion' (p. 47).

Before copying more from *The Policy of the Turkish Empire* describing the rise of Islam, Biddulph assured readers that everything reported so far must be true, not because he took it from someone else's book, but because it confirmed Daniel's prophecy.

> God would have this prophecie to be extant for a strengthning of the godly against the crueltie of Turks, and when they should see the event to answeare to the prophecie, they might not be offended at the stumbling blocke of so great persecution, and of such revolting from the true Church. And therefore being thus forewarned by the Prophet, let us take to our selves against this Turkish tyranny and wickednesse, especially seeing how the event hath answered to the prophecie. (p. 49)

This prophetic framing appears to be Biddulph's own. Unlike the anonymous author of *The Policy of the Turkish Empire*, Biddulph was not interested in drawing historical and racial distinctions between Arabs, Saracens and Turks, since to him the history of Islam was one continuing tyranny inspired by the devil and first foretold by Daniel. Like most Western Christian commentators of the time, Biddulph had no desire to understand Islam; he 'wanted merely to refute it'.[12] Repeating Luther's claim that Muhammad took his earliest followers from the unpaid soldiers of Heraclius,[13] Biddulph cast the Prophet's subsequent success in terms both human and unholy:

> This champion first a thiefe, afterwards a seditious souldier, then a runnagate, after that a Captaine of a rebellious hoste, perswadeth light heads, enemies to the true Religion, how hee is the messenger of God; whereby wee may gather how great the power of Satan is in them, which imbrace not the truth. Wherof it is, that at this day that adversaries of God defendeth his blasphemies against God, by Turkish and *Mahometicall* force, according to the prophecie of Daniel. (p. 51)

While using prophecy to refute Islam, Biddulph then described eight maxims of 'this devilish religion', but had difficulty finding very much wrong with them. Once again he follows *The Policy of the Turkish Empire* by reducing Islam to these eight 'commandments', but offers a summary discussion in his own words.[14] He objects to the Islamic Witness, that there is 'one onely God, and Mahomet is the Prophet of God' (p. 52) since it elevates Muhammad over

Christ and denies the Holy Trinity. But the list of subsequent injunctions – to obey one's parents, to 'doe unto others as thou wouldest be done unto thy selfe', to pray five times a day, to keep holy fasts and to give to charity – barely whispers of Satanic logic. Could it be that Biddulph had spent too long living among Muslims to be able to condemn everything he had seen and learned?

When he reached the 'seventh commandment' concerning marriage, Biddulph had to admit that the English could learn lessons from Islam. Without passing judgement on either the purchase of brides or polygamy, Biddulph admired the way he imagined that married life was conducted in Muslim households. Wives, he believed, 'never sit at table', but only serve their husbands at meal-times, and they 'never goe abroad without leave of their husbands' (p. 55). A dutiful wife typically 'riseth up, and boweth herselfe to her husband' whenever he enters a room. 'If the like order were in England,' he concluded, 'women would be more dutifull and faithfull to their husbands than many of them are' (pp. 55–6).

Once on the topic of English women, the preacher in Biddulph warmed to the imaginative possibilities of punishment. 'And especially,' he continued:

> if there were the like punishment for whores, there would be less whoredome: for there, if a man have an hundred women, if any one of them prostitute herselfe to any man but her owne husband, he hath authoritie to binde her, hands and feet, and cast her into the river with a stone about her necke, and drowne her. And this is a common punishment amongst them; but it is usually done in the night. And the man, if he be taken, is dismembred. (p. 56)

Did Biddulph entertain fantasies of emptying the London brothels by throwing prostitutes into the Thames at night? The associated image of male dismemberment led Biddulph to report how the daughters of the 'great Turk' were presented with special daggers on their marriage, 'and whensoever their husbands... displease them, they may and doe cut off their heads'. Still on the topic of ritual killing, Biddulph related how newly appointed sultans strangled their brothers 'to avoid treason'. Mehmed III, he reminds us, 'put to death 19. of his brethren', but in such matters he considered the '*Persians* are somewhat better, (although too bad) where the eldest sonne is king after the death of his father, and all the rest of their brethren have their eyes put out, yet live' (p. 56). With this gory image, Biddulph returned to the topic of marriage: 'Other Turkes have three wives, and have as many women-slaves as they can keepe, whome they use as wives, and esteeme them equall with their wives' (p. 57). When contemplating Islamic society, admiration and horror distinctly mingle in the Protestant clergyman's imagination, as do violence and sexuality, concubinage and dismemberment.

Returning to his version of the eight maxims of Islamic doctrine, Biddulph could say little about what he calls 'their eight Commandment' since it 'is the same with our sixt: *Thou shalt not kill'*, and so was clearly not satanic (p. 58). Instead, he described ways he claims to have seen Turks behaving among themselves and others. Biddulph could not help finding faults that threatened godly Christians. Although he had often heard Turks arguing with each other, he reported: 'never did I see or heare of two Turkes in their private quarrels strike one another.' They will, on the other hand, 'strike Jews and Christians oftentimes, who dare not strike them againe' (p. 58). What was worse, he argued, is that Muslims do not obey their own laws. By way of illustration, he offered a detailed report of a murder involving two Englishmen which took place in Aleppo during his stay there.

Whenever a murder took place, he began, the 'master' of the house or the 'parish' where it occurred must find the criminal or be held responsible 'unto the Subbashaw' to pay 'so many hundred Dollers as shall be required' (p. 58). According to Biddulph, the inveterate greed of the 'Subbashaws' to collect on this arrangement encouraged many of them to 'hire some desperate person to kill a man in the night' (p. 58). This must have been the cause of what happened in Aleppo the night of 18 September 1603:

> We had an Englishman, not long since, who sleeping on the *Tarras* (that is, on the top of the house) in the night, (as the custome of the contrie is in the heate of Sommer) who had his throat cut being asleepe in bed, by two or three wicked men, who came from the streete by a ladder to the top of the house; and after they had committed this murther, being discried by the barking of a dog, and seene also by the master of the house, through his chamber window where he slept, (but not plainely discerned being somewhat darke) they made haste downe againe, and were never knowen. But on the morrow after, the master of the house (an Englishman also) was in trouble himselfe, because he could not find out the murtherers, and it cost him an hundreth Dollers at the least before hee coulde bee freed, and the whole *Contrado* or Parish, was also fined. (p. 59)

A marginal gloss names the luckless victim as William Martin and the house-holder as 'Jeames' Stapers, presumably a son of Richard Stapers, one of the founders of the Levant Company, who had travelled out with Henry Timberlake on board the *Trojan* early in 1601.[15] Of this incident I can find no other account, but in terms of Biddulph's purposes it usefully closed his discussion of the eight maxims of Islam with a dire example of the dangers ever present to innocent Englishmen among the covetous and treacherous Turks, regardless of Islamic law.

Without losing sight of the eschatological framing of his version of Islam, Biddulph continued by relating illustrative anecdotes that offer advice to

Christian travellers on how best to avoid certain kinds of danger. In addition to the eight commandments, Biddulph reckoned that Muhammad 'fortified his law with foure bulwarks or strong defences', enjoining followers to kill those who speak against the '*Alcoran*', not to hold conference with or extend credit to 'men of a contrary sect', not to believe anything 'beside the *Alcoran*', and finally 'to separate themselves altogether from other men, and to say *Let me have my law, and take you yours*'. Of this last Biddulph duly observed:

> and herein I hold it better for Merchants and other Christians to sojourne and to use trade and trafficke amongst Turkes then Papists; for, the Turke giveth libertie of conscience to all men, and liketh well of every man that is forward and zealous in his owne religion. But among the Papists no man can buy and sell, unlesse hee beare the markes of the beast as *S. John* foretold, *Revelation* 13:17. (pp. 60–1)

With apocalytic symbolism ever in mind, Biddulph advised readers that trading with Turks may be one thing, but 'whosoever will live in quiet amongst them, must neither meddle with their Law, their Women, nor their Slaves.' This warning still fresh, millennial horizons continued to open up in Biddulph's imagination. As for Islam, did not its own Prophet also foretell how he would return 'at the end of 1000. yeeres (as he promised them) and bring them to Paradise'? Biddulph must have taken special delight in pointing out that by the Prophet's own reckoning, '*Mahomets* comming to judgement was expected 20 yeeres since'. And he surely felt especially condescending when reporting how Muhammad's credulous followers had invented excuses: 'which time expiring, and he not comming, they have dealt more favourably with him, and given him longer time; for they say he was extremely sicke when he was asked of the time' and may have been misheard (p. 61).

Biddulph was not alone in taking pleasure from the notion that Islam contained the millennial seeds of its own destruction, noting that if the Prophet failed to return at the end of 2,000 years, 'they will looke for him no longer, nor beleeve in him any more, but become Christians' (pp. 61–2). Such wishful fantasies were not uncommon among Anglo-Protestants when they contemplated Islam.[16] But there is something very revealing about the way Biddulph chose this moment of anti-Islamic prophetic enthusiasm to introduce an image of himself, personally triumphing, dressed in the habit of an English churchman. The Turks, he informs us:

> reverence Churchmen of all nations, and call them holy men, Saints, and men of God.
>   I my selfe have had great experience heerof both in the place of my abode at *Aleppo*, and in my journey towards *Jerusalem*, and in other places. In *Aleppo*

as I have walked in the streets, both *Turkes*, and *Moores*, and other nations, would very reverently salute me after the manner of their Country: yea their very souldiers, as I have walked in the fields, with many other of our Nation, without a *Ienesarie* to guard us, thought have beene many hundreds together, yet have they not offered either me or any of my company wrong, for my sake . . . At *Jerusalem* many strangers of sundry Nations understanding I was an English Preacher, came and kissed my hand, and called me the English Patriarke. (p. 62)

What is most remarkable about this rather smugly aggrandizing self-portrait, especially in contrast to the ways Dallam inhabits his text, is just how stark and remote the figure being conjured up for us is. In ways simply unimaginable to the organ-builder, Biddulph promenades in a ritualized performance of his clerical role and robes. Through the streets of distant cities with ancient histories and biblical associations, the English clergyman strolls for no apparent purpose, it would seem, other than to displace anxieties and boost his self-esteem by receiving gestures of respect and reverence from strangers.

On the evidence of his own account, Biddulph, the travelling figure inside *The Travels*, seldom did anything other than sightseeing, enjoying hospitality from local communities and pointing out their erroneous beliefs. Unlike Dallam, without whose constant interventions the voyage of the *Hector* would have been quite different, Biddulph never once reports lending a hand or otherwise contributing to the practicalities of his journey. Instead, he complains that the considerable importance of his clerical office was usually slighted by other Englishmen, 'and by them chiefly whom it chiefly concerned to protect me from wrongs: yet have I found them most forward to offer me wrong only for doing my duty, and following the order of our Church of England: knowing that I had none of the Reverend Fathers of our Church to defend me' (p. 62). Evidently peeved at the memory of an unspecified affront, Biddulph failed to see the irony in his next comment, that the very same Eastern strangers who honoured and respected him for his clergyman's office 'also account fooles, dumbe men, and mad men, *Santones*, that is *Saints*' (p. 63). Abroad in the company of fools and mad men, an easily affronted English preacher with the vision of the apocalypse before him might have felt very much at home.

Expatriate observations

Once Islam had been firmly disarmed by prophecies from Daniel, Revelations and its own millennial traditions, the remaining sections of the letter from Aleppo continue to draw lessons from the religious folly and strange customs of others. Here Biddulph clearly relied on a mix of hearsay and personal experience, presumably including conversations from which he gained some elementary knowledge in the Arabic, Turkish and Persian languages. Increasingly, Biddulph offers advice to future travellers. After reporting on two venerated naked madmen of Aleppo, noting the existence of the Dervish order and the absence of printing, Biddulph comments:

> The poore, amongst the *Moores* and *Turks* at *Aleppo*, beg oftentimes in the streets in the name and for the sake of *Syntana Fissa*, who was (they say) a whore of charity, and would prostitute her selfe to any man *Bacsheese* (as they say in the *Arabicke* tongue) that is *gratis* freely.[17] (p. 65)

From here, an idiosyncratic chain of associations led him to report that the 'Diet of the Turks is not very sumptuous', followed by a description of his own favourite dishes, instructions on how to greet people in both Arabic and Turkish, and a guide to names and titles. 'They call one another diversly, and not alwaies by their names...sometimes by the father qualities, as *Eben Sacran*,[18] that is, *The sone of a Drunkard*...sometimes by their markes as... *Cowsi Sepher*, that is *Sepher* with the thinne beard...sometimes by their humours, as *Chiplac*,[19] that is, *A naked man*; or, *One who was of a humour to weare no cloathes but breeches*' (p. 68).

If Biddulph could not avoid choosing examples that are derisive and demeaning – beggars, whores, drunkards and trouserless men – it may well have been because he found naming such types in their own language to be highly amusing. But where and from whom did he learn such words? Under what circumstances did he hear the term for the son of a drunkard? Might Biddulph himself, with his 'gotes beard' as Sanderson called it, have been called thin-bearded 'Sepher', one who was a mere 'sıfır' or nothing, one incapable of growing facial hair?[20] He clearly had something of an ear for the sounds of other tongues, including, it seems, their comic possibilities. We know Biddulph was especially scornful of pilgrims, and he took evident delight in anglicizing the Islamic term for those who made the pilgrimage to Mecca, repeating it as frequently as he could when informing us that pious travellers to Mecca 'at their returne are called *Hogies*, that is, *Pilgrimes*, as *Hogie Tahar, Hogie Mahammet*, &c which is counted a word of great grace and credit amongst them. And the witnesse of an *Hogie* will be taken before any other' (pp. 68–9).

Arabs and Jews

In a separately titled section, 'Of the Arabians', which follows, Biddulph was less subtle in voicing his contempt. He simply could not resist the temptation of correcting the errors of others. The 'Arabians', he claimed, do not even know their own ancestry since they call themselves '*Saracens, of Sara*', when they 'are rather *Ishmalites*, of *Ishmael*' though 'some take them to be of the race of the

Sabaens...which people came of *Sheba'* (p. 69). From their ancient origins until the present time, the Arabs have achieved nothing since they live entirely 'by theft and robberie', being by nature 'a base, beggerly, and rogish people; wandering up and downe, and living by spoile, which they account no sinne' (p. 69). Yet having once made such claims about these ancient and fierce desert warriors, Biddulph immediately defused any present sense of threat or danger that they might have posed by resorting to a trivializing anecdote.

To illustrate how these 'Arabians' were so barbarous and backward, Biddulph reported how one of their 'kings' was astonished to be presented by an Englishman with a mince pie:

> But as *Diogenes* accustomed to feed on roots, having a peece of a tart given him to eat, and as he was eating it, being asked what it was, answered that it was bread; and when he was laughed at for his answer, he said again, Either it is bread of a very good making, or bread very wel handled in the baking: So this Synicall or Diogenicall king accustomed to feed grossly, having never seene a pie or pastie before, marvelled what it was: And when he saw it cut up and opened, and perceived smoke to come out of it, shrunke backe, fearing it had beene some engine to destroy him, and that the fire would follow after the smoke. But when he perceived no fire followeth the smoke, he was content to taste of it, and highly commended it, as the daintiest dish that ever he tasted of in his life. (p. 70)

It took only the daintiest of dishes to transform a mighty 'Arabian' king into a comic primitive, a frightened figure of folly. The one concession that Biddulph offered in favour of the Arabs was that, unlike the Ottomans, they were so backward that they still 'retaine the use of speaking their naturall tongue to this day'. The Ottomans were far more hybrid: 'for as the Turkes Religion is a mixed Religion, compounded of many Religions, so is their language also a medly language, or (as I may justly call it) a linsie wolsie Religion and language, compounded of many other languages, wherein nothing is written' (p. 71). Biddulph's certainty that the Arabic he was hearing in Aleppo was indeed the ancient tongue, the 'natural' tongue as he called it, serves as further testimony to his unbounded conceit.

Biddulph was clearly something of an early Orientalist, a self-authorizing expert for whom knowledge of the East consisted in describing how present conditions differed hardly at all from what he understood of their ancient origins from books such as the Bible, backing up his observations with reflections based on his newly acquired skill in local languages. Since they were but recent arrivals in the area, the Turks and their religion were of little account, a mixture of feeble stuffs, without a proper language of their own. Of the Arabs, Biddulph remarked on the antiquity of their putative stagnation, the unchanged and unchanging national qualities that rendered them not only different and amusing, but also grotesque and bizarre, at times not entirely distinct from the way English readers might think of sheep and cattle. He wrote:

> for the most part their lodgings are on some dunghill or other . . . their wives weare rings in their noses . . . They are people who can and doe endure great hardnesse and miserie. (p. 70)

Lest readers doubted his authority to pronounce on these matters, he provided a chart listing how to count from 1 to 20 in the four 'Orientall tongues . . . most spoken in these parts, *Arabicke, Turkish, Armenian*, and *Persian*' (p. 71).

Both in method and prejudice, the rest of the third letter contributes to the Orientalist project of making the East knowable by describing how the other 'nations' to be found in and around Aleppo were all backward, wicked or ridiculous; sometimes all three at once. After the Arabians and other 'Mahometans' he had 'already named', Biddulph devoted sections to the 'Jewes', the 'Christians of sundry sorts', including the 'Nostranes', the 'Chelfalines', the 'Greekes' and finally the 'Franks'. Biddulph is as good an example of religious hypocrisy as one will find among the English clergy of his time.

A pious churchman, Biddulph made no bones about his dislike of Jews, whom he found 'contemptible and of base account, according to the cry of those crucifiers, *His blood bee upon us and our children*, which is fulfilled this day. He clearly enjoyed reporting how the Turks hated Jews worse than Christians, while for their part, 'the poore Christians sojourning and dwelling in these partes doe hate them very uncharitably'. To add fuel to the fire of religious hatred, Biddulph reported how, on Good Friday, the Christians of Zante threw stones at the Jews, 'insomuch that they dare not come out of their houses all that day' (p. 73). Although quick to condemn this lack of charity, Biddulph was happy to announce that the Jews were murderous and to condemn their rabbis as 'blasphemous wretches.'

Just as he was eager to point out how Islamic tradition contained a prophecy of its own destruction, Biddulph enjoyed condemning the Jews from their own report. Under Ottoman rule, the Jews 'observe still all their old Ceremonies and feasts, Sacrifices only excepted' because, so Biddulph seems to have believed:

> they were wont amongst them to sacrifice children, but dare not now for feare of the Turkes. Yet some of them have confessed, that their Physitians kill some Christian patient or other, whom they have under their hands at that time, instead of a sacrifice. (p. 74)

Biddulph's report is exactly the kind of self-serving rumour that he would have taken notice of, remembered and recorded for posterity. On one of the few occasions that he reported talking with local people, he damned the Jewish community of Aleppo again by their own 'confession':

> I have sundry times had conference with many of them; and some of them, yea the greatest part of them, are blasphemous wretches, who (when they are pressed with an argument which they cannot answer) breake out into opprobrius speeches, and say Christ was a false Prophet, and that his Disciples stole him out of his grave whiles the souldiers (who watched him) slept: and that their forefathers did deservedly crucify him; and that if he were now living, they would use him worse than ever their forefathers did. (p. 75)

Putting an end to the casual disposal of female infants was among Muhammad's greatest social achievements.

Throughout *The Travels*, Biddulph was profoundly interested in tracing the ancient roots of the peoples and practices he met, and he was unstinting in finding fault with Christians. But he was, after all, a professional Christian himself, so the necessary logic of his faith and times required him to find Jews peculiarly obnoxious. What is most disturbing is the evident delight he took in dehumanizing them.

Christians in the East

When turning to the different kinds of Christians to be found in and around Aleppo, Biddulph distinguished those locally born from the expatriate communities of European merchants. Although the former were permitted their own ecclesiastical officers, they remained under Ottoman authority, 'all slaves unto the great Turk' (p. 75). The 'Nostranes', or Maronites from Mount Lebanon, are reported to be generally trustworthy and serve as 'Cookes, and servants unto English Merchants'. Biddulph was much taken by a Maronite wedding ritual, whereby the happiness of the marriage would be predicted by the groom's ability to keep hold of his bride's hand while 'the mother of the maid commeth with some sharpe instrument made for the purpose, and all bepricketh the new married mans hand, and maketh it bleed' (p. 76). Another custom he found worthy of mention was how a father would be renamed on the birth of his first son. 'I have knowen a *Nostrane* whose name was *Mou-se*, that is *Moses*,' he wrote, become '*Abou Useph*, that is, the father of *Joseph*' (pp. 76–7).

Unlike these quaint cultural practices, what made the Christian community of 'Chelfalines' from the Persian border especially memorable to Biddulph was their error about the place where they lived, since he can treat their claim to come from the site of the Garden of Eden as simply preposterous. Not only Genesis, but Plato, Aristotle and Lactantius are pressed into service to prove this belief mistaken. 'These *Chelphalines* are ignorant people,' he wrote, and make this claim even though they 'have no reason to proove that they now dwell in the place which was called *Eden*' (p. 79).

Trained in the prejudices of his Church, Biddulph's observations of other nations largely reinforced prejudices that he had brought with him, but at the same time they reflect the different degrees to which he felt foreign customs threatened Protestant belief. His derisive contempt for the backwardness of the Arabs, his hostile distaste for the perfidy of the Jews, his condescending tolerance of the quaint behaviour and erroneous legends among Eastern Christians, are all as characteristic as the smutty horror and indignant fascination with which he reported on the sexual behaviour of the expatriate Greek community. Generally a very 'superstitious, subtle, and deceitfull people', the Greeks in Aleppo

> are very poore, for they are there (for the most part) but Brokers or Bastages, that is, Porters; and many of their women light as water; maintaining their husbands, themselves and their families, by prostituting their bodies to others. And their owne husbands are often times their Pandars or procurers to bring them Customers. (pp. 79–80)

Biddulph, who believed that Jews practised human sacrifice, also evidently thought sexual licentiousness to be characteristic of the Greeks, presumably based on local hearsay. He certainly did not find such practices described in Nicolay's *Navigations*, although he would there have found Plutarch's account of how Lycurgus encouraged the Lacedemonians to breed selectively among themselves, even encouraging extramarital sexual activities in the interests of increasing the population.[21]

Ottoman justice

Despite his compulsive correcting of other people's errors, Biddulph was content to repeat hearsay whenever it suited his purposes. He closes his third letter by turning to a theme much favoured by English travel writers, the tyranny of the Ottoman state and the cruelty of its judicial system. He described how the Franks, the 'other sortes of Christians' to be found among the English, French, Italian and Dutch communities in Aleppo, were the only 'Freemen' in the city: 'For all the rest, even from the greatest Bashaw or Vizier unto the poorest peasant, are slaves unto the Grand Signiour' (p. 82). Interested in Ottoman tyranny and how it produced slavish attitudes among subject peoples, Biddulph offered anecdotal illustrations of the subservient attitudes and cruel punishments common among those enslaved by the 'slaves' of 'the Grand Signiour'. He reported how one 'Bashawe of Aleppo', falling into the disfavour of the Sultan and discovering that he had been condemned to be strangled, asked only to be allowed to pray first: 'which performed, hee yeeldeth his head and was strangled, sitting on his horse before all his followers, which were at the least 100 men, and no man durst speake one worde against it, much lesse to offer to resist him, but said, it was Gods will it should be so' (p. 82).

The same tale of passive compliance, however, was told in somewhat greater detail by William Lithgow, who claimed to have been in Aleppo when it occurred, noting 'the dead corps were carried to Aleppo and honourably buried, for I was an eye witnesse to that funerall feast'.[22] According to Lithgow, the incident occurred in 1611, more than two years after Biddulph's *Travels* had appeared, so it is impossible to know where or when the story might have originated. From whatever source it might have come to him, Biddulph had no compunctions about repeating such durable legends.

Biddulph describes other punishments and tortures – bastinadoing, impaling, strangling. In a rare moment of comparative analysis, he concludes: 'Unspeakable is their tyranny to those that fall into their hands, not unlike the tyrannie of the Spaniards towards the poore *Indians* who never offend them' (p. 84). Under tyrants, the innocent suffer; under the Turks, even the Franks suffer despite being 'Freemen' who are legally protected by their consular officials. 'And notwithstanding their Consuls and Ambassadours too, yet they are oftentimes abused by Turks both in words and deeds ... This miserie abroad will make us love our owne contrie the better when wee come thither' (p. 84). Empowered by years spent in the Holy Land, surviving the contamination of Islamic heathens and hypocritical Christians, the preacher in Biddulph closed his third epistle in fine hortatory style:

Oh how happie are you in England if you knew your own happinesse! ... So many in England know not their own felicitie, because they doe not know the miseries of others.

But if they were here in this heathen Countrie, they would know what it is to live in a Christian common wealth, under the government of a godly king, who ruleth by law and not by lust; where there is plentie and peace, and preaching of the Gospell, and manie other godly blessings, which others want. (p. 85)

What Biddulph left out

Remarkably, given his concerns with foreign dangers and the benefits of life in England, Biddulph never once mentioned how, during his stay in Aleppo, the region was regularly the scene of armed rivalry between the Ottoman-appointed provincial governors of Damascus and Aleppo. 'For most of the sixteenth century,' one recent historian writes, 'the province of Aleppo was continually subjected to forays by Damascus based troops to collect taxes while its governors were either hard pressed to respond or completely impotent to stop them.'[23]

In 1599, the year of Biddulph's arrival, the situation was ameliorated when the governor of Aleppo, Ibrahim Pasha, successfully petitioned Sultan Mehmed III to have a permanent garrison of Janissaries stationed in his city. But the respite was only temporary: 'with the governor's removal from office in the following year, the garrison was disbanded and chaos returned.'[24]

Biddulph's silence regarding these local disturbances is surprising. From the point of view of the English merchant community in Aleppo, disruptions in trade were further exacerbated when Husein Pasha, sent into Anatolia by Mehmed as an inspector, double-crossed the Sultan and joined the rebel leader, Kara Yazici ('the Black Scribe').[25] Toward the end of November, Thomas Freake in Aleppo wrote to Sanderson in Istanbul that, from their stronghold in Urfa, 'the rebells...dayly breaketh fourth upone the Vizears forces and hath killed many of the janessaryes of Damasko; so as nowe we are in hope to live more at quyett here then before'.[26] The next day the Aleppo consul, Richard Colthurst, wrote to Sanderson: 'This day, [it] is thought, our bashawe goeth towards them with an newe supply of men and mynycion. I doubt this place will groue verry troublesome.'[27] By late February, word had reached as far as London that 'The Bassa of Caramania, revolted from the Turk, has overthrown the Bassa of Aleppo, taken the town, and ranges over Syria.'[28] But as was so often the case, the news was out of date before it reached London. The rebel Kara Yazıcı had, in the meantime, made peace with the Sultan by double-crossing his new ally Husein Pasha and sending him captive to Istanbul to be summarily executed. In a letter to Colthurst of 6 February 1600, Sanderson described going with Lello to see

> the trator Ussine Bassa upon the gaunch, first in the duan having one of his armes and a legge broke, and caried bound to a croose of wood with two candles burning in the flech of his backe, with a chope behinde one the nape of his neck. Dead he was before he was put one the gaunch. (p. 191)

Into the political void that then opened up in Aleppo and northern Syria stepped two Kurdish chieftains, Huseyn Canbuladoğlu and his nephew Ali, who had already gained considerable local influence in Aleppo by organizing resistance against the Damascus Janissaries.[29] In recognition of their services, the Sultan appointed Huseyn governor of Aleppo in 1603, 'the first local figure to be so honored', but the appointment so greatly angered the existing governor that the Kurdish chieftain had to fight his way into the city.[30] Huseyn, the first Kurd ever to be appointed governor in the Ottoman Empire, lasted in office barely two years. Summoned to assist in the campaign against the Persians in 1605, Huseyn and his troops arrived after the Ottoman army had already been defeated and was executed on the spot by the angry Ottoman general. In retaliation for his uncle's death, Ali Pasha quickly seized Aleppo, negotiated directly with the European consuls there, 'guaranteeing them that trade would be protected and unlawful exaction and bribery ended under his regime'.[31] The youthful Sultan Ahmed I, however, eventually sent an army against Ali in 1607, defeated the Kurdish army and exiled Ali Pasha to Romania.[32]

Biddulph, who was in Aleppo to witness these events, seems, on the contrary, not to have noticed anything untoward. Even Sir Thomas Glover, from the safe distance of Istanbul, thought fit to write to Sanderson in London about Ali Pasha's defeat.[33] Perhaps the clergyman was oblivious to, or simply uninterested in, such local matters.[34]

10
Journey to Jerusalem

It haveing been the Custome of most English Merchants resideing at Aleppo, either out of Curiosity or Devotion or both, to Visit Jerusalem, & the Holy Land, so renowned in Ancient writings, & more especially for that twas the Place where Our Salvation was wrought by the Death & Passion of Our Blessed Lord & Saviour Jesus Christ.

Richard Chiswell the younger, 1697[1]

For Europeans living in Aleppo, a visit to Jerusalem held obvious appeal. Biddulph made the journey overland during the spring of 1601, and once again demonstrates indifference to the locals and their lives except in so far as what he witnessed confirmed what he already wanted to believe. At the time, Jerusalem was a city of fewer than 10,000 people, its wealth and population having increased rapidly following the Ottoman occupation by Selim I in the final months of 1516, though the population had already started contracting by the end of the sixteenth century.[2] Under Suleiman I, 'the Magnificent' (1520–66), the water supply was improved, the walls and gates stoutly rebuilt, a splendid new covered market constructed and a law court established to which even Christian and Jewish residents took their grievances.[3] Commerce was encouraged and many well-placed local families grew prosperous.[4]

Under the Ottomans, Jerusalem was booming when Biddulph visited. Increasing wealth and population, however, were starting to strain the administrative system, with the result that 'tensions were already apparent between local governors – sons and slaves of former senior officials, or Bedouin shaykhs in the area – and their colleagues appointed by the Ottoman government'.[5] Constant fears that another crusade might be launched to recapture the city made the Ottoman authorities suspicious of Christian visitors and pilgrims.[6] Entry to the city was carefully controlled, no travellers being admitted without sponsorship from local representatives of their own nation or sect. The walls and underground passageways were kept under armed guard at all times, and the city gates were locked at night. The Muslim community was spread throughout the city, but while 'no limitation was imposed on Christians or Jews wishing to buy houses in Muslim neighbourhoods...most preferred the safety of their own communities'.[7] At the start of the seventeenth century, Jerusalem was already a city internally divided.

In his account of Jerusalem, Biddulph remained as remote as possible from the natives. Fynes Moryson took the trouble, at least, to express contempt for those he saw: 'All the Citizens [of Jerusalem] are either Tailors, Shoomakers, Cookes, or Smiths...and in generall poore rascall people, mingled of the scumme of divers Nations, partly Arabians, partly Moores, partly the basest inhabitants of neighbour Countries.'[8] But Biddulph seems to have seen nothing and noticed nobody. His perspective remained resolutely that of an English Protestant clergyman with little or no interest in the social, cultural or political life of those around him, beyond repeating an occasional or sensational anecdote that confirmed a prejudice: the tyranny of the Ottomans, the perfidy of the Jews, the superstition of the Catholics or the backwardness of the Arabs. At the same time, he carefully distinguished between what he himself was doing, travelling as a representative of the Church of England and being a pilgrim intent on visiting sacred sites in hopes that doing so would guarantee his personal salvation.

No pilgrim he

Unlike the Catholic and Muslim pilgrims whom he reviled, Biddulph did not travel in order to venerate holy relics, to pray to bits of ground, bone or stone, and he constantly ridiculed those who did. Moryson, who had visited Jerusalem five years earlier, also felt the need to ensure his reputation was free from any suspicion of superstition, announcing 'first I thinke good to professe that by my journy to this City, I had no thought to expiate any least sinne of mine; much lesse did I hope to merit any grace from God'.[9] Biddulph similarly proclaimed himself true to his calling, insisting that he and his companions were 'not mooved as Pilgrimes with any superstitious devotion to see Relikes, or worship such places as they account holy; but as Travellers and Merchants, occasioned by dearth and sicknesse, pestilence and famine in the City where we sojourn' (p. 87). Godly English Protestants made sure that none should suspect their motives.

Biddulph left Aleppo on 9 March 1601 in company with four other Englishmen and an escort of Janissaries.[10] Three of his companions, Jeffrey Kirbie, Edward Abbott and John Elkin, were all merchants; the fourth, Jasper Tient, was a jeweller who had previously visited Jerusalem in company with Fynes and Henry Moryson in 1596: Sanderson thought him a 'devill'.[11] The overland journey to Jerusalem took them the rest of that month. For reporting his visit to the holy city, Biddulph adopted an abbreviated reportorial style, noting dates and places, recounting dangers, moments of occasional hospitality, sights of particular splendour or biblical importance, and commenting on what he terms 'charo', the tolls levied against Christian travellers by local leaders, Ottoman officials and the Catholic authorities in Jerusalem.[12] Since we can confirm some of his details from other sources, it is clear that in the case of this journey, we are being given a more reliable itinerary than usual.

Along the way, Biddulph continued his tirades against Islamic pilgrims, Jews and Jesuits, and offered what he considered sage and indispensable advice for future travellers. From time to time he introduces readers to various members of his party by name, including some of the Janissary guards who protected and advised the travellers. Yet at the very moment when, after many strenuous adventures on the road, he finally rode toward the gates of Jerusalem, he and his companions might very well have been mistaken for enthusiastic pilgrims racking up points that would get them into heaven:

> understanding that *Jerusalem* was but ten miles off, we went on in our way somewhat faintly five or six miles, and then beholding the prospect of the Citie, wee were somewhat cheered and revived, and solaced our selves with singing of Psalmes, untill we came neere unto the Citie. (pp. 115–16)

Despite the devotional nature of his approach, Biddulph's trip to Jerusalem was not so much a spiritual odyssey as an exciting and often uncomfortable adventure in sometimes inhospitable territory that served to confirm him in his own convictions.

Jerusalem itself proved to be not so much a space of ecstatic revelation as an authoritative ground where a Protestant witness might set the record straight on matters of importance to reformed Christian belief by exposing the superstitious credulity and hypocrisy of Catholicism. The land and its biblical sites were historically significant, but not to be worshipped. Certain events happened in particular places because the Bible says they did, but local legends, especially when reported by the resident Franciscans, were to be heard with caution if not with suspicion. Whatever its past, Jerusalem for Biddulph proved to be an exercise in analytical classification, a site where 'things' were best 'divided into *three parts*' – true, untrue and doubtful (p. 123). Once again, Biddulph resembles his near-contemporary, Fynes Moryson, who argued 'he that conferres the situation of the City and of the monuments, with the holy Scriptures . . . shall easily discerne what things are necessarily true or false, and what are more or lesse probable'.[13]

In describing the sights of Jerusalem, Biddulph's aim was to confirm holy writ. In this he was unlike the more sceptical travellers who soon followed, men such as John Greaves, William Halifax and Henry Maundrell, who began the trend for drawing careful plans and taking exact measurements of ancient sites in an attempt to extend knowledge of the ancient world by means of scientific method, even when their findings might cast doubt on scriptural authority.[14] For Biddulph, the measure of truth remained the Bible.

The road to Damascus

Biddulph provides sufficient details of his itinerary from Aleppo to Jerusalem for us to follow his route on a map.[15] Indeed, part of his purpose may have been to describe the places he visited and provide future travellers with a detailed guide to a regularly travelled route. Two days' journey from Aleppo, for example, he reports stopping for the night at 'Marrah', today called Ma'arret en Nu'man, where 'for protection against theives', the treasurer of Aleppo, '*Amrath* (commonly called *Morat*) *Chillabee*', had 'built a stately strong Cane like unto Leaden-Hall in *London*, or rather the Exchange in *London*' (p. 88). Today, the Murad Pasha Khan, as stately as ever, is a museum housing mosaics from Syria's many Roman villas and Byzantine churches.

Biddulph was impressed by the practice of constructing such hostels, caravanserais and khans where passing merchants could rest in something resembling comfort and safety.[16] But he warned against accepting hospitality without payment:

> there are faire upper roomes for great men in their travels, and the nether roomes are for ordinary travellers and their horses, but in hot weather the best make choise to sleepe on the ground in lowe roomes, rather than in their chambers. The founder hereof also ordained that all Travellers that way should have their entertainement there of his cost. He alloweth them Bread, Pilaw and Mutton which our Jenesaries accepted off; but we scorning reliefe from Turkes without money, sent unto the village, where (besides our owne provision which wee brought with us) wee had also other good things for money. (pp. 88–9)

Biddulph's reluctance to eat the provisions freely provided was less a matter of distaste for what was on offer than a refusal to become too closely assimilated into the local Islamic culture and customs. By paying for their food, at least, the English travellers were able to keep a needful distance between themselves and the Ottoman system, thereby maintaining a certain degree of financial independence that prevented them becoming too obliged to their Muslim hosts. This question of what and how to eat seems to have been anticipated well in advance, and clearly involved prior trepidation and distrust of local arrangements. On arrival in Damascus, Biddulph reported how 'our servants bought our meat, and dressed it themselves, as they did also all the rest of the way where we could get anything. To this end we tooke a Cooke with us, and other servants from *Aleppo*, to dresse our meat' (p. 93).

The modern highway between Aleppo and Damascus closely follows the route Biddulph travelled. From Ma'arret, he headed for Hama, stopping at an impoverished village he calls 'Lacmine' (pp. 89–90) which seems to have disappeared. In Hama itself, he 'lodged in a faire *Cane*', but it too has gone, perhaps destroyed in February 1982 when most of the old city was flattened by the Syrian army.[17] From Hama, Biddulph went to Homs and doubted the belief of local Christians that Job once lived there (p. 91). Between Homs and Damascus 'is a desart, uninhabited, and a theevish way' except that there are 'certaine Canes to lodge in'. Unlike khans near cities, he complains, those built along highways are poorly maintained and 'worse than stables' (p. 91). By 15 March, he was in Hassia (Hisyah) and, finding no khan at all, 'lodged in an old Castle', of which little remains today. From here, Biddulph visited Charrah (Qara) where there was, and still is, a substantial number of Christians. There is a church dedicated to SS. Sergius and Theodorus, of whom there are magnificent wall paintings, and an ancient community of monks and nuns dedicated to St John the Baptist which has recently received massive financial support following a visit from Pope John Paul II in 1998. Biddulph visited a church dedicated to St Nicholas, noting that here 'both Christians and Turkes pray therein', but local wisdom has it that the building is now only a mosque (p. 92).

Biddulph stopped twice more before reaching Damascus and seems to have become confused. After visiting Charrah he reports stopping in 'a poore village called *Nebecke*, or (as they pronounce it) *Nebhkeh*, where we lodged in an old Cane', then travelled the next day to Cotifey (Qutaifah), 'where we lodged in a very state new Cane, built by Synan Bashaw' (p. 92). In Biddulph's report, this khan 'doth far exceed that at *Marrah*' because it includes 'a fair new Church and a Bazar' with 'a faire large fountaine of water, of hewed stones foure square, wherein there is exceeding good water for Travellers to drinke, and chambers for their lodging' (p. 92). Near Qutaifah today, the only khan to be found is the isolated, but well-kept 'Khan of the Bridegroom', a simple, single-storey structure still used by local herdsmen for bringing in their mixed flocks of sheep and goats at night. Meanwhile, in the midst of the bustling town of An'nabk is to be found the Sinan Pasha Khan, exactly as Biddulph describes it. From the street entrance a covered stairway on the left leads from the street to upstairs rooms, while straight ahead opens onto a cloistered courtyard from which, on the right, a small, immaculately kept mosque boasts a fine blue dome. When editing his notes, Biddulph evidently confused Nebecke and Cotifey.

On arrival in Damascus, Biddulph stayed inside the old walled city at the '*Cane Nebbe*, that is, the Cane of the Prophet; but by the Turkes, *Cane Haramin*, where we hired three chambers for our mony' (p. 93). The next thing he did was to reach for his Bible. Relying on the timeless logic of scripture to interpret whatever he saw, he reflected, 'Damascus is a most ancient City, and as *Esay* spake of it in his time, *The head of Aram is Damascus: Isa.7.8.* so Damascus is the chiefest City of *Syria* to this day' (p. 94). Sometimes the Bible provided him with more information about a place than could be gleaned from those living there. While in Damascus, they hired a Greek guide who 'shewed us first a stately Muskia, or Turkish Church', but thanks to his Bible, Biddulph was able to recognize that the Ummayid mosque had been 'erected in the place where the Temple of *Rymon* stood, mentioned 2. *King.* 5' (p. 94). He failed to mention that the red domed tomb of Salah ed-Din, the Kurdish military leader who famously united Muslim nations against the Crusaders, stands guard at the entrance. Instead, he continued with further observations that show him more willing to trust the Bible than local Christians:

> And two other memorable matters, mentioned *Act.* 9.25. viz. the place where the Disciples let downe Paul in the night through the wall in a basket, whereof the Christians there dwelling, keepe an exact memoriall; taking upon them to demonstrate the very place of the wall; which we not beleeving, they confirmed it with this reason, that Damascus was never overcome; and that there have beene Christians dwelling there ever since the time of Paul, and therefore might keepe a memoriall of the very place: But to let the place passe, the thing it selfe we know to be true. (pp. 94–5)

The second memorable matter was a visit to the underground house where Ananias 'lived in secret for feare of the Jews'. Rather than his usual doubts, Biddulph registered frustration that 'many Christians comming thither to see that place, with a coale write their names on the wall, and there are so many names there already, that there is scarce roome for any other to set his name' (p. 95).

Once in Jerusalem, however, one member of Biddulph's party evidently had somewhat better luck finding a biblical site on which to scratch his name. In July of the same year, none other than John Sanderson visited the house in Jerusalem where Lazarus was reputed to have been raised from the dead; here he 'read the name of Jefferie Kerby upon the wall, written by himselfe in that sepulcher' and could not resist the temptation to add his own, commenting rather sanctimoniously, 'and not in any other place in all my pilgrimadge'.[18] Biddulph, however, took a certain modest pride in setting himself apart from such activities. From his own report, he never felt the urge to leave his name behind in this manner, either in Damascus or Jerusalem, though he took habitual pleasure from recording places where other Englishmen had done so.

Today, no trace remains of early European graffiti in the house of Ananias. The walls are damp and crumble to the touch. Damascene Christians living in the old city near Bab Sharqi still proudly show visitors the dense collection of churches and mosques as evidence of a peaceful coexistence that Biddulph might not have anticipated, although he knew Christians had lived there since the time of Paul.

On leaving Damascus, Biddulph passed through Daraya and had no difficulty avoiding the customary response of 'Christians of sundry Nations, viz. *Armenians, Greeks, Chelfalines, Nostranes*, and sundry others' who, in hopes of divine privileges, superstitiously fell 'on their knees' at 'the place where Paul was converted' after falling off his horse. A good Protestant, Biddulph took pleasure in being rather more singular in his behaviour, never prone to enthusiastic excess. Staying on his horse, Biddulph passed on, yet reckoned that there were 'foure or five hundred people' moving slowly on their knees (p. 97). Today such activities would cause a traffic jam.

Advice from the Golan Heights

Biddulph derived distinct enjoyment from parading himself in public places and relished the frequent signs of respect he received from pious onlookers of different nations. On reaching Quneitrah, which he calls '*Contera*', he found it a 'pleasant' place to rest a few days, especially after the 'tedious travell' of getting there. He greatly enjoyed walking and 'beholding greene pastures and running rivers near unto it', and wrote of his pleasure strolling in the cloistered 'Bazar' among the people of 'sundry Nations', who were happily 'assembled together from sundry places' (p. 98). Indulging the typically British habit of going for a stroll, he attracted some potentially hostile attention that led him to reflect on how cultural differences were sometimes simply a matter of the climate:

> in a Bazar (like unto a cloister) adjoining to the Cane, wee tooke pleasure to walk up and downe some few turns, which the Turks beholding wondred at us: (for it is not their custome in those hot Countries to walke up and down as wee doe in cold Countries, but to sit still on the ground like brute beasts) and one of them came unto us, and asked us what we meant to walke up and downe in such sort, and whether we were out of our way, or out of our wits. If your way (said he) lieth toward the upper end of the cloister, why come you downwards? And if at the nether end, why goe you backe againe? We answered him, For our pleasure. He replied, that it was the greater pleasure to sit still, than to walke up and downe when we need not. But their brutish sitting still on the ground was as strange unto us, as our walking up and downe was to them. (p. 98)

There have been a great many changes since Biddulph's visit. Seized by the Israeli army in 1967, Quneitrah is now a ghost town under United Nations control on the edge of the demilitarized zone separating Syria from the Israeli occupied Golan Heights. Before leaving, the Israeli army forcibly evacuated the entire population of 37,000, diverted the rivers to flow into the occupied territories and destroyed the houses and ancient cloistered market where Biddulph strolled. Quneitrah today is a museum trip. You are accompanied by a police guide who directs you round a deserted upland plain strewn with destroyed houses. Everywhere you look there are collapsed roofs that seem to be slowly growing back into the land. A Greek church and a minaret still stand from before the occupation, and a small museum displays prehistoric, Roman and Byzantine finds. The fabled Golan Hospital still stands, with its windows blown out and its stonework riddled with bullet holes. And its sign really does announce: 'Destructed by Zionists and changed to a firing target!'

Biddulph was confident that the Protestant way of doing things was the right way, but despite moments of ostentatious self-display he was no foolish provoker of hostility. Soon after leaving Quneitrah, his group met 'many Turks and Arabs, with maces of Iron and other weapons' who stop the travellers and demand '*Caphar* or tole money'. Without hesitation, Biddulph and the other Englishmen paid up. 'But,' he hastened to notice, a '*Caravan* of Christians, who came after us' refused to pay and were 'shrewdly beaten with their iron mases' (p. 99). Biddulph noted that there was a Jesuit among this group 'who escaped not without stripes, whereat (as I have heard) he rejoiced, and counted it meritorious, in that he suffered such misery in so holy a voyage' (p. 99). Ever eager to point out what he considered Catholic nonsense, Biddulph continued: 'But I know, had it not beene more for love of his purse than for love of Christ, he might have escaped without stripes, yea with these kinde speeches, *Marhabbah Janum*, that is, *Welcome my friend or sweet-heart*' (p. 100).

In Biddulph's view, Catholics in all their piety were invariably more contemptible than the most aggressively covetous Muslims, since the latter became friendliness personified as soon as one played by their rules and paid the road tax. He mentions meeting a Friar who, 'bragging of his good workes', claimed that 'he had done so many good workes, that if he should kill three men, his good works would make satisfaction', and merit remission for them all. Unable to brook such casuistry, 'one in my company answered, that by his murder he might merit indeed a double reward, viz. death in this life, and damnation in the life to come, for blood will have blood' (p. 100).

Indeed, Biddulph would certainly have agreed with Milton's Adam warning Eve not to seek temptation. Leaving aside 'these *Jesuiticall Jebusites*, or *Jebusticall Jesuites*' who invite physical hardship in the hope of spiritual reward, he directly offers advice. 'Heere,' he wrote, 'I may fitly take occasion to teach those that purpose to travell into Turkey, how to behave themselves', and in the style of a puritan pedagogue, conjures a vivid visual emblem:

Travellers into those parts must looke upon the picture of a servant as of old he was wont to be painted, that thereby they may learne how to behave themselves in travell.

I read, that of old they were wont to paint the picture of a servant at the doores of their houses, that their servants might see how they should behave themselves. And he was painted on this manner; With the snout of a Swine, the eares of an Asse, the feet of an Hart, with hands open, with his garments cleanly, and on his head a bonnet, having on his backe a coule staffe, with two vessels, the one having in it fire, the other water. (pp. 100–1)

The swine's snout, he explained, shows a willingness to eat whatever is available; asses' ears show patience when hearing abuse; harts' feet show swiftness; open hands show lack of deceit; clean garments show personal cleanliness; the bonnet shows humility; the staff shows willingness to work; while the buckets of fire and of water show discretion, since travellers, like servants, must not mingle fire and water together. 'Most of these qualities,' he concluded, 'are required in Travellers' (p. 101).[19]

Meetings with fellow travellers

In the pages that follow, Biddulph continued interleaving advice to future travellers with anti-Catholic anecdotes, personal reminiscences and vindictive insinuations. Passing through Galilee, Biddulph and his companions paused at various biblical sites. They visited the village where Christ turned water into wine, 'nowe a poore village inhabited by Turks' (p. 104), climbed Mount Tabor where Christ 'was transfigured...(as we read *Matth*.17.1.2.& c)' (p. 106) and paused to drink at Jacob's Well: 'The water thereof goeth down very pleasantly, like unto milke' (p. 114). Finally, on 29 March, they arrived at 'the west gate of the Citie called *Joppa* gate', where they were met by 'two Italian Friers' who 'kissed our hands, and bade us welcome, and told us that two other Englishmen were at their house, *viz*. master *Timberley*, and master *Borell*' (p. 116). Biddulph had nothing more to say about Timberlake and Burrell, while for his part, Timberlake barely once mentions meeting Biddulph when writing his *True and Strange Discourse*. The two English travellers presumably disliked each other.

Biddulph avoided Muslims whenever he could, yet accepted the help of Catholics whenever it proved useful to do so. 'After supper' on the first night in the monastery, he reports

wee delivered them our letter which wee had brought from the *Venice* Consull of *Aleppo* and other *Italian* Merchants there in our behalfe. Which when they had read, the Guardian said, our custome is, when strangers come to us, to call them the first night to Masse, and to Confession, and to give every man a candle to hold in his hand at Masse time...But for us, they understood by letters what we were; and told us that wee were so highly commended by their Patrones and Benefactors, the *Venice* Consul, and Merchants of *Aleppo*, that if they should shew us halfe the favour which was required at their hands, they should themselves lie without doores, and suffer us to rule and *dominier* at our pleasures. And that therefore they would not urge us to any thing against our consciences, but give free libertie both of persons and consciences as if we were in *England*, or in our own houses else-where. (p. 117)

Biddulph understood only too well that his group avoided attending mass, making confession and carrying candles not simply because they produced letters from the Venetian consul, but 'the rather because they understood our Merchants were rich, and hoped to gaine by us' (p. 117). Shortly after, he provided more specific details, noting:

And this kindnesse and liberty of conscience, which we found amongst them, we imputed not so much to the men, as to our owne money; for it cost us *charo*, viz 100. duccats for our entertainment: for we knew them to be of the Court of Rome, and were not ignorant that,
> *Curia Romana non captat ovem sine lana.*

that is,
> The Court of Rome no *sheepe* doth receive,
> Unlesse to them her fleece she leave. (p. 119)

Given the delight Biddulph took in criticizing his fellow countrymen whenever he could, another of his versified observations may have been inspired by Timberlake and Burrell. 'But,' he wrote,

although they dealt thus kindly with us (at the instance of their benefactors) in giving us liberty of conscience, yet they dealt not so with others. For some I do know who have been there, and made no conscience to doe as they have done, according to those verses:
> *Cum fueris Romæ,Romano vivito more:*
> *Cum fueris alibi, vivito more loci.*

That is,
> When they are at Rome, they doe what there is done:
> When they are elsewhere, they doe as they doe there. (p. 118)

The implication that Timberlake might have done rather more than carrying a candle at mass is certainly in keeping with the accusation Biddulph made in the Preface to his *Travels* that, while in Jerusalem, the other English traveller was seen not only 'going to Masse', but also 'observing many other ceremonies' (sig. B).

In much the same way that Dallam, an Englishman with no particularly strong religious convictions, found his life more in peril from the Spanish than the Ottomans, Biddulph considered English visitors to the Holy Land faced greater risks from the servants of Rome than the followers of Islam. 'True it is,' he observed, 'that the *Turkes* give liberty of conscience unto all that come thither; but they give not entertainment unto any Christians in their houses' (p. 119). As a result, the major challenge facing Protestants visiting Jerusalem was choosing between staying in the Franciscan monastery or at the house of the Greek Orthodox Patriarch. 'Wherefore,' he warned:

> I admonish those who have a desire to travell to *Jerusalem* heereafter, to take heed to themselves, that they make not shipwracke of conscience; for if they come not well commended, or well monied, or both, there is no being for them, except they partake with them in their idolatrous services. (p. 119)

For his own part, Biddulph insists that 'though we were fleeced amongst them, yet had we libertie of conscience, and safety of persons' (p. 120). Presumably Biddulph's hostility towards Timberlake arose from the way he exemplified what, for the clergyman, was the gravest danger confronting Protestants visiting the Holy City, that of spiritual contamination from Catholic ritual.

Truths, untruths and things doubtful

The final pages of *The Travels* offer a different kind of advice, a further admonition that future visitors to Jerusalem should maintain a sceptical attitude towards the claims made by the various local guides who, partly from superstitious belief and partly for cash, show the unwary visitor many dubious sites. As for the guide who conducted Biddulph and his companions, 'who had dwelt there fourteen yeeres', he recalled, 'we gave him the hearing of all, but did not beleeve all' for 'such things as we saw at *Jerusalem*' need to be 'divided into three parts... 1. Either apparant Truths. 2. Manifest Untruths. 3. Or Things Doubtfull' (p. 123). In the former group, he admitted only those things 'which I could confirme by reading, or reason'. These include the fact that Jerusalem itself is built on the site of the ancient city (pp. 123–4), that Bethlehem 'is the very place where our Saviour Christ was borne' (p. 126) and that the Sepulchre – to see which 'every man paied nine Shekines' – 'standeth on the same place as the Sepulcher did wherein the bodie of our Saviour Christ was laid ... because it was agreeable to the circumstances of Scripture whereby the place is described'

(p. 127). Manifest untruths include the site of the manger where Christ was born, 'now a beautifull place built of stone' complete with marble statues of Mary and baby (p. 130), and a hole in the roof where the star 'which directed the three kings' is said to have fallen (p. 131).

Biddulph's objective, as we might expect, was to cast scorn on Catholic ritual and belief. He could not resist reporting 'a superstitious custom' whereby the 'chiefe Frier...every Palme Sunday' rides on an ass towards the city gates from the Mount of Olives while onlookers 'cut downe branches from the trees, and straw them in the way'. In characteristic fashion, he took the opportunity to comment, 'Wiser are the Turkes herein then they':

And that Turke was to be commended, who (when the Friers followed their *Guardian* in such sort riding on an Asse) seeing a simple Christian woman strip her selfe so farre, as in modesty she might, and spread her garments in the way; tooke a cudgel and all to belabored her therewith, saying, Thou foole, art thou so mad to thinke that this is Christ? (p. 134)

Once again, the Protestant clergyman's imagination took evident pleasure from the prospect of physically punishing a (semi-naked) woman.

Among his catalogue of the many 'Doubtfull things', Biddulph included the 'Celler under the ground' where it was claimed 'Lazarus lay dead when Christ raised him up to life' (pp. 141–2), which is presumably the same place where, some weeks later, Sanderson found Jeffrey Kirbie's name written on the wall. He doubts too whether the slab of marble at the entrance to the Sepulchre really was the place where Christ's body was placed before being taken inside. Yet he reports witnessing

many simple people (both men and women) kneeling round about that stone, wringing their hands weeping, and crying, as if they had seene the dead bodie of our Saviour Christ there present before their eies. And they all to be-kissed that stone. Yea, more then kissed it, for some of them rubbed their lips up and down upon that stone very often, untill they had rubbed off the skin and made their lips bleed. (p. 141)

Such enthusiastic forms of worship were not to his taste, and he corrected himself for not placing this stone among the manifest untruths: 'For if there had been any such stone, it would have been either caried away by pieces, or removed whole to *Rome*' (p. 141). With this list of 'lying wonders' that 'these lazie Friers' show 'silly strangers' in order to 'bring them into a wonder and admiration,' (p. 139), Biddulph's *Travels* comes to an end.

Return to England: What Biddulph did on Zante

> Upon request they [the Zanteans] will carry you to the *Lazaretto* (which is in the nature of a Pest-house) there to abide untill the date [of quarantine] be expired.
>
> George Sandys, *Relation* (1615), p. 6

Scholars sometimes remark that accounts by travellers so far resemble each other as to be nearly indistinguishable, but this does not seem to be an entirely reliable observation. Dallam and Biddulph, at least, are so very distinct in manner, attitude, style and perspective that their shared national origin clearly did not prepare them to view the world in the same way. On the contrary, their shared Englishness provided them with a richly mixed and varied common culture, not a uniform set of opinions. Travellers do, it is true, often notice and report in remarkably similar ways on seemingly identical features of exotic landscapes and foreign customs. In many cases this can lead, as we have seen in the case of Biddulph, to going so far as to transcribe someone else's account as if it were his own. Even so, Biddulph did add personalized details to what he was copying; when transcribing Nicolay, he introduced English examples, and when borrowing an account of the life of Muhammad, he placed that life in an apocalyptic context not present in his source.

Yet all travellers' writings, even when they record visits to the same place, are also about the traveller, and as such they cannot help but reveal fascinating differences not only of individual personality but also of social perspective, even when they originate from a common cultural background. The views of a mechanical engineer and talented musician will necessarily differ from those of a pious and moralizing clergyman who travelled with his Bible ever ready to hand. Dallam's unlettered condition enabled him to see directly and freshly. Sometimes he was mistaken in his understanding of what he saw, but seldom does he convey the impression that he was seeing things that he had already expected to find before setting out. Biddulph, on the other hand, took with him a great deal of learned baggage, including all the presuppositions of his clerical office. His interest in other religions, especially Eastern varieties of Christianity, was conditioned by how much he felt they threatened his Protestant position. He was intrigued by the manner of life enjoyed by the upper clergy of other religions, especially other Christian Churches, but he was less interested in understanding than he was in refuting, dismissing or ridiculing their practices and beliefs. Yet it was also his very particular interest in other religious groups that caused him to notice what a secular eye might have missed – such as the existence of the Yezidis.

On the basis of his *Travels*, Biddulph was greatly interested in clerical culture and intrigued by some of the peculiarities of other belief systems. He also recorded, from both hearsay and personal experience, many of the popular themes used to characterize and vilify the Turks, Arabs, Jews and other Eastern nations – he comments on their strange diet, backward conditions of life, the tyrannical nature of the Ottoman social order. He was also constantly on the lookout for strange and immoral sexual practices wherever they might be found. He noticed anything, in short, that might constitute a threat to the pieties of reformed Christian morality and, in doing so, echoed many of the prejudices that would surface in later Orientalist discourse.

Unlike Dallam, who never published a word of what he wrote, Biddulph evidently had a variety of aims in writing and publishing his *Travels*: to refute and ridicule Islam, Catholicism and Judaism, to correct the errors of others and prove what he already doubtless believed before he even set out, that life in England was better than many who had never left believed it to be. But he also published his account, it would seem, for some peculiarly personal reasons which included vilifying Sir Thomas Glover and getting even with Timberlake, whose best-selling report no doubt incited authorial jealousy. Glover offers a little insight into his side of things, calling Biddulph factious, and it seems more than likely that Biddulph took great offence not only because he found Glover insufficiently respectful towards his calling as a clergyman, but also because he disapproved of the way Glover conducted his personal relations with servants and women.

As so often, however, the judge takes notice of and condemns that of which he is himself most guilty. In the four edited letters that comprise the greater part of his *Travels*, Biddulph says nothing about his journey home. The preface by Theophilus Lavender, however, ends with a lengthy and detailed narrative relating how Biddulph escaped from an especially dangerous storm at sea while sailing from Istanbul to Zante. Arriving among the Cyclades, the ship was becalmed, when 'suddenly this calme was turned to a storme' which 'so confounded the *Ragusean* Mariners (being no skilful Navigators) that they knew not where they were'. Thanks to the 'providence of God', rather than the skill of the crew, the ship was not dashed on any of the rocky islands but sent out to sea by the strong winds. 'The storme,' however, 'still increased more vehemently, and continued three daies and three nights together; during which time, they could neither eate nor drinke, nor sleepe'. Panic broke out among the captain and crew who, being 'of divers nations, so of divers natures: and as they differed in religion, so likewise in their conversation and cariage, during the continuance of this tempest. Being of a superstitious nature, the *Raguseans* and *Italians* called upon all the gods and goddesses, the Hee Saints, and She saints,' but all to no avail. It was only when the Englishmen on board, 'having learned out of the Scriptures (Psal. 46.1) *That God is a present helpe in time of trouble* ... gave themselves jointly and severally to prayer' that the storm ceased and the ship came safely to port (sigs. Bv–B3).

But this is not, as it happens, the only account we have of Biddulph paying a visit to the island of Zante on his return.

On 6 May 1609, John Kitely wrote to John Sanderson about Biddulph's behaviour on that island, taking particular delight in elaborating some excruciating puns and tortuous conceits on the clergyman's name. Biddulph, he wrote:

> ever hath shewed more beard then witt or religion in all his 10 years travils. Witnes his behaviour at Aleppo, here [i.e. Istanbul], and now lastly at Zante in the Lazarotto where he was found by the guardians in the very action rem in re, with that Inglishe strumpitt who I formerly described unto you. This Bed-woolfe or rather a woolfe in bed limed to a bitch, being so taken, fayned him selfe Lunitique, and beinge thus openly shamed became past all shame and was seene reeleing-drunke publiklie every day to the scandall of our religion and shame of our whole nation to see the Greekes pointing at him saying ecco il vicario de l'inferno e imbriago. For my part I am of the Greekes opinion with this last imposition betimes that he may be well termed the vicar of hell.[20]

Apprehended *in flagrante*, or 'rem in re': so much for the pious and righteous self-image conveyed throughout *The Travels*. We will probably never know what Biddulph got up to in Aleppo and Istanbul. But one needs no training in psychoanalysis to see in Biddulph's indirect attempts to castigate Glover's sexual habits, in the delight he took in imagining punishing prostitutes and reporting how a Turk set about beating a semi-clad woman, in his compulsive desire to set the record straight by illustrating the 'lying wonders' of the Catholic Friars and in his self-representations as a pious, upright and venerated member of the Church of England, what William Blake might have called the lineaments of ungratified desire.

Moreover, since it seems most likely that Biddulph had been aboard the *Hector* on her voyage out from England, we cannot help but wonder whether he was among the unnamed 'gentlemen' who had received 'all kinde entertainment' on Zante in late April 1599.

Part III

Blount's *Voyage*: The Ottoman Levant, 1634–36

11
Sir Henry Blount, 15 December 1602–9 October 1682

In her will dated 21 February 1678, Sir Henry Blount's wife Hester refers to 'my Husband's Little Picture set in Gold' as part of her legacy to their youngest son, Ulysses.[1] Perhaps it was Hester's attachment to family portraits that encouraged Henry to have his portrait painted at least three more times after they were married. I have been unable to locate the heirloom miniature, but the earliest portrait of Henry still hangs alongside a companion portrait of Hester at Tittenhanger Hall, the family seat in Hertfordshire where Henry was born in 1602.[2] It seems likely that these were painted after their marriage in 1647, when Hester was a wealthy widow in her thirties, and Henry a bachelor of forty-five. In the fashion of the times, Henry is shown wigless and soberly clad in scholarly black: the high collar, high forehead and hair loose to the shoulder strongly recall Robert Walker's portrait of Cromwell painted around 1649.[3] The motto, 'Radicem Pete', or 'Seek the Root', is entirely in keeping with Blount's radical thinking.

The companion portrait of Hester, whose first husband, Sir William Main-waring, had died during the siege of Chester (1643–6),[4] shows her confidently baring her shoulders and returning the spectator's gaze, an intelligent and wellborn lady of means. Her pearls may suggest the wealth that Hester had inherited from her father, Christopher Wase, before her first marriage.[5]

Henry sat twice again at later stages in his life for portraits by two of the most important and celebrated artists of the times, Jacob Huysmans and Sir Peter Lely.[6] The Huysmans portrait, also still hanging at Tittenhanger, is the only one that links him with his fame as a traveller. The Flemish artist Huysmans painted Henry fully-wigged in the courtly style that returned with monarchy at the Restoration, and the painting may well date from 1661 when Blount was appointed High Sheriff of Hertfordshire by Charles II. The striking gesture of the left hand, while the right rests on a globe and points obscurely in an eastward direction, are characteristic of Huysmans, who was prone to such 'elaborate use of attributes'.[7] Huysmans also saw the prominent lower lip, strong nasal labials and fleshy nostrils noticed in the earlier painting, while he figures a more fully pronounced jaw and a stronger, more directly focused set to the eyes.

Clearly from a later date, Sir Peter Lely's portrait, now in the National Portrait Gallery, shows Henry Blount in old age and relying for support on a walking stick.[8] Time and care have hung folds on the flesh of his face, but the eyes remain active, bright and intelligent, the mouth and chin retaining resolve and fortitude evident from the earlier portraits. Lely's portrait is the most likely model for the oval engraving of Henry Blount, published in 1801, which associates him with a second motto, 'Loquendum cum vulgo, sentiendum cum sapientibus' or 'You should speak with the crowd, but perceive with the wise'.[9]

The character shown by the portraits accords well with written accounts of Blount's personality. The antiquarian Anthony Wood reported: 'He was esteemed by those that knew him a Gentleman of a very cler judgment, great experience, much contemplation (tho not of much reading) and of great foresight into Government. He was also a person of admirable conversation, and in his yonger years was a great banterer, which in his elder he disused.'[10] Although a later historian of the Blount family adds that 'in his Younger years too He was a great drinker of strong Liquors',[11] all the evidence agrees that following his return from Ottoman lands, Henry Blount became famous for abstaining from any drinks other than water and coffee. 'For the first forty years of his life he was a boon companion,' one biographer reports, 'and much given to railery; but in the other forty, of a serious temper, and a water drinker.'[12] Recollecting a meeting on 30 September 1659, the diarist John Evelyn called him 'the famous Travellor & water-drinker'.[13] According to John Aubrey: 'When Coffee first came in he was a great upholder of it, and hath ever since been a constant frequenter of Coffee houses.'[14] As we will see, Blount doubtless owed his taste for coffee and his aversion to alcohol to his travels in Ottoman lands.

A further legacy from his travels may appear in the name chosen for his last son, Ulysses, born when Henry Blount was sixty-two. Both parents seem to have been exceptionally fond and protective of Ulysses. When writing his will in February 1681, Blount took considerable care to protect him, and any family he might have, in the event of his own death before Ulysses reached the age of eighteen.[15]

Yet there is little evidence of the bantering, hard-drinking young Henry Blount in any of the extant portraits. Rather, we are shown an idealized country gentleman who looks sober, thoughtful and trustworthy. Blount was a successful member of an important family with roots reaching back to the Norman Conquest. His father, Thomas Pope Blount, was among the very first to be knighted by James I when the Scottish king arrived in 1603, the year after Henry was born. By the time he died – Sir Henry – on 9 October 1682 at Tittenhanger Hall, his contribution to the family fortunes was considerable, especially given the economic uncertainties and political upheavals of mid-century England. In 1638, following his return from the East, he inherited the manors of Arlestone and Syndefine in Derbyshire as well as Blount's Hall in Staffordshire, 'being anciently the Younger Brothers Portion for preferment from our Ancestors'.[16] When his older brother Thomas died without an heir in 1654, Henry succeeded to the Tittenhanger estates as well as extensive properties in Middlesex, Bedford, Leicester and elsewhere 'in the Commonwealth of England'.[17]

By the mid-1650s, Henry was a legal advisor to the republican government and does not seem to have been short of funds. Employing Inigo Jones' most brilliant pupil, John Webb, he quickly had the old Tudor house demolished and replaced with the substantial four-storey gentleman's house in the Palladian style which still stands today.[18] Rebuilding on this scale required a liquid cash flow and good credit line. Although I have found no records of the costs of rebuilding Tittenhanger, Blount's finances must have been in excellent shape for the 1650s when few others could afford to build on this scale, and he seems to have traded and invested wisely throughout his adult life. Aubrey noted that his 'estate left him by his father was 500 pounds per annum, which he sold for an annuitie of 1000 pounds per annum.'[19] Besides shrewdly annuitizing, by the time he made his own will, Blount had also engrossed the family estates by acquiring copyhold lands locally in Ridge, Tithurst and Kendall, Hertfordshire, as well as further afield. To Ulysses he left all 'Lands Tenements & Hereditaments called the Downes in the County of Surrey & all other my Lands Tenements & Hereditaments whatsoever in the County of Surrey,'[20] as well as all 'copihold lands and tenements in the village of London Colney, Hertfordshire, purchased in the name of my son Ulissees'.[21] Besides ratifying his wife's will – Hester brought to the marriage a considerable fortune of her own – Blount left further securities worth about £1,650 as well as households in London and Westminster, both fully furnished with silver plate, books, coaches and horses. For a younger son, Blount had done rather well for himself and his family, especially given the revolutionary period in which he lived.

Henry Blount was born at Tittenhanger on 15 December 1602 and christened a week later.[22] Lady Frances (*née* Piggot), his mother, died in 1616,[23] and that year Henry entered Trinity College, Oxford, which had been founded by Sir Thomas Pope, his paternal grandfather's sister's second husband. At Trinity, according to Robert Harley, 'he became a gentleman-commoner, and there, not so much upon his relation to Sir *Thomas Pope* founder thereof, as upon account of his own intrinsick worth, and the facetiousness of wit so peculiar to him, he had, in a particular manner, the deference and respect of the said college'.[24] In 1780, the literary historian Thomas Warton reports that Blount's tutor was Robert Skynner, fellow, and later bishop of Bristol, Oxford and Worcester.[25] In 1620 Henry was admitted to Gray's Inn to which, three years later, the disgraced Francis Bacon would retire.[26]

During those early London years, Blount evidently moved in political and literary circles, dining regularly 'at the Heycock's ordinary, near the Pallsgrave-head tavern in the Strand, which was much frequented by Parliament-men and Gallants'.[27] His earliest publication, verses 'Upon the Tragick Muse of my Honour'd Friend, Mr. Wm. Davenant', prefacing William Davenant's *The Tragedy of Albovine* (sig. A2v), appeared in 1629 alongside similar verses by Edward Hyde, later Lord Clarendon, Richard Clark, Robert Ellice, William Habbington, Roger Locke, Thomas Ellice and Henry Howard. At the time, Davenant was being hailed as the new Shakespeare. More examples of Blount's own attempts at poetry survive in several manuscript copies of amatory verses in the conceited cavalier style, but none can be dated with any certainty.[28] During these years he may first have met Henry King, who would later become Bishop of London and write verses praising Blount's *Voyage*. Blount sailed from Venice in May 1634, so he would have been in London during the lengthy preparations at Gray's Inn for James Shirley's *Masque of Peace*, performed at Whitehall the previous December. With machinary designed by Inigo Jones, this was the most spectacular event of its kind ever staged and cost the combined Inns of Court more than £20,000.[29] Life at Gray's Inn and friendships with the likes of Davenant, Hyde and King would easily have brought Blount into contact with luminaries of literary London such as John Donne, Ben Jonson, George Sandys, Izaak Walton and James Howell.[30] For the second edition of his *Instructions and Directions for Forren Travell* (1650), Howell borrowed liberally from Blount's *Voyage* when adding 'a new Appendix for Travelling Into Turky and the Levant Parts', while Blount and Howell together received dedications in *Organon Salutis* (1657), a celebration of the medicinal properties of coffee and tobacco by Walter Rumsey, a fellow member of Gray's Inn.[31]

Of Blount's early career in law, I have found no trace, but residency at Gray's Inn provided gentlemanly access to the secret service, founded for Elizabeth by Sir Francis Walsingham, a member of the Honourable Society himself. Blount claims that he had already travelled to '*Italy, France*, and some little of *Spaine*', but the occasion and circumstances remain obscure.[32] But certain it is that Blount left England for the Levant, sailing from Venice down the Adriatic coast to Dalmatia, thence overland to Belgrade, Niş, Sofia, Edirne and Istanbul, where he stayed only five days before setting off with a Turkish fleet for Rhodes, Alexandria and Cairo. In Egypt he visited the pyramids at Giza and the 'labyrinth' or mortuary temple at Hawarah in the Fayyum, which Herodotus considered surpassed the pyramids. Blount cancelled plans to visit Joppa and Jerusalem and returned in a hurry via Sicily instead, after realizing he was likely to be arrested for spying in Alexandria.

Blount's account of this eleven-month journey, *A Voyage Into the Levant*, was published in 1636 to considerable and lasting acclaim: 'This book made him known to the world, and much taken notice of; so that shortly after, King Charles I., who desired to fill his court with men of parts, appointed him one of the band of Pensioners, then composed of gentlemen of the first families in the kingdom.'[33]

Blount was knighted on 21 March 1640 and appointed tutor to the royal children.[34] He accompanied the royal court during the early stages of the Civil War and 'had charge of the young Princes at Edgehill during the battle' according to a legend attached to the frame of the Huysmans' portrait at Tittenhanger. After the battle, however, Blount joined the court in Oxford only briefly before returning to London where, according to Aubrey, he

> walkt into Westminster Hall with his Sword by his side; the Parliamentarians all stared upon him as a Cavaleer, knowing that he had been with the King; was called before the House of Commons, where he remonstrated to them he did but his duty, and so they acquitted him.[35]

At some point in 1647, he and Hester married. Following the king's execution in 1649, Blount accepted parliamentary commissions to investigate legal reform (1651) and trade abuses (1655). During the 1650s 'he shew'd himself Active aginst the Payment of Tythes, & endeavour'd that every Minister should not have above £100' a year.[36] In 1653, he was appointed alongside Sir Anthony Ashley Cooper to judge the Probate of Wills.[37] The next year he served as a judge at the trial of the Portuguese ambassador's brother.[38] At the Restoration he was appointed High Sheriff of Hertfordshire and continued to advise the government on matters of trade and navigation.

Hester gave birth to at least eleven children: even Henry's great-grandson, the indefatigable family historian, Sir Harry Pope Blount, never risked a definitive account of the number of her offspring. In addition to Ulysses, at least three other sons named Henry and Christopher died in infancy, and Hester may have given birth to as many as five daughters.[39] Their eldest son was the parliamentarian Thomas, who was followed by Charles, the celebrated deist.

In 1693, Charles published *The Oracles of Reason*, a series of epistolary essays on materialism that includes the Latin text of 'a Discourse of Sir H.B's *De Anima*' composed at Ludgate-hill on 8 February 1679, three years before Sir Henry died. Charles offered 'this undigested heap of my Father's Thoughts concerning the Soul's acting, as it were, in a state of Matrimomy with the Body' as evidence that 'all Philosophy, excepting Scepticism, is little more than Dotage'.[40] Charles's notorious suicide the same year inspired his friend,

Charles Gildon, to issue a defence of the man and his ideas that opens with the following:

> His Father was Sir HENRY BLOUNT, the *Socrates* of the Age for his aversion to the reigning Sophisms, and Hypocrisies, Eminent in all Capacities, the best Husband, Father, and Master, extreamly ageeable in Conversation, and just in all his dealings.
>
> From such a Father our Hero deriv'd himself, to such a Master ow'd his generous Education, unmixt with the nauseaous methods, and prophane Opinions of the Schools. Nature gave him parts capable of Noble Sciences, and his industrious Studies bore a proportion to his Capacity: He was a generous and constant Friend, an Indulgent Father, and a kind master.[41]

We have no reason to imagine Gildon was fabricating.

Blount's *Voyage* was reprinted seven times before 1671. I have quoted throughout from the first edition: 'A Voyage Into the Levant. A Breife Relation of a Journey, lately performed by Master *H.B.* Gentleman, from *England* by way of *Venice*, into *Dalmatia, Sclavonia, Bosnah, Hungary, Macedonia, Thessaly, Thrace, Rhodes*, and *Egypt*, unto *Gran Cairo*: With particular observations concerning the moderne condition of the *Turkes*, and other people under that Empire, London, Printed by J. L. [John Leggatt] for Andrew Crooke, 1636.'

A German translation appeared in 1687, while an illustrated Dutch translation was issued twice, in 1707 and 1737. The map of Blount's journey and the plan of Rhodes, are taken from the second edition.

12
On Becoming a Passenger

> I was of opinion, that hee who would behold these times in their
> greatest glory, could not find a better *Scene* then *Turky*.
>
> Blount, *Voyage*, p. 4

Henry Blount's strenuous self-representations in the opening pages of his *Voyage to the Levant* (1636) outline his preparations before starting on a journey from Christian Europe into the Ottoman Empire. Known for his precocious wit, Blount portrays himself as a well-educated man of his times, a learned and yet sceptical observer seeking to contribute to knowledge currently unavailable from the records.

Casting himself from the start as a man of the new Baconian scientific method, Blount proposes a comparative and rationalist inquiry into the Islamic world, offering evidence that Christian supernaturalism may not have dominated discourse about the East before the French Enlightenment as Edward Said has suggested. Blount insists that his desire to travel to Ottoman lands was both sceptical and rational; he sought to test tradition and authority and find out if the '*Turkish* way appeare absolutely barbarous, as we are given to understand, or rather another kind of civility, different from ours, but no lesse pretending' (p. 5). For Blount, civilizations and cultures were evidently distinct but also relative, to be valued on their own terms and not those of an opposing perspective. Perhaps the Turks would prove to be not as terrible as they had often been made out to be.

Istanbul: Blount in haste

> The times grow verie variable in Turkie, all things have latelie changed
> farre, the Gran Signior is grown most bloodie, laying hold of slight

ocations to shedd it, and his insatiableness therein is such, as manie times he doth it with how owne hands, but daylie it is done in his sighte.

Sir Peter Wyche to Secretary of State Sir Edward Coke,
28 December 1633[1]

Blount reached Istanbul in the summer of 1634, yet 'stayed here but five dayes' (p. 24). It had taken him, he records, 52 days travelling overland from Spaletro (Split), so he must have arrived in July, two months after leaving Venice. Although frustrated that he 'had not leasure for much observation' while in the imperial Ottoman capital, he notes that he was 'in this hast' without further explanation. Yet we can easily adduce several reasons, not least of which was his desire to take the earliest passage for Egypt. While he was there, Istanbul was certainly not at its best. From November 1631 until May 1632, regular rioting between Janissaries and Sipahis had made the city streets the scene of widespread violence. In May 1632, however, Sultan Murad IV began to emerge from his minority by forcefully asserting a bloody command over the imperial government. On the 18th, Murad ordered the Grand Vizier, Topal Recep Pasha, to be strangled.[2] He then swiftly ended revolts in Anatolia, led by Abaza Mehmed Pasha, and set about internal reforms of the army, 'executing 20,000 men in the process'.[3] A nineteenth-century historian imagined the scene as follows:

> Every morning the Bosphorus threw up on its shores the corpses of those who had been executed during the previous night; and in them the anxious spectators recognised Janissaries and Spahis, whom they had lately seen parading the streets in all the haughtiness of military licence.[4]

Except for those partial to morbid fancies, these early years of Murad's personal rule would not have been a good time for sightseeing in Istanbul.

To make Istanbul even less attractive, a great fire in late August 1633 had destroyed extensive sections of the old city, including the Janissary barracks and state archives, in addition to which, Blount noted, 'they report seventie thousand houses to have perished' (p. 25). The contemporary Ottoman historian Kâtip Çelebi put the number lower, at 20,000.[5] During those few summer days that Blount spent in the city, Murad himself was in Scutari, planning his campaign to recapture Erivan and Tabriz from the Persian Savafids.[6] Once he had taken command, Murad expended his energies on political reforms and border wars, leaving him little time or inclination for improving his capital or engaging in ceremonial displays. Moreover, for several months, Europeans living in Istanbul had been subjected to an unusual degree of harassment. Since 1629, regular hostilities between English, French and Venetian merchant communities over shipping made the Frankish communities unpopular with the Ottoman authorities. By 1633, according to Thomas Nabbes, the 'suspition had of strangers' in the capital 'began now to move the wheels of some practises upon them'. The houses of Christians 'in general' were searched, and 'all stranger merchants, in whose houses they had found a sword, a gunne, or pistoll, or any the least weapon whatsoever' were summarily imprisoned, to be ransomed 'at 2000 dollars apiece'.[7]

When Blount arrived, the English ambassador, Sir Peter Wyche, had already resigned his post and may well have been sufficiently disgruntled not to be especially welcoming. For his part, Blount was interested in the politics of international trade but not engaged in any, and he had no commercial business to transact while in Istanbul.

> In that I observed no more of so great a *Citie*, I doe not much accuse my selfe; for the chiefe time I had to view, was my first two dayes, when I lodged with the *Turkes*, in the *Hane* of *Mehemet Basha*; afterward I shifted into *Christian* habit, and went over to *Galata*, where I was very courteously entertained in the house of an *English Gentleman*, to whom I was recommended; next after I had kissed the hands of the right Honourable, *Sir Peter Weych Lord Embassadour* for *His Majesty of England*, I tooke an instant opportunitie of passage for *Egypt*, upon the *Blacke Seas Fleet*, which three dayes after departed for *Alexandria*. (p. 26)

In a single sentence, he records formally presenting himself to the ambassador and then 'instantly' taking ship with the Black Sea fleet for Egypt (p. 26).[8]

For all his haste, Blount appears to have made efficient use of his limited time in Istanbul. After all, he aimed to observe the Ottoman Empire in 'its greatest glory', not to add another traveller's description of its ancient capital. To have written such an account would, in any event, have necessarily plunged him into those games of diplomatic bluff and intrigue that Dallam could not avoid and Biddulph could not resist. Being in haste, Blount put his 'thoughts upon two points; First, to view the chiefe *publique sights*, then to consider the judgement of those ancient *Emperors*, who so often thought of transferring the Seat of the *Empire* from *Rome*, thither' (p. 24). On the first count, Blount was suitably disappointed given the current condition of the city. Murad and his court were 'then at *Scutari*', so there was no possibility of seeing 'the *Emperours* Person'; a visit to the Topkapi Palace 'as farre as Strangers use, having accesse into the second Court' revealed only 'low' and 'meane' buildings; a more thorough view 'throughout' the Suleymaniye complex proved it 'no way equall to his other at *Andrinople* [sic], which in my eye is much more Magnificent, then any of those at *Constantinople*' (p. 25).

Yet his reflections on the 'chiefe part of my contemplation' are emphatically enthusiastic about Istanbul's claim to be the world's greatest city. With global empire evidently in mind, he declared that Istanbul 'of all places, that I ever beheld, is the most apt, to command the world', continuing with arguments that have little to do with original observations and everything to do with imperial envy:

> so as for *strength, plentie*, and *commoditie*, no place can equall it: Then it stands almost in the middle of the World, and thereby capable of performing commands over many Countryes, without any great prejudice of distance . . . for hee who considers the sudden accidents of *State*, with the difficulties of remote *Forces*, and other *dispatches*, must needs acknowledge the necessitie of (as it were) a *Mathematicall* correspondence from the *Center*, to the *Circumference*. (pp. 25–6)

Unlike Biddulph, Blount did not set out to prove the correctness of his religious beliefs. His terms of reference have less to do with confirming biblical geography than with questions of supply, trade and military power on a global and imperial scale. The mathematical metaphor is no accident. It is a sign of Blount's method and purpose in writing his *Voyage*: to test received opinion of the Ottoman Empire in order to understand how it worked. Although he does not use instruments and take measurements like later generations of travelling amateur archaeologists, Blount regularly counts things to do with volume of trade and the size of the Ottoman army: horses, donkeys, camels, coaches, wagons, foot soldiers. And he regularly uses arithmetical, geometrical and mathematical terms to account for the structures of the Ottoman Empire: the size of its armies and fortifications of its cities, the splendour of Sinan's architecture, the distribution of the population, the geographical location of its capital.

For Blount, physically being in the great imperial city where Europe and Asia meet served to confirm what he might otherwise have known from a map; that to a Western European, Istanbul was in an ideal geographical position to control a massive empire. Even a few days proved sufficient to persuade him of what other visitors had felt before and would feel again, that Istanbul was rightly situated to command the world.[9]

Spies, intelligencers, passengers

> Perhaps severe and froward censors may judge it an apish vice thus to imitate other nations, but in my opinion, this obsequiousness of conversation, making us become all things to all men, deserves the opinion of a wise man, and one that is not subject to pride.
>
> Moryson, *Itinerary*, 3: 397

The not having any other *Christian* in the *Caravan* gave mee two notable advantages: First, that no mans errors could draw either hatred, or engagement upon me; then I had a freedome of complying upon occasion of questions by them made; whereby I became all things to all men, which let me into the breasts of many.

Blount, Voyage, p. 5

The bookish Anthony Wood may have thought Blount disinclined to 'much reading' because he repudiated the habit of including learned quotations from earlier writers into every paragraph, a practice familiar to readers of, for instance, George Sandys' *A Relation of a Journey* (1615), reprinted for the fourth time in 1632. And Blount would no doubt have offended the antiquarian Wood by insisting on the superiority of the knowledge that can be gained only from experience and careful observation over that to be found in the writings of others 'for,' he argues,

> relations are not only in great part false, out of the relaters mis-information, vanitie, or interest; but which is unavoidable, their choice, and frame agrees more naturally with his judgement, whose issue they are, then with his readers ... Wherefore I desiring somewhat to informe my selfe of the *Turkish* Nation, would not sit down with a booke knowledge thereof, but rather (through all the hazard and endurance of travell,) receive it from mine owne eye not dazled with any affection, prejudicacy, or miste of education, which preoccupate the minde. (pp. 3–4)

Yet the very vehemence with which Blount prosecutes his case on behalf of learning from travel and empirical observation over information gleaned from 'booke knowledge', and the evidently well-informed care with which he describes preparing for his journey, are evidence enough that he must have read extensively in advance.

Unlike Biddulph, who was content to transcribe large sections of earlier authors, and unlike travel writers who felt compelled to point the finger at the errors of previous authors in asides and footnotes, Blount was not only anxious to correct 'mis-information', but also content to follow good advice when he found it. When sneering at the vanity, interest, prejudice and 'miste of education' afflicting many authors, Blount must surely have had Richard Knolles' influential and much reprinted *Generall Historie of the Turkes* in mind since the schoolmasterly Knolles himself characterized his own work as 'these homely fruits of mine endevors' which had been collected from previous authors.[10] Knolles' old-fashioned humanist methodology and self-confessed 'zeale' on behalf of 'the Christian Commonwealth' would also have ill-suited the advocate of empirical enquiry, who felt contemptuous of 'those who catechize the world by their owne home' (p. 4).[11]

More to Blount's taste would have been the 'Precepts for Travellers' which Fynes Moryson included in the published version of his *Itinerary* (1617), the second of which emphatically begins: 'Let each Traveller forecast with himselfe his owne purposes and ends.'[12] Blount might well have known Moryson, whose patron, Charles Blount, Earl of Devonshire and Eighth Lord Mountjoy, was a distant relation. Certain it is that throughout his *Voyage*, Blount echoes and exemplifies several of Moryson's precepts. In addition to examining his motives before setting out, Blount stays with local inhabitants (8, 12), talks on occasion with women and children (8), avoids travelling with fellow countrymen and other Christians (12), carries a book for companionship instead (13), adopts local costume (19), refuses to engage in religious disputes or talk too much about his own country (21), employs a Janissary for guidance and safety (23), and engages in strategic dissembling when not to do so would lead to danger (24).[13] Perhaps more importantly, Blount also shared Moryson's pragmatic and utilitarian perspective. 'Let him constantly observe this,' Moryson advised the traveller, 'that whatsoever he sees or heares, he apply it to his own use, and by discourse (though forced) make it his own.'[14]

Blount's account reveals how his particular methods of travelling were fully in line with Moryson's advice to apply all he saw and heard and to make it his own. Ever since stepping ashore on the Dalmatian coast, he had been 'clad in the *Turkish* manner' (p. 98). On arriving in Istanbul, he avoided the expatriate community in Pera for as long as he could, staying instead among the Turks in a commercial khan, only changing into '*Christian* habit' to present himself to the English Ambassador just in time to leave again. Blount clearly had a mission, as Dallam and Biddulph had theirs, but far from requiring him to perform as a representative member of his nation or his religion, Blount's plans required him to be as inconspicuous as possible while in Istanbul in order to avoid involvement in diplomatic wrangling.

Blount terms himself a 'passenger' (p. 2), by which he means a number of interesting things: taking passage to travel along local trade routes with companies of traders, wearing local costume, avoiding other Christians, paying Janissaries to warn him of any plots against him and, most of all, travelling according to schedules and routes over which he had no control, but which would enable him to observe the nature, range and practices of Ottoman power and authority. Unlike Dallam and Biddulph, Blount sought not to display his national origins, but to pass as unnoticed as possible in order to view the Ottoman Empire at work without being seen to do so. In the event, as we shall see, he frequently found himself obliged to behave like a spy whenever it proved impossible to avoid. What such moments illustrate, however, is that for Blount, behaving like a spy was a reluctant interruption from his normal sense of himself, an imposed activity requiring a special performative mode. While travelling, Blount might not have been able to avoid being mistaken and misunderstood by those he encountered, but the emphatic details of his opening pages serve to distinguish him quite clearly from the contemporary sense of spies or state 'intelligencers' who, in the words of Sir Thomas Palmer, 'are sent out by the mediation of the Councell in most States, or by some of the principall'. The professional calling of the state intelligencer, unlike that of the Ambassador, was 'not honorable', but Palmer notes how they were, nevertheless, selected from

> persons of notable esteeme to support the policie of the Estate by the knowledge of the secrets of forreine powers and daily occurrences that chaunce in them. Whereby Princes may shew all offices unto their friends and confederates, and be sufficiently armed with knowledge to resist the malice of their enemies or encounter such as are held in jealousie.[15]

Blount confidently assumed that readers would not confuse him with the other kind of 'base intelligencer', characterized by Palmer as 'necessarie evils in a State', those base persons who 'prie into the hearts of men to know how such stand affected'.[16] Nor is Blount a spy in a third sense, one he himself uses, that of a soldier who goes ahead of an army on the move. But so many of the personal qualities Palmer listed when defining state intelligencers resemble features of Blount's characterization of himself as an inquiring passenger, that the association is compelling. Palmer requires that intelligencers display knowledge of necessary languages, the ability to 'imitate the common gestures and behaviour of those nations', and that they 'endure the accidentes of Sea or land; as stormes, heate, colde, excesse of meates and drinkes, sicknesse, much riotte of speech, simplicitie and such like'.[17] Nowhere does Blount suggest that he had been appointed by any national authority, yet in many respects his book fulfils Palmer's requirements of providing knowledge useful to the state.

From the start, Blount proposes a comparative inquiry into the Ottoman Empire that would be free from the fearful prejudices of Knolles and the clerical certainties that animated Biddulph. Blount's very first words – 'Intellectuall Complexions' – would either immediately implicate readers in the terms of his project or would put them off continuing to read. Against the traditional authority of Christian zealots, Blount sought to find out 'whether to an unpartiall conceit, the *Turkish* way appeare absolutely barbarous, as we are given to understand, or rather another kind of civility, different from ours, but no lesse pretending' (p. 2).[18] Only by visiting their empire himself could Blount discover whether the Turks were as terrible as they were thought to be.

Bishop Henry King praises Blount's *Voyage*

Sir, for this work more than my thanks is due
I am at once inform'd and cur'd by you.
Bishop Henry King

Blount describes how preparing himself for his journey required an extended process of unlearning, a preparatory period of self-scrutiny resulting in nothing less than a 'putting off the old man' and a freedom 'from all former habit of opinion' (p. 4). In describing this Baconian rather than Pauline rebirth, Blount outlines a carefully prepared programme involving a complete personal, intellectual, cultural and spiritual makeover on the part of the inquiring visitor. Such a programme would have shocked the pious Biddulph, but in its own day, Blount's *Voyage* was praised by no less than a learned bishop for transforming travel writing by refiguring the agency of the British visitor to Ottoman lands. In panegyrical verses 'To my Noble and Judicious Friend Sir Henry Blount upon his Voyage', Bishop Henry King explains how Blount's exemplary method of travel teaches others how best to manage their business in the lands of the Turks. Apparently, reading Blount's *Voyage* did not so much add to King's previous knowledge of Ottoman imperial history as alter his attitude to it by informing him of useful things that British travellers to the East needed to know. According to King, Blount's reports of encountering and contending with cultural differences transformed the familiar registers of both travel writing and the knowledge they offered about the Ottomans into a new form of practical knowledge, a guide to the kinds of agency available to future British travellers. For King at least, Blount's secular, sceptical and comparative approach was perfectly proper and did not violate Church orthodoxy.

Bishop King's claims on behalf of Blount's *Voyage* are important enough to deserve close attention for several reasons: they provide evidence of what a well-read and important churchman of the time knew of the Ottomans from maps and books; they demonstrate the comparative and global terms in which national identities were being imagined at the time; and they show how British interests in the Ottoman Empire were typically characterized by pragmatic concerns with trade, power and the control of empire. The first half of King's poem summarizes what he knew and thought about the Ottomans before reading Blount's book. King reports familiarity with the origins of the Ottoman Empire, partly from looking over the maps of Ortelius and Mercator, but also from reading.[19] Moreover, the Anglican prelate admits that 'those two baits of profit and delight' (line 4) had often tempted him, while reading traveller's reports and looking over maps, to feel 'strong and oft desires to tread/Some of those voyages which I have read' (lines 7–8). He describes an imaginary journey north through Africa, pauses in Cairo, then sets off to Istanbul:

> Once the world's Lord, now the beslaved Greek,
> Made by a Turkish yoke and fortune's hate
> In language as in mind degenerate
> And here, all wrapp'd in pity and amaze
> I stand, whilst I upon the Sultan gaze.
>
> lines 38–42

King offers the common view that the ungodly Turkish empire brought slavery and degeneration to the once glorious Greeks. The degenerative effects of empire on those imperialized proved to be one of Blount's recurrent themes, but here, in King's imaginary moment of gazing on Istanbul, the bishop imagines himself gripped by pity and amazement at the spectre of the Islamic sultan:

> To think how he with pride and rapine fir'd
> So vast a territory hath acquir'd;
> And by what daring steps he did become
> The Asian fear, and scourge of Christendom:
> How he achiev'd, and kept, and by what arts
> He did concentre those divided parts;
> And how he holds that monstrous bulk in awe,
> By settled rules of tyranny, not Law.
>
> lines 37–50

These lines provide an explicit declaration of the malicious hatred of Ottoman imperial success, which I have called imperial envy. What King ponders is the way God has allowed the ungodly to use terrible means to achieve and maintain control over so vast an empire. To the Anglican divine, the Islamic Ottoman Empire is both a moral and a theological problem: how can God allow pride, rapine and tyranny, the emperor's base motives and base means, to continue enabling him to hold such a monstrous bulk of an empire together? The answer, of course, has already been provided in the terms of the question: the Ottoman Empire is the scourge of Christendom. It may seem to operate 'settled rules', but they are godless, 'tyranny, not Law'.

> Sure, who e'er shall the just extraction bring
> Of this gigantic power from the spring;
> Must there confess a Higher Ordinance
> Did it for terror to the earth advance.
>
> lines 53–6

Following this reassurance of Christian providentialism, King summarizes the rise of Islam up to the capture of Istanbul in 1453 and includes sketches of

Osman, the eponymous founder of the Ottoman dynasty, Murad II, and his son Mehmed II to whom the holy city of Byzantium fell.

> This, and much more than this, I gladly read,
> Where my relators it had storyed;
> Besides that people's manners and their rites,
> Their warlike discipline and order'd fights;
> Their desp'rate valour, hard'ned by the sense
> Of unavoided Fate and Providence.
>
> lines 77–82

Emphasizing Ottoman passions, King catalogues features of life under the Ottomans he had gleaned from reading travel books. He repeats one of Blount's key observations regarding the hospitality of Turks towards Christian travellers, but even here King insists that he already knew about 'What quarter Christians have; how just and free/To inoffensive travelers they [the Turks] be' (lines 89–90).

King's survey of what he already knew about the rise of the Ottoman Empire before reading Blount prepares the way for his tribute to a writer who has transformed travel writing from 'the commonplace of travelers, who teach/But table talk' (lines 114–15) into a systematic programme of knowledge that will directly serve England's national interests in the East. King confesses that his earlier reading among travel writers was 'for wonder, not for use', so an immediate effect of reading Blount's *Voyage* is that the Bishop now feels himself 'cured' of his own desire ever to travel from his 'native lists'. Blount's 'experienc'd and authentic pen', King writes:

> Taught me to know the places and the men;
> And made all those suspected truths become
> Undoubted now, and clear as axiom.
> Sir, for this work more than my thanks is due
> I am at once inform'd and cur'd by you.
>
> lines 92–8

But King expands his personal obligations to Blount into a matter deserving gratitude on a national scale. 'By your eyes,' he writes:

> I here have made my full discoveries;
> And all your countries so exactly seen,
> As in the voyage I had sharer been.
> By this you make me so; and the whole land
> Your debtor; which can only understand

How much she owes you, when her sons shall try
The solid depths of your rare history.

lines 105–12

Employing language linking knowledge and discovery with sharing in a trading
venture, King's conceits reveal the nation's debt to Blount for providing future
'sons' with the 'solid depths' of learning they will need to travel among the
Turks. The nation should, he argues, 'canonize' Blount's book as a 'rule to all
her travellers', because of the increased profits reading it will encourage. King's
mercantile metaphors reveal the commercial motives underlying imperial envy:

I cannot less in justice from her look,
Than that she henceforth canonize your book
A rule to all her travellers, and you
The brave example; from whose equal view
Each knowing reader may himself direct,
How he may go abroad to some effect,
And not for form: what distance and what trust
In those remoter parts observe he must:
How he with jealous people may converse,
Yet take no hurt himself by that commerce.
So when he shall embark'd in dangers be,
Which wit and wary caution not foresee;
If he partake your valour and your brain,
He may perhaps come safely off again,
As you have done; though not so richly fraught
As this return hath to our staple brought.

lines 124–38

In an important sense, Blount's book itself is the rich freight, the 'return' to the
nation's 'staple', the knowledge of how to travel and 'come safely off'. Dismissing
those who travel 'for form' and not 'effect', King praises Blount's 'example'
since future 'sons' here will learn how they might most profitably pursue their
nation's commerce, going abroad 'to some effect'. Blount, the exemplary guide
to 'dangers' unforeseen, describes needful strategies to future travellers encountering the threats of everyday life inside a supremely powerful but nervous
empire. According to King, Blount deserves national recognition and reward
for writing a book that extends British agency within Ottoman territories by
providing such a detailed account of how Britons might visit, avoid dangers
and deal profitably.

How well does Blount's *Voyage* live up to the learned bishop's praise and its own
proposals? King justifies his secular interests and imperial perspective by arguing

from the mysterious workings of providence – Said's 'Christian supernaturalism' – in order to explain both the rise and success of the Ottoman Empire as divinely inspired events. Yet there is nothing supernatural about his concern regarding the military power of the sultan or, for that matter, the commercial metaphors he uses to praise Blount. King was doubtless correct in drawing attention to the usefulness of the knowledge Blount gained for encouraging British trade. Blount himself, however, also sought to advance other kinds of knowledge.

From the start, Blount's account is couched in secular logic which seeks to demystify and owes rather more to Bacon and the new scientific methods of empirical analysis and explanation than to Christian belief. He does not defend travelling for promoting religious faith, but for advancing knowledge by means of rational inquiry that will dispel, as it were, the idols of the tribe. By shifting understanding of the Ottoman Empire from a religious to an empirical frame of reference, Blount's achievement was not only to demystify the ingrained certainties of national prejudice, but also to offer ways of understanding the Ottomans and how their empire flourished that were practical and useful. Further, Blount describes travel to be an exercise in self-reconstruction that must begin, if it is to succeed, with the suspension of normative domestic perceptions and attitudes, a stepping outside native religion and hearsay. Far from perceiving the Ottoman Empire to be an orientalized space awaiting Western penetration and dominance, Blount argues that understanding the great Eastern empire required European visitors to put aside received opinion well in advance of setting out. Before there could be any question of Europeans taking advantage of the East, they first had to make themselves capable of recognizing and understanding what was already there, firmly in place, rather than simply denouncing Eastern culture for being ungodly and barbarous.

Bishop King was not alone in his assessment of Blount's *Voyage*. James Howell evidently agreed and summarized Blount's work when offering advice 'for Travelling Into Turky and the Levant Parts'. Judging by a reprint history that would have made Biddulph jealous, booksellers found a steady market. There is every reason to think that, during Blount's lifetime, the book and he were both well known and widely respected. Yet neither Blount nor King could have imagined that *A Voyage* would still be playing a part – a small one it is true – in the drama of British interests in the Ottoman world more than two centuries later. They would have been staggered at the reach and purchase of Britain's own empire in the East by 1856. In June of that year, Private John Casey of the 41st Regiment stationed in the Crimea won a prize for rifle shooting. He was duly presented, by command of one C. B. Phipps at Buckingham Palace, with a copy of Blount's guide for sons of future empire, 'the third Edition' of 1638 to be precise, from the Queen's own library.[20]

Blount gets ready

> Thus if ever any race of men were borne with Spirits able to beare downe the world before them, I thinke it to be the *Turke*.
>
> Blount, *Voyage*, p. 97

Blount wrote *A Voyage* in formal sections: an introductory account of his reasons and preparations for travelling, a narrative description of the journey itself, and a substantial final analysis of the Ottoman Empire in terms of its '*Armes*, *Religion, Justice*, and Morall Customes' (p. 61). Repeatedly insisting that he went to learn and explain how the Ottoman Empire works within a general historical theory of world empires, Blount and his project strongly anticipate the phase of rational inquiry into the Islamic world that Edward Said's *Orientalism* suggests would appear only much later, and first in writings by French authors. Blount draws directly on Bacon for his methodology and suggests ways the origins of Orientalist discourse preceded the Englightenment.

Blount opens with a self-fashioning gesture, which constructs both himself and his readers as subjects of the new scientific age, mutually engaged by a rational enquiry into the history of human nature. 'Intellectuall Complexions,' he begins, desire '*knowledge*', especially 'of humane affaires'. Proposing that '*experience* advances' knowledge of human institutions 'best', Blount argues that knowledge will increase proportionally with the degree of novelty and difference experienced. 'So my former time spent in viewing *Italy, France*, and some little of *Spain*,' he swiftly concludes, 'being countries of Christian institution, did but represent in a severall dresse, the effect of what I knew before' (p. 1). Knowledge is acquired in proportion to cultural difference, and cultural difference can best be experienced free from religious similarity.

The logic of Blount's argument is clear enough: the human intellect desires knowledge, and since experience of difference increases knowledge in proportion to increase in difference, the desiring intellect craves experience of radical difference. Within this scheme, Blount's designation of 'Christian' countries suggests a cultural and political category that suspends those religious differences between Protestants and Catholics that were, at the time he was travelling and writing, devastating Europe. Nowhere in Blount's *Voyage* do we find any trace of the Christian providentialism so evident in King's poem, or any evidence of concern for the Thirty Years War; except in a casual aside to praise the orderliness of Ottoman troops on the march relative to Christian armies. For Blount, nations and the institutions that attend them are as much historical products of geography, nature and climate as they are of religious belief. Neither a product nor evidence of a theo-genetic or providential design, national, cultural and religious differences appear to knowledge as matters of distinctive geophysical spaces that have their own histories. Since no culture could appear more different to an inquiring observer from the 'Climate' of the '*North-west parts of the World*' than that practised by 'those of the *South-East*' (pp. 1–2), Blount proposes that knowledge of the geographical space where Islam currently rules must necessarily prove most different and therefore most specially desirable to those seeking knowledge. Here, south of the Danube, 'the *Turkes*' have established an empire 'and fixt it selfe such firme foundations as no other ever did; I was of opinion, that hee who would behold these times in their greatest glory, could not find a better *scene* then *Turky*: these considerations sent me thither' (p. 2).

In 1634, when Blount set out, the lands north-west of the Danube were still being destroyed by rival Christian armies. Starting in 1618, the Thirty Years War had reached its peak of intensity when Gustavus Adolphus of Sweden joined the field in 1630. South-east of Vienna, on the other hand, the Ottomans – 'the only moderne people, great in action' (p. 2) – were successfully managing a vast and glorious empire which, when Blount visited, constituted the most stable regime in that region for some time.[21] How could anyone of an intellectual complexion not want 'to behold these times in their greatest glory' by going to see for themselves just what was going on inside the magnificent Ottoman Empire? Yet it may well be that Blount had other, undisclosed motives. As we shall see, he was not infrequently presumed to be engaged in some form of intelligence gathering, and the presumption was most likely correct.

Even as he appears to draw to a close, Blount elaborated once more on his purposes and preparations before setting out. He describes four 'particular cares': observing religion, viewing the various 'sects' coexisting within the Ottoman Empire, examining the Ottoman army and visiting Cairo. Expecting to find 'another kind of civility, different from ours, but no lesse pretending', Blount distinguishes himself from expatriate 'inhabitants'. It is here that he describes himself as a 'passenger' for the first time, a context that indicates a traveller with an 'unpartiall' mind, a comparative project and a healthy disrespect for the common prejudices of Christians about Turks (p. 2). Passengers might never achieve the perfect knowledge available to 'inhabitants', but nor do they simply pass by without seeing what is around them. Blount, the exemplary passenger, sets forth with an agenda that requires stopping long enough to test received opinion by means of experience. Urged by rational motives, passengers travel to seek critical distance from their own cultural prejudices, already expecting to find that things may not be the way they are commonly said to be. And to achieve this condition, Blount points out, passengers need to be capable of imagining and even attempting to live through the possibility that other cultures might be 'different from ours, but no lesse pretending' (p. 2). Here he uses litotes – the rhetorical figure of negative understatement – which is never, of course, a trope of simple equivalence but one of relative negation; 'no lesse pretending' points to the absent foundations of European (or any other) normativity.[22] For Blount, no culture, religion or civilization can claim to be fundamentally right, true or eternal. The Ottoman Empire might show the present times in their greatest glory, but Blount explains this as an historical phenomenon, a product of global trade together with a geographically specific military, political and juridical organization. He has no need for arguments from providential design.

Each of Blount's declared reasons for travelling illustrates his general and pervasive interests in the links between trade and imperial organization. His concerns are those of a political economist mainly interested in cultural, social, juridical and religious beliefs and practices when they affect the running of the imperial state. How do the Ottomans manage to rule such a diversely constituted empire? Blount writes that he wanted to 'acquaint my selfe with those other sects which live under the *Turkes*, as *Greekes*, *Armenians*, *Freinks*, and *Zinganaes*, but especially the *Jewes*' (p. 2). The seemingly peaceful coexistence of so many distinct and potentially antagonistic communities within Ottoman society consistently fascinated British visitors and readers. Here and throughout the *Voyage*, Blount uses the term 'sect' to distance himself from every religious persuasion, Christian or otherwise, just as we might expect from the father of Charles Blount, the celebrated freethinker.

His third professed reason for travelling was 'to see the *Turkish* Army, then going against *Poland*, and therein to note, whether their discipline *Military* encline to ours' since doing so would enable him to judge 'whether it be of a frame apt to confront the Christians, or not' (p. 2). Whatever Blount's interests in the activities of Christian armies might have been, he must have known something of the terrible conditions throughout much of continental Europe after two decades of war. Blount's desire to view the Turkish army might well have been inspired by Sir Thomas Glover's account, in Purchas's *Hakluytus Posthumus* (1625), of how Elizabeth's first ambassador, Edward Barton, had accompanied Mehmed III and his army on the march against Hungary in 1596. Lord Byron was inspired by reading Knolles, and there is every reason to think that Blount might have imagined himself accompanying the famed Ottoman army. But reading may not have been the only inspiration, since it is extremely unlikely that Blount would have known anything about the Ottoman incursion into Poland unless he had friends in high places. The campaign itself was a relatively unimportant affair; no accounts were published before Blount left England. The earliest report in England is a letter, dated 28 December 1633, from Sir Peter Wyche to the Secretary of State, Sir Edward Coke, relating how 'Abasa Bassa made an inroade into Polande, with twenty thousand people where he did some spoyle, but (as it is reported) receaved greater; and so withdrew'.[23] Less than a month later, on 25 January 1634, Wyche again wrote to Coke, emphasizing the secrecy surrounding the campaign:

> Concerning the affaires in generall, yt is most probable that the Gran Signior in person, will fall into Polande, and sett from hence upon that expedition, within a month, or two at the fartheset, verie great treasure hath bin gathered togeather, and although the Grand Vizier wilbe upon the confines of Persia with a good parte of the armie . . . yet the Grand Signior maie enter into Polande with neere upon three or foure thousand men, and as the Moscovitts do fall in another waie, God knowes what maie happen; for questionless they nevere supported this resolution of the Turke, for it hath bin verie much disguised.[24]

Ottoman attempts to keep the campaign 'very much disguised' were not entirely ineffectual: the Venetian ambassador in London seems to have known nothing of such matters until August 1634, and by that time Blount had already fulfilled his desire by meeting and travelling with the Ottoman forces gathering at Belgrade.[25] So, unless Blount added this detail of his rationale after the fact, it suggests that he had been particularly well connected and well informed before setting out, providing further reason to suspect that his journey had undisclosed motives.

The fourth of Blount's major reasons for travelling, the one that sent him speedily packing from Istanbul, was the desire to visit Cairo, 'and that for two causes' (p. 3). The first was his wish sceptically to interrogate received Christian opinion about Ottoman administration. The second, more interestingly, was 'because *Egypt* is held to have been the fountaine of all *Science*, and *Arts civill*, therefore I did hope to find some spark of those cinders not yet put out' (p. 3). This suspicion that Christian images of Ottoman 'sottish sensuality' might greatly misrepresent existing conditions is indeed 'shrewd', as Samuel Chew once remarked.[26] But it again draws attention to Blount's persistent interest in empires and imperialism. How do empires arise, and what happens when they fall? He wants to assess the nature, range and authority of Ottoman power by seeing if anything remains of the great African imperial civilization that might provide a clue to its demise.

While describing his interests in the workings of Ottoman imperial state-craft, Blount notably avoids the Christian moral-providential arguments of King's poem, where the ungodliness of the Turkish tyranny caused Greek degeneracy. While Blount does view ancient history in terms of degeneration narratives, he also insists on the need to understand and even justify specifically non-Christian practices by evaluating them in appropriate terms. He retains a clear moral sense based on civil virtues and vices, yet judges nations, races and religions historically rather than in terms of their conformity to any ideal-ized norm, Christian or otherwise. For Blount, understanding the rise and fall of nations and races is a matter of the rise and fall of learning within the empire. He declares, for example, that the vast multitudes living in Cairo are 'deeply malicious', but does not hold the Ottomans responsible for current conditions in the city he calls the 'greatest concourse of Mankind in these times' (p. 3). Instead, he expresses admiration at the Ottoman ability to rule a city and people that had been brutalized by centuries of invading armies and repressive regimes.

Blount, the Oxford rhetorician and wit, who knew what he was doing with words, boldly mixes metaphors when acknowledging Egypt to have been the 'fountaine of all *Science*, and *Arts civill*', in the hope of finding 'some spark of those cinders not yet put out' (p. 3). By the 1630s, evidently, the European Renaissance had not entirely erased knowledge of the African roots of civilization and civility, a matter regarding which Blount is strangely lacking in his usual scepticism.

On avoiding Christians

> ... wherefore he who passes through the severall educations of men, must not try them by his owne, but weyning his minde from all former habite of *opinion*, should as it were putting off the old man, come fresh and sincere to consider them.
>
> Blount, *Voyage*, p. 4

Throughout his opening pages, Blount distinguishes himself from writers on Turkey who never went there, for whom 'Turk' was synonymous with Islam and therefore principally an enemy to be feared and righteously destroyed. By travelling as a 'passenger', he seeks to keep himself open to the kinds of experience that will produce knowledge of a sort unavailable from reading the frequently false reports of other travellers. Having found himself 'desiring somewhat to informe my selfe of the *Turkish* Nation, [he] would not sit down with a booke knowledge therof', but had to see for himself in order to avoid any 'affection, prejudicacy, or mist of education', all of which necessarily 'delude' the mind with 'partial *ideas*' (p. 4). Passengers may know less than inhabitants, who can provide visitors with reliable, local information – such as the 'Family' who had been resident in Cairo for twenty-five years, who 'informed me of many things, with much certaintie' (p. 38). But passengers will learn more than those who stay at home and read books full of authorial prejudice and opinion. In this role of a sceptical passenger, Blount performed most of his travelling from the moment he left Venice on 7 May 1634, a passenger on a Venetian galley amidst 'a *Caravan* of *Turkes*, and *Jewes*' (p. 5). It would be their trading interests that determined the route and schedule followed all the way to Istanbul. Passengers may have to accommodate themselves to the plans of others, going where and when they are ready, but the well-prepared passenger is never simply passive and dependent.

Blount reserves one of his more startling revelations of what being a passenger can mean for the moment just before his journey actually begins. About to set forth, Blount retrospectively assures us that his 'preparation' served him well, bringing about nothing less than a form of personal reconstruction essential for all who would travel 'through the severall educations of men' (p. 4). To achieve this condition, Blount insists, one 'should as it were putting off the old man come fresh and sincere to consider' prior opinion (p. 4). Even as he evokes the Pauline injunction to the Ephesians to put aside the 'old man', Blount secularizes the trope, transforming this commonplace figure of spiritual rebirth into a Baconian injunction to unlearn received opinion and prejudice. Passengers of an intellectual complexion need to put aside their ingrained domestic pieties and provincial judgements, since only by doing so will they prepare themselves – in mind and body – for the change of diet, lodging and cultural expectations they will undergo.

Thus prepared, Blount sets out. But his narrative has barely begun before circumstances once again demand that he engage in yet another striking moment of self-reconstruction by stepping outside Christianity. He is delighted to find himself sailing among Turks and Jews, 'not having any Christian with them besides my selfe'. In line with Fynes Moryson's precepts, Blount explains that travelling without other Christians offered two advantages: he would not get into trouble because of association with the dangerous views of other Christians; and second: 'I had a freedome of complying upon occasion of questions by them made; whereby I became all things to all men, which let me into the breasts of many' (p. 5).

Once he has set sail, Blount does not simply imagine himself prepared to step outside his own culture, he joyfully shakes it off and declares himself better able to perform without it. He often notes the inconveniences of being noticed for being a 'stranger', observing how Tartars are notoriously keen on seizing known Christians and selling them into slavery (p. 69). And he continually finds any association with Christianity burdensome. Later, he describes himself not 'loving company of *Christians* in *Turky*' (p. 38), and avoids them whenever possible. Seeking to travel free from any customary cultural identification as an Englishman and Christian, Blount seeks to become both confidential and compliant. 'All things to all men', he becomes the prototypical agent who, keeping himself unobtrusive and secretive, finds a way into 'the breasts of many'.

In these opening pages, Blount details multiple reasons for travelling, but by the time one has finished reading his report of the journey, it is hard not to suspect that he has been rather reticent from the start; certainly with respect to his material means, but also about possible undeclared motives for adventuring into Ottoman lands in the first place. His book begs readers to suspect that, amidst his elaborately stated intentions and elsewhere, crucial aspects of his 'purpose' might have been too obvious to require comment. Although he provides constant circumstantial reminders and asides about travelling conditions, not once does Blount feel any need to tell us directly how it was that he undertook this journey in the first place. Who paid? After offering his detailed rationale, Blount simply and suddenly projects himself to Venice, where he discovers himself employing a Janissary to serve as travel agent to organize his trip as far as Istanbul.

Here, the terms of King's verses may help us grasp the contemporary sense in which it may have been the very act of writing the *Voyage*, of publishing the book, of describing in detail and illustrating with exemplary episodes how to be a passenger, that constituted both Blount's most obvious and therefore unspoken motivation and, according to King, his great achievement. By writing to instruct future sons of an as yet unimagined empire how they might most profitably travel among and, more importantly, deal with the Turks, Blount perhaps fulfilled a mission that did not need explanation. As Sir Thomas Palmer observed in 1606, since princes no longer travelled abroad themselves, they needed others to do it for them.[27] Bishop King's verses should be read as a professional letter of reference, perhaps a commendation for the knighthood which Blount received from Charles I in 1640, four years after initial publication of *A Voyage*. For Blount investigating the Ottoman Empire was a shrewd career move.

13
The Sinews of Empire: Venice to Istanbul

> Now bicause Goulde is the Sinowes of Warres: & as if it were Spirit or Soule, gives life & motion to an Army: I will remember some thinges, that I have understoode of the Turkes Riches.
>
> Humphrey Conisby (c.1600)[1]

Among Henry Blount's virtues as a writer is his ability to balance the excitements of personal adventure with detailed information. In telling the story of his journey, he keeps up a fast pace, describing conditions of travel and interesting incidents along the way without losing sight of more abstract principles. Recounting his sea journey from Venice and the overland trek across the Balkans, Blount's major concerns are with those complex economies of extracting, moving, and protecting trade goods and military supplies that enable the Ottoman Empire to run.[2] Although, like Biddulph, he wants to set the record straight, he does not have all the answers beforehand. By travelling from Venice as a paying passenger among a caravan of Turkish and Jewish merchants, he enables himself to notice and describe conditions along the Venetian–Ottoman trade routes as well as the efficiency and strength of local administration. Almost immediately, he observes how the commercial–military connection allows trade to take place between the Venetians and the Ottomans. Sailing down the Adriatic, he comments on the fortifications at Venetian ports, observing that Zara (Zadar) is 'apt to command the whole *Adriatique*' because of its central location (p. 6). A stopover of three days after leaving ship in Spaletro (Split) afforded him the opportunity to witness how the strategic trade links between Venice and the Ottoman Porte operated at this major Venetian entrepôt. Here, the resident Ottoman 'Emir', who collected duty on the goods carried to Venice on huge galleys, was backed up by Ottoman forces only four miles away, stationed in what Blount declared to be the 'strongest land fortress I ever beheld' (p. 6).

Trade routes and dangers: The Balkans

When valuable goods are on the move, borders are to be crossed and there are armed soldiers about, adventures must be lurking nearby. From Split, Blount and the caravan took to horse and wagon and headed overland for Sarajevo. Within nine days they reached 'the city *Saraih*... the *Metropolis* of the king-dome of *Bosnah*' (pp. 7–8). Noting the 'meanely built' condition of the city and its abundant supply of excellent water, Blount and his company set off for Belgrade, accompanied by a drunken soldiery.

> ...at our departure, we went along with the *Bashaw* of *Bosnah* his troopes going for the warre of *Poland*; they were of *Horse*, and foote betweene sixe or seven thousand, but went scattering, the *Bashaw* not yet in person, and the taking leave of their freinds[*sic*], Spirited many with drinke, discontent, and insolency; which made them fitter company for the *Divell*, then for a *Christian*: my selfe after many launces, and knives thretned upon me, was invaded by a drunken *Ianizary*, whose iron mace entangled in his other furniture gave me time to flee among the Rockes, whereby I escap'd untoucht: Thus marcht we ten dayes through a hilly country, cold, not inhabited. (p. 8)

Despite his precautions, Blount cannot avoid arousing suspicion concerning his religious origins. Being a passenger could be dangerous when one was undeniably a stranger, as Blount would later call himself, among armed, dis-affected and inebriated soldiers on the move. What is more remarkable is that he clearly did not spend every night hiding among the rocks.

In several subsequent accounts of life-threatening adventures, Blount repeat-edly emphasized the importance of humility, wit and speed to stay out of danger, and would praise Ottoman justice towards strangers. He would have more to say about travelling among Ottoman forces, in particular their hospi-tality towards him, but for the moment what is notable is how free Blount seemed to be from prejudice when he ascribed this incident to circumstantial causes. Drink, discontent and insolence are liable to provoke violent behaviour among departing soldiers whatever their nation or religion. After ten days, however, Blount was clearly happy when the caravan set off again without the military rabble. No sooner had they set off on the road than the merchants began making plans against anticipated attacks by bandits.

> ...we left them [the soldiers] behind, and being to passe a Wood neere the Christian countrey, doubting it to be (as confines are) full of Theeves, we divided our Caravan of sixscore Horse in two parts; halfe with the Persons, and Goods of lest esteeme, we sent a day before the rest, so that the thieves having a bootie, might be gone before we came; which hapned accordingly;

they were robbed; one thiefe, and two of ours slaine; some hundred *dollars* worth of goods lost. The next day we passed, and found sixteene thieves, in a narrow passage, before whom, we set a good guard of *Harquebuze*, and *Pistols*, till the weaker sort passed by: so in three dayes, we came safe to *Belgrada*. (p. 9)

Dryly, and without further comment, Blount notes how it was proximity to 'Christian countrey' that put the caravan at risk. Along borders lacking guards and customs officials, brigands were at work exacting tolls instead, thereby driving up the cost of the goods being carried. Without pausing over the incident, Blount maintains his focus on conditions of moving trade goods and various strategies for coping with difficulties and dangers along the road. Although at personal risk from being recognized as a Christian, Blount was evidently paying enough for his passage among the merchants never to be in any danger of being classed among those persons 'of lest esteeme', but it must have been strange to watch that first party of victims setting off.

Belgrade and Ottoman justice

Blount was interested in Belgrade mostly because it was an important imperial Ottoman outpost. Given its strategic position on the rivers Sava and Danube, Belgrade had long been a key frontier fortress. Since capture by Suleiman I in August 1521, it had marked the frontier of Ottoman conquests into Europe.[3] From here, generations of sultans would enviously gaze towards Vienna. Here, according to Blount, 'is kept a great part of the *Gran Signieur* his treasure, to be ready when he warres on that side the *Empire*' (p. 11). He further comments on the strength of the city walls, the location between two rivers with outlying fertile floodplains, and the impressive arsenal held in a castle, featuring 'a round Tower, called the *Zindana*, a crueltie not by them devised, and seldome practised' (p. 10). Meaning 'dungeon' in Turkish, 'zindan' here has clearly come to designate a place of torture.[4] Blount describes how the beams inside the Belgrade tower are 'stucke frequent with great flesh-hookes' onto which 'the condemned was naked let fall amongst those hookes, which gave him a quicke, or lasting misery, as he chanc'd to light' (p. 11). Early travellers were often keen to report on the suddenness and cruelty of Ottoman justice, and after nearly two decades of practising law in London, Blount had a particular stake, as it were, in bizarre and unusual juridical practices. But that cannot fully explain what he was doing nosing about while in Belgrade:

Within this great Castle, is another little one, with works of its owne; I had like to have miscarried, with approaching the entrance, but the rude noise, and worse lookes of the Guard, gave me a timely apprehension with sudden passage, and humiliation to sweeten them and get off: for as I after learnt, there is kept great part of the *Gran Signeior* his treasure. (p. 11)

Retreating hastily and humbly from an angry-looking guard was clearly a good move. In reporting moments such as this, Blount stays true to his purpose and seeks rational explanations for things: he does not treat Ottoman soldiers as essentially cruel, vicious or malevolently violent by nature. He is, moreover, always able to outwit or outrun them when caught snooping.

Travel with the Ottoman army

When Blount visited in 1634, Belgrade was, as so often in its history, a city of amassing armies.

> Here the *Basha* of *Temesvar* joyning the people of *Buda*, and his owne, with those of *Belgrado*, and *Bosnah*, they were held incamped on the South-Side of the Towne; yet not so severely, but the *Spahyes, Ianizaries*, and *Venturiers*, had leave to goe before to the generall *Rendivous*, as they pleased, though most of them stayed to attend the *Bashaes*; they there expected *Murath Basha*; he five dayes after our arrivall, came in with few Foot, but foure thousand Horse, of the *Spahy Timariots*; such brave Horses and men so dextrous in the use of the Launce I had not seene. (p. 11)

Despite his initial encounter with unsupervised Bosnian soldiers, Blount was nevertheless greatly impressed by the various troops assembling under Ottoman banners. From his language here, he presumes readers will understand something of the geography and Ottoman military terminology. The forces being marshalled to go against Poland by the Bey of Temesvar are typical of Ottoman forces on European frontiers. Under a serdar, or field marshal, local troops joined regulars of the Ottoman army: by Blount's time the Sipahi regiments of skilled cavalrymen represented an established feudal elite, while the Janissary corps was a force to be reckoned with. By 'venturiers' he presumably means the irregular volunteer cavalrymen, called akıncı or 'raiders', who had formerly played a major part in Ottoman military tactics, advancing before the regular army to plunder and lay waste. By the late sixteenth century, however, akıncı forces were deployed in the Balkans only.[5] Blount's 'venturiers' might have included some of the celebrated 'deli' or 'mad' horsemen who served along the European frontier zone, wearing 'skins of wild animals and feathers for decoration'.[6]

If Blount's admiration for the Sipahi cavalrymen bespeaks the horseman in every Englishman of his class at this time, his initial lack of comment on the hanging of straggling soldiers perhaps bespeaks the professional lawyer seeking to assess a regulation by its efficiency. For the next twelve days, Blount and the caravan of merchants travel to Sophia with the assembled army, now under the rule of Murad Basha, and he has nothing but admiration for how the entire operation runs smoothly, in large part because of that command being strictly enforced.

> In this and our former march, I much admired, that we had a *Caravan* loaded with *Clothes, Silkes, Tissues*, and other rich commodities, were so safe, not only in the maine Army, but in stragling troopes, amongst whom we often wandered by reason of recovering the *Iewes Sabbath*; but I found the cause to the crueltie of *Justice*; for theeves upon the way are empaled without delay, or mercy; and there was a *Saniacke* with two hundred Horse, who did nothing but coast up, and downe the countrey, and every man who could not give a faire account of his being where he found him was presently strangled, though not known to have offended. (p. 12)

While travelling through the Balkans, Blount never reports witnessing Ottoman summary justice in action.[7] Instead, he makes sense of the system, arguing that 'although not so rash as we suppose', making examples of the innocent 'works as well as if he were guiltie indeed' since 'the resentment so violent terrifies the more'. 'Therefore,' he continues, 'to prevent disorders sometimes, in the beginnings of warre, *colourable* punishments are used, where *just* ones want.' (p. 12). Having, no doubt, some understanding of how competing Christian armies had wrought havoc across most of central Europe during the previous twenty years, Blount goes so far in his endorsement of the Ottoman system as to criticize Christian practices. 'This speedy and remorcelesse severitie,' he continues:

> makes that when their great Armies lye about any *Towne* or *passe*, no man is endamaged, or troubled to secure his goods; in which respect, it pretends more effect upon a bad age then our *Christian compassion*, which is so easily abused, as we canot raise two, or three Companies of Souldiers, but they pillage, and rifle wheresoever they passe. (p. 13)

Clearly being able to attach your trading caravan to an Ottoman army on the move, providing it was going your way, was the best means of travelling in the Balkans, especially since 'through all Turky...are many *Mountainers*, or *Out-lawes*' (p. 13). Even under Ottoman control, the overland routes available to the Venetian trade were costly, difficult and dangerous: yet without the support of an Ottoman army, keeping the brigands at bay could prove impossible.

Life on the road

Besides admiring the efficiency of capital punishments in wartime, Blount was also struck with wonder at the Ottoman system of military supply:

> In all our march, though I could not perceive much *discipline* as not neere an adverse partie; yet I wondred to see such a multitude so cleare of *confusion, violence, want, sicknesse*, or any other *disorder*, and though we were almost three score thousand, and sometimes not a towne in 7. or 8. dayes; yet was there such plentie of good *Bisket, Rice*, and *Mutton*, as wheresoever I passed up, and downe to view the *Spahyes*, and others in their tentes, they would often make me sit, and eate with them very plentifull, and well. (p. 13)

The Ottoman army on the march is not the disorderly horde of prejudiced legend. Biddulph, it will be recalled, recoiled from accepting food offered by local people, but for Blount accepting such hospitality was an essential element of what he was there to do: find out as much as he could by making himself as amenable as possible. Blount clearly felt himself free to roam, viewing the different ranks of soldiers while in camp. He halts his narrative to describe the scene, noting how the several generals travelled with opulent courts, 'each of them having three or fourscore *Camels*, besides five or six score *Carts*, to carry the *Baggage*' as well as '*Coaches*, covered with *Cloth of Gold*, or rich *tapestry*' to carry their wives, of whom 'some had with them *twelve* or *sixteene*' (p. 13).

Blount seems more impressed by the scale and efficiency of the operation than by the luxurious manner in which Ottoman generals went to war. Expressing no surprise or moral judgement, he report that 'beside these wives, each *Basha* hath as many, or likely more *Catamites*, which are their serious loves; for their Wives are used (as the Turkes themselves told me) but to dresse their meat, to Laundresse, and for reputation' (p. 14). Without commenting one way or the other on the use of boys for sexual pleasure, Blount describes instead what they looked like and how they too served to display the wealth, power and prestige of the various generals:

> The Boyes likely of twelve, or fourteene yeares old, some of them not above nine, or ten, are usually clad in *Velvet*, or *Scarlet*, with guilt *Scymitars*, and bravely mounted, with *sumptuous furniture*; to each of them a Souldier appointed, who walkes by his bridle, for his safetie; when they are all in order, there is excellent *Sherbert* given to any who will drinke; then the *Basha* takes Horse, before whom ride a dozen, or more, who with ugly Drums, brasse Dishes, and wind instruments, noise along most part of the Journey... These are the chiefe ceremonies I remember. (p. 14)

Blount, we might say, commodifies the boys by turning them into valuable items of property on display, each supplied with costly clothing, a richly caparisoned horse and a personal bodyguard. Rather than moralize over their sexual function, he indicates how the boys usefully serve multiple purposes. In Maurizio Calbi's words, 'Eastern sodomy, in Blount's case, is represented as contiguous with military might rather than as its mighty opposite.'[8] Blount's interest in homosexual behaviour among the Ottoman army proves far more utilitarian than that of other English commentators of his time.

Sexual behaviour among the Ottomans

By the 1630s, Western writing on the Ottomans in English had widely circulated a tradition of condemning those they called Turks, and indeed most Eastern, African and Islamic peoples indiscriminately, for indulging excessively in a variety of ungodly sexual practices.[9] Blount himself would later dismiss as idle nonsense what he took to be the widely held belief that Jews are especially libidinous. Yet as recently as 1632, in dedicating his translation of Michel Baudier's *The History of the Imperial Estate of the Grand Seigneurs* to Sir Harbottle Grimston, Edward Grimestone had published his view that to understand the Ottoman Empire required seeing how 'the State of the proudest and most powerfull Monarch of the World'[10] was about to collapse from sexual corruption. Grimestone endorsed Baudier's argument that the strength and stability of the Ottoman Empire depended on, and could be assessed in terms of, the sultan's sexual behaviour. Arguing from general precept in the manner of a Renaissance humanist, Baudier writes:

> Among all the passions which rule the affections of Princes, Love (as the most powerfull) triumphs more over great men, then all the rest together, for they obtain no victories, but to increase its glory: Covetousnesse heaps up to furnish the charges, Ambition aspires to make it great. So we see the most powerfull princes after they had subdued all other passions, are vanquished by Love.[11]

Consequently, every aspect of life within the Ottoman Empire falls subject to the personal behaviour of the tyrannical sultan and the sexual culture of his court:

> That which we have formerly written of the entertainment of the Turkish Prince with his women, is not the most blameable of his affections. The greatnesse of his power, which makes all mens wils obey him, and the contagious example of his Courtiers, carries him to the detestable excesse of an unnaturall passion. Hee burnes many times for the love of men and

the youngest Boyes which are in the *Levant*, the flowre of beautie and the allurement of graces, are destined to the filthinesse of his abominable pleasures... The Prince is the Physician of the State; but how can hee cure it if hee himselfe bee sicke? Hee is the heart; but what meanes is there to give it life, if it hath weakness and faintings: Hee is the eye, and how can he see and lead others, if it be troubled and darkened with passions? Every Prince that loves his Throne, his Scepter, and his Estate, must flie vice and cherish wisdome: For a wise Prince is the assurance of those, and the support of his people.[12]

It was exactly such traditional moral judgements about the Ottomans that were the target of Blount's aim in traveling in the first place. No doubt his years at St Albans School, at Oxford and later among lawyers and literati in London towards the end of James's reign had taught him not to be surprised by unorthodox sexual behaviour, whatever his own early tastes might have been. He certainly knew better than to judge an empire by a ruler's personal habits or to evaluate a political system on the basis of the sexual culture of its court, or by the way it controlled and licensed sexuality. Indeed, he set out to discover whether accusations of Ottoman 'sottish sensuality' could possibly be true. By representing the boys as objects on display who contributed to the splendour, spectacle and *esprit de corps* of the Ottoman army on the move, Blount effectively argues the irrelevance of moral judgements of the kind Baudier, Grimestone and others wished to advance for a sound assessment of the health and strength of the Ottoman Empire.[13] Rather than reply to those who would damn the sultan and his empire because of his 'abominable pleasures', Blount ignores moral arguments about sexual behaviour in order to describe what he considered to be an important feature of an undeniably efficient army on the move.

Blount's naming and description of the 'Catamites' is the first direct reference to sexual behaviour in the *Voyage*. Reserving judgement strategically prevents traditional Christian moralizing, yet Blount's relative silence is also in keeping with his general attitude towards Ottoman social life. In the narrative sections of his book he most commonly ignores social matters except when they are relevant to his immediate concern with local resources and supply. At this moment of describing military procedure, when judging sexual behaviour was directly on the agenda, he remains curiously reticent: which is surely odd because, during his eleven months travelling, Blount must have had many personal thoughts on what he saw and how he felt.

In a later section of the book, he will observe: 'there are foure severall *Orders* in their *Religion*; all very malicious against *Christians*; otherwise I have not noted them vicious, excepting their profest *Sodomy*, which in the *Levant* is not held a vice' (p. 79). The comparative method once again allows a different culture to operate in its own terms. Blount does not so much condemn 'Sodomy' as turn the notion of a moral 'vice' into a question of cultural difference which enables him to treat the practice itself as no more than a fact of being in a world constituted by differences. Some readers might think it rather strange that the next thing he thinks about is reporting on an ascetic sect. 'The *Calenderim*,' he writes, 'upon *Chastity*, wearing an *iron Ring* through the skin of his yard; in some I have noted it capable of being taken of with small difficultie' (p. 79).

Blount's seemingly impersonal attitude towards matters sexual finally stretches and breaks out even as he describes features of the libidinal economy of the Ottoman army on the move, and clearly deserves further thought. Thomas Dallam, it will be recalled, while travelling in his twenties, felt by turns perplexed, fascinated and mildly threatened by the erotic possibilities of the Ottoman Mediterranean: he hurried back to England, married and had children. William Biddulph could barely contain himself from revealing his fantasies of drowning London prostitutes while secretly pursuing the sport himself. Blount, still single in his early thirties at the time of his travels, had spent his entire life in all-male institutions. When he arrived in London from Oxford in his late teens, the major sex scandals of James's reign were old news, but for a witty young lawyer, the London literary circles in which he moved would have provided opportunities for all manner of sexual behaviour and experience. Blount was 45 when he finally married and became a father. In his old age, he was especially solicitous on behalf of his youngest son, Ulysses.

John Aubrey's testimony should dissuade us from imagining that such a profile indicates Blount was specially attracted to young boys or other men for his 'serious loves', or condemned the vice of sodomy merely for form. 'He was pretty wild when young,' Aubrey writes, 'especially addicted to common wenches.' Such was Blount's reputation that Aubrey notes he was lampooned 'for spreading abroad that abominable and dangerous Doctrine that it was far cheaper and safer to lye with Common Wenches then with Ladies of Quality' (p. 26).[14] Writing in 1680, Aubrey was recalling a personal acquaintance with Blount of more than twenty years: 'Drunkeness he much exclaimed against, but wenching he allowed' (p. 26). Absence of evidence may not be evidence of abstinence, but it is difficult to imagine that Blount would have gained such a reputation if he had frequently turned to the bodies of young men for sexual pleasure. He certainly enjoyed the company of men throughout his life, and late in the *Voyage* would write fondly of Ottoman mariners, favourably contrasting their manners with those of English sailors. But even this observation is once again in keeping with Blount's aim of setting the record straight in order to dispel unfounded prejudices.

If the case were to be made that Blount was especially attracted to boys, and that such an attraction explains why he was non-judgemental in his account of homosexuality among the Ottoman troops, only indirect in condemning sodomy and generally impersonal about matters sexual, such a case would depend greatly on the episode immediately following his description of those 'Catamites'. After describing the boys riding off as part of 'the cheife ceremonies', Blount informs us that he came to know so much because he made a particular friend of one of Murad Basha's favourites on the very first night.

> That which secured and emboldened my enquiry and passage these twelve dayes March, was an accident the first night, which was thus: the *Campe* being pitch'd on the Shoare of *Danubius*, I went, (but timorously) to view the Service about *Murath Bashaes* Court, where one of his favorite Boys espying me to bee a Stranger, gave me a Cup of *Sherbert*; I, in thanks, and to make friends in Court, presented him with a Pocket *Looking Glasse*, in a little *Ivory Case*, with a *Coombe*; such as are sold at *Westminster-hall* for four or five shillings a peece; The youth much taken therewith, ran, and shewed it to the *Bashaw*, who presently sent for me, and making me sit, and drinke *Cauphe* in his presence, called for one that spake Italian. (pp. 14–15)

This is the longest he has paused so far to describe a personal encounter. The ingredients are very similar to Dallam's account of hospitality on Zante, but the erotic possibilities are surely being understated in what is, after all, a published text. Performing as an inquisitive stranger and exchanging gifts with one of the 'favorite Boys' in order to gain admittance to the big man certainly sounds like striking an erotic bargain. Yet Blount mutes the sexual possibilities in order to represent himself as exemplifying strategic travelling. Unlike Dallam's awkward and confused fumblings over gift giving, Blount knows what is going on from the start; his timorous approach is clearly planned, a prelude to the gift that is designed to invite further hospitality and bring him closer to Ottoman imperialism at work. He says no more of the boy once he has gained admittance to the field marshall's tent, or otak. This night marked the beginning of Blount's taste for coffee, but there is evidence that he also indulged a taste for boys.

Coffee drinking by the Danube

Blount may not have known the Turkish saying to the effect that 'if we drink one cup of coffee together, we will be friends for forty years'.[15] But two decades later he must have recalled that evening in June 1634 when writing 'The Answer of Sir Henry Blount Knight, to the preceding Letter of his worthy Friend Judge Rumsey' on the medicinal properties of coffee and tobacco. Walter Rumsey, a self-proclaimed 72-year-old member of Gray's Inn, had dedicated his *Organon Salutis* (1657) to Blount, declaring: 'I lately understood that your discovery, in your excellent Book of Travels, hath brought the use of the Turkes

Physick, of Cophe in great request in *England.*'[16] Printed five years after the opening of the first coffee house in London, Rumsey's subtitle – *An Instrument to Cleanse the Stomach, As also divers new Experiments of the Virtue of Tobacco and Coffee: How much they conduce to preserve humane health* – explains his purpose in writing. Rumsey's praise of Blount confirms Aubrey's report that Blount was a great champion of coffee drinking. And if Rumsey's praise is more than simple flattery, and Blount's book and public reputation really did help stimulate the market for coffee in England, then his evening by the Danube with Murad Basha in the summer of 1634 might be said to have been a formative moment in the development of coffee-house culture in seventeenth-century England, a key prelude to the development of what has come to be known as the public sphere. The late nineteenth-century historian Edward Robinson, in his valuable study of the English coffee-house, certainly thought so, declaring that Blount 'has some claims to be regarded as the father of English coffee-houses'.[17]

In describing his performance that evening, Blount does not sound self-aggrandizing. On that first evening drinking coffee with the Ottoman general, he has to depend on his native wit when overwhelmed by Ottoman hospitality:

> it was my fortune to hit his humour so right, as at last, he asked if my Law did permit me to serve under them going against the *Polacke* who is a *Christian*; promising with his hand upon his breast, that if I would, I should be inrolled of his Companies, furnished with a good Horse, and of other necessaries be provided with the rest of his Houshold. (p. 15)

Like Dallam in Istanbul, Blount discovered how gaining friendly access to Ottoman authorities can lead to a tricky diplomatic predicament requiring ingenuity to avoid offending a hospitable, but potentially life-threatening, representative of absolute power. Unlike Dallam, however, Blount could rely on his education and years at law, and did not need to invent a fictional family waiting at home as an excuse. Instead, he offered substantial reasons for turning down the invitation, while at the same time solidifying the political alliance between the Ottomans and English, and even managing to flatter his host in the process.

> I humbly thanked him, for his favour, and told him that to an *Englishman* it was lawfull to serve under any who were in league with our *King*, and that our *King* had not only a League with the *Gran Signior*, but continually held an *Embassadour* at his Court, esteeming him the greatest *monarch* in the *World*: so that my Service there, especially if I behaved my selfe not unworthy of my *Nation*, would be exceedingly well received in *England*; and the *Polacke*, though in name a *Christian*, yet of a *Sect*, whom for *Idolatry*, and many other points, we much abhorred; wherefore the *English* had of late, helpt the

Muscovite against him, and would be forwarder under the *Turkes*, whom we not only honoured but also loved, for the kinde *Commerce* of *Trade* which we finde amongst them: But as for my present engagement to the warre, with much sorrow, I acknowledged my incapacitie, by reason I wanted language, which would not only render me uncapable of *Commands*, and so *unserviceable*, but also endanger me in *tumults*, where I appearing a Stranger, and not able to expresse my affection, might be mistaken, and used accordingly; wherefore I humbly entreated his Highnesse leave to follow my poore affaires, with an eternal *oblige* to *Blazon* this honourable favour wheresoever I came. (pp. 15–16)

Even humble passengers must sometimes play at international diplomacy and Blount seems to have been rather good at this kind of impromptu negotiation. He cannot avoid being a stranger, but he was at least able to negotiate his own terms when his prying into Ottoman tents brought him to the attention of the authorities. Surely this is exactly the kind of encounter which Blount's method of travel was designed to invite? Blount may well have known Sir Thomas Glover's account of how Edward Barton had joined Murad III on campaign against the Hungarians in 1596, gaining the respect of the Ottomans without compromising his reputation among his own countrymen. At that time Elizabeth herself endorsed the view that the war against idolatry justified league with the Ottomans against Catholic nations. Clearly the argument still worked when backed up with sound economic arguments such as the 'kinde *Commerce* of *Trade*'. Apart from explaining his unsuitability for military service, however, Blount does not tell us if or how he explained to Murad why he was travelling. Perhaps, since he accompanied a trade caravan, he identified himself as a merchant with business in hand. The question is of interest since, as we shall see, Blount later describes how soldiers usually assumed he was a spy.

Blount's friendship with the general failed to insulate him from the hazards of the road or protect him from a dangerous incident outside the town of Niş. Once again, Blount attributes the problem to drunkenness rather than to any essential character failing. 'Wine having possest a *Janizary*, and one other *Turke*, who rode in my Coach,' he begins, 'they fell out with two countrey fellowes, and by violence tooke an Axe.' Blount intervened and returned the axe, but these 'fellowes dogg'd us', broke into the Coach that night and gave the Turk 'two blowes with Scymitars' and fled. The attackers recognized Blount and left him alone, but his problems were not over:

I was found there all bloudy, and so taken, and surely the next day beene executed, but that within lesse then halfe an houre, the hurt person, comming to his senses, cleared me, telling how it came, and by whom.
Thus in twelve dayes, wee came to Sophya. (p. 16)

All Blount's incidental narratives prove exemplary, serving not simply to illustrate a traveller's need for ingenuity, good sense and luck, but also how life in the Ottoman Empire rarely confirmed received opinion. Here Blount is rescued by the honesty of the Turk who, though severely wounded himself, and otherwise prone to drunken violence, acts not out of malice, that fabled attribute of his nation, but out of a clear sense of justice.

Imperial remains and imperial cities

Reserving for later several exemplary incidents from his journey across the Balkans, Blount recorded no further perils between Sophia and Istanbul, commenting instead on the imperial history of the towns and other sites along the route and reporting on current conditions under the Ottomans. Having fulfilled his ambition of observing the Ottoman army marching against Poland, he turns his attention to the imperial past of the lands through which he travels. Approaching the Ottoman capitals of Edirne and Istanbul, the roads become safer and the historical sites and monuments more impressive. Like Lady Mary Wortley Montagu seventy years later, Blount first felt himself to have entered an Ottoman city on arrival in Sophia, with its many 'brave' mosques, 'magnificent Colledge' and 'exquisite Bathes' (p. 17). Nor was Blount's experience based on an aesthetically untrained eye; his later detailed descriptions of Sinan's mosque in Edirne, features of Ottoman and Egyptian domestic architecture and the Pyramids themelves show that he had possessed considerable understanding of what he was looking at when observing built structures. His praise for the Ottoman contribution to Sophia's architecture gives the lie to contemporary reports of Ottoman negligence regarding urban areas under imperial control, often based on observations of fortresses and cities along the North African coast.[18] While in Sophia, in addition to noting the splendour of the Ottoman buildings, Blount parted company with the Janissary who had accompanied him from Venice. Rather than run the risk of becoming caught up in the impending wars, Blount's unnamed companion stays on to pursue his personal trading interests.

Blount had evidently prepared himself for the final leg of his overland journey from Sophia to Istanbul during which he engaged in some serious archaeological tourism. Like Biddulph touring the Holy Land with his Bible as his guide, Blount had brought along Caesar's 'Commentary...which on purpose I carried to conferre upon the Place, for the better impression' (p. 20). On leaving 'Potarzeek' (Pazarcik), Blount noted it to be a town 'full of antiquities' and records beginning an extended discussion with 'a learned *Jew*, (to whom I owe most of my information)' (p. 18) about the site of Thermopolyae and other famous battles reportedly fought along the route through Thrace. When in sight of a 'large mountaine... the *Jew* held it to be the *Thermopyla*' and then, he told me that *Easterne* custome of wearing *Turbants* came from thence; and that how once the *Barbarous* people having the *Grecian Army* at a great advantage, there was no other remedy, but that some few should make good that narrow passage, while the maine of the army might escape away; there were brave Spirits who undertooke it; and knowing, they went to an unevitable death, they had care of nothing but *Sepulture*, which of old was much regarded; wherefore each of them carried his *winding* sheete wrapt about his head, and then with losse of their owne lives saved their fellowes; where-upon for an honourable memoriall of that exploit, the *Levantines* used to wrap *white linnen* about their *heads*, and the *fashion* so derived upon the *Turke*. (pp. 18–19)

Blount accepted the site to be Thermopylae, but considered the story about the origins of the turban to be a version of the tale of '*Leonidas* with his three hundred *Spartanes*, but corrupted by time, and tradition' (p. 19). As the caravan moves on, he noted how 'the *Champaigne* betweene this Mountaine and *Philippoplis*' still gave evidence of the great battles anciently fought there. Recalling burial mounds on the 'Downes of *Marleborough*, where the *Saxons* as it is thought had a great Battell', Blount noted how 'just in that manner, there yet remaine the heapes were the slaine were buried' from the Roman civil wars (p. 19). He attributes his detailed observations of the area to spending 'two dayes' in 'a little Town' along the way that 'gave me leasure to reade Caesar his Commentary thereon' (p. 20). Adding up the numbers of those reportedly slain in different battles, Blount assesses the sites according to the size of the burial mounds before him.

Blount's archaeological interest in touring imperial Roman remains seldom dulled his engagement with the imperial Ottoman present. Moving eastwards, Blount observed how the sultan kept stables in Phillipi for 'five thousand Camels, which carry his provision when he Warres on this side his Empire' (p. 20). Passing through 'many pretty Townes of *Thrace*' (p. 21), Blount and the caravan arrive finally at Adrianople, modern Edirne. 'Untill the conquest of *Constantinople*, it was the Turkes Emperiall Seat' (p. 21). Here he is struck with such enormous enthusiasm for a mosque built on top of 'the highest, and larg-est' of three hills, 'as the crowne and glory of the other buildings' (p. 21), that he devotes an entire page to a detailed description, concluding:

This edifice is not great, but of structure so neate, and that so advantaged by scituation, as renders it not only stately, and magnificent, but with such a delicacy as I have not seene in any other place, no not in Italy.[19] (p. 22)

This time, Blount has supported his judgements with geometrical details of how the body supports the great dome. Clearly he is describing the magnificent mosque Sinan built for Selim II between 1569 and 1575. What counts here is not simply Blount's admiration for one of Sinan's greatest buildings, but his recognition of how Ottoman culture has contributed to human achievements unequalled in Christendom. He may not have known Sinan's name or who commissioned him to design which buildings, but Blount clearly appreciated the Ottoman architect's genius, unsurpassed in world architecture at the time, and was eager to pass on his enthusiasm to his readers.

Between Edirne and Istanbul, Blount continued to admire the profusion of public buildings for being not only useful but also beautiful. Arriving in the great Ottoman metropolis, he ends this stage of his journey by observing how 'it is in *Turky* as in other Kingdomes, the neerer to the *Emperiall Citie*, the more stately is the countrey inhabited' (p. 23). After five days in Istanbul, he set sail for Egypt with the Black Sea Fleet of 86 vessels, booking 'the Gunners Roome' on the '*Admirall Galeon*', together with a Frenchman and a Flemish 'gentleman' (p. 27) of whom Blount makes no further report. Nor does he comment on the fleet, or its purpose in sailing for North Africa. Passing through the Dardanelles, he observes the artillery aimed at passing shipping and comments on Troy, Samos, Chios and Patmos as he passes by each (pp. 27–9).

14
Ottoman Egypt: African Empire in Ruins

> ...because *Egypt* is held to have been the fountaine of all *Science*, and
> *Arts civill*, therefore I did hope to find some spark of those cinders not
> yet put out.
>
> Blount, *Voyage*, p. 3

From the start of the *Voyage*, Blount emphasized how important visiting Egypt
would be. At the time, Cairo was the most important trading centre in the
Ottoman Empire, but Blount was less concerned with commerce alone than
with analysing how it related to imperial authority at work and with looking
for signs of Egypt's ancient learning. What had caused the knowledge and
power of the ancient Egyptians to decay? From this distance of time, many
details of his travels in Egypt read like a holiday brochure: itinerary, means of
transport and famous sites; camels in the desert, sailing on the Nile, visiting
the Pyramids at Giza, riding horses to Saqarra, seeing tombs and mummies in
the sand. But in 1634, an Englishman travelling through Ottoman Egypt was
still relatively unusual: of other Europeans he mentions meeting only an Italian
consul, his Flemish host and an illustrious Italian travelling companion.

Other conditions of public life in Ottoman Egypt also differed too. Safety
could still be an issue: from time to time while travelling, Blount encountered
bandits, but they were invariably repulsed when he and others discharged their
weapons. In Cairo itself, he took note of ancient monuments and modern
buildings, the aqueduct and urban water supply, the masses of people, the
densely crowded streets and the gardens by the Nile made lively by street
vendors who 'passe up, and down with *Pipes*, & *Roguy Fidles*, in Boats, full of
Fruits, *Sherberts*, and good *banqueting stuffe* to sell' (p. 43). Still intrigued by
Ottoman imperial administration, Blount hoped to find out as much as he could
that would help explain how 'all the ingenious *fancy*' of the Egyptian 'Nation'
had been 'corrupted into *ignorance* and *malice*' (p. 49). For Blount, one key to

understanding the history of imperial nations was the status of knowledge and the advancement of learning within the empire.

Throughout the travel sections of *A Voyage*, Blount often observed the methods and means of Ottoman imperial control. In Egypt, he distinguished Egyptians from the Arabs of the desert, from the Ottoman imperialists, from Moors and Jews, and also from the renegades to be found aplenty in Cairo. He describes Egyptians either living in abject slavery to the Ottomans or enjoying a compromised luxury as traitors to their own country: degenerate, ignorant and malicious either way. By Blount's reasoning, what had caused the great Egyptian nation to decay was the tradition of keeping 'the most *important* peeces of their *Philosophy*' obscure or, in Blount's term, 'vayled' (p. 48). Contemporary Egyptians were, for Blount, necessarily degenerate, having lost their ancient learning through '*frequent* oppressions; especially in those two of late ages; this of the *Turkes*; and the former of the *Circassian Mamalukes*' (p. 49). In this second phase of suffering under foreign imperialism, the Egyptians could be kept ruly only by the most extreme means available to Ottoman law. In Egypt, Blount reports witnessing gruesome spectacles of summary justice quite different from anything he had seen elsewhere. Amidst the oppressed Egyptian people, their decayed learning and dusty monuments, it was only in the bloodlines of the asil, or thoroughbred, Egyptian Arabian horses that Blount found any trace of Egypt's former native glory still alive.

On being a spy

> ...though held a *Spy*, they scorned to afflict mee, but rather chusing to glorifie their State in my Relation at home, informed me of all, and much against my will.
>
> Blount, *Voyage*, p. 66

Blount does not, at any time, deny being a spy, though he invariably reserves the term to describe something he is not. More to the point, he emphasizes how being presumed to be a spy and behaving accordingly could often prove very much to his advantage. In such moments he most closely resembles those 'secret' agents who, like James Bond, depend on being recognized by those in the know, and so are not really 'secret' at all. When Blount arrived on Rhodes, for example, he was promptly assumed to be a spy. Bearing in mind how he had described himself behaving in the *Voyage*, this is not at all surprising. Later, Blount reveals more of what was going on during the trek through the Balkans besides observing military discipline and drinking coffee. But let us return to Blount's travels with the Ottoman army before investigating his arrival on Rhodes.

Of soldiers on the move to Belgrade, Blount reports that there were 'above seven hundred thousand':

> which number was told me, with many other of their notes, by some of the *Timariots* in the *Army*, where though held a *Spy*, they scorned to afflict mee, but rather chusing to glorifie their State in my Relation at home, informed me of all, and much against my will, forced mee in their presence to write it all downe; which I did in *Italian*, and in termes so respective, as when the *Interpreter* expounded, they received me exceedingly kindly, making me *eate, drinke,* and *lodge* in their tentes all night. (p. 66)

Unable to deny that he would be making some form of 'Relation at home', Blount had been reluctantly behaving like a spy for some time by the time he arrived on Rhodes. Like the initially innocent protagonists in Eric Ambler's spy-thrillers, Blount has unavoidably become an agent, reluctantly caught up in circumstances that made it impossible for him not to go along with a dominant (mis)perception of who he was and why he was travelling: especially since that perception was backed up by a military apparatus. As a recipient of Ottoman hospitality, Blount learnt and saw more than he otherwise would be able to. He seemed especially anxious about being obliged to keep a written account of such information. Whether he liked it or not, Blount could not avoid performing, some of the time, in ways that might be expected of a spy. When he arrived on Rhodes, Blount was carrying a notebook written in Italian in his own hand, containing details, facts and figures regarding the strength and strategies of the Ottoman army on the march. And he was also carrying a letter of introduction signed by the Dutch ambassador in Istanbul. Whether the notebook and letter were known about or not, Blount must have aroused suspicion among his fellow passengers since setting sail from Istanbul with the Black Sea fleet.

In the event, Blount discovered a certain advantage in 'being taken for a Spy' while on Rhodes. Since Christians had no right of trade there, his mere presence itself was suspect:

> here we stayed three dayes, which gave me some view of the place, and that so much the more by being taken for a Spy; for in *Rhodes* is no pretence of Merchandize for a *Christian*; and but that my excuse of going upon wager into *Egypt* seemed possible, I had beene lost: yet in that *Suspition*, some of them out of such a bravery, as I had once before found in their Campe, shewed mee the Palace. (p. 30)

Although being 'taken for' a spy gained him access, rather than confinement, Blount so far mutes the possibilities of danger as to leave readers guessing what being 'lost' might have entailed. Rather, he invites us to notice how being thought a spy though inevitable was not necessarily a disadvantage. Clearly, any guise of being a merchant would not serve him here. Instead, the local forces proudly displayed some of their most powerful defences, presumably hoping to impress Blount so that he would report on their impenetrability. In the event, Blount claims to have been shown several monumental buildings and military fortifications that he would otherwise have missed on Rhodes had he not been suspected of ulterior motives.

Unable to control perceptions of why he was there, Blount avoided the danger of being 'lost' by an effective 'excuse': that he had undertaken a wager payable on his return. It would once have been by no means uncommon for someone like Blount, a younger son, to cover the costs of overseas travel by taking on a lucrative bet. By the 1630s, however, courtiers and gentlemen would have considered the practice beneath their dignity.[1] But for Blount, the 'excuse' helped clarify why he was not in possession of trade goods worth confiscating and also helped explain his curiosity as both idle and innocent in terms that served his turn: the authorities on Rhodes were evidently familiar with the practice of young gentlemen who travelled on a wager. Even so, by allowing himself to be taken for a foreign agent, Blount placed himself at risk.

> Upon my first landing I had espyed among divers very *honourable Sepultures*, one more brave then the rest, and new; I enquired whose it was; a *Turke* not knowing whence I was, told me it was the *Captaine Basha*, slaine the yeare before by two *English Ships*; and therewith gave such a Language of our *Nation*, and threatning to all whom they should light upon, as made me upon all demands professe my selfe a *Scotchman*, which being a name unknowne to them, saved me, nor do I suppose it any quitting of my Countrey, but rather a *retreat* from one corner to the other; and when they enquired more in particular, I intending my owne *saftie* more then their *instruction*, answered the truth both of my *King*, and *Country*, but in the old obsolete *Greeke*, and *Latine* titles, which was as dark to them as a discourse of *Isis* and *Osyris*; yet the third day, in the morning, I prying up, and downe alone, met a *Turke* who in *Italian* told me ah! you are an *Englishman*, and with a kinde of malicious posture, laying his *fore-finger* under his eye, methought he had the lookes of a *designe*, he presently departed, I got to my *Galleon*, and durst goe to land no more: The next morne we departed for *Alexandria*. (pp. 32–3)

Manipulating political and linguistic confusion over nationality only got him so far. But after three days of being seen prying up and down, Blount knew it was time to take such warnings seriously.

Following storms at sea, Blount landed in Alexandria. He commented on the antiquities and present conditions under the Ottomans (pp. 34–5). Crossing the desert to Roseta, he took a boat to '*Gran Cairo*, 360. miles off: In five dayes we arrived' (p. 36).

Cairo: Poverty, palaces, horses

Ottoman Cairo in 1634 was the busiest trading city in the entire Mediterranean and required, according to Blount, 28,000 armed guards to patrol it every night (p. 38). According to the modern historian of Islamic cities, André Raymond, urban development after the Ottomans overthrew the Mameluke state in 1517 had brought Cairo to 'the pinnacle of an 800-year history – the realization of an urban program launched in 969, reoriented southward by Saladin in 1176, and extended by Muhammed Al-Nasir with his attempt to settle the western districts'.[2] While Blount was there, developments 'south of Bab Zuwayla' were in progress under the direction of Ridwan Bey, who 'managed to impose a quasi-monarchical authority over Egypt' between 1631 and 1656. Improvements included a 'remarkable' monumental souk, 'which largely survives to this day'.[3] But Blount was impressed not so much by what he saw of Cairo's recent municipal development as he was by the domestic palaces of the wealthy.

> This *Citie* is built after the *Egyptian* manner, *high*, and of large ruffe stone, part of *Bricke*, the *streets narrow*: it hath not beene yet above an hundred yeares, in the *Turkes* possession, wherefore the old buildings remaine; but as they decay the new begin to be after the *Turkish* manner, *poore, low, much of mud*, and *timber*: Yet of the *moderne Fabrickes* must I except divers new *Pallaces*, which I there have seene, bothe of *Turkes* and such *Egyptians*, as most engage against their owne Countrey, and so flourish in its *oppression*.(p. 40)

Thanks to a letter of introduction provided by Sir Cornelius Haga, ambassador of the Dutch Republic in Istanbul, Blount stayed while in Cairo with 'the *Illustrissimo Signior Sancto Seghezzi*', who 'had there beene resident twentie five years' (pp. 56, 38).[4] In company with 'the *Illustrisimo* with whom I lived', Blount was often a guest in such palaces of the newly powerful and wealthy. Without telling us more of his hosts or distinguishing between Ottoman and Egyptian domestic architecture or local and expatriate hospitality, he offers a highly detailed report of being entertained in a typical palace by a wealthy Cairene.

Having spent the better part of three months travelling, how could Blount not be impressed by Cairo's urban opulence? Indulging his interest in architectural detail, Blount is nevertheless overwhelmed by the magnificence of his entertainment. After passing through an outer walled courtyard with shady trees and exotic birds and beasts, fountains and fruit orchards, Blount describes inner rooms with marble floors, carpeted platforms for eating and elaborate water courses with 'Secret *Pipes*' feeding interior pools 'with a kinde of fish of two or three foot long, like *Barbells'* that will eat bread from the hand (p. 41). Having brought his readers through these marvels, Blount observes:

> But that which to mee seemed more *Magnificent* then all this, was my *entertainment*: entring one of these Roomes, I saw at the upper end, amongst others sitting crosse-legg'd the *Lord* of the *Palace*, who beckoning me to come, I first put off my *Shooes* as the rest had done; then bowing often, with my hand upon my breast, came neere, where he making me sit downe, there attended ten or twelve handsome young *Pages* all clad in *Scarlet*, with crooked *Daggers*, and *Scymitars*; richly gilt: foure of them came with a sheete of *Taffity*, and covered me; another held a golden *Incense* with rich *perfume*, wherewith being a little *smoked* they tooke all away; next came two with sweet *water* and *besprinkled* mee; after that, one brought a *Porcelane* dish of *Cauphe*, which when I had dranke, another served up a draught of excellent *Sherbert*: then began discourse, which passed by *interpreter* by reason of my *ignorance* in the *Arabick* there spoken. (p. 42)

Such evenings spent in formalized male conviviality drinking coffee and conversing, even through interpreters, no doubt inspired Blount's later championing of coffee-house culture in 1650s London. Blount was clearly delighted with the experience of being hosted in style by the lords of the 'divers new *Pallaces*', recognizing that some had been built by 'such *Egyptians*, as most engage against their owne *Countrey*, and so flourish in its *oppression*' (p. 40). Although we are invited to imagine Blount making many such visits among Cairo's merchant elite, he never specifies who any of his hosts were, and suggests that discussions regularly centred on matters of horse breeding. At this moment in *A Voyage*, at least, Blount reports back nothing more of what he might have learned from conversations during these visits, and reserves what he did learn about Ottoman administration in Egypt for later in the book.

Blount's account of his time in Cairo no doubt reflects what he was shown as much as his attitudes toward what he saw. Certainly, his preference for the buildings of the rich over Ridwan Bey's urban development schemes is fully in keeping with what is elsewhere evident of his architectural taste and personal delight at being exotically entertained in sumptuous settings. But judging from what he reports of conversations among the elite, administrative details were less compelling than the breeding of local horses.

> in some remote part of the house, they have their *stable* of Horses, such for *shape*, as they say are not in the world, and I easily beleeve it, but *unusefull* in other *Countryes*, by reason of their tender *hoofes* never used to any ground but *Sand*: They have one sort of a *peculiar* race, not a jot outwardly different

from other *Horses*, nor alwayes the *handsomest*; but they are rare; and in such esteeme, as there is an *Officer* appointed to see the *Fole*, when any of that race is *Foled*, to *Register* it, with the *colour*, and to take *testimonny* of the right brood; one of these at three years old, is o*rdinarily* sold for a *thousand peeces* of *eight*, sometimes more: the reason is because they will runne, without *eating* or *drinking* one jot, foure dayes and nights together; which some *Egyptians* wound about the body and helpt with little *meate*, and lesse *sleepe*, are able to ride: this is of infinite *consequence* upon sudden *dispatches*, to passe the wildernesse, where neither *water*, nor *grasse* is found. (p. 43)

Unfortunately Blount does not tell us more about that studbook. He may not have known whether it was an Ottoman innovation or a Mameluke tradition, but his report of a written, rather than oral, record suggests a innovative departure from local practices.[5]

Blount is no natural historian, but as an Englishman he fancies he has an eye for a horse. He is clearly both fascinated and astonished at the reported price of a breed that, considering its feet and size, appears to him to be useless elsewhere in the world. But he does provide what may be the earliest report in English that a studbook was being kept of Egyptian Arabian horses during the Ottoman period, a matter of considerable interest in itself, which also evidences a peculiarly English interest in Eastern bloodstock. Commercially, English interest in Arabian horses for breeding was negligible in the seventeenth century, although they were greatly admired. In 1609, Nicholas Morgan's *Perfection of Horsemanship* had ranked Arabians at the top of thirteen breeds, followed by Thessalians, Neapolitans and Barbs: no British breeds made it into the rankings.[6] Although Blount considered them unsuited for work in a damp climate like Britain's, the asil or thoroughbred Arabian horse was nevertheless prized for its justly celebrated stamina, and several Arabians had been introduced into Britain since the sixteenth century for cross-breeding purposes. King James kept Arabians, which Blount might have seen, but the great era of English thoroughbred breeding from Arabian stallions would follow the Restoration. Among the English, what one historian calls 'Fanaticism for the Purity of the Blood' came even later, during the eighteenth and nineteenth centuries.[7] It was this very fascination with the asil Arabian that would bring other Blounts, Wilfrid Scawen Blount and Lady Anne Blount, to Egypt nearly three centuries later in their search for horses for their Arabian stud at Crabbet Park.

From discussions with Cairo's elite, and from living in and visiting the city, Blount reports numerous other items of local interest: diseases come chiefly in the winter, like the recent plague which killed '*eighteene hundred thousand and odde*', and winter's odiferously hot southern wind, Blount notes, could keep him constipated for up to ten days at a time whenever it blew (p. 44). Historical sites abound, and 'many rarities of living creatures', including musical serpents (p. 45). Blount visited the Pyramids, rode to Thebes, and examined ancient tombs and the mummies they contained. Though wonderful, all these ancient remains led Blount to ponder the decay of empire and of ancient learning, forearmed as he was with a special interest in 'that admirable Table of Isis... lately Printed in Italy' (p. 48). Was there a spark of the ancient learning still left alive? Imitating venerable examples such as Herodotus and Julius Caesar, Blount starts by asking priests, since they are most likely to know. When the Egyptian priests prove 'utterly ignorant of all things not *Mahometan*', Blount immediately reflects, 'Nor can I wonder' (p. 49), since it seems to him that the ancient learning has been wiped out by two waves of imperialism, first the Mamelukes and now the Ottomans. As a result, Egyptians have been rendered ignorant and malicious by an uninformed priesthood engaged in promoting superstition in the service of imperial authorities. 'Thus,' he concludes, 'is all light of *Egypts* old devotion, almost quite extinct' and Ottoman authority supreme (p. 51).

In Blount's summary judgement, Ottoman rule in Egypt presents a parody of its own claims to '*Justice, Zeale, Clemency, Publique-good*, and the like' (p. 53). The Ottomans are specially rigorous in ruling over the Egyptians, believing them 'to be *malicious, treacherous*, and *effeminate*, and therefore dangerous, not fit for Armes, or any other trust' and requiring 'more frequent, and horrid executions' than anywhere else in the Ottoman Empire (pp. 51, 52). To 'breake the spirit of the People the more', the Ottomans keep Egyptians poorer than any other Muslim nation under their Empire, oppressing the poor and exploiting 'all wealthy Persons' by various forms of extortion, including lease-farming practices that keep farmers impoverished and landless: 'whereby without scandall, the nation is made *effeminate* and *disarmed*' (pp. 53, 54).

Before leaving Cairo, Blount pondered visiting the Red Sea, but went instead to some closer ruins, finding himself there briefly caught up in a sandstorm: 'this fright made us returne neerer the *Nile*, where I saw two *Crococyles* running together' (p. 56). After taking leave of his host and describing the seven tributaries of the Nile, Blount sets off on the return trip to Alexandria, intending to sail for Joppa. In Alexandria, however, plans go awry since he cannot resist doing a little snooping about, especially when he finds that access to the port 'was severely prohibited ... contrary to the usuall freedome of Turky' (p. 58). Suspecting that something valuable was being hidden, he returned the next day 'secretly' to find out what, but was spotted and 'dogg'd' by an Egyptian from the garrison, 'whose *violence* produced an accident that made me forget all my other *designes*, and flye for safety of my life'. Abandoning plans to sail for Joppa, he hurried off in 'a little French Barke, which I knew was that day, to depart for Sicily' (p. 58). Further dangers were to come as the bark barely avoided a skirmish between Maltese and Ottoman ships (p. 59). Once in Palermo, Blount took passage for Naples, and set off overland for Venice:

> where I arrived the eleventh moneth after my departure from thence: having in that time, according to the most received divisions of *Turky*, beene in *nine Kingdomes* thereof, and passed six thousand miles, and upward, most part by land. (p. 61)

The journey over, Blount turns to reflect upon what he has learned.

Empires, armies and history

> The most important parts of all States are foure, *Armes, Religion, Justice,* and *Morall Customes.*
>
> Blount, *Voyage*, p. 61

In Ottoman Egypt, Blount found the ancient Egyptian empire forgotten or in ruins, little more than pyramids and mummies in the sands. Only in the blood horses did any reminder survive of the once great Egyptian empire, now reduced to servitude if not slavery. Yet in Blount's view of imperial history, such is exactly what is bound to happen to empires founded on concealed knowledge, on superstition and false religious beliefs. This will be the general argument of the rest of his book: that the eventual weakness of the Ottoman Empire will prove to be, like that of the Egyptian empires of ancient times, the habit of concealing knowledge and thereby halting the advancement of learning in favour of superstition and orthodoxy in religion. His journey over, Blount analyses the current condition of the Ottoman Empire by developing earlier arguments about the links between imperialism and learning. Remarkably enough, he has reserved several surprising personal anecdotes to illustrate his analysis. In these and numerous other incidental details, Blount often reveals ways of thinking about empire, state and religion that reflect more on contemporary England than the Ottoman territories.

In the final section, Blount's *Voyage* moves English writing about the Ottomans from Renaissance narratives compiled from chronicles towards the new political history demanded by Bodin, Guicciardini and Bacon, a move which might be said to herald the Orientalism of the Enlightenment. In re-tuning his notes from narrative to analysis, Blount pauses long enough to recall how the intellectual basis of his enquiry aimed to be comparative and political from the start. In considering the '*Armes, Religion, Justice, and Morall Customes*' of the Ottoman Empire, Blount will not do as 'most men' who merely 'set downe what they should be' and judge 'by their owne silly *education*'. Instead, Blount promises 'in remembering the *Turkish* institutions,' that he will judge them according to only one simple rule, 'that of more, or lesse *sufficiency* to their ayme, which I suppose the *Empires* advancement' (pp. 61–2).

This focus on what is sufficient to promote imperial advance enables Blount swiftly to recall and describe the efficiency of the Ottoman military system. His facts and figures detailing the number, size and strength of Ottoman forces fielded against the Poles, it will be recalled, were especially accurate because told to Blount against his will by 'some *Timariots* in the *Army*', who thought him a spy and forced him to write it all down (p. 66). In his account of the Ottoman navy, Blount manages to pillory the Dutch for cowardice at sea (p. 74) and record 'the strangest thing' that he 'found among the Turkish Mariners', which was 'their incredible civilitie':

> I who had often proved the *Barbarisme* of other Nations at Sea, and above all others, of our owne, supposed my selfe amongst *Beares*, till by experience, I found the contrary; and that not only in ordinary civility, but with so ready service, such a patience, so sweet, and gentle a way, generally through them all, as made me doubt, whether it was a dreame, or reall; if at any time I stood in their way, or encombred their ropes, they would call me with a *Janum*, or *Benum*, termes of most affection. (p. 75)

A comic moment, this incident recalls times aboard the Black Sea fleet *en route* to Rhodes and Alexandria. These civil *'Beares'*, the sailors in question, experienced at surviving the terrifying storms of the Black Sea and keeping their temper while tripping over Englishmen tangled among the ropes, were quite likely to have been skilled Greek or Laz-speaking mariners for whom those terms of affection involved a second language. In that sense they were not really 'Turks' at all.

The Ottoman religion

> *Opinion* which moves all our *Actions*, is governed by the *Apparancy* of things, not by their *realitie*.
>
> Blount, *Voyage*, p. 78

Leaving matters military behind, Blount turns to religion but only, by his own admission, in order to treat 'the *Politicke* Institutions' (p. 77) of Islam as they affected the Ottoman state. Muhammed, he suggests, had imperial ambitions from the very start. Taking notice of other religions and their ceremonies, he founded Islam not on the worship of idols or miracles, but on the worship of the sword, 'which with more assurance commands *Mankinde*'. With strategic wisdom, Muhammed preached '*Paradice*, more then *Hell*', thus favouring *'hope* above *feare*, thereby filling the minde with good *courage*; which was much to his *Military* purpose' (p. 78). What Muhammed understood in offering a future paradise to those who lived by the sword is that 'Mens opinions are in great part, complexionall, and habituall', so it is

> no wonder to see them taken with *promises*, which to us seeme beastly, and ridiculous; they as much despise ours; and in a more *naturall* way, every thing is received, not at the rate of its owne worth, but as it agrees with the receivers *humour*; whereby their *hopes* and *feares* though false, prevailes [*sic*] as strongly as if true, and serve the *State* as effectually, because *Opinion* which moves all our *Actions*, is governed by the *Apparancy* of things, not by their *realitie*. (p. 78)

Blount is pointing to what he considers the weak moment of irrationality where Ottoman imperialism will eventually come unstuck. But he admires how Islam serves imperial interests. He is much taken with the fact that the sultan appoints religious leaders, since this 'makes the *Turkish Theology* excellently to correspond with the *State*, as depending thereon; & seemes of reason more *Politick*, then if his head *Ecclesiasticke* were of another Countrey, or otherwise *independent* upon [i.e. from] the *Prince*' (p. 79). Even so, religious differences can also interfere with state interests.

Unlike other English writers of his age who casually refer to Islam as the 'Turkish' religion and to all Muslims as 'Turks', Blount respects certain distinctions. Of the Koran he notes 'it is prohibited to be translated; which both preserves the *Arabicke* tongue, and conceales *Religion*'. As if that were not bad enough, he continues with the theoretical problem of interpretation: 'All set *Texts* are obnoxious to severall *Expositions*; thence growes *distractions*' (p. 80). Blount describes four competing Islamic sects: each interprets the Koran 'according to the *Genius* of its *Nation*; the *Tartars simply*; the *Mores* and *Arabs Superstitiously*; the *Persian ingeniously*; the *Turkes* with most *liberty*' (p. 80). Of these, only the Persians and Ottomans use religious difference as a pretext for war, and Blount notes that many 'Turks', 'in publique acknowledge the *Persians* better *Mahometans*, then themselves' (p. 81).

Blount often writes admiringly of how certain features of Islam were successfully designed to appeal to 'the minds of men'. He notices how two features of Islamic culture – polygamy and the prohibition on wine – serve imperial interests. He finds their origins in the Prophet's 'cunning' understanding that 'seconding humane inclination' is certain to make Islam attractive, hence these

> two politicke acts of the Alcoran: the one permits *Polygamie*, to make a numerous People, which is the foundation of all great *Empires*: The other pretending a divell in every grape, prohibits *wine*: thereby it hardens the Souldier, prevents disorder, and facilitates publique provision. The first as

pleasing to nature is generally received: the other is borne downe by appe-
tite, so as more drinke wine, then forbeare. (pp. 82–3)

Blount would later advocate drinking water and coffee, and while he never
seems to have approved of polygamy, he was satirically accused in 1647 – the
year of his marriage to Hester – of 'publishing an hereticall and dangerous
Doctrine, *viz. That it is better to side with and resort to common Women then ladyes
of Honour*'.[8] What later caused even greater dispute was how, in treating the
Prophet like a Renaissance prince skilled in the ways of imperial statecraft, and
in pointing to ways that state religions serve the imperial turn, Blount so far
kept clear of religious bias that he shows no special affinity for Protestant
Christianity either. This offended the Oxford historian Thomas Warton who,
writing more than a century later, makes the *Voyage* sound like a dangerous
and ungodly tract which may infect readers with enthusiasm for taking up
polygamy:

> But to say the truth, this little work is the voyage of a sceptic: it has more of
> the philosopher than the traveller, and would probably never have been
> written, but for the purpose of insinuating his religious sentiments. Yet
> his reflections are so striking and original, and so artfully interwoven with
> the thread of his adventures, that they enliven, instead of embarrassing, the
> narrative. He has the plausible art of colouring his paradoxes with the
> resemblance of truth. So little penetration had the orthodox court of Charles
> the first, that merely on the merit of this book, he was appointed one of the
> band of Pensioners. (p. 207)[9]

This was in 1780, and Warton was writing with the high-handed contempt
and prejudiced hindsight of one who has shown himself greatly offended by
the writings of Henry's son Charles, the celebrated deist, and by a short Latin
tract on the materiality of the soul posthumously published and attributed to
the traveller himself.

   In the late 1630s, the earliest readers of Blount's deft observations on Islam
may also have found themselves considering general questions of state religion
pertinent to the Church of England. If so, no one seems to have been offended
that Blount implied such questions as: Were bishops mere mouthpieces of the
King? Was the Bible interpreted simply to serve a contemporary political
agenda? Since Blount's *Voyage* was praised by a contemporary bishop for contributing to the nation's imperial mission, Warton's concern over orthodoxy
perhaps says something about episcopal authority of the time, but should also
alert us to how Blount's account of Islam announced ways of criticizing state
religion which applied to the Caroline Church of England. During the 1650s,
Blount pressed for clerical incomes to be levelled at £100. Despite Bishop

King's kind verses, Blount was no friend of the professional clergyman, what-ever his nation or sect.

Religion and the Ottoman empire

While praising the suitability of many Islamic principles for the growth of the early Ottoman Empire, Blount has been preparing to suggest there are founda-tional weaknesses too, and that these follow from a weakness common among nations based on religions that restrict reason. To Blount at least, any religion that 'seconds humane inclination' by allowing polygamy and banning wine from the public sphere so successfully works upon human 'passions' that 'rea-son' has little room or reason to flourish. Blount returns to the opening words of his book to recast his general enquiry into what we would today call the ideology of religious belief:

> Now the greatest number of men being governed by *passions*, in all *people* they have beene entertained, for the present life, with Justice; for the future, with *Religion*: yet there were ever found some few Intellectual complexions, in whom the Understanding prevayled above the Passions: those discerning wits could not receive the grosse supposals, upon which the Heathenish superstitions relyed. (p. 83)

Blount continues by listing future heavens promised by Homeric legend and Platonic speculation, but one can see why an eighteenth-century Anglican like Thomas Warton would have been offended by Blount's approach. By not insisting on the superiority of his own religion, Blount renders all religious beliefs subject to the criticism that they appeal to passionate ignorance rather than rational understanding.

However, Blount has the Ottoman case firmly in mind throughout, announ-cing 'To which purpose I have oft considered, whether *learning* is ever like to come in request among the Turkes' since they have so far allowed themselves to be ruled by passionate belief (p. 83). An entirely different kind of reason is at work among the Ottomans since they have become long accustomed to a phase of imperial expansion during which '*learning* is not admitted'. Such, he reflects, often happens at 'the beginning of *Empires*', but once imperial greatness sets in, 'sloth' and 'other *effeminacies* come in', including '*letters*' (pp. 83–4). Moreover, since the Ottoman Empire now includes countries which bred '*speculative* wits' and 'the greatest Divines, Philosophers, and Poets in the World', it seems most likely climate and marriage with local people will '*Gentilize*, and infect' Ottoman military culture 'with the ancient softnesse *naturall* to those places' (p. 84). So learning is likely to come to the Ottomans as soon as their empire settles down among the peoples it has conquered, but will meet fierce resistance from some 'as a corruption most pernicious to their *Religion*, especially the *searching* parts of *Philosophy* . . . Thereupon, the *Academy* which began to rise up at Bagadat was supprest' (p. 84).

But Blount is not at all sure what form the arrival of learning among the Ottomans would take, since he reckons that their 'Wits seeme more abstruse, and better fixt for *contemplation*' than those of the English, 'but ours more nimble and ready; so as their *discourses* are more profound; ours more superficiall, and plausible'. Having pondered the Ottomans and made all allowances for differences of what he coyly terms '*Language, Tyranny, Warre*, and *Intresse Ecclesiastique*', Blount insists that the key difference is 'this different relish and straine of our *fancy* from theirs . . . our very *Reason* differs' (p. 85), so it would be idle to speculate what impact learning might have other than to meet continued resistance from religious interests. Concerning works of charity, Blount turns unusually caustic when describing foundations such as khans, hospitals, mosques, bridges, and fountains:

> These faire works so caused, seemed to mee like daintie fruit growing out of a *Dung-hill*; but the *vertues* of *vulgar* minds are of so base a nature, as must be manured with foolish *hopes* and *feares*, as being too grosse for the finer *nutriment* of *reason*: These were the chiefe points I observed in their *Religion*. (p. 87)

So much for the Ottoman religion: suited to governing in times of imperial expansion but liable to hold back the advancement of learning, producing only dainty fruit from a general dung-hill.

Law and social customs in the Ottoman empire

Blount observes Ottoman justice, on the other hand, to be more '*Severe, Speedy*, and *Arbitrary*' than in other nations and finds it, accordingly, eminently suitable for governing an imperial state 'made up of severall People different in *Bloud, Sect*, and *Interesse*' (p. 89). Admiring the swiftness of court procedures, he offers personal instances of how '*Turkish* Justice' can prove impartially 'honourable to *Strangers*' (pp. 92–3). Since 'the *Turkish Empire* is originally composed to amplify by *warre*', the severity, speed and arbitrary nature of Ottoman civil justice are in keeping with an originary military rationale that still holds good. Blount even defends '*Sultan Murat* now reigning' for 'supposed errors' when acting in agreement with the '*violent* nature of the *Government*, wherein' Murad's acts of arbitrary violence 'are not so pernicious as the *Christians* imagine' (p. 95). Blount was not in Istanbul long enough to see Murad in action, but his point in any case would hold: terror can be an effective way to drive a militarized empire forward while keeping the people in check.

16. This engraving of a 'Curous Musical Instrument' appeared in the *Illustrated London News* (20 October 1860) from a lost original. It represents a prototype model for Dallam's organ.

Femme de l'Isle *de Malthe*

17. 'A Woman of Malta' from the first French edition of Nicolay's *Navigations* (1568), one of William Biddulph's sources, which reports on how to recognise prostitutes on several Mediterranean islands.

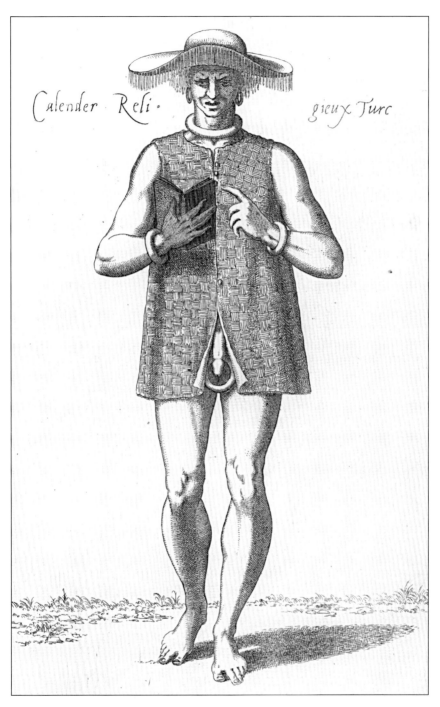

Calender Reli·   gieux Turc

18. Henry Blount reported: 'The *Calenderim* upon *Chastity*, wearing an *iron ring* through the skin of his yard; in some I have noted it capable of being taken of [*sic*] with small difficultie.' From Nicolay's *Navigations* (1568).

19. An upstairs corridor in the Khan al-Gümrük, where the European community lived, ate and slept when William Biddulph was Protestant chaplin. Aleppo souk, Syria.

20. The lower courtyard at the Khan al-Gümrük is still used for warehousing by wholesale textile merchants.

21. The Sinan Pasha Khan, An'nabk, Syria.

22. The Murad Pasha Khan, where William Biddulph and other Englishmen refused to accept free victuals, is today a museum. M'arret en Nu'man, Syria.

23. The 'Khan of the Bridegroom' is still used by local herdsmen. Qutaifah, Syria.

24. All that remains of the 'Old Castle' in 'Hassia', where William Biddulph stayed the night of 15 March 1600. Hisyah, Syria.

25. In the Khan Haramain, William Biddulph and his companions found accommodation so cheap they 'hired three chambers for our money'. Damascus souk, Syria.

26. In 'Contera', William Biddulph enjoyed strolling in the cloistered 'Bazar' among 'people of sundry Nations' happily 'assembled together from sundry places'. Quneitrah, Syria.

27. The underground house of Ananias, where Englismen once wrote their names on the walls. Bab Sharqi, Damascus.

28. Nineteenth-century view of Sir Henry Blount's house at Tittenhanger. Drawn by J. P. Neale and engraved by H. Hobson.

29. Engraved portrait of Sir Henry Blount, published 1 November 1801 by Wm. Richardson, York House, 32 Strand. The motto reads: 'Loquendum cum vulgo sentiendum cum sapientibus' (You should speak with the crowd, but perceive with the wise).

30. Tittenhanger House from the south-west. Pencil drawing dated 18 April 1832 by the topographical artist John Buckler, FSA (1770–1851).

31. Map of Henry Blount's journey, which accompanied the translation of his *Voyage* into Dutch. From *Zee-en Land Voyagie Van den Ridder Hendrik Blunt, Na da Levant*, 1737 edition.

aan peder hoek een. Wan booten staat 'er in 't , by be menschelijke gedagten / sig selven berhessen

32. A view looking eastward towards Istanbul and the Sea of Marmara along the Dardanelles. Fom *Zee-En Land* . . .

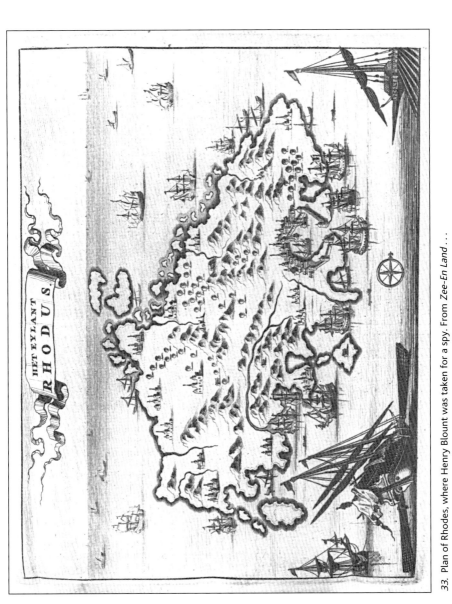

33. Plan of Rhodes, where Henry Blount was taken for a spy. From *Zee-En Land* . . .

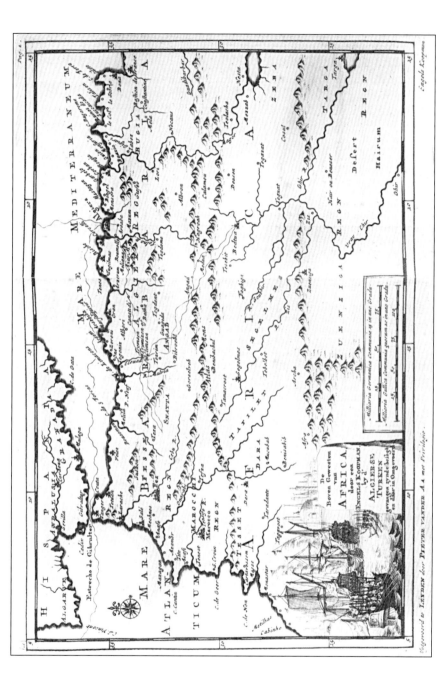

34. Map of T. S.'s journey, from *De Ongelukkiege Voyagie van Mr. T. S. Engels Koopman, Gedaan in den Jaare 1648*, 1737.

35. The slave market in Algiers, from *De Ongelukkiege Voyagie* . . .

36. Torture in Tlemcen; the brazen lion is visible in the centre. From *De Ongelukkiege Voyagie . . .*

As for the morality of the Ottomans, Blount equivocates over attributing particular qualities to any nation or race, but concedes that 'if ever any race of men were borne with *Spirits* able to beare downe the world before them, I thinke it to be the *Turke*'. He has in mind the Ottoman manner, which he calls 'magnanimous', and finds it perfectly suited to imperial rule, remorseless to those who resist, but generous to those who show them respect. Much of Blount's subsequent analysis of the Ottoman Empire depends on these key notions of imperial dignity and respect. 'I had', he exclaims, 'almost hourely *experience*' of how to deal with the well-known haughty manners of the imperial Ottomans, but 'not to weary my pen' notes only two examples. On his second day travelling in the Balkans, Blount rides ahead of the caravan and stumbles on four '*Spahi-Timariots*' who recognize him for a Christian. Blount describes how he

> stood still, till they menacing their weapons, rose, and came to me, with lookes very ugly; I smiling met them, and taking him who seemed of most port, by the hand, layed it to my forehead, which with them is the greatest signe of love, and honour, then often calling him *Saltanum*, spoke *English*, which though none of the kindest, yet gave I it such a sound, as to them who understood no further, might seeme affectionate, humble, and hearty; which so appeased them, as they made me sit and eate together, and parted loving. (p. 98)

Being confidently ingratiating worked for Dallam too, and Blount is surely right that armed Ottoman horsemen deserved respect, certainly within their own empire. Shortly after, the same soldiers encountered a 'Merchant of quality' who was 'clothed in the *Italian* fashion, and spruce'. But the merchant, failing to consider 'how the place had changed his condition', argued with the soldiers and 'stood upon his *termes*, till they with their Axes, and iron Maces (the weapons of that *Country*,) broke two of his ribs, in which case, we left him behind, halfe dead, either to get backe as he could, or be devoured of beasts' (p. 98). The merchant in question, a '*Rhagusean*', had presumably joined the caravan from Venice in Ragusa, or Dubrovnik, and would have had a journey home of only two days. Even so, Blount hardly makes travel in the Balkans sound very appealing to the faint-hearted. He follows up with a further anecdote involving threats with a knife that end with an invitation to eat and drink once the quarrel is over and Blount has performed being 'respective' (p. 99).

Blount advocates avoiding dangers among the Ottomans, and these violent episodes exemplify what he has been arguing from the start, that travellers must undertake suitable preparations, suspend customary expectations and wear suitable clothes. Hostility toward travellers 'clothed like a *Christian*', Blount learned, was 'a peece rather of *institution*, then *incivilitie*; for they desiring perpetuall *hostilitie* with the Christians, must estrange the People from their

Customes as utterly as may be' (p. 99). For the most part, Blount admired the 'Turkish Nation' and eulogizes their personal cleanliness, social institutions and diet, before returning to the dangers of travelling among them. 'The only beastly peece of injustice I found among the *Turkes*', he writes, was their habit of catching and selling any stray Christians that might come their way (p. 102). Blount knew how to stay clear of trouble when it arrived. 'I have divers times beene put to defend my selfe with my *Knife*,' he confesses, 'from being shoved into houses, by those who would have kept me slave' (p. 102). But his main defence against 'the worst part of my danger' was 'two wayes of prevention' (p. 103), which turn out to be representing himself as too poor to warrant seizing for ransom, while at the same employing paid protectors and spies. By handing out wine and cash, he writes: 'I ever kept in secret pension some of the *Caravan* who understood the *language*' and 'in each place of abode, I acquainted my selfe with some *Renegadoe*, whose story after he had delivered, I knew how to make him so much my friend, as in case of danger, would have helpt me to flye, or conceale: herein was the most expence, and unquiet of my voyage' (p. 103). Whether it was the threat of danger or the cost of protection that caused Blount unquiet remains unclear.

Otherwise, Blount writes favourably about social life inside the Ottoman Empire. From mixing with locals, he has learned that Anatolian shepherds with no taxes to pay are reputed to live so exceptionally well that 'their quiet, and plentie' must not be 'published among the adjoyning *Christians*' (p. 104), who would immediately change sides from self-interest. He quietly admires severe punishments for public drunkenness and offers a short disquisition on coffee and how it is prepared and drunk, showing how coffee-house culture provides 'a harmlesse entertainment of good fellowship', unlike the ale-houses and taverns of England (p. 105). He finds Turkish music a mystery worthy of investigation. Declaring 'through all those vaste Dominions, there runnes one tune' but no musician 'can play the same twice over,' Blount sometimes felt the need to 'experiment':

> I have ventured to play at divers meetings, pretending the ayers of my countrey, to note whether they had skill or no, and tooke so well as they have often made me play againe; then I found their skill and mine alike, for I never understood the least touch of any instrument. (p. 106)

Perhaps they were too amused by the spectacle not to ask for an encore. But Blount clearly found the matter troublesome since it disturbed his sense of how to understand people: 'Nothing could more disguise their *Genius* unto me, who was used to guesse at the *fansies* of men by the *ayres* wherewith I found them most taken, almost as much as by their discourse' (p. 106).

Otherwise he observes that manners are formal, sometimes extreme, and involve dignity and respect. Jealousy he notes to be a characteristic feature, 'wherein a *Turke* exceeds an *Italian*' (p. 106). Men may divorce their wives, while a wife may seek divorce only on grounds that 'her husband would abuse her against nature' (p. 107). While beggars are few because food is abundant, there are the '*Santones* who are able cunning *Rogues*' and resemble 'our Tom of *Bedlams*' though they *act* in a more *grave, sublime*, and *meeke* way than ours' which may be why they are respected (p. 107). Greetings are courteous, while conversation shows them 'free from that rudenesse, whereof they are accused' (p. 107). Funerary monuments demonstrate respect for the ancestral dead.

In part because of that very imperiousness of manner which testifies they have achieved that 'vanity of Nations, to esteeme themselves civeller, and more ingenious' than all other nations, Blount concludes by condemning the Ottoman Empire to the ways of past empires. He argues that by keeping the Ottomans on military alert, only two great enemies, the Christians and the Persians, prevent a collapse into vice and corruption which would be worse than that of Rome 'for then it would have a farre greater Empire than ever the *Roman* was' (p. 108). If the Christian and Persian threats were ever 'removed', Blount is in no doubt that the Ottoman Empire 'would soone corrupt' from belief in its own supremacy:

> thus of old, the *Ægyptians* despised the *Grecians*, they the *Romanes*; the *Romanes* all the World; and at this day the *Papists* us; the *Jewes* them; the *Mahometans* all. (pp. 108–9)

So, Blount would have us believe, it will be with the Ottomans if ever their massive empire were no longer to face great antagonists.

Sects and subject nations

> After this discourse of the party imperiall, I must not forget those other Sects which it has in its subjection.
>
> Blount, *Voyage*, p. 109

How does the mixing of nations and religions work under the Ottomans? For Blount, the Christians living under Ottoman rule, whether '*Latines, Armenians, Greekes*, or of another sort' were treacherous, divisive and best avoided (p. 109). They are repressed by the Ottomans, not by being banned, but by a policy of tolerant immiseration that renders them 'poore, wretched, taxed, disgraced, deprived of their children, and subject to the insolence of every Raschall' (p. 110). Many, in consequence, convert to Islam, but greater respect is accorded to 'Convertites' who are 'serious, voluntary, and Persons of important condition'

(p. 111). By frequently talking with renegades, Blount found most who converted voluntarily to be atheists who were simply interested in improving their living conditions, with no special hatred towards Christians, except those who revile them for apostasy. 'Then take heed,' Blount warns, 'for in your ruine they get both revenge, and reputation of zeale' (p. 112).

Among involuntary converts, the desire for revenge could be even fiercer, as in the story Blount tells of a 'Eunuch of the Garrison of *Belgrade*'. One of those spies Blount had paid to keep an eye out on his behalf, he lived in a house by the Danube where Blount found him one evening, 'alone very drunke'. In this condition, he 'fell to rayle against the *Turkes*' and admitted that nearly every week for the past six months he had taken his revenge on the Ottomans for the way they had 'marred his game'. Pointing to the river, the Eunuch of Belgrade announced that, he had 'throwne some of their children therein, and told mee that formerly in other places, hee had done many such secret revenges, for their gelding of him' (p. 113). After meetings with such men, Blount abandoned any former thoughts that Islam attracted converts by promising paradise. Instead, he observed that they were persuaded 'manifestly with respects worldly, wherefore seeing how many daily goe from us to them, and how few of theirs to us; it appeares of what consequence the prosperity of a cause is to draw men unto it' (p. 113).

Of other nations subject to Ottoman rule, Blount writes, 'the chiefe Sect whereof I desired to be enformed, was the *Jewes*; whose moderne condition is more condemned, then understood by *Christian*-writers, and therefore by them delivered with such a zealous ignorance, as never gave me satisfaction' (p. 113). Although better informed than Biddulph, Blount's account of the Jews is no less hostile. He repeats the theory of racial decay, of how a race of *'primitive'* Jewish shepherds were corrupted by 'frequent Captivities' and rendered 'from their old innocence' into what they are today, 'Merchants, Brokers, and Cheaters' (pp. 113, 114). The change was also brought about by 'no small necessitie from their Religion', which sets them apart and 'renders them more generally odious' (p. 114). Survival under such conditions means that 'they are generally found the most nimble, and Mercuriall wits in the world', for which reason Jews are employed throughout the Ottoman Empire as advisers (pp. 114–15).

Beyond admiring their knowledge of local history, Blount was personally unimpressed by the Jews with whom he spoke. His report of what must have been a lengthy conversation with a 'principall of the *Synagogue* at *Sophya*' begins by detailing the rabbi's 'malice' towards and wilful misunderstanding of Christians and Christianity (pp. 115–16). From the same source, Blount asked for and obtained a rudimentary account of the Cabbala which, he writes, 'I had alwayes held the great secret of the *Jewes*; I demanded whether it consisted in that *Arithmeticall* signification of *letters* as we suppose' (p. 116). 'In part,' came the answer, but only in Hebrew. Then the rabbi 'added the story of it; telling me that *Caball* signifies *tradition'* (pp. 116–17). Revealed four times since Adam, knowledge of the tradition was last given to Esdras. 'When I considered this Art,' Blount comments, 'it put me in mind of what the Prophet sayes to the Church of Israel – *Thy habitation is in the midst of deceivers'* (p. 118, citing Jeremiah 9:6). One of the few times Blount alludes to the Old Testament, this instance serves to condemn Jewish belief in the words of a Jewish prophet. Sceptical of all superstitious beliefs, Blount considered 'this devise of *Caball'* to have been

> well framed to take with the *Jewes*, who generally are light, ayeriall, and fanaticall braines, spirited much like our hot *Apocalyps* men, or fierce expounders of *Daniel*, apt to worke themselves into the fooles Paradise of a sublime dotage. (p. 119)

Although Blount held all superstitious beliefs in similar contempt, his conclusion that Jews were characteristically responsive to fanatical beliefs indicates the limitations of his empirical and experiential method. While lacking in Biddulph's overt malice, Blount's account of the Jews confirmed received opinion rather more often than otherwise. By blending rumour with description, he seems to affirm the truth of both: Jews are particularly lascivious, and 'suffer no women to enter the Synagogue' (pp. 120, 122). Like his summary assessments of Armenians, Greeks, Arabs, Moors and other groups, Blount's report of what he understood from personal encounters among a small number of witnesses is clearly limited. His version of Jewish history, a tale of lost nomadic innocence decayed into avaricious fanaticism, fits rather too neatly with his general thoughts on the history of nations and empires. He dismisses the possibility of a Jewish state ever arising from two major causes, 'beside the many disadvantages in their *Religion*':

> First the *Jewish* complexion is so prodigiously *timide*, as cannot be capable of Armes...the other impediment is their extreme corrupt love to private interesse; which is notorious in the continuall cheating and malice among themselves; so as there would want that justice, and respect to common benefit, without which no civil societie can stand. (p. 123)

Given Blount's general theories of nations and empires, this is just what he was most prone to think, given whom he was likely to have met and talked with. He ends his account of the Jews with a valediction: 'These are the chiefe notes which I gathered in conversing with the *Jewes*' (p. 123), which may indicate why his view is so prejudiced, but barely explains why, at the beginning of the book, he announced a special interest in seeing the Jews under Ottoman rule.

Of the gypsies, or 'Zinganaes', Blount has little to say beyond describing their poverty: 'their habitation is hovels, and poore houses in the suburbs, contempt secures them, and with that, I leave them' (p. 124). The book is about to end and he is eager to offer some final statements.

First, of 'the *Turkish* Empire', Blount considers it a 'sweet *Monarchy*' to the '*Turkes*', but a heavy burden to 'other Sects' (p. 124). Next, of the sultan: he seems to rule without the inconveniences of being a tyrant or an elected 'civill Prince... wherefore he seemes absolute as a Tyrant, as happy as a King; and more establisht then either' (p. 124). The stability of Ottoman rule has been shown by the rule of 'five weake Princes' without disruption or disorder (p. 125), while the current Sultan Murad IV 'is of Spirit like to equall the bravest of his predecessors' (p. 125). The problem facing Murad, in addition to Persian armies to the east, is the Janissary corps which recently showed itself capable of deposing and executing his immediate predecessor, Osman II. According to Blount, it was all Ahmed I's fault for allowing his brother, Mustapha, to live and become a pretender to the throne instead of dispatching him according to Ottoman habit. In Mustapha, the 'insolent' Janissaries found a candidate of the 'line' suited to replace Osman once he had been executed. By allowing Mustapha to live, Ahmed thus gave the Janissaries 'occasion to taste the Bloud Royall, whose reverence can never be restored, without abolishing the order of *Janizaryes*, which hath beene the Sword hand of the *Empyre*' (p. 126). And that, to Blount, is the predicament facing Murad, an armed soldiery with experience of killing heads of state. Having established that he can be more bloody than his army, Murad has shown himself to have the right 'spirit' but, 'by reason of his age... hath not yet put into action' the bravery of which he must prove himself capable (p. 125).

For the nonce, Blount ends by returning to Ahmed and declaring that his action, in allowing Mustapha to live, was a 'vertue' and indeed 'a high one', but a virtue that might not be appropriate 'in such a feirce *Government*'. 'Thus,' Blount concludes:

> have I set downe what I noted in the *Turkish* Customes; all instruct, either as errors, or by imitation: Nor is the minde of man a perfect paradice, unlesse there be planted in it the Tree of *Knowledge* both of *Good*, and *Evill*. (p. 126)

He ends not with a bang but with a sop to the moral censors, if any were attending.

Bishop King claimed that Blount's *Voyage* transformed travel writing from gossip into useable knowledge for future travellers. The volume's reprint history indicates its sustained importance. Though partly cast in the form of a personal travel narrative, Blount's *Voyage* may also be said to have helped transform Ottoman historiography in English. Coming after Knolles' *General History* and before Paul Rycaut's *Present State*, Blount's *Voyage* demonstrated the need for serious analysis of the Ottomans based on extended personal experience as well as sound Baconian methods.

Part IV

'T.S.' in Captivity: North African Slavery, 1648–70

15
The *Adventures* of 'Mr. T.S.' and Restoration England

> Little is known even now of the history of Algeria under the Turks; it is a period which has not aroused much interest.
>
> Marcel Colombe, *Encyclopedia of Islam*, 1960[1]

A tale of five years captivity set in Algeria on the western limit of the Ottoman Empire, *The Adventures of (Mr T.S.) An English Merchant, Taken Prisoner by the Turks of Argiers* (1670) presents several enigmas, which make it an ideal work with which to end. I want not only to complete but also to complicate this study, since to do so shows how, by the late seventeenth century, narratives of travelling into the Ottoman Empire had entered into that murky mix of fact and fiction from which would emerge the novel. Some of the incidents reported here doubtless took place, while certain descriptive passages could have been written only by, or with the advice of, someone who had visited Ottoman Algeria. Yet there is as much of fiction as there is of fact in T.S.'s adventures, such that several pages detailing some of the more spectacular episodes were reprinted as if they were the 'adventures' of another English captive, this time known only as 'R.D.' A brief quarto pamphlet, *A True Relation of the Adventures of Mr. R.D. an English Merchant, Taken by the Turks of Argeir in 1666* appeared in 1672, shortly after the English admiral Sir Edward Spragge attacked an Algerine fleet moored at Bugia and obtained articles of peace with the Dey.[2]

Who was 'T.S.'?

The identity of 'Mr T.S.' remains entirely obscure. A prefatory epistle draws attention to the fact by insisting, 'My Name will be useless to the Judicious Reader' (p. 4). Although the intitials 'T.S.' have sometimes been identified as those of 'Thomas Smith', I have found no authority for this attribution which would, in any case, help little, since the name is too common to be traced with any certainty from the few biographical details supplied in the narrative.[3]

The names of other Englishmen appearing in the book do not help establish its authorship or authenticity. Richard Norris, an 'Industrious and Experienced Seaman', is named as author of a short treatise on tides in the Western Mediterranean which appears at the end of the book (p. 247), but of Norris I can find no further account. The title-page informs us that A. Roberts edited the author's work and that Moses Pitt printed and sold *The Adventures* from Little Britain.[4] The editor Roberts opens the volume by dedicating 'the *Memoires* of our Deceased Friend' to Thomas Manley 'Esquire,' who can attest to 'the integrity of the AUTHOR' (sigs A2, A2v–A3) and hence the reliability of the narrative. Roberts observes that while readers who 'have seen nothing but their Cradle' might dismiss the book as 'a well humoured *Romance*', Manley's name guarantees its veracity. Unfortunately, knowing whether this witness to truth might be the same Thomas Manley who, in 1652, translated a Latin poem praising Oliver Cromwell, as well as 'the whole booke of Job...into heroicall verse, metaphrastically',[5] would not help clarify the identity of T.S. or the truth claims of his memoir. That I have been unable to find any clear evidence concerning who T.S. might have been means only that I have failed to find it, and not that the identity and story are entirely fictitious. However, Roberts must have had his reasons for alerting readers that some would doubt the authenticity of what they would find in these pages.

Restoration romance?

The book is most likely to be historically based fiction of the kind associated with Aphra Behn and Daniel Defoe. *The Adventures* is evidently not entirely imaginary, since it does describe real places as well as customs, architecture, flora, fauna, landscapes and features of life in Algeria that can be confirmed by contemporary reports. Yet as the editor Roberts understood only too well, the book might attract readers by promising something new and unusual. 'Two or three Passages look like Miracles', he notices, but even they could be confirmed by reports from unspecified 'Merchants and Travellers, that have seen in those parts the things related' (sigs A3–A3v), a claim repeated almost word for word by R.D.[6] How readers are supposed to find one of these witnesses remains unclear.

Roberts' short prefatory epistle is too anxious that readers should believe every detail to be entirely convincing. Challenging readers by stretching plausibility is too common a feature of travel writing, and of captivity narratives especially, to require such protests unless the editor is seeking to attract readers by insinuation. Roberts' claim that *The Adventures* may be mistaken for a 'Romance' by those who 'have seen nothing but their Cradle' addresses itself to sophisticated readers who feel themselves to be too knowing, too worldly, indeed too mature, to make such an infantile error. Yet announcing that the book could be mistaken for a romance helps to hook readers looking for something more than another story of surviving Algerian captivity.

In generic terms, this tale of a physically irresistible young man's sexual adventures among Maghrebian women might more accurately be called a picaresque than a romance. Towards the end of the book T.S. announces: 'Had my design been to make Conquests in the Empire of Love, I think none could have been more happy' (pp. 213–14). But by this point in the tale, the declaration is a weary one. By now our hero has been worn out, being the constant object of desire among a variety of women – married, widowed, rich. All of them, in various ways, have helped him rise among the ranks of slaves, but he has tired of the sport and longs to see 'again my Native Soil' (p. 217). Several escapades and liaisons later, T.S. cannot help but pronounce himself fatigued by inhabiting his too, too desirable flesh. 'I was once so troubled with addresses,' he mourns, 'that I wished my Face had been disfigured, my stature more contemptible, and that all the promising Characters of my person had never appeared in me' (p. 223). Such rakish gesturing is entirely in keeping with the bawdy tastes of contemporary readers caught up in the 'deluge of libertinism' sweeping England at the time,[7] but this is not the only reason to think that the book was crafted to fit Restoration literary tastes.

Published exactly ten years after the Restoration when Charles II made licentious behaviour fashionable, *The Adventures* provides a palimpsest of elements popular with Restoration readers. Purporting to take place between 1648 and 1652 – years that saw the execution of Charles I and the ascendancy of Oliver Cromwell – *The Adventures* tells of a fate-tossed English hero who returns from foreign parts with an education in the ways of the world. Besides proving irresistibly attractive to women, the hero possesses personal courage and ingenuity that earn him the position of chief adviser to the Ottoman governor of Tlemcen, on the border between the regency of Algeria and the kingdom of Morocco. His services advising and negotiating on behalf of Ottoman interests, together with his pimping for the governor, are eventually rewarded by considerable wealth and the freedom to return to England. For this remarkable Englishman, captive exile proves to be not only a test of Christian fortitude, but also an education in diplomacy and imperial management. Royalist writers had been making similar claims regarding Charles II since 1660, translating his years of exile in foreign courts, following the battle of Worcester (1651), into a period of schooling, a Grand Tour that enabled him to increase British trade, power and prestige abroad.[8] The argument that travel, even exile, provided an education in imperial politics preceded Charles, who was regularly compared in this respect with Aeneas. In 1662, the marriage settlement between Charles II and Catherine of Braganza brought England its first African colony, Tangier, stimulating interest in the adjacent port of Algiers. While *The Adventures* offers nothing like a political allegory, it nevertheless offers a narrative pattern remarkably suited to the nationalist fantasies of its historical moment.

Completing a circuit of the Mediterranean by taking us to the western edge of the Ottoman Empire, where the sultan's power was stretched to its limits and where captive slavery was not an uncommon experience, *The Adventures*, occupying as it does the border between fact and literary fiction, marks an important moment in the historical development of writing about the Ottoman Empire.

Imperial envy

Curiously enough – and it is perhaps more coincidence than significant enigma – I discovered quite late in the writing of this book that *Die Wijd-Beroemde Voyagien Der Engelsen In Twee Deelen*, containing the second edition of the illustrated Dutch translation of Henry Blount's *Voyage*, immediately followed it with 'De Ongelukkiege Voyagie van Mr. T. S. Engels Koopman, Gedaan in den Jaare 1648, en vergolgens', complete with a translation of Roberts' letter to Manley, a map and imaginary scenes of the slave market and Algerian justice. Delighted to have found near-contemporary illustrations for my book, I was also struck by the possibility that a common logic for selecting T.S.'s *Adventures* to follow Blount's *Voyage* might have governed both the Dutch editor's decision and my own. Unfortunately, he has left no clues to his rationale.

For my own part, I want to follow how, decades later, when the English were seriously pursuing imperial ambitions in the East, Blount's interests in the operations of Ottoman imperialism took different form with different emphases. T.S., far from being 'Ongelukkiege' or misfortunate, ends his Algerian adventures a wealthy man, whose services to an important Ottoman official had been richly rewarded. Unlike Blount, who went to observe for himself how the Ottomans ran their empire, T.S. claims to have entered the Ottoman administrative elite, helping them to govern the empire's sensitive border with the kingdom of Morocco. I can only speculate that it is because putting these two works together so neatly illustrates major developments in imperial ideology during the second half of the seventeenth century that that this pairing also appealed to a European editor working closer to the events.

I have quoted throughout from the first English edition: 'The Adventures of (Mr. *T.S.*) An English Merchant, Taken Prisoner by the *Turks* of *Argiers*, And carried into the Inland Countries of Africa: With a Description of the Kingdom of *Argiers*, of all the Towns and Places of Note thereabouts. Whereunto is added a Relation of the Chief Commodities of the Countrey, and of the Actions and Manners of the People. Written first by the Author, and fitted for the Publick view by *A. Roberts*. Whereunto is annex'd an Observation of the Tide, and how to turn a Ship out of the *Straights Mouth* the Wind being Westerly; by *Richard Norris*. *London*, Printed, and are to be Sold by *Moses Pitt* at the *White Hart* in *Little Britain*, 1670.'

16
Captive Agency

...and providence their guide.

John Milton, *Paradise Lost* (1673), 12: 647

Dallam travelled to imperial Istanbul and became caught up in diplomatic negotiations. In the Ottoman Levant, Biddulph intrigued among the expatriates and survived the contagions of Catholicism when visiting Jerusalem. Blount travelled through the Balkans and to Egypt to see for himself how the Ottomans ruled. T.S. claims to have set out to make money and earn a reputation as a traveller: he got no further than Algeria, and his name failed to survive.

Where Blount suspends prejudice and belief in order to establish knowledge of the Ottomans based on direct observation, *The Adventures* immediately invokes traditional religious conceptions in order to explain how providence guided this English captive to become an important agent of Ottoman imperialism. The difference is partly a question of form – they are different kinds of travel writing. But more importantly, I think, the difference also signifies changes in English attitudes towards the Ottomans, towards the world and towards themselves, which were taking place between the 1630s and the 1660s. Providentialist explanations for the rise of the ungodly Ottoman Empire remained on the agenda, as we saw from Bishop King's poem to Blount, but they already belonged to an older way of thinking that Blount was keenly eager to challenge in the name of the new scientific method. At the Restoration, traditionalist belief in providence took on a new life, not only to explain away details of the King's exile, but also to herald his return as the dawn of English global power. John Dryden was not alone in declaring Charles the new Augustus who promised a new age of English imperialism.

Far from following the ambitions of Blount's Baconian enquiry, *The Adventures* returns to the pre-Enlightenment Christian supernaturalism characterized by Edward Said as the strategy most often employed to legitimate, and indeed naturalize, the sense that Britons should, and soon would, rule not just the waves, but other people's empires for them too.[1] New ideas are seldom the best way to advance ideological and political programmes, so it is hardly surprising that the imperial ambitions of the Restoration should be justified, as they were by this story of captivity, in terms of a providential theory of history which, though mysterious at times, insists upon the existence of a divine plan.[2] The appearance of Paul Rycaut's *Present State* in the late 1660s indicates how Restoration interest in the Ottoman Empire sustained developments in the serious understanding of that empire in the manner initiated by Blount, combining analytical method with knowledge gained from firsthand experience. But *The Adventures* points to another specifically literary direction in which English interests in the East, the Mediterranean, the Ottomans, and indeed the entire world, were heading: the rise of the novel.

The case of Samson Rowlie

One feature that doubtless helped make many tales of captivity in the Maghrebian regencies of the Ottoman Empire so popular with English readers was the hero's eventual success in overcoming the most extreme of adverse circumstances and living to tell the tale. Regularly adopting features of spiritual autobiography and providentialist allegory, accounts of rescue and escape from Islamic slavery invariably projected nationalist ideals through the representative heroism of a captive who survived. As Linda Colley has observed, captivity narratives need 'to be read and interpreted in a wider English and global context' because they 'were never simply stories about individuals under stress, but commentaries on, and by-products of changing power relations over time'.[3] What this means is that the form itself, the narrative of captivity, has a precise and definite history, with specific, if historically variable, conventions that helped shape the personal experience of captivity as well as its literary representation.

   That T.S. cannot be identified does not mean that well-documented examples of captive agency among enslaved Englishmen in Algeria cannot be found.[4] The best example is Samson Rowlie, who rose to great power and influence among the Ottoman military-administrative elite in Algeria.[5] Unlike T.S., the historical Rowlie did not leave a text describing his life and times. He is known primarily from a watercolour portrait made in about 1588 and from diplomatic letters published by Richard Hakluyt in the *Navigations*. Despite the different kinds of evidence, the comparison proves instructive because both these Englishmen are represented as identifying with the Ottoman imperial administration in Algeria rather than with any of their fellow countrymen or with any native peoples. Both are shown to have overcome their enslavement by bonding with their imperial captors rather than with the oppressed local population. Instead of finding common cause with others similarly struggling against Ottoman power, both Rowlie and T.S. entered the administrative ranks. It seems that to be English in the Ottoman Maghreb was not only to be from somewhere else, but to act as an imperial agent collaborating in the running of a global empire.

Taken from a German traveller's picture book of 1588, the portrait of Rowlie shows him in full Ottoman garb, an Englishman performing East. He is, we might say, acting the part of Assan Aga, Eunuch and Treasurer to Uluç Hassan, Ottoman Beylerbey of Algiers.[6] Judging by the opulence of his robes and the dignity and authority suggested by the gilt throne on which he relaxes, Rowlie has done rather well for himself. His pose and smiling expression suggest a man happy and healthy amidst the comforts and responsibilities of his position. Despite captivity and, we must presume, castration, wearing the white turban of a convert to Islam has provided this merchant's son with status, political influence and access to wealth unimaginable at home. Nabil Matar rightly insists that we keep in mind just how attractive life in the Islamic Mediterranean was for many classes of Englishmen, even those taken against their will.[7] For Rowlie, performing East, 'turning Turk', wearing local costume and becoming a eunuch were not choices exactly, but transformations under pressure of cata-strophic circumstances – piracy, captivity, slavery.

In spite of his conversion, Rowlie continued to be regarded by the English ambassador as a fellow Englishman who could be called upon to do his duty by other Englishmen who were victims of piratical predation. Readers of Hakluyt's *Navigations* also met Rowlie in this role of inadvertent diplomat, performing East perhaps less colourfully but in more detail than in the portrait. From Hakluyt, ever interested in celebrating English power abroad, readers could learn that Rowlie had become the most influential Englishman in the Ottoman regency of Algiers, having the direct ear of the 'king'. In 1577, Francis Rowlie, a merchant from Bristol, and his son, portentously christened Samson, had been aboard the *Swallow* when she was seized; her crew and passengers were all taken captive to Algiers.[8] Three years later, the English signed trading capitulations with the Ottoman sultan and appointed an ambassador, William Harborne, to be resident in Istanbul. Among his duties was to intercede on behalf of English captives within the Ottoman sphere of influence. Hakluyt includes a letter from Harborne dated March 1585, eight years after the *Swallow* was taken, insisting that John Tipton, the English consul in Algiers, do something about releasing English prisoners still being held there.[9] Harborne includes the names of three men captured on the *Swallow*: 'Rich. Crawford, Anthony Elvers, Wil. Rainolds'. Hakluyt also published Harborne's subsequent letter written a year later; dated 28 June 1586, it seeks the release of yet another English prisoner, one William Hamore. This time, however, Harborne bypassed the consul Tipton – whom John Sanderson called 'a wicked athiesticall knave'[10] – and addressed himself directly to one 'Assan Aga, Eunuch & Treasurer to Hassan Bassa king of Alger, which Assan Aga was the sonne of Fran. Rowlie of Bristow merchant, taken in the Swallow' – thus Hakluyt's text.[11]

Details remain unclear of how the captured Samson came to occupy 'an office of great trust and importance as the Beglerbeg of Algiers' Treasurer'.[12] For a provincial Ottoman governor to imitate the Ottoman devşirme by promoting a promising and intelligent captured English boy would not be unusual, particularly in Algeria at a time when, as Tal Shuval has argued, the Ottoman elite regularly recruited its members from outside the country.[13] As for Rowlie's influence, Harborne deemed him powerful enough to persuade his master to release an English prisoner. 'I am inforced by duetie to God & her majesty,' Harborne wrote, 'as also by the smal regard your master had of the Grand Signors former commandements, to complaine unto him.' Comparing him with the Ottoman sultan himself, Harborne further flatters Assan Aga by expressing confidence in his influence, writing: 'by your means, he will not contrary this second commandment.'[14]

Both the portrait and Hakluyt's account insist that the price Rowlie paid for wealth and power was his biological manhood, though few renegades and captives were castrated. Although the face in the portrait is no more feminized than others by the artist of this collection, the sloping shoulders make no concessions to virility. The artist shows Rowlie slouching in a negligent way, while the flow of his skirts across his leg and over the groin seems to invite the eye to picture absence. Being a eunuch, even if in official title only, removes Rowlie from the settled certainties of heterosexuality and opens up speculative possibilities. To be a eunuch after all meant being allowed to do something that ordinary men were forbidden to do: enter the harem. What he could not do, presumably, was take advantage of the potential pleasures to which he had admittance or to father children. Here Rowlie parts company with T.S., whose first-person autobiography claims that he managed to achieve both. Avoiding paying the price that Rowlie paid, T.S. invites readers to imagine those very heterosexual possibilities denied to Rowlie, but available to an English captive who endured slavery without 'turning Turk' or enduring castration.

17
For the Vainglory of Being a 'Traveller'

> They left me an Estate which might have obliged me to reside at
> home, had not the desire of seeing Foreign Places, and the vain-glory
> of being named a Traveller, with my Masters Commands, forced me
> abroad.
>
> T.S., *Adventures*, p. 5

Captive agency, which for Rowlie was a fact of life, for T.S. was a providential
achievement, a blessing only partly deserved. While the opening words of
Blount's *Voyage* narrowed its readership down to those of an 'Intellectual Complexion' interested in considering the need to see beyond traditional ideas, the
first paragraph of *The Adventures* offers a conventional discussion of how 'Gods
Providence' governs historical events. Biblical and historical examples are cited
to illustrate how the unknown workings of the divine and mysterious plan
raise some 'from a Cottage to a Throne', while tumbling 'others down to the
most despicable condition'. We are invited to recall how 'A proud *Bajazet* who
makes the World bow to his Scepter, serves many times for a Footstool to his
Enemy' (pp. 1–3). Having reformulated commonplaces regarding providence,
the authorial 'I' reappears in the second paragraph only to back off from offering
further explanations of 'the Reasons and secret Actings of Gods Providence'
since that is the 'business of a Divine, and not of one whose Profession is to
Trade' (p. 3). Instead of testing received opinion in order to further knowledge,
The Adventures aims to illustrate the mysterious workings of providence
through the author's life story. And in many ways that is exactly what the book
achieves. However, in common with other captivity narratives of the time,
both autobiographical and fictional, the very conventionality of the providential
argument in T.S.'s narrative constitutes pious packaging for other designs and
purposes.

Right from the start, T.S. experiences slavery as a gender crisis, a problem
of adopting to unfamiliar roles that call his masculinity into question. The

opening pages place T.S. in a number of subordinate, passive and sometimes effeminized positions from which he invariably emerges triumphant. As we might have anticipated, he claims to be publishing his 'Observations' only at the request of 'Some of my Friends' (p. 3), and keeps his name hidden since it 'will be useless to the Judicious Reader'. He characterizes himself further as a younger son, passively constructed as one 'first designed for a Scholar' until an imperious teacher 'gave me such an aversion for Learning, which formerly I esteemed, that I could not endure the sight of a Book' (p. 4). Rebelling against further education, T.S. enters a five-year apprenticeship to a London merchant, leaving him prey to forces outside his control. His apprenticeship in London ends with a curious coincidence of events 'in the Year 1648' when his master appoints T.S. factor to Izmir, 'my Father dies, and my Elder Brother was kill'd in our unhappy Troubles', leaving him free to indulge his 'desire of seeing Foreign Places' and pursue 'the vain-glory of being named a Traveller,' an indulgence he will later regret (pp. 4–5).

T.S. is the first of the travellers considered here who felt the need to offer this kind of autobiographical reflection on his birth, education and family as motive for travel. While other providentialist captivity narratives, such as William Okeley's *Eben-ezer, or, A Small Monument* of *Great Mercy* (1675), included such details along the way, this structure of establishing, from the beginning, an authorial persona whose circumstances of family and class background made travel desirable or necessary, shows us a key convention of the early English novel in the making; one later to be much practised and developed by Daniel Defoe in *Robinson Crusoe* (1719) and *Moll Flanders* (1722). In the manner of Defoe's fictitious narrators, T.S. was from birth destined to travel.

Captured by 'Turks'

Following his first moment of self-assertion and muted oedipal rebellion, T.S. begins assuming more active, dominant, heroic and emphatically manly roles. At the same time, he continues to be tossed back and forth by superior, potentially hostile, but invariably providential powers, such as winds and 'Turks', until he lands in Algeria and is sold into slavery. From that point on, his story becomes not simply one of steady redemption despite setbacks, but of achieving unimaginable power and wealth while engaging in an astonishing number and variety of sexual 'adventures'.

Circumstances having conspired to leave him the head of his family, T.S. takes control of his future by rashly selling off part of his inherited estate in order to set himself up with trading goods of his own: 'With this and some Goods belonging to my Master' he set sail from London in July 1648 aboard the *Sancta Maria* of Hamburg. Initially, fair winds favoured them and they crossed the Bay of Biscay without incident, reaching Cape St Vincent in twenty days.

But crossing the Bay of Cadiz, the sight of 'two Ships to Windwards, making all sail to come up with us' brought consternation, confusion and fear aboard the Protestant ship. 'Many idle Conjectures did spread amongst us,' T.S. reports, as to whether they were French, 'Turks' or 'Ostenders' (p. 6). Once the predators hoisted a French flag and 'commanded us to strike Sail', some aboard immediately recognized the 'Tricks of Pirates', but the 'giddy headed Skipper' ignored them and followed his own 'Design which we never could well understand' (p. 7).

Pious readers might here wish to consider the analogy between the captain's inscrutable behaviour and the mysterious workings of divine providence – an interpretation entirely in keeping with the purported frame of the story. But T.S. does not pause to draw the analogy; rather, he rushes into the thick of things as soon as it is discovered that the two Men of War are indeed 'Turks': 'Then began our Skipper to be amazed, our Company to be frighted, and every one to bestir himself' (p. 8).

In these early pages at least, narrative excitement interferes with, but never quite overwhelms, the illustration of how providential design operates behind the scenes. To build suspense, T.S. pauses before describing the bloodthirsty battle. First, he tells the amazing tale of how a disabled mariner suddenly overcame his gout and proved able to 'handle the Guns as if nothing had ever ailed him', and then describes preparations to fight: 'We had then aboard about a hundred Men with the Passengers of several Nations, and thirty great Pieces of Ordnance, with other smaller Guns' (p. 8). The battle, when it comes, lasts for four hours of bloody violence, demonstrating such heroic determination among 'Our men' that some of them miraculously continued to fight even after they had been seriously mangled and, in some surreal instances, after they had been killed:

> Our men behaved themselves gallantly; neither Death nor Wounds could force them from their Charge and Posts. Some when their Limbs were all bruised, their Bones shattered, and their Bodies torn with Splinters, did obstinately continue to handle and manage the Guns. (p. 9)

But all to no avail. When providence drives events, even the dead who heroically man their posts cannot prevent the 'Turkish' victory. In the end, only eighteen will survive and be taken as slaves into Algiers, including our narrator whose reputation for having fought so bravely increases his market value.

Providential reflections en route to slavery

From these initial self-representations, T.S. emerges with all the marks of a new kind of national hero, one that Defoe would popularize in Crusoe, and that Swift would brutally satirize in Gulliver. T.S. is at once upwardly mobile, prey to family circumstances that led him to sea and providentially fortunate throughout. He figures for us, like Crusoe, the fully imperializing traveller, confident master of all he surveys despite all the reversals, trials and humiliations, which serve only to test and strengthen his self-righteous fortitude. Without apparent difficulty, he proves capable of taking on multiple roles: ethnographic observer, sex-slave, soldier on the march, war correspondent, big-game hunter, diplomat and political adviser.

For such a hero, evidence of a divine plan can be discovered in any and every incident and event, even in military defeat. As soon as the battle at sea is over, T.S. tells how 'We found that near 300 of their men had been killed' against only 82 from his ship (p. 11). Finding himself defeated despite being on the side that achieved a higher kill rate causes T.S. to recollect a bad omen:

> One thing passed during the Fight worthy our Notice, and which I did then look upon as an ill Omen: at a Broad Side one great Shot was forced back again, and split in pieces; we did conceive that it met with a more violent one, which had driven it upon us. (pp. 11–12)

Such incidents provide the kind of authenticating detail that early novelists regularly used to lend verisimilitude to their fictions. Someone, somewhere very likely witnessed two cannon balls colliding in just this way, and whether it was T.S. on the occasion described is less important than the effective placement of the retrospection here at the moment of our hero's defeat by stronger forces. Besides adding a realistic touch, it helps transform a moment of superior firepower into a providential sign whose meanings our hero is about to discover for us.

The 'ill Omen' recalls two conventional attitudes towards the Ottoman Empire: the 'Turks' are 'the terrour of the world', as Richard Knolles put it back in 1603, while the superior military power of the Ottomans could render armed resistance worse than futile. Ways other than force were needed to deal with the 'Turks' who, as so often, enter the account as figures of duplicity, irregularly behaving contrary to expectations. These 'Turks' prove to be remarkably friendly after such a long and bloody fight, and become even more so when they learn of the rich prize they have taken:

> The *Turks* treated us very generously, that we expected not from Enemies which we had angered by so long a Resistance. They commended our Courage, and wondered at our Resolution. And when they saw the rich Loading that they had got into their hands, they quickly pardoned us the Injuries we had done them. (p. 12)

Perhaps if T.S. had not abandoned his studies so early in life he would have been less surprised to discover that the 'Turks', however duplicitous, were thought to remain covetous above all else: even Thomas Dallam knew this stereotype. But T.S. needs to discover things for himself in order to demonstrate for his readers the unfolding of his own place and life story within the providential scheme of things. This is not Henry Blount's empirical and sceptical examination of book learning, but the dutiful self-scrutiny of a certain kind of Protestant hero seeking to find the workings of grace and salvation operating within the circumstances of his own life.

'I made some Reflections upon my former Condition,' T.S. writes:

> and wished my self upon some Christian shore as poor as *Job*; Liberty was sweet to me that was taken a Slave: I remembred then that excellent advice, *Trust not unto uncertain riches, &c.*, I then condemned the joy I had felt for the rich Patrimony that was left me, and the earnest desire for to see Foreign Places. Now to my sorrow I began to remember my former Condition; but all these Reflections and Regrets could not turn the Wind, nor stop our Course from *Argiers*. (p. 13)

Passages like this, recalling the narrative pattern of how alternately feeling saved and then damned describes the workings of divine grace, are common in captivity narratives and spiritual autobiographies of the period. Returned captives, writing of their experiences, may genuinely have felt that they had been specially chosen to survive.

Invoking divine intervention and providence to explain what had happened to them, of course, also provided an acceptable cover for any suspicion that they might have reneged while in captivity. William Okeley regularly pauses while telling of his years in Algerian captivity to interject a pious aside pondering how an incident exemplified divine intervention. In *The Adventures*, however, too many details and incidents fit rather too neatly into the providentialist scheme proposed by the first paragraph. Although among a small and, indeed, elect group of those saved from death, T.S. cannot help but recognize how his captivity means that he is being punished for feeling joy at his inheritance, and for using that new wealth to indulge his vain desire to acquire the name of a traveller who had seen 'Foreign Places'. But rather than expressing belated grief at the death of his father and brother, or pondering how he might have used his financial independence to a more public or pious good, T.S. finds himself unavoidably being swept off by a wind different from that which brought him so swiftly to the Bay of Cadiz.

While providential winds carry him ever closer to a slavery he can no longer avoid, T.S. swiftly negotiates his new position among the brutalities of life at sea after a battle, the remarkable hospitality of his captors, the treachery of fellow English renegades and the dangers of Spanish ships. Recalling the gruesome scene of throwing 'Our dead Bodies and those that were wounded desperately...to feed the Sharkes and other Ravenous Fishes of the Sea' gives him occasion to reflect upon the horrors and beastliness of the alien space into which he has travelled (pp. 13, 14). Almost immediately, however, that personal '*Our* dead' by which T.S. identifies himself with the living, slides into an identification with a very carefully constructed community among those being held captive:

> During our stay a shipboard, we were as civilly treated as we could expect from *Turks*, and did feed as they did upon Garlick & Rusk, poor *John*, Rice, & such like food. I observed them very inquisitive to find out our Qualities, and the Estates that we had remaining, our Friends, and what Assistance and Favour we might expect from them. To know these Particulars, we were examined a part: We had been forewarned of this Proceeding, and therefore we had prepared our Answers, that we might not be found in a contradiction. I had desired our Company to make me pass for a poor Fellow. (pp. 14–15)

The sequence of personal pronouns in this passage as T.S. identifies with the other captives (we) against their captors (they) only to emerge isolated (I), captures what Joe Snader calls a 'fundamental crisis of identity produced by the situation of captivity'.[1] Where and with whom does the captive find points of identification? For T.S., the possibility of alliance with other captives proves fragile and fractured from the start, given how fearful members of that 'Company' are of being 'found in a contradiction'. Under the scrutiny of his captors, T.S. proves successful in this attempt to appear poorer and less important than he is until 'some *English* Renagadoes' recognize him, expose his fraud and leave him to fend for himself:

> I laboured to excuse my Rashness, and to justifie my former Declaration; nevertheless one word made me to be suspected for an eminent Person, powerful in Friends, and Acquaintance, which made them put a higher Value upon me, and hope for a greater Ransom.
>   We sailed into the *Streights*, and at the Entry, over against *Gibraltar*, we met with a *Spanish* Man of War at some distance from us. (p. 16)

Before arriving in Algiers, T.S. offers this final anecdote that produces a new 'we', one that collapses the distinction between captives and captors when confronting a common enemy; in this case the Spanish.

Such is the slippery identity of the Englishman who has been taken prisoner at sea and is destined to be sold into slavery in Algeria. For the rest of the book, T.S. continues to identify in this way with his so-called 'Turkish' captors. He dislikes some of his masters, but will never again recognize a common bond with any except those with power over him. He may deplore some aspects of the imperial rule with which he finds himself complicit, yet he serves and prospers within that system according to the dictates of personal self-interest and divine providence.

18
Slavery in Algeria

> To the general reader the most interesting part of the history of Algiers commences with the rule of the Turks, and of the brothers Barbarossa, the famous pirates.
>
> *Cook's Practical Guide to Algeria and Tunisia* (1908), p. 25

Ottoman Algeria

When T.S. arrived, Algeria was the most important centre of Ottoman power in the Maghreb, providing an essential bulwark against Spanish expansion, offering a strategically situated naval base for privateers and housing a Janissary force that was, in the estimation of Albert Hourani, 'perhaps the largest in the empire outside Istanbul'.[1] For three centuries before the Ottomans arrived, the kingdoms throughout Morocco, Algeria and Tunisia had been in continuous conflict following the break-up of the Almohad Empire. When the Merenids occupied Tlemcen in the mid-fourteenth century, the rest of Algeria became little more than a vassal state, variously serving Morocco or Tunisia. Between 1505 and 1510, however, imperializing manoeuvres by the Spanish provoked local resistance, including that of the Kabylies of Bougie who employed a pirate, Oruç, with a base on the island of Djerba, to help them throw off Spanish control. Oruç and his brother Hayreddin are said to have been Greek renegades from Mytilene, on Lesbos, where their family name was Barbarossa.[2] Oruç, recognizing 'that the country could be mastered only by the occupation of the interior as well as of the coastal zone', set about recapturing most of the ports together with important inland centres as far west as Tlemcen.[3] Oruç lost his life fighting the Spaniards by the river Salado in 1518.[4] So it was his younger brother, Hayreddin, who consolidated power in the area by offering homage to Sultan Selim I. In return, he received from Selim the title of beylerbey, thereby making Algeria an Ottoman province, or vilayet. Assisted by Istanbul, Hayreddin drove the Spanish out of the rest of Algeria except Oran, which they held until 1792. Thus it was that

Algeria became the extreme western province of the Ottoman Empire, and a Greek-born renegade pirate known as Barbarossa became its first governor.[5]

Ottoman control in Algeria regularly faced local opposition, but brought economic stability that soon altered the demography of the ports and inland trading cities. Hourani notes that the population of Ottoman Algiers 'was dominated by three groups: the janissaries, mainly brought from Anatolia and other eastern parts of the empire; the sea-captains [*reis*], many of them Europeans; and the merchants, many of them Jews, who disposed of the goods captured by the privateers through their contacts in the Italian port of Livorno'[6] By the mid-seventeenth century the balance of power was shifting more and more away from Istanbul and into the hands of local authorities. In 1587, Murad III reduced the position of beylerbey to that of pasha, or general, with a three-year terminal appointment. Aimed at curbing the personal power of the beylerbeys, the change altered the position itself, such that the pashas, having so short an appointment, ruthlessly pursued personal wealth for three years, leaving the country to be run by the *reis* and the aghas in command of Janissary units. 'For a short time in the middle of the seventeenth century the aghas, or chiefs of the militia, seized power and reduced the pashas to impotence, but there was perpetual conflict, and in 1671, the rais gained control, and elected one of their captains to the office of dey, or protector.'[7] Such were the political conditions when T.S. arrived and in which he soon found himself embroiled.

Seventeenth-century Britons considered Algiers – or Argiers as it was most often called – as a notorious centre of piracy and slavery. Both Hakluyt and Purchas included scare stories of how English ships and mariners were regularly threatened by pirates operating from Algiers. In his 'Africa' volume, Purchas reprinted Nicolay's account of the city, which includes a version of the tale of Barbarossa, and points out that the

> most part of the Turkes of Algier, whether they be of the Kings Household or the Gallies, are Christians renied, or Muhametised, of all Nations, but most of them Spaniards, Italians, and of Provence, of the Ilands and Coasts of the Sea Mediterran, given to all Whoredome, Sodometrie, Theft, and all other most detestable vices.[8]

In other words, not 'Turks' at all really, but renegade Europeans acting in ways they thought 'Turks' behaved. Purchas continues with an account of Sir Robert Mansell's celebrated naval expedition 'against the Pirats of Algiers' in 1620. Aimed at reclaiming captives, Mansell's heroic failure to rescue anyone achieved little more than to waste munitions and the lives of several of his captains and many sailors.[9] In order to redeem this notable failure 'to the glory of God, and honour of the English', Purchas immediately followed it with anodyne reports of 'two strange deliverances' of British ships from 'the Turkish Pirats of Argier'.[10]

By the Restoration, the fact of Algerian slavery was so culturally embedded within the fabric of public life that one day in February 1661, Samuel Pepys found himself drinking all afternoon in the Fleece Tavern, listening to 'stories of Algier and the manner of the life of Slaves there'.[11] To a popular balladeer, the association of Algeria with captivity could serve as a metaphor for the slavery of being in love, picking up a familiar erotic fascination with hot Islamic lands.[12]

T.S. becomes a horse

For T.S., Algeria is a land of beasts, where beastliness takes many strange forms and slavery entailed imagining himself to be an animal, ever fearfully suspicious of men and their intentions, but also proudly conscious of being a fine performer. Feeling like a horse being sold at market was a familiar trope in captivity narratives, and T.S. extends the metaphor with subtlety and nuance, though the Dutch illustrator made nothing of it. On his arrival in Algiers, T.S. negotiated with a Cornish-born slave trader who told them 'that if we came on shore, we should be led to the Market, and there sold as Horses' unless they promised to pay him off (p. 18). The narrative keeps readers as uncertain as T.S. was at first concerning the renegade Cornishman's intentions and honesty, though he later calls him 'the Deceitful *Turk*' (p. 20) once his malicious self-interest and duplicity have become clear. Narrative strategies are handled deftly throughout the *Adventures*, keeping readerly interest in what might happen next to the fore. Titillating moments of sexual innuendo appear early on and accumulate resonance. Once he lands in Algiers, T.S. describes how being a slave is rather like being not simply any horse in any market, but a prized, well-bred and noble stallion among a harem of mares.

Wearing chains (p. 23), T.S. was led through the streets and into the palace to be inspected by none other than 'the King of *Argiers*' (p. 24).[13] In a cool palace courtyard, the slaves were kept waiting, 'for being about Noon, he had been bathing himself, and afterwards taking another Recreation, which is usual at that time of day in the hot Climates' (p. 24). Hot climates, noon, bath house, chained slaves lounging about in oriental palace: once ashore, alongside the ethnographic voice, T.S. begins to favour coy idioms, sexual innuendo and bawdy implications in keeping with the tastes of the Restoration readers for whom the work was first published. Most readers would have had little difficulty imagining what the king was doing while engaged in 'another Recreation' 'usual' 'in the hot Climates'. In concert with the Orientalist stereotype, we are soon told that 'the good old man was a greater Lover of his Pleasures [with boys] than of Money...a strange Fancy possesses the minds of all the Southern People; they burn with an unnatural Fire, which consumed *Sodom* and *Gomorrah*' (p. 28).

While covetousness overwhelms the typical 'Turk', the Maghrebian potentate longs for youthful male flesh. Being a fine and fully mature stallion, T.S. finds himself in little danger from the beylerbey's 'unnatural Fire', and it will be heterosexual women who pursue him. With typical narrative efficiency, Algiers has already been established as a slave market where all manner of different sexual possibilities come to be exchanged.

Once the King has emerged from his noontime recreation, T.S. finds himself being looked over for points of conformation as if he were a horse. He recuperates the moment by taking on, once again, the confident ethnographic voice of one capable of standing aside from the circumstances of the moment. These acts of becoming immediately expert in the foreign culture in which he finds himself, these moments of putting the other under scrutiny, momentarily set the English slave mentally free, enabling him to look directly back into the eye of the 'King of *Argiers*' and recognize a fellow expert:

> He look'd upon us with a stern Countenance, and took notice of our Features and Stature; for it seems the *Turks* are excellent in the Art of Physiognomy; they know a man and his Inclinations at the first view, as well as an expert Farrier can the good or ill Qualities of a Horse. (p. 27)

All 'Turks'? All the time? When he writes of being looked at in this way, T.S. wants us to see that, under the gaze of a human flesh expert, he really measures up as a fine specimen. What would be the point of being assessed in this way if not by a judge with all the instinctive abilities of an expert farrier, one risking his back every time he lifts the hoof of an unfamiliar and powerful animal?

Once he has come up for sale, a slave with no other options, T.S. needs to look like a good performer, and he is immediately rewarded by the judgement passed. T.S. writes that the King 'cast a Jest upon every one of us' and of T.S. 'he said, That he advis'd him that should be my master, not to trust me too much with his Women' (pp. 27, 28). What T.S. is not is a boy with a boy's body. With this shrewd testimonial from an expert in the points and qualities of a man, our stallion finds himself kept on by the King for his personal service. The rest of his stay in Algiers uses conventions of comic romance to arrange a palimpsest of tropes from captivity narratives, but never once is T.S. the object of homoerotic desire.

A stallion among the mares

Sometimes imagining yourself a horse means that you get to perform like a stallion at stud among the Eastern mares. While in captivity in Algiers, T.S. confirms the beylerbey's judgement of him. Unable to escape or effect a rescue,

T.S. becomes a victim of his desirable body. After establishing the comic mode with moments of merriment in the kitchens, where he served briefly as a cook, T.S. found himself 'by a wonderful change of Fortune' promoted 'Keeper of the Kings bath'. The change of fortune and accompanying change of scene bring the kitchen slave to the bath house and the stallion closer to the mares. 'It seems,' T.S. writes, 'some of his Women had seen me in the House, and interceded for me...I thought myself then a pretty Fellow, and not inferiour to my former Estate' (p. 34). Immediately after these reflections on his good looks and good luck, he describes being seduced in the baths: 'One of the Kings Wives... sought a fit opportunity to discover her self to me, and make use of my Bath when the King was abroad' (p. 34). Making use of facilities other than just the bath, the King's wife embodies the sexual intrigue Europeans had come to associate with bathhouses. A Spanish maid appears on the scene to serve as go-between and we are left to imagine the rest.

T.S. soon discovers that one problem with being a useful and valuable stallion is that you are likely to be sold on. The King has heard rumours 'which were sufficient to cause him to remove me from my pleasant Office, which', T.S. notes, 'angered me more than any thing that happened to me all the time of my Slavery' (p. 35) – a remarkable testimonial to the pleasures of the bath-house. Finding himself on the way to market, T.S. resumes his equine identity long enough to describe himself performing in a moral tableau: 'When I saw my self with an ill favoured *Turk*, leading me by a Chain, as a Horse or a Bullock, thorough the streets, I then began to lament my hard fortune, and remember my former Estate; I knew not what Providence had prepared for me, nor what surly Master I should meet with next' (p. 37). In the event, T.S. was surreptitiously bought by his former lover, the appreciative wife of the King, who kept him for the next two years for her own purposes. But in this expressive lament and moment of anxiety over the next 'surly master', surely we hear a voice common in captivity narratives. Remembering their childhood, some English readers may hear the voice of Black Beauty.

In the clanking of those chains can we (not) also hear some moment of camp being performed? He reports delight at finding himself a sex-slave: 'I thought my self happy to be a Slave to so excellent and kind a Lady: I never dreamt of a Change whilst I belonged unto her: I had no reason; for nothing was wanting unto me useful to the Life of Man' (p. 40). It is perhaps not so astonishing after all that his next sentence qualifies this general assertion by indicating how the 'Man' in question must welcome a 'Life' involving bondage and discipline: 'I only wore a Chain out of Formality,' he confesses, and 'I did also employ my self in slavish work...but not above measure' (pp. 40–1). Limits are desirable in all things, it would seem, especially in sex games; but we are not told what tasks he refused to undertake. Wearing his chains now merely for formal, decorative purposes, T.S. only hints at his daily tasks.

The Lady became very devout after my coming to that place; she seldom mis'd a day, but came in some Disguise to pay her Devotions at the Mosquette, from whence there was a passage into my Lodgings. (p. 41)

Still claiming to be a good Protestant, with providence sometimes acting as his guide, T.S. cannot resist hiding irregular sexual adventures behind the doors of a reviled religion: mosque or convent is all one. The joke turns on how the implicit sexual performance of the English slave becomes occasion for the superstitious to find, in his mistress's daily devotion, evidence of her saintliness:

By this frequent and constant Attendance at Publick Prayer, she purchas'd unto her self a very great esteem with the People, and a favour with her Husband; and ever after she was named a Saint.
  I continued her Slave about two years . . . (p. 41)

Happy times indeed! If only, T.S. recalls thinking, she would marry him! (p. 56). Instead she becomes sainted for her piety and dies six months after being 'brought to Bed of a pretty little Girl, somewhat whiter than ordinary; the old Fool thought himself to be the Father of it. I was once admitted to see it; but now my Mistress was dead, I was left to the Misfortunes and Miseries of a slavish Life' (pp. 57–8). 'It', the unnameable thing left behind, simply disappears from the account. Whatever problems his sexual desirability might have entailed, fatherhood was evidently not one of them.

Sexual adventures while captive in Algiers help to compensate T.S. for his slavery but leave him in it. While they provide a limited degree of personal agency despite his circumstances, the stylized innuendo and farcical content that transform North African slavery into picaresque adventuring hardly fit earlier concerns with exemplifying providence: piety has given way to what might look like titillating implausibility. Given the sheer conventionality of his sexual escapades, it is difficult not to suspect them of being imaginary. Were it not for the detailed historical and topographical descriptions that follow, one might suspect that *The Adventures* as a whole was fabricated.

19
On Tour with the Ottoman Army

A new master

Following his adventures as a sex slave, T.S. finds himself being sold to several bad masters before entering the service of 'an Officer of the Militia called *Hally Hamez Reiz*' (p. 61). Since the title of *reis* was often given to 'officers of certain military corps',[1] it seems less likely that Hally Hamez was a renegade sea captain than a member of the regular Ottoman forces drafted to Algeria from Anatolia. T.S. does not tell us, but he does describe how his new master's personality was in keeping with certain stereotypes: 'He was very passionate and lascivious, nevertheless Valiant; as I did afterwards learn' (p. 63). Entering service to Halley Hamez and following the Ottoman drums of war released T.S. from his sense of being a horse, but in the performance of his duties to his new master, he will eventually return to his devotions to Venus.

T.S.'s account of his years in service as adviser and sometimes pander to Hally Hamez Reis shows just how far the captive agency of an ingenious Englishman could allow him to rise within the Ottoman scheme of things. During their three years together in Tlemcen, T.S. provided such exemplary advice in diplomatic negotiations with recalcitrant Moorish and Arab tribes resisting Ottoman taxation, that the two of them became major agents of Ottoman imperialism on its western periphery. Both T.S. and his master grow fantastically wealthy once Hally Hamez uses his position in the historically important market city to his own advantage. At the end of his appointment, his master is promoted back to Algiers and T.S. is set free. In describing these years, T.S. provides a firsthand insider's account of Ottoman imperial administration at work, and of his own interventions within it. He writes as if providing the scoop on how the Ottoman taxation system really worked, with reports on campaigns against local resistance movements and advice on how to negotiate with powerful Moorish kings.

Once in service to Hally Hamez, T.S. no longer feels like a horse but instead like an Ottoman. Although T.S. will return to England at the earliest possible moment, his status as a slave seldom troubles him now as he internalizes the imperialist's perspective. He clearly flourished in this new position, which offered him opportunities to visit dangerous and exciting places seldom visited by Europeans, not simply to witness but also to be a part of how the Ottomans handled insurgency on the westernmost border of their empire. For T.S., the chance to earn that much desired name of traveller, rather than slave, seems to have materialized. Marching across the Algerian desert with the Ottoman army, T.S. reports on numerous adventures hunting wild game and offers field notes on local flora, exotic creatures, historical sites and local cultures. Not once does he question what the Ottomans are doing in North Africa, nor does he ever once seem at all sympathetic towards any of the colonized inhabitants.

On the road

I have yet to find any evidence confirming, or disproving, the historicity of many events T.S. describes while he was in the service of his Ottoman master. It may well be that the details he provides of various military and diplomatic expeditions in which he participated are a reliable historical source for the names of Moorish and Arab leaders. In his account, T.S. shows insider knowledge of Algerian political geography under the Ottoman occupation, and provides data concerning trade and local customs. It is from this later section of *The Adventures* that some of the more sensationalistic reports were taken and reissued as *The Relation* of 'R.D.' in 1672. The map of T.S.'s travels provided for the Dutch translation follows the imaginative geography of T.S.'s narrative rather more closely than the situation of actual towns and rivers in Algeria would allow. For example, the map follows T.S.'s report of a desert town called 'Bedtua' and situates it accordingly, though no such town is to be found there: T.S. may have meant Bettiwa on the coast.

According to T.S., an Ottoman army of 12,000 men set out from Algiers to gather taxes under a field commander, Ben Osman Bucher, 'and to relieve *Tremsen* or *Climsan*, a strong and populous City in the Country' (p. 62). This enormous force set out during the June harvest when 'the Country was able to furnish the yearely Revenue either in Corn or Money'. The army then divided into three, one army to collect along the coastal 'Western Circuit' as far as Tetuan under Abel Hamed Simon, another to collect as far east as Tunis under two 'Chieftains, *Halaç Rigla Reiz*, an old Renagado of *Spain*, and *Haleç Sim Haly*, a young blade that had more Precipitation than Wisdom' (p. 65). Under the direct command of Ben Osman Bucher, T.S. and Hally Hamez joined the third army with orders to march inland and 'enter the Country' to collect taxes from reluctant Moors and rebellious Arabs who 'do hate the Turks, because they are imperious, and because they are obliged to pay unto them an yearly Tribute' (p. 64). For the Ottomans soldiers, this 'middle Circuit' was the most heroic and hazardous of all, since it brought them up against 'a sort of People very valiant and stout, that sometimes make a strong Resistance to the *Turks*, and when they see their advantage, they refuse Tribute' (p. 67). For the first stage of their march, however, T.S. and Hally Hamez meet nothing more dangerous than wild beasts and natural hazards.

The names of none of these Ottoman officers appear in any records that I have been able to find, but they do reappear in R.D.'s *Relation*, which simply changes the dates and tells how an Ottoman army commanded by one *'Ben Osman Butcher*, a Man valiant and Faithfull to his Charge', set forth 'in *June*, 1667'.[2] Providing factual-sounding details of this kind – names, dates, places – could persuade readers that otherwise implausible occurrences did take place; it mattered little whether the names, dates and places were accurate.

Some beastly encounters

Of the march inland, T.S. records sights and incidents in the voice of an inquisitive note-taking traveller rather than a captive Englishman forced to serve in the Ottoman army. Along the way, he comments on local customs, describes exotic flora and fauna, and kills his fair share of game. With great excitement, he reports on sporting encounters with dangerous lions and marvellous beasts, and on a less than sporting encounter with a horrid scorpion. He translates inscriptions from ruined monuments, and comments on visits to ancient inhabited caves. He describes the landscape attentively, and notes which trees and plants bear fruits that are good to eat. He comments favourably on Ottoman policy in the region, and describes the military campaigns and diplomatic tactics by which they maintain rule with sympathy and more than a hint of pleasure at his personal complicity.

Travelling with the Ottoman army in Algeria suited T.S. from the start. Though still a slave, he now led a life that differed very little from that of the other men. In a soldierly manner, he grumbles about having to carry 'my Masters Lance, and a Gun', but these are weapons after all, a manly burden not to be confused with those earlier chains, and he admits that the journey into the desert from Algiers 'was very pleasant' (p. 70). An early chance encounter enables T.S. to reaffirm his own loyalties to nation and religion, but this will be almost the last we hear of them (or of providence) until the end of the book. Falling in step with 'an *English Turk*' who was 'desirous to seek his escape', T.S. piously reminded this faithless Englishman of the true religion and thereby reduced him to tears (p. 71). Without further regard for England, T.S. hastens to report how much he enjoyed 'several Accidents that we met with, that gave us a great deal of sport' (p. 71). One involves a soldier who, having attacked a lion with only 'his Cymeter in his hand', would have been 'instantly devoured' if T.S. and the others had not shot 'above 100 Bullets' into the body of the lion (pp. 72, 73).

But the manly and adventurous life of an armed soldier does not entirely distract T.S. from a slightly less violent relation to the natural world. After shooting the lion:

> We journeyed about three Leagues and we came to a little Valley very fruitful of Palms and Olive Trees, a small Rivulet, covered with Strawberry Bushes, did run through it, and water the Plain; at each end a Grove did grow. (p. 73)

Like many a traveller, when T.S. looks at the landscape, he sees things to eat. The scene achieves its magical effect by following an aesthetics of productive modes rather than pictorial qualities: those fruiting trees and bushes need no human hands to tend them, just as the rivulet that waters the plain naturally enables those groves to grow without human intervention. Thoughts of food, however, disappear immediately when, from within one of those groves, right from this source of untamed nature, appears the most magical sight of all:

> I saw a Flying Serpent, about the bigness of an ordinary Dog, with a long Tail, and a head like an Ape, with a larger mouth, and a long Tongue, the Body had about four Foot in length; we shot at it, but could not kill it: It threatened some of our men when they ventured to come near it, and could not be obliged to depart until a great number of us were arrived at the Place. I saw it near a pleasant Fountain that did rise in one side of the furthermost Grove. I enquired of the Name, but could not learn it; it had Wings of divers Colours, the chief were Red and White: It hovered long over our heads, and had not the Noise of our Guns frighted it away, I think it had ventured amongst us again. I could not distinguish of what substance the Wings were; they were bigger than those of our winged Fowls; all the Birds that saw it at a distance were glad to fly. I imagined it to be a kind of Basilisk, a desperate Serpent. (pp. 73–5)

One hundred bullets might kill a raging lion, but this 'desperate Serpent' proves impenetrable to bullets and earns elaborate description instead. Since none of the other men had ever seen such a creature, T.S. expertly concludes that 'it was some In-land Creature not usually seen near the Sea-Coast'. For T.S. and his readers, encounters with strange and wonderful animals in exotic settings transformed captivity into an exciting adventure.

But adventures among foreign beasts entail personal dangers too. Four days from Algiers, T.S. was bitten by a 'great Scorpion', living to tell the tale thanks to those in the know who instantly applied the creature's blood to the wound. 'It was wonderful to see the present cure that the Blood gave', he noted with clinical interest, 'it has no sooner touch'd the tumor, but it began to decrease, and out of the little prick came forth a Liquor white as Milk' (p. 81). For a further 'three days together' after his recovery, T.S. and the army cross wild terrain inhabited only 'by Monsters and Wild Beasts' (pp. 83, 82). They kill a goodly number of them, sometimes for food, but most often from fear or fascination. To the guns of the troops fall a four-legged bird, several lions and a great 'Monster of a large Bulk':

> the Head was like a Lion, the Paws like a Bear, the hinder parts much like to an Ass; when it was killed, every one in the Army had a sight of it; I then did remember the Saying of the *Romans, Africa semper apportat aliquid novi*; every year there is some strange Creature of other to be seen in these remote places.(p. 85)

While the wild goats escaped the soldiers' bullets by climbing into the steep rocks, T.S. catalogued a creature like a dog, 'but yielding an extraordinary stink' that the Moors call '*Subsib*'. and a local fox known as '*Thaloub*' (p. 86).

Such episodes from *The Adventures* indicate how sightings of bizarre and unusual creatures contributed a sense that these lands belonged to a different order of nature from that familiar to the English, one in which the human inhabitants were sometimes little different from the savage beasts alongside whom they lived. Reports of beastly encounters belong to a strategy that, by shifting, blurring or even erasing the border between nature and culture in strange Islamic locations, brought local peoples and animals into a common register below the superior human level which Europeans imagined for themselves. What this strategy permitted early travellers, who perhaps only partly understood what they were seeing, was the ability to feel less threatened and humbled by their potentially subordinate position within the exotic Ottoman imperium. Regular reports of infestation by invisible perils, alien insects and other vermin not before seen by Englishmen, contributed to previously existing structures of xenophobic prejudice.

Passing over 'several other sorts of Serpents and Beasts', T.S. claims that he 'almost forgot' to report one beast that proved to be the most extraordinary of all the bizarre creatures he encountered:

> I had almost forgot one of a strange Nature; it appear'd unto us a as a White Lamb, something differing in the shape, as we were marching through a Valley; but when it perceived us to approach in such Numbers, it fled before us...I had Order to pursue it, and accompany the Hunters. As we came within a hundred Paces of it, it made more haste than ordinary, and began to shift for itself amongst the Trees; but as it could not well escape from us, because it was already weary, and very fat, we overtook it at the entry in of the Bushes; but perceiving us so near, it ran under one, and that we might not find it, it changed in an instant its white colour in to the same with the

Bush, which unexpected alteration gave us a great deal of trouble. We had never found it again, had not one of the Company discharged a Musket; at the Noise it rose up in a fright, and began to run for its Life; we little thought it to be the same; nevertheless, some of us did venture after it, and some remained in the place, seeking the white Beast: The Pursuers shot off one of its Legs, and then cried to us to forbear seeking, and that the counterfeit Lamb was caught. (pp. 87–8)

On close inspection, the counterfeit lamb proves to have fine wool, a wolf-like head with sharp teeth, but the 'Hinder-parts were like a Sheep', causing T.S. to reflect how, with its shape and colour-changing abilities, the creature provides 'a good Emblem of an Hypocrite'. Without further comment, T.S. tells of spending a further 'three days climbing over these mountainous places, and fighting with strange and unknown Creatures' before they come in sight of the army of the insurgent Arabs camped by the river Tafna (p. 89).

Interlude: Archaeological sites and military danger

For T.S., the march into the North African desert was also a march into the past, as he pondered monuments raised on ancient battlegrounds and imagined finding mementoes left by primitive Christians. Sights and incidents along the way shift from sporting opportunities and natural history, to ancient sites that prompt reflections on the vicissitudes of human history and the arrival of cautionary news concerning Arab tribes in revolt. On the first day's march from Algiers, T.S. stopped at some ancient marble monuments celebrating a battle once fought there. An unnamed Moor instructs T.S. that the inscription tells how Zidi Dockra Moukadem, in service to Prince Abel Hamed, led 2,000 men to victory against 6,000 'Brabbers' under the command of Azoret Moudem, whom he personally killed (pp. 75–6). Only 'a League farther' on, T.S. stopped once more to engage in some amateur archaeology by inspecting some caves. Spotting some crosses carved into the walls, he imagined the caves 'to be a Place made for the Dwelling of some solitary *Anachoret* of the Primitive Christians' (p. 77).

During the march inland, T.S. increasingly writes of matters military in the voice of an experienced soldier. He displays a shrewd sense of military tactics and campaign strategies rather than formal training in the arts of war. The night after his visit to the caves, the army reached '*Boumelli*, a good Town situate upon a River', where the 'Inhabitants furnished us with all things necessary' (pp. 77, 78), including information that certain Arab tribes, resisting Ottoman taxation, were gathering 'beyond the River *Talna* [Tafna]', in the hope of engaging the Ottoman forces. 'All their Substance,' T.S. learns, 'they had transported to the Top of a high Mountain, called by the Inhabitants *Azar*, unto which they were resolved to flee, if they did lose the Day' (p. 79). Just west of the eastern fork of the river Tafna lies the plain of Angad, dominated to the south by the great mountain ridges of Ras Asfour – T.S.'s '*Azar*' – which, at over 5,000 feet, provide an excellent bolt-hole in which a defeated army might seek shelter.[3] Geographically, the description is accurate enough to suggest how experienced local Arabs were at strategic military planning. It would have been no coincidence that they had gathered for battle close to the border where the Ottoman vilayet of Algeria became the kingdom of Morocco.

The revolt of Isha Muker and Elmswar Tapnez

According to T.S., the Arab revolt against Ottoman control in western Algeria during the summer of 1651 was led by one Isha Muker, a 'Person of a Noble Family' from the kingdom of Fez. Reputed to be an eminent commander, and with the backing of his personal wealth, Isha Muker had gathered an Arab army 'to shake off the *Turkish* yoke'. Apparently, he had stirred up widespread anti-Ottoman sentiment without much trouble simply by representing how 'imperious' the 'Turks' were and by declaring how 'the poverty of the Year' meant local herdsmen and farmers would not be able to 'furnish the Tribute-Money' as well as feed their families (pp. 92, 93). Arousing fear and rebellious indignation was not difficult. Where Isha Muker ran into problems was in attempting to incite men to take up arms against Ottoman forces. In order to lend religious legitimacy to his rebellion, he declared that '*Turks* were not true *Mohametans*', but were so very heretical in thought and vicious in deed that 'it was not lawful to submit to' Ottoman rule but rather a duty to resist it (p. 93).

   Finding 'the multitude' still reluctant to fight, Isha Muker resolved upon a clever 'Strategem'. He persuaded one Elmswar Tapnez, recently returned from the pilgrimage to Mecca, to feign lameness. Next, he produced a letter purporting to be from 'the Keeper of *Mohamet's* Temple', certifying that Elmswar Tapnez had been visited while there by a vision of the Prophet who had 'commanded him to signifie unto them that it was his Pleasure to assist them this year in a notable manner, and free them from the Slavery of the *Turk*' (p. 94). News of this letter attracted the attention of local 'Grandees' who met in council. Once Elmswar Tapnez, appearing before them, was miraculously cured from his lameness, all doubts vanished; the Arab leaders declared him 'a Holy Man' and resolved 'they would no longer pay Tribute to the *Turk*' (pp. 94, 96). So successful was Isha Muker's strategic deception that, much to the alarm of T.S., an army of 'thirteen thousand Horse and Foot' had assembled under his command fully prepared to do battle with the Ottoman army (p. 97). By exposing their superstitious credulity, T.S. efficiently undermines any possible sympathy for, or reason to make common cause with, the insurgent Arabs. He never once doubts that he belongs on the Ottoman side. In this land which breeds lions, basilisks and hypocrite sheep, local human inhabitants are also to be distrusted, feared and even killed without a second thought.

With all the casual confidence of a victorious conqueror, T.S. narrates his first battle. Despite standing orders not to engage with the enemy until the other two Ottoman armies had caught up with them, Ben Osman Bucher decides to rout the Arab camp. In the hour before dawn, the Ottoman troops attack:

> As soon as we came within a quarter of a Mile of the Enemy, we found a small Party lodged in a hundred Tents, which we surrounded according to our Orders. We killed all that we found alive, with very little noise. (pp. 99–100)

And so the slaughter continues until the entire camp has been overrun and the surviving Arabs have fled into the hills. Contempt for the Arabs is only increased by the things they left behind:

> The Plunder of the Camp was but small; such things we found that Beggars would scarce lift from under their Feet; a few nasty Tents were erected of such pitiful Stuff that I never saw the like. It seems the *Arabs* delight not in rich Household-stuff, but in numbers of Sheep and Camels.
>
> Some few Horses fell into our hands the next day. (p. 102)

T.S. has lost sight of the fact that he is a captive slave; or rather, he has so far identified with the superior military power of his captors that he now has a personal stake in those horses falling into 'our hands'. His assimilation into, and acceptance of, the military and imperial mission of the Ottomans in Algeria has become second nature as it were. In the afterglow of victory, T.S. has himself become an Ottoman.

T.S. takes the Ottoman side whenever reporting military encounters and statistics. 'In this attempt,' he writes, 'we lost about 50 men, and 435 of the *Arabians* were kill'd' (p. 102). Nearly one Ottoman for every ten Arabs, this kill-rate is close to the ratio he uses when describing how the Arab foot soldiers were so very poor and miserable that 'ten of them do not dare to look a *Turk* in the Face' (p. 104). Arab horsemen, however, prove to be a different matter from their pedestrian colleagues. Soon after the arrival of the Western army under Abel Hamed Simon, a combined Ottoman cavalry is ambushed by Arab horsemen. With the danger of the rebellion close at hand, T.S. reveals his sympathies. 'Our poor men,' he writes with unusual compassion of the slain Ottoman cavalry, 'were surrounded, disordered, and killed like so many Sheep' (pp. 106–7). Humbled by defeat, Ben Osman Bucher awaits the arrival of the Eastern armies before mounting any further full-scale attack.

When news arrives that, a full day's march away, the troops under Halaç Rigla Reis and Haleç Sim Haly have been pinned down under a hill by Arab horsemen, T.S. proudly declares: 'It was my Masters and my Fortune to accompany the Army' that were ordered to free the Eastern contingent (p. 109). After dispersing the Arab forces at 'a place called by the *Arabians Stefee*', the rescue party are initially viewed with suspicion by their fellow Ottomans:

> Our Men were possest with so strange a fear and apprehension, that when our Vanguard came near the place, they imagined them to be the Enemy; their joy was no less than their fear, when they perceived their errour. They received us as their Protectors. (p. 111)

In the annals of captivity narratives, it would be difficult to find a similar degree of concern being shown by an English captive for beleagured Ottoman troops – 'our men'.

According to T.S., the Arab rebellion is soon broken up by the combined Ottoman armies. 'Our men,' he notes, 'were so enraged by their former Losses' that they pursued the Arabs into their retreats on Mount '*Houlahka*', slaughtering all 'that fell by chance into their hands' (pp. 112, 113). With the enemy finally on the run, T.S. took time out to describe the mountainous woodlands into which the Arabs had retreated, before noting how 'Our Generals shared amongst themselves the danger and the honour of the Victory' in which the Ottomans 'drove the *Arabians* quite out of the Wood with great slaughter' (pp. 116, 117). Once the great battle was over, the Arabs had lost 'above 1500 Men' and the Ottomans had seized 'many hundred Head of Cattel, Sheep, Oxen, Cammels, and all sorts of Beasts' (p. 118). All told, the plunder 'did abundantly satisfie for the yearly Tribute' (p. 119). After a further three weeks of minor skirmishes and negotiations, Isha Muker and other Arab leaders accepted a truce, promising 'to be alwaies obedient to the Grand Seignior, and to the City of *Argiers*' (pp. 120–1).

Unknown to the Ottomans, not all the Arabs had complied with this settlement. Under the leadership of Elmswar Tapnez many were still armed and planning to resist payment of tribute money. Barely had T.S. and the Ottoman army set out for Tlemcen when they were surrounded and attacked in a 'narrow passage between two high Hills' by a heavily armed enemy (p. 121). Days pass fruitlessly in attempts to make a way through the passage before an opportunity finally presents itself in the shape of 50 maurauding Arabs sent to steal cattle. Carefully selecting speakers of Arabic from among his best troops, Ben Osman Bucher sent them off dressed in the clothes of the captured Arabs, each armed with 'four Pistols', and driving a herd of cattle before them (p. 128). Coming to the Arab camp, they soon gained entrance, killed the guards and enabled the Ottoman troops to enter and drive out the soldiers and seize the women and children. Beware Ottomans dressed as Arabs with cattle accessories – they do not bring gifts! Finally overwhelmed and, with their families taken hostage, the remaining Arabs accepted terms from Ben Osman Bucher. All, that is, except Elmswar Tapnez, who fled to Oujda beyond Ottoman control (p. 131).

With the revolt of Isha Muker and Elmswar Tapnez finally quelled, the Ottomans moved on to Tlemcen, gathering taxes from compliant villagers along the way and providing T.S. with occasion to reflect on the wisdom of Ottoman policy. In the aftermath of rebellion, the Ottomans exact from the Arab villagers no more than what they held to be owing to them in the first place. T.S. praises the way that 'Our Army' did not seize goods and sell Arab women as 'Bond-slaves', knowing 'that this dealing would serve to no other purpose' but to provoke future resistance (p. 134). The evident wisdom of Ottoman policy in this case moves T.S. to sententious reflection on the nature of state power and authority:

> It is never good to deal with Men as with Beasts; the latter are awed into obedience, but the first must be perswaded: The Magistrates sword may scare me, but it shall never win me. (p. 134)

Ben Osman Bucher receives particular praise for securing the truce by entertaining local Arab leaders and distributing gifts among

> some of the Arch Rebels, imitating the practise of those Princes that bestow their Favours upon those that are suspected, or that have been rebellious, to oblige them to be more faithful to their Interest for the future. (p. 135)

The rebellion over, the Ottomans set about wisely ruling by rewarding obedience, both present and future, rather than precipitating further unrest by vengefully punishing past insurgency.

Village wedding

As if to illustrate even further the benefits of obedience to Ottoman rule, T.S. reports how the army paused once more on its march to Tlemcen and became honoured guests at a wedding. Besides bridging the divide between military action and peaceful imperial rule, the wedding brings together not only two local families but also the Ottomans and the regional elite. Although T.S. never reveals whether the Moors at the wedding had been involved in the rebellion, Ottoman control over the area is signalled immediately by the fact that they have changed the name of the town where the wedding takes place from its local original. 'At a small Town,' T.S. writes, called by the *Turks, Canatudi*, and by the *Moors, Canahaal*, there was a great Feast kept for the Marriage of one *Elmswar Bidow Ben Hemmed*, an *Alcalde* of one of their Tribes; our General coming to the place at that time, honoured the Solemnity with his presence, and caused all his Captains and *Chouses* to pay their respects to the Bride and Bridegroom.(p. 135)

From the Ottoman point of view, which T.S. inhabits, there can be no question of Ben Osman Bucher requiring an invitation: rather, the triumphant general confers honour on the occasion by his presence and ostentatious display of authority. The wedding may bring Ottoman and Moor together, but the imperial relation between them remains intact, if not strengthened, following such direct and personal contact. Elmswar Bidow Ben Hemmed may well be an *alcalde* of his tribe, but Ben Osman Bucher is a general of an imperial army, and that difference is what counts.

The wedding interlude also provides T.S. with further opportunity to develop his ethnographic voice. He acquires something of the character of the imperial 'seeing man' described by Mary Louise Pratt, the travelling polymath who instinctively understands everything he sees before him and, unthinkingly confident in that knowledge, seeks to gain authority over it.[4] 'I cannot pass further,' T.S. announces in a tone that would have been familiar to those attending lectures on foreign customs and cultures delivered before the Royal Society, such as Thomas Smith's *Remarks* of 1678,

> until I take notice of what is observed by this People in such occasions; the young man that hath a mind to marry, demands the Daughter from her Father, or next Kindred; if they grant her, he never troubles himself to win her consent; this is an excellent way to spare a great deal of hypocrisie, and to save the poor men much Courtship. (p. 136)

Marriage on demand strikes T.S. as a sensible system. The woman's consent is irrelevant and courtship mere hypocrisy. Yet the wedding preparations are not without ceremonies, which induce anticipation on both sides. Seven days of gift-giving are followed by the big day itself when the couple finally meet and are conducted, the bride still veiled, to a tent where prayers are said 'to favour this Conjunction' (p. 138). T.S. records several authenticating and amusing details along the way: on the sixth day of courting, the bride receives 'a Cock and a Dog, to teach her Diligence and Watchfulness' (p. 137). The bride keeps her veil on until finally taken to 'her Husbands House... because Modesty is no longer in season, nor proper to that place' (pp. 138–9). Only after Elmswar Bidow Ben Hemmed and his bride are properly and seasonably alone does T.S. reveal how his own desires and investments have led him to report the occasion. 'I was,' he proudly announces, 'an Eye-witness of several Ceremonies observed in this occasion, which are related in other Travels' (p. 139).

As much as anything else, what T.S. wants readers to recognize are his credentials for admission to that select group of eye-witness travellers who have been there and seen for themselves. After all, he left England in the first place fired by 'the vain-glory of being named a Traveller' and cannot help exploit opportunities for achieving that ambition. At the wedding in Canahaal, or Canatudi, T.S. acquires a new authorial voice, no longer that of a soldier on the road or a war correspondent, but that of a man on his way to becoming an imperial administrator in a foreign outpost, getting to know the locals over whom he is to rule.

20
Tlemcen: Life in a Desert City

In a word, Tlemcen was one of the most civilised towns of the world about 1553, when the different nations of Europe were hardly awakening from their long lethargy.

Cook's Practical Guide (1908), p. 166

Ottoman Tlemcen

T.S. arrived in Tlemcen on 3 October 1651 and spent the final three years of his captivity there. At that time, the ancient city had been in Ottoman control for a century. With Ottoman support, Oruç Barbarossa had entered Tlemcen in 1518, but only long enough to drown 'a great number of princes of the blood-royal' in the Sahrij, the great basin built during the fourteenth century to the west of the city walls, before meeting his own death at the hands of the Spanish.[1] By the time the Ottomans occupied Tlemcen in 1555, the corpses had no doubt gone, but according to Alfred Bel, 'the material, moral and intellectual collapse' of this once glorious Berber capital had only just begun. 'The administrators, often without conscience, led a scandalous life,' Bel moralizes.[2] The Ottoman occupation, it is still said, drove away into Morocco all the wise men who had gathered there for centuries under the pious and civilizing patronage of the Ziyyanid dynasty, which had governed their kingdom from Tlemcen from the end of the Almohad empire. A century after T.S. returned to England, the satiric poet Benemsaib compared his native Tlemcen under Ottoman rule with a frog caught in the maws of a serpent.[3]

Much of what T.S. reports of his activities and attitudes while in Tlemcen confirms Bel's assessment of the city's intellectual and perhaps even moral collapse ('affaisement') under the Ottomans. But economic and material life flourished. Immediately on his arrival, T.S. noticed the fertility of the land outside the city, where prodigious quantities of 'Fruits, Apples, Pears, Melons of divers kinds, Grapes' and dates grew. But he was immediate in his contempt for the local people, observing how 'the Climate wants nothing but People worthy to receive and enjoy the good things that it affords' (pp. 139, 140–1). Fully identifying himself now with the Ottoman imperial point of view, T.S. was bound to think so.

T.S.'s account of Ottoman Tlemcen suggests continued prosperity and considerable importance despite local hostility to Ottoman rule at the time. He recognized Tlemcen was 'one of the ancientest Cities of the World' and admired the beautiful architecture of the 'stately *Mosque*', the 'Governors Palace' and the 'Town-House', ornamented with marble pillars, which houses a library 'full of the ancient Records of the Arabians' (pp. 142–3). While strolling through the city, he admired the Law Courts and 'curiously painted' houses, before passing through the marketplace and among the many 'Cloisters of the Religious men'. Of the madrasah adjacent to the Grand Mosque, he notes:

> One is more remarkable than the rest, because of the excellent Worksmanship and ancient Fabrick, and because of a great Library, a curious thing amongst this rude People: I know not with what manner of Books it is stored; for Christians have never the liberty to handle them; but as I did learn from the Keepers of the Door, they were Books that had been pick'd up in all the parts of *Africa* by one of their Princes, and laid in that place, for the benefit of the Students, whereof there are very few, unless it be of Magicians, and men that study the Virtues of Simples. Other Arts and Sciences as *Astrology*, *Logick*, the *Mathematicks*, &c. are almost extinct amongst them. (pp. 145–6)

A few pious scholars may have fled, but the cultural and material fabric of the ancient city remained intact during the Ottoman period. The colonial administration encouraged trade and commercial prosperity, and several administrative buildings in Tlemcen today were built by the Ottomans. If formal learning declined, it by no means disappeared. Another colonial historian, Auguste Cour, reluctantly admitted that under the Ottomans Tlemcen 'remained one of the intellectual capitals of the Maghreb'. In 1907, Cour catalogued the Arabic manuscripts remaining in the madrasah that T.S. was unable to visit, and noted how the failed French occupation of Tlemcen in 1836, and the successful attempt of 1842, caused a 'great number of families' to leave, either taking manuscripts with them or burying them 'to prevent them falling into the hands of the infidel' ('pour les soustraire aux mains des infidèles').[4] Professor Abdelhamid Hadjiat of the University of Tlemcen informs me that, while the extensive collection of manuscripts started by the Ziyyanid Sultan Abu Hammu I (1308–18) was dispersed into France or destroyed, a valuable collection of printed books from the Tlemcen madrasah are still in the Grand Mosque, or in Meknes, and provide an important source for the history of the Ziyyanid Empire.[5]

Tlemcen's ancient library is but one of several authentic details reported in *The Adventures*, suggesting how the book is not entirely fabricated. T.S. mentions the nearby tomb of the marabout Sidi Bou Medienne, which was an ancient site of pilgrimage and healing for centuries before Islam arrived. There really are curious natural rock formations near Tezrim, though none as spectacular as the one T.S. describes; and there were minor earthquakes in the mid-seventeenth century that damaged one of the city mosques. Professor Hadjiat assured me that the damaged mosque in question was a recent Ottoman building.

Like colonial administrators before and after him, T.S. quickly became fascinated by local history. He planned a full history of Tlemcen, but was ever too busy to write it (p. 150). Yet imagining that he might do such a thing reveals T.S. assimilating the colonial point of view and suggests just how far the former equine sex-slave has advanced his rank in life. T.S. increasingly adopts Orientalizing views, discovering traces of a glorious and all but forgotten past encrusted within a degenerate living present. Henry Blount set out for Egypt looking for embers of empires he knew were long gone, but T.S. creates a sense of discovery, of finding for the first time an ancient and unrecorded past, and of feeling newly empowered by imagining he might record for the first time that particular history. This sense of empowerment surely is among the founding impulses of Orientalism and imperialism both.

Embassy to Bedtua

T.S. never wrote his history of Tlemcen because he was too engaged with important affairs of state. With Halley Hamez he was soon called to an ancient city he calls Bedtua, where one Sultan Moyses Zim Kush ruled beyond Ottoman control. For eight days they marched into the autonomous region of Angad, through sandy valleys and over the plain of '*Scidduahr*', before sighting 'the Walls of *Bedtua*' (pp. 153–7). Like courtiers in all ages, T.S. is so captivated by the ceremoniousness of the reception granted the Ottoman delegation by the local potentate that he adopts a formal and pompous style suited to the dignity of the occasion:

> The Ceremonies observed on this Occasion I took exact notice of. The Princes Guards cloathed with a thin Stuff of a Scarlet Die, with red Bonnets and white Feathers flying upon it, yielded a most pleasing sight. (p. 158)

Details of the procession, exchange of gifts and formal pleasantries follow, during which T.S. noticed 'nothing of that rudeness, which our People imagine to be in all the Parts of *Africa*' and regretted only their 'barbarous' language which he could not understand. (p. 161).

The Ottoman delegation wanted several concessions from Moyses Zim Kush, notably free trade and resolution of disputed borders. But there were thornier issues concerning regional support and supplies for 'rebels'. When negotiations started to drag on too long, T.S. quietly took charge of the situation, offering Halley Hamez advice on how to break the deadlock. 'This was not the first time,' T.S. boasts, 'that I had been useful unto him to help him out of difficult Affairs.' Halley Hamez readily listens: 'Sir, said I to my Master, Trouble not your self, I will cause the Prince to give you full satisfaction' (p. 170). First, though, T.S. insists that Halley Hamez promises him freedom 'at his return to *Argiers*, in case he should be successful in this business.' Once that promise has been offered and accepted, T.S. reports how well his plan worked for the Ottomans.

The Ottomans recruited one Zidi Hamed Hochbush, a young and popular nephew of Moyses Zim Kush, by plying him with wine and promises of imperial support if he were to depose his uncle. Everything goes according to plan because 'the young man perceived not my Masters Design, but began to conceive very haughty thoughts of himself and Abilities.' It is not very long before the ambitious Zidi Hamed, in a drunken moment, insults his uncle and factions break out. Furnishing him with 'a Horse, an excellent Courser', Halley Hamez sent the young nephew out of town to raise an army with further promises of Ottoman support, and news soon came that Zidi Hamed had reappeared 'at the head of 10000 men' (p. 177). Once rumours that 'the Turks of *Argeirs* were resolv'd to assist him were not their Demands granted', Moyses Zim Kush gave way and granted Halley Hamez all he requested (p. 177). Everything had gone exactly as T.S. said it would.

Return to Tlemcen

> In this City of *Tremisen* or *Climsan* we made our abode longer than my Master at first designed.
>
> T.S., *Adventures*, p. 201

After reconciling uncle and nephew, T.S. and Halley Hamez returned to Tlemcen where they found glory and promotion, but not the recall to Algiers that would earn T.S. his freedom. 'My Master had the honour of it,' T.S. notes,

> although it was effected by my Contrivance. He ever after employed me in his difficult Affairs, and admitted me into his private Council; An Honour that a Slave could never expect from the *Turks* Severity. (p. 180)

In Ottoman Algeria, however, the life of a clever slave is better than that of a Moor. To emphasize his final point about 'the *Turks* severity', T.S. devotes several pages to descriptions of horrendous methods of torture and execution employed by the Ottomans in Tlemcen to enforce their rule over local people. These lengthy accounts of cruelty recall for us how terrible life was for many living under Ottoman rule in Tlemcen, where T.S. was destined to remain another two years. His master's reward for success in Bedtua was promotion to governor of Tlemcen, so perhaps the rather excessive eye- and ear-witness accounts of the great brazen lion into which criminals – sometimes whole families – are thrown to roast in the sun show us T.S. exorcising memories of events in which he felt some complicity: 'during my stay in that place, I saw above twenty cast into that Oven' (p. 185). Such an extremely unusual form of torture would surely have left some trace in local memory, but none of the historians in Tlemcen I spoke with had ever heard of such a thing.

Sensationalistic as they are, T.S.'s accounts of seeing and hearing the tortured dead and dying provide moments when he tries to distance himself from those he calls 'Turks'. He returns compulsively to the family inside that brazen lion:

> There was no regard to Innocency it self: The poor Child was forced to accompany his Parents in Death ... Their different Voices and cries did yield a most pleasant although a cruel Harmony, which was not ungrateful to the *Turks*, who never pity the *Moors*. (pp. 187–8)

What is most startling is how T.S. emphatically agrees that those cries 'did yield a most pleasant although a cruel Harmony', whether grateful to him or not. In his morbid fascination, T.S. even asks readers to imagine being a man who has been tied to a cross, his tongue cut out and left naked to watch as the eagles and vultures circle above before arriving to feed: 'It is observed, that the Eagles seek first for the Heart; they tear up the Brest till they have found it, without any regard to the rest of the Body, until that be devoured' (p. 189). Perhaps this is meant to be reassuring – you would be dead before they came for your eyes – or a grim warning to watch out for birds with different habits that might feast elsewhere on your body while you watched. For T.S., imagining the sight of birds tearing human flesh is linked to a memory of how he nearly shrugged off his 'Turkish' identifications. 'It is a sight,' he tells us

> that may move any bodies compassion, but that of the *Turks*, to see one of the same nature thus torn and ript up by these cruel Birds: I was never so much concern'd at any thing in my life as I was at it: had I not feared the Censure of the Law, I had ventured to protect the miserable Body of one poor man from those Ravenous Birds; but it is no less than death to hinder the Execution of the Judges Sentence.(p. 190)

Once again T.S.'s instinct for survival kept him alive and out of trouble with the law.

Having abandoned his projected history of Tlemcen's founding dynasties, T.S. describes instead a few local sites, such as a natural spring and a marabout's tomb – most likely that of Sidi Bou Medienne – where miracles are said to occur. 'In this City,' he complains, 'we made our abode longer than my Master at first designed' (p. 201). Thanks largely to excellent counselling from his English adviser, Halley Hamez is promoted to governor, an opportunity for becoming rich while awaiting recall to Algiers. For the next two years, T.S. helps Halley Hamez find wealth and compliant women and in doing so gains his freedom.

Growing rich and pandering

In the final sections, T.S.'s *Adventures* return to the picaresque and bawdy. While helping Halley Hamez use his authority to grow rich, T.S. starts behaving like the slaves in Roman comedies who act like men about town, constantly on the make while arranging affairs for themselves and their masters. T.S. recalls the King of Algiers's judgement of him when he was first being sold as if it had been a prophecy:

> In the meane whiles, I was not idle; I had several Affairs that concerned my private Interest, and that I was to manage with Care and Industry. The *Sultan* of *Argiers* gave a judgment of my Ability and Person, which was not contradicted by the Women with whom I was afterwards acquainted. (p. 203)

Claiming to have as many 'difficult Encounters' and 'Strange Adventures' among the widows who wanted him to convert to Islam in order to marry them as his master 'had in treating with the Arabs' (p. 203), T.S. turns to Hally Hamez for advice when one woman becomes especially pressing. From here, his homosocial triangulated relation to his master starts to develop:[6]

> I declared the busines to my Master, and made him the Confident of that Love. He...desired me, if I were so reserved, that I would pleasure him by giving him a favourable Meeting with that Lady...he grumbled at me that I had not sooner declared it unto him...I excused my self, and told him that had I known his pleasure, he should have been already satisfied. (pp. 209–10)

Pandering to his master, T.S. approached the lady, who 'still continued her kindness to me' (p. 210), found her agreeable and successfully arranged her first visit, in disguise, to his master's house.

> She found the Guard very favourable to her, and my Masters Lodging far more; for he was prepared to receive her with as much civillity as she did desire: She quickly returned muffled up...

When Women once lose their honesty, nothing can keep them from that pleasure which they fancy so sweet. This Woman having found so good entertainment at the first, was resolved to make a second tryal of our Kindness. She continued to visit us, as often as her industry could find an escape. (p. 213)

'Our Kindness', 'visiting us' – it sounds as if pandering may have included joining in.

T.S.'s triangular bond with his first master in Algiers was entirely structural and displaced, experienced at a distance; they had sexual access to the same women, but not at the same time or place. With Hally Hamez, however, T.S. embarks on an entirely different arrangement. 'I did him sometimes the favour,' T.S. reports, 'to cause him to share with me in my good Fortune, and furthered the satisfaction of his Inclinations, an Office not ungrateful to an old Lover, that hath scarce any thing acceptable in him, but the desire of doing well' (p. 224). Being so attractive to Algerian women himself, T.S. could not help but find himself sought after by so many lusty widows that he had no difficulty finding women to share with his master, who could not attract them on his own. 'Had my design been to make Conquests in the Empire of Love,' he reflects, 'I think none could have been more happy' (pp. 213–14). When possibilities of a legitimate marriage to a rich and loving widow come along, T.S. is sorely tempted until recalling that marriage would require he convert to Islam, and then he would have but 'small hopes left of seeing again my Native Soil' (p. 217). But T.S. has lost his earlier delight in whoring, and comes to wish that he was not so attractive to women. 'I was once so troubled with addresses,' he complains, 'that I wished my Face had been disfigured' (p. 223).

In his final pages, T.S. wearily reports what seems to have become a routine life in an imperial colony: women, local uprisings, acquiring wealth. When Bembouker, 'King of *Fez*', sets out to rob a caravan carrying gold for the Ottomans, Halley Hamez and T.S. successfully thwart his plans with some loss of life. They safely bring back the caravan which 'did enrich us, and fill the City with plenty of Gold, Ivory and other Commodities' (p. 231). As his time in Algeria draws to an end, however, T.S. seems to have lost the energy and excitement that animated his retellings of earlier adventures. Instead, he adopts a somewhat clipped and summary style as if he is packing the few remaining incidents in before leaving town. In rapid succession he reports that the Great Mosque collpased in an earthquake; a woman gave birth to 'a strange Monster' with ape-head and lion-claws; rebellious Arab forces were thwarted 'at a Town called *Tezrim*' (pp. 232, 234, 237). At the mention of Tezrim, a town about six leagues from Tlemcen, T.S. is reminded of something:

One thing I cannot omit very memorable in this place. At some distance from *Tezrim*, in a little Meadow where excellent Grass grows, I saw the perfect

Statue of a man Buggering his Ass: it was so lively that at a little distance I fancied they had been alive, but when I came nearer, I saw they were of a perfect Stone. (p. 238)

Knowing full well that the local Moors and Arabs 'naturally hate all sorts of Representations', T.S. inspects the statue and is soon persuaded that it was a divine act that 'in the very moment of the Beastly Act...changed the fleshly Substances of the Man and of the Ass into a firm Stone' (p. 239). T.S. is not the only Englishman to report seeing this statue, and as if suddenly aware of sceptical readers, he reassures us that other 'Merchants, and Traders' will confirm that such stone monuments are to be seen elsewhere in North Africa, all evidence of divine agency (p. 242).[7]

With the stone monument to the man and his donkey, T.S. neatly ends his book by bringing prurient interests and pious claims together in this display of God's providential judgement:

From those that travel into these place every one may better satisfie themselves concerning the truth of these wonderful Examples of Gods Justice, much like that of *Lot's* Wife turned into a Pillar of Salt. (p. 244)

On returning from this campaign, T.S. finds that his time of captivity is nearly up. Halley Hamez has been recalled, 'we took our bag and Baggage' and they left for Algiers.

My master was grown very rich, and powerful, he had got...much Wealth. According to his Promise he gave me my Liberty, and a sum, of Money to carry me home. (p. 246)

T.S. had made the most of his captivity. He had risen above abjection, resisted and eroticized his slavery, earned the trust of a powerful Ottoman pasha and grown rich. He had numerous adventures amidst the wildlife of North Africa, discovered remains of ancient civilizations, learned how to administer a colonial outpost without always resorting to brute force. Like Thomas Dallam, T.S. took the first boat home.

In short, and if a word of this book is to be trusted, T.S. achieved his initial goal of travelling in order to have something to write about.

Epilogue: What About the Women, Then?

The spectres of Lady Mary Wortley Montagu

> I dare say You expect at least something very new in this Letter after
> I have gone a Journey not undertaken by any Christian of some 100 years.
>> Lady Mary Wortley Montagu to Alexander Pope,
>> 1 April 1717, from Adrianople[1]

Lady Mary Wortley Montagu keenly wanted the reputation of being an original. She was fortunate in this ambition; there are very few records of English women visiting the Ottoman Empire before her. There are the important exceptions of the Quakers Katherine Evans and Sarah Cheevers, who set out in 1659 to convert the people of Alexandria but were held captive by the Inquisition on Malta. But apart from their account of their captivity, no women travellers wrote in English about visiting the Ottoman Empire before Lady Mary.[2]

Women clearly went. Their names sometimes appear in lists of redeemed captives. In 1647, for instance, an expedition from Algiers and Tangier returned with 242 former captives, including nineteen women from England, Ireland, and Scotland.[3] Traces of expatriate women also occasionally appear in rumours of disreputable goings-on. William Biddulph was reported to have met an 'Inglishe strumpitt' on Zante, while even the extremely broadminded Samuel Pepys was staggered by the behaviour of women living in the English colony at Tangier.[4] Women also accompanied their husbands on trading and diplomatic missions, taking daughters and maids with them.[5] Lady Mary was by no means the first wife of an English ambassador to accompany her husband, but she was the first to write about it.

The strange case of Anne, Lady Glover

After marrying Sir Thomas Glover in 1606, Anne Lamb became Lady Glover, and as part of the deal, also became the first wife of an English ambassador to

221

Istanbul to accompany her husband on his posting. Lady Glover was herself accompanied by at least two maids. One of them returned to England in 1608 and promptly accused Sir Thomas of getting 'one of the maids which went over...with child'.[6]

Of Lady Glover's life before she embarked for Istanbul, I have found very little evidence. From William Forde's sermon preached at her funeral, we learn she was 'Daughter to M. Lamb of Padley in Suffolke' and that she claimed Lady Wentworth, to whom the published version of Forde's sermon is dedicated, as her patroness. Beyond this, Forde fails to tell us very much, resorting instead to some obvious puns on her maiden name – this 'Lambe in name...Lambe in nature' – which is not surprising since he had never met her.[7]

The date when Lady Glover died from plague is uncertain – Forde says 30 October while John Sanderson heard it was 'the 2 day of November 1608'.[8] What Forde knew, but discreetly never mentioned, and what many attending the funeral also knew, was just how grotesque it was to describe the 'bodily forme and outward feature' of Lady Glover as being 'full of grace and beautie' since the body they were burying had been dead for three and a half years, preserved in bran and stored in the cellars of the Levant Company house in Pera.

The evidence also conveys little about Lady Glover's life in Istanbul. John Sanderson was in London in 1606 when Thomas Glover received his knighthood and ambassadorial appointment, and he considered the marriage to be an even greater blessing than either of these career achievements. In August 1606 he wrote about the preparations that were then underway for the newly appointed ambassador's entourage to sail for Istanbul, commenting:

> God, you see, hath highelie advansed the nowe Ambassator every way. The place he is in is no smaule favoure of God; the Kinges favoure a great matter; but in his wife I hould him to be more blessed; for he hath matched with a most disreete, wise, milde, a very gentill gentillwoman; a lamb by hir father and no lesse in hir owne nature; a lady worthy to be ever most best beloved. I pray God continewe hir health ther and keepe hir husbands hart ever lovinge unto hir.[9]

Perhaps Forde, who did not know Anne Lamb, took advice from Sanderson, who did. If not, then the name of Lamb, understood as a predictor of character, was too potent an association to avoid. Sanderson knew and liked Glover, so he may well have been writing hopefully, keen that a good wife would inspire good works in her sometimes erratic and flamboyant husband. A year later, Sanderson sent Lady Glover some books, including a work translated into English by an 'honorable' lady 'out of French' in the hope that it might inspire her to undertake similar translations from Italian and Greek authors, 'for methinks I see hir most apt inclinations to all good'.[10]

In addition to self-improvement through study, Lady Glover was required to perform a public role in the social life of the Ottoman court. As the first English ambassadorial wife to live in the capital, she was also the first to be the focus of curiosity at the Ottoman court. Thomas Gainsford, a member of Glover's retinue, recalled a meeting with Sultan Ahmed I during September 1607 – perhaps around the same time that Ahmed destroyed Dallam's organ. Ahmed, a 'gallant young-man of nineteene yeeres olde,' Gainsford noted, was

> somewhat fat and well favoured: yet did the pock-holes a little ecclipse the sweetnesse of his aspect: his countenance was sterne and majesticall, and his apparrell a plaine crimsen satten gowne. He wore no gloves, nor suffered any to do so in his presence, which likewise all their women observe, especially the *Sultanesses*, whom when the Lady *Glover* was admitted to visit, they caused her to put her gloves aside.[11]

This would by no means be the last time the wife of an English ambassador would be called upon to remove some of her clothing for an Ottoman court.

Lady Glover's death upset Sir Thomas greatly, and his subsequent strange behaviour became a matter of no small concern among the English community. Glover's friend, the physician John Kitely, was much vexed by the ambassador's agitated state and especially by his plans to send Anne's body home to England for burial. Reassuringly, Sanderson advised Kitely that he thought Glover 'to be of too manly and heroyacall spiritt to be amated [i.e. dismayed] at the decease of one wife'. Sanderson's editor, William Foster, glossed 'amated' as 'dismayed', but we might sense something more strongly felt at the loss of a 'mate', akin to losing one's reason or behaving irrationally. Sanderson offered sober advice:

> Counsell His Lordship to interr hir ther. My opinion is that in the monstary of Calcose Ile, where that wourthy Bartons body lieth, ether by or therabout, with some marble monument, wilbe more laudable then to bring hir corps for Ingland. You knowe it is Christian buriall; and peradventure, yf by sea she should be transported, every storme would hassard hir truncke [i.e. coffin] to be buried overbourd; most mariners ar superstitiouse in that respect. And al resoun and order would that, wher the tree faulteth, ther it should lie.[12]

Plans to transport Lady Glover's body back to England were abandoned. Yet even with the imitable precedent of Edward Barton before him, Glover could not be prevailed upon to bury her in Istanbul, preferring instead to wallow in his grief, as Kitely reported to Sanderson in May:

> I shewed your letter and likewise perswaded a private funerall in the place you named; but as yet cannot prevaile. He answers shee is buried already in

branne, which is a kind of earth, and it is no sinne to keepe her. Get Master
Leate and Master Stapers to persuade to intere her, for sight of her herse
oftentimes revives his melancholy passions.[13]

Nearly two years would pass before Sanderson in London wrote directly to
Glover urging him to do something about a proper funeral:

> It is heare also reported that you doe the dead lady, your wife, wrong,
> because you have not yet geven hir Christian buriall, but have laid hir in the
> butery at the end of the selore [i.e. cellar] underground.[14]

So matters remained at an impasse for several more months: the merchants
worried about their ambassador, Sir Thomas indulged his grief, while Lady
Glover remained unhygienically housed in the ambassadorial buttery. In
September 1611, King James ordered Glover back to England and appointed
Sir Paul Pindar in his place. Surely this was the stimulus that Glover needed
in order to act. However, another seven months elapsed before William Forde
presided over the funeral obsequies.

The funeral was the event of the season that spring in Istanbul. Edward
Grimestone's continuation of Richard Knolles's *Generall Historie* for the year
1612 offers an account that begins:

> On the 14 of Aprill, the Lady *Anne Glover*, wife to Sir *Thomas Gloover*,
> Embassador residing at Constantinople for the English, was buried with
> very great solemnity, the like had not bin seen in that countrey, since the
> Turks conquered Constantinople.[15]

Grimestone seldom reveals his sources, yet there is every reason to think that,
in addition to drawing on Forde's sermon, he owed the story of Lady Glover's
funeral to Sir Thomas himself.[16] And Grimestone was in no doubt that the
occasion, however sad for some of those attending, was a major propaganda
victory for the Protestant English in Istanbul:

> There were present at this funerall of most nations in the world, the sermon
> was preached in a large garden under a Cypresse tree: and although but few
> of those present did understand it, yet it wrought this effect, that whereas
> the Jesuits and Friers had formerly possest both Jewes, Turks, and other
> people, that the English nation since the change of their religion, had nei-
> ther churches, nor any form of divine service; hereby they perceived, that
> they had both, and served God far more decently and devotedly than they
> themselves; insomuch that the Jesuits being ashamed of their impostures,
> and slanderous untruth, durst not for a while after walke the streets, for

feare of the Turks, who threatned them for so much belying the English. The Sermon being ended, the body was caried from Pera unto the English graves, which were almost a mile from the place . . . The tomb was of faire marble, built foure square almost the height of a man, having an Epitaph engraven thereon.[17]

The site where the English were buried – 'almost a mile' from Pera – is now part of Taksim Square, Istanbul's busiest hub. Of her marble tomb and engraved epitaph, no trace can be found. Yet William Forde was right to observe in his sermon that 'Her life procured love, her death, fame'.[18]

Lady Wych disrobes

A second ambassadorial wife who preceded Lady Mary Wortley Montagu to Istanbul was the consort of Sir Peter Wych, who held the post between 1628 and 1639. In 1653, the rather pious John Bulwer reported the following incident in order to illustrate the folly of courtly costumes, especially such flamboyant female attire as the hooped skirts that were fashionable at the Stuart court before 1649. 'I have been told,' Bulwer writes:

> that when Sir *Peter Wych* was Embassadour to the Grand *Signeour* from King *James*, his Lady being then with him at *Constantinople*, the *Sultanesse* desired one day to see his Lady, whom she had heard much of; whereupon my Lady *Wych* (accompanied with her waiting-women, all neatly dressed in their great *Verdingals*, which was the Court fashion then) attended her Highnesse. The *Sultanesse* entertained her respectfully, but withall wondring at her great and spacious Hips, she asked her whether all English women were so made and shaped about those parts: To which my Lady *Wych* answered, that they were made as other women were, withall shewing the fallacy of her apparell in the device of the Verdingall, untill which demonstration was made, the *Sultanesse* verily believed it had been her naturall and reall shape.[19]

The incident anticipates by at least 78 years Lady Mary Wortley Montagu being importuned to undress by ladies in the bathhouse at Sophia in 1717. Grandiloquently claiming to have 'past a Journey that has not been undertaken by any Christian since the Time of the Greek Emperours', Lady Mary was clearly not the first English woman to experience such moments of intimate cultural curiosity over her body and clothes, whatever her other claims to originality might be.[20]

Notes

Prologue and Argument

1. Murad III, 1574–95.
2. Mehmed III, 1595–1603.
3. Ahmed I, 1603–17.
4. Koran 51: 28.
5. The biblical Abraham, who destroyed his father's idols.
6. The Palace gardeners, who were also responsible for policing.
7. Koran 20: 97.
8. Kinzer, *Crescent and Star: Turkey between Two Worlds*, p. 3.
9. For an excellent and balanced study of the historical and regional complexities, see Goddard, *History of Christian–Muslim Relations* (2000), and the pioneering essays in Blanks, ed., *Images of the Other* (1997).

1 Thomas Dallam (c.1575–c.1630)

1. *CSPD, 1598–1601*, 31 January 1599, p. 156.
2. 'The family is named after the hamlet of Dallam in Lancashire, now part of Warrington. Thomas was born at nearby Flixton in 1575. There is evidence to show that the Dallams (and later their in-laws, the Harrises) were recusant Catholics, and several suggestions that the family was of noble lineage,' writes Bicknell, *History of the English Organ*, p. 72. But see Bak, 'Who Built the Organ for the Sultan?' for speculation that Thomas himself did not build the organ. See also Edmonds, 'The Dallam Family'; Sumner, 'The Origins of the Dallams'; and Cocheril, 'The Dallams in Brittany'.
3. See Skilliter, 'Three Letters'.
4. Chew, *The Crescent and the Rose*, p. 172.
5. See Prologue to this book, and Necipoğlu, *Architecture, Ceremonial, and Power*, p. 155, citing from the two-volume manuscript copy of the *Zubdetu't-tevarih* in the Topkapi Palace Library (Revan 1304) ff. 39r–39v.
6. See Bent, ed., *Early Voyages and Travels*.
7. Pamuk, *Benim Adım Kırmızı*, trans. Erdag M. Goknar, *My Name is Red*.
8. G.E. Abbott, who thought Dallam's editor a lunatic, would not have been surprised at the truly alarming number of errors that have crept into subsequent reports of Dallam and his organ where misconceptions and errors of fact concerning both man and organ abound. Dallam's biographer Mayes, for instance, repeatedly refers to Dallam condescendingly as a 'little Lancashireman', though nothing is known of his height. The historian Brandon Beck claims that Elizabeth sent Dallam and the gifts in 1595, the year Mehmed III acceded, while his two short quotations from Bent's edition of the manuscript – Beck calls him 'Dent' by the way – average three

226

errors every five words, not counting entire sentences silently omitted, or the ungrammatical and unidiomatic rendering 'the sight whereof did almost make to think that I was in a different world' for 'the sighte whearof did make me almoste to thinke that I was in another worlde', *From the Rising of The Sun*, pp. 32, 113, and compare p. 39 with Bent's transcription, p. 69. The literary historian Kamil Aydin repeats the double error of the travel writer Eric Newby, by calling Dallam 'a cockney organ-maker, sent to Constantinople in 1599 to erect in the Selamlik an hydraulic organ he had built', *Images of Turkey*, p. 49, following Newby's *On the Shores of the Mediterranean*, p. 218, almost word for word. By no stretch of the imagination could Dallam be called a cockney; he worked in London but came from Lancashire, and the organ in question was clockwork. More recently still, in his history of Istanbul, John Freely writes of 'an extraordinary water-organ' built by 'Thomas Dallaam', *Istanbul*, p. 213, misspelling 'Dallam' throughout. Newby and Freely, however, manage to quote Dallam's eccentric Elizabethan prose without error and get the dates right, unlike Laurence Kelly, who fancifully reports that Dallam 'had just finished the erection of the organ in King's College, Cambridge' before being sent to Istanbul, *Istanbul*, p. 224. Dallam constructed the organ at King's several years after returning from Istanbul, and it is likely that he received the commission as a result of his success in the Ottoman capital. Most recently, Boyd Tonkin, writing of Orhan Pamuk's novel, comments: 'Pamuk mentions the showy clock given by the Queen to the Sultan as an emblem of mutual amity and curiosity. A generation after their treaty, the clock stopped. Now is the time to make sure that it ticks again', *The Independent Magazine*, p. 380.

9. Readers of Turkish can benefit greatly from the introduction, additional notes and appendices provided by Mehmet Halim Spatar in his translation of Mayes's book, *Sultan'ın Orgu*, which also may have helped inspire Pamuk's novel.

10. See Yerasimos, *Les Voyageurs*.

11. A notable exception is the account of an overland journey written by the servant Fox; see *Mr. Harrie Cavendish*.

12. Yerasimos, *Les Voyageurs*, p. 11; for a catalogue of the various translations into German, French, Dutch, Italian, Polish, English, Serbo-Croatian and Czech, see pp. 159–63. The first English translation, *The Offspring of the House of Ottomanno* by Hugh Goughe, appeared in 1570.

13. See Parker, *Books to Build an Empire*, for a useful survey of the professionalization of travel writing in early seventeenth-century England.

14. In *Religion and Empire*, Louis B. Wright provides what is still one of the best critical introductions to the ideological efforts of Hakluyt and Purchas.

15. The purchase date is marked in a ms note on the false title-page of the manuscript, BL Add. Ms 17480. First notice may have appeared two years earlier when the British Library acquired a *Catalogue of the Collection of Works of Art and Vertue, comprising pictures, books, prints, sculpture...formed by Henry Rhodes* (1846), but this work is now marked 'destroyed'.

16. Personal letter from Dr M.C. Breay of the Deparment of Manuscripts, British Library, 5 July 1999.

17. Anon., 'Relics of the Past', p. 380.

18. Rimbault, *Early English Organ Builders*, pp. 45–50.

19. Thomas's son Robert (1602–65) entered the business and, with his father, constructed an organ for Durham Cathedral between 1624 and 1627, and later for both Jesus College, Cambridge and New College, Oxford.

20. Abbott, *Turkey, Greece*, p. 85 n. 1.

2   On First Setting Out

1. See Phelps Brown and Hopkins, *A Perspective of Wages and Prices*, p. 11.
2. Normally, a Venetian gold coin, the *zecchino* Dallam encountered may have been a Turkish variation. Three decades later, Henry Blount writes of 'a *Zeccheen* Turkish [which] I value nine shillings sterlin', *Voyage*, p. 98.
3. Sanderson to Thomas Simonds, 21 September 1599, in Foster, p. 181. Subsequent page references to this edition are given as 'in Foster', except when I have quoted directly from Sanderson's manuscript, BL MS Lansdowne 241.
4. See, for example, the letter from Richard Staper and Edward Homden to Robert Cecil trying to get him to intercede on their behalf with the Queen to send a present to the new Sultan; 6 December 1595, *CSPD, 1590–98*, p. 486. The officers of the Levant Company repeated the request a year later with greater urgency.
5. See 'The Travailes of John Mildenhall', in Purchas, 2: 297–304.
6. John Mildenhall names the captain as Richard Parsons, who had previously made the trip as captain of the *Great Susan*, see in Purchas, 2: 297; and see Foster, ed., *Early Travels in India*, p. 52. The *Hector* was next commissioned as part of the fleet sent to the East Indies, on which voyage her purser was one George Parsons, with John Middleton captain; see Stevens, ed., *Dawn of British Trade*, pp. 33, 94, 100, 121, 154.
7. While in Istanbul, Buckett was commissioned by Henry Lello to paint a portrait of Queen Elizabeth for a gift to the Sultan's mother. On return to England, he was employed by Robert Cecil, 1st Earl of Salisbury, on decorations to Salisbury House and Hatfield House between 1608 and 1612, becoming one of the most notable painter-stainers of his generation; see Croft-Murray, *Decorative Painting*, 1: 32–3, 194.
8. For Conisby, see *DNB* entry for his son, Sir Thomas (d. 1625).
9. Sir Dudley North, 'Relations of some voyages and forrein Transactions And Avianas in Turky. Extracted from the papers of an honorable person deceased, with A Proposall Intended to be made in parliament in order to Regulate the Coyne, in 1683', BL Add. Ms 32522, f. 34v–35.
10. Drabling: Bent glosses the term 'drabler, or a piece of canvas laced on the bonnet of a sail to give it more drop', p. 9, n. 2, anticipating the *OED*, which gives 'an additional piece of canvas, laced to the bottom of the bonnet of a sail, to give it greater depth', citing Greene and Lodge, 1592.

3   Mediterranean Encounters

1. Sandys, *Relation*, p. 8.
2. Lithgow, *Totall Discourse*, pp. 58–9. Begun in 1533, the English trade in Zante currants was, according to Lithgow, worth '160000 Chickins . . . every Chickin of gold being nine shillings English' at the time of his visit, ibid.; and see Epstein, *Early History*, p. 6.
3. News that the *Hector* had arrived in Iskenderun must have reached the English community in Aleppo by 18 May, the date several letters thence were addressed to Sanderson; BL Lansdowne 241, ff. 308–308v.
4. The inventory for the *Hector* compiled for her second voyage can be found in Stevens, ed., *Dawn of British Trade*, pp. 15–16. On 23 August 1633, Richard Dike wrote to his brother Edward Nicholas: 'Two English ships, the Hector and the William and Ralph . . . were met with by 60 galleys of the Turks and were both fired and sunk,' but this might not have been the same *Hector*; *CSPD, 1633–34*, p. 190.

5. The role of the *Hector* on her return in the action against two Spanish galleons of much greater size remains unclear. Dallam's account of this episode corresponds exactly with two missing pages in the manuscript. Of this action, John Chamberlain wrote to Dudley Carlton on 10 May 1600, that nine or ten 'good merchant ships' from the Levant have come in near North Cape. They had met with two Spanish galleons, 'sunk one, and took the other', later letting her go; *CSPD, 1589–1601*, p. 434.

6. Marginal gloss, BL Add Ms 17480, f. 30.

7. Marginal gloss; BL Add Ms 17480, f. 30v.

8. Biddulph, *Travels*, p. 39. Peter Mundy wrote: 'Scandarone or Allexandretta is the Sea port of Alleppo, some three daies Journie distant. It is very unwholesome by reason of the hugh high hills hindringe the approach of the Sunne Beames, untill nine or ten a Clocke in the morning, lyeinge in a great Marsh full of boggs, foggs, and Froggs' (*Travels*, p. 19). Charles Robson visited in 1625 noting: 'At last (by Gods favour) we arrived in safety at *Alexandretta alias Scanderone*, which we found full of the carcases of houses, not one house in it. It having been a litle before sackt by the Turkish Pyrats. The unwholesomest place in the world to live in, by reason of the grosse fogges that both descend from the high mountaines, and ascend from the moorish valleys. The hilles about it are so high, that till ten of the clocke in the morning the Sunne seldome or never peepeth over them. Here wee tooke horse, (not daring to stay above two houres) for *Aleppo*, paying two and twenty Dollars for a *Ianizarie* to be our guide, six Dollars and a halfe a man for our horses, besides halfe a Dollar a day to find our horses meate: our noone and nights lodging were the open fields, our victuals such as wee brought from *Scanderone*; our guide proud and surly, our journey the most troublesome that any before (by relation) ever had' (*Newes From Aleppo*, p. 11).

9. Maye had been in Aleppo since 1596 at least, at which time he was involved in adjudicating a local dispute among the English merchants; see George Dorrington to Sanderson, 11 August 1596, in Foster, p. 155. He had made himself unpopular, however, soon after; see Elizeus Sotheren to Sanderson, 5 March 1598, in Foster, p. 175.

10. Nicolay, *Navigations*, p. 37. George Sandys, whom we might have expected to provide some classical poet to illustrate his point, simply noted: 'The women celebrated of old for their beauties, yet carry that fame: I will not say undeservedly. They have their heads trickt with tassels and flowers. The bodies of their gownes exceed not their arme-pits: from whence the skirts flow loosely, fringed below; the upper shorter than the neather; of damasks or stuffes lesse costly, according to their condition' (*Relation*, p. 14).

11. Yerasimos identifies these small towns as Şarköy and Gaziköy, but they do not appear on the detailed maps he provides, and I have been unable to find them on other maps; see Yerasimos, *Voyageurs*, p. 435 and map 19.

4 Istanbul

1. BL Ms Cotton Nero B.xi, f. 215–215v.

2. Sanderson to the Levant Company, 25 August 1599 in Foster, p. 177.

3. Capello to the Doge and Senate, 18 September 1599, *CPSV, 1592–1603*, #814.

4. Lello to Cecil, 8 September 1599, PRO *SP 97/4*, f. 45. See Mayes, *Organ*, pp. 171, 183; and Peirce, *Imperial Harem*, pp. 225–8.

5. Capello to the Doge and Senate, 21 August 1599, *CPSV, 1592–1603*, #806.

6. Capello to the Doge and Senate, 18 September 1599, *CSPV, 1592–1603*, #814.

7. Capello reported that the English gifts included 'many suits of cloth which they say are all mouldy and ruined', 18 September 1599, *CSPV, 1592–1603*, #814.
8. Capello to the Doge and Sentate, 2 October 1599, *CSPV, 1592–1603*, #817.
9. For a different account of relations between Dallam and Lello, see Mayes, who considers that Dallam was flattered by this 'somewhat unnecessary speech', *Organ*, p. 193.
10. See Girolamo Capello to the Doge and Senate, 21 August 1599 and 18 September 1599, *CSPV, 1592–1603*, #806, 814.
11. BL Ms Cotton Nero B.xi, f. 1.
12. BL Ms Cotton Nero B.xi, ff. 1–16.
13. See Mayes, *Organ*, p. 208.
14. For a different discussion of the episode, see Fuller, 'English Turks'.

5   Biddulph's Ministry: Travels around Aleppo, 1600–12

1. Forde, *Sermon*, sig. A2.
2. See Purchas, 8: 248–304.
3. Kimber and Johnson, *Baronetage*, 2: 303.
4. Clark, *Register of the University of Oxford*, 2: 127.
5. Curiously, a certain Theophilus Biddulph of Westcombe, Kent, was created baronet in 1664, and the name reappears in the family for some generations; Kimber and Johnson, *Baronetage*, 2: 304.
6. Parker, *Books to Build an Empire*, p. 187. Timberlake's manuscript is to be found at BL Ms Sloane, 2496, ff. 62–9; reprints appeared in 1608, 1609, 1611, 1612, 1616, 1620, 1631, 1683, 1685, 1692, 1695 and 1699.
7. Palmer, *Essay*, sig. A2v.

6   Preacher among the Diplomats

1. Stevens, ed., *Dawn of British Trade*, p. 276.
2. A copy of the letter appointing Glover ambassador, dated 'die decimo sexto mensis Augusti, Anno Domini 1606', PRO *SP 97/5*, f. 76. Glover refers to the date of his appointment in a letter to Robert Cecil, 3 April 1607, PRO *SP 97/5*, f. 131.
3. Sanderson to Glover, 16 November 1608, in Foster, p. 257. On Eldred, see Foster, p. 6. Sanderson disliked Eldred, calling him 'my ould mortall illwiller'; letter to Nicholas Salter, 29 March 1600, in Foster, p. 199.
4. Sanderson to Glover, 15 December 1608, in Foster, pp. 257–8; here corrected from BL Ms Lansdowne 241, f. 197.
5. Strachey may have been related to the merchant John Strachey who, in 1601, was a signatory to a petition to the Company regarding wages for Thomas Glover; see Foster, p. 220 n.1.
6. See Glover to Lello, 'The Coppie of my tre writne from Sio unto Mr Henrie Lello in Constantinople',' PRO *SP 97/5*, f. 85; a second copy appears at PRO *SP 97/5*, ff. 129–30. Lello had already been instructed to leave behind all the household goods by a letter from the Levant Company, dated 20 June 1660, in which he was also advised that Anthony Abdie had been instructed to pay him 600 chequins: PRO *SP 105/143*, f. 6. Some weeks later, another letter was addressed to Lello similarly instructing him to give up the house and advising him that he would be receiving a total of 3,100 chequins: PRO *SP 105/143*, f. 7v.

7. Ottaviano Bon to the Doge and Senate, 8 November 1606, *CPSV, 1603–7*, #617; see also 9 January 1607, #657; 28 March 1607, #712; and 27 April 1607, #724.

8. Glover to Cecil, 18 March 1607, PRO *SP 97/5*, ff. 114–15.

9. Glover to Cecil, 1 April 1607, PRO *SP 97/5*, ff. 121–6; another copy of the document appears at PRO *SP 97/5*, f. 127.

10. Glover to Cecil, 3 April 1607, PRO *SP 97/5*, f. 131.

11. Sanderson to Glover, 30 April 1607, in Foster, p. 235.

12. Glover to Cecil, 16 April 1607, PRO *SP 97/5*, f. 142.

13. Lello to Robert Cecil, 17 April 1607, PRO *SP 97/5*, ff.146–7.

14. Petition to Cecil, 17 April 1607, PRO *SP 97/5*, ff. 150–1.

15. Glover to Cecil, 19 June 1607, PRO *SP 97/5*, f. 173.

16. A report that Lello had stopped over in Venice and addressed the Doge and Cabinet, 17 September 1607, *CSPV, 1607–10*, #65.

17. Sanderson to Glover, 27 August 1607, in Foster, p. 239.

18. See Glover to 'Sir Tho. Berlie, the old knight' (i.e. Sherley), 10 August 1607, *Historical Manuscripts Commission* 9, p. 212. Glover repeated the accusation in a letter to Thomas Sherley the younger dated 25 August 1607, PRO *SP 97/5*, f. 207.

19. Biddulph to 'Mrs. *Gratzwicke*,' 14 July 1607, PRO *SP 97/5*, f. 181.

20. Among other accusations that, according to Percivall, George Coxden brought against Glover were that 'one mournynge my Lord went into his closett in his shirt and nyghtgowne only (under pretext to write letters) wheare his wench stayed for him; And Abraham the drogurman seeing that sayd (somewhat to his offence) feythe [it] is a naughtye man that havinge a fine gentlewoman to his wife would notwithstaindinge doe thise thinges', and further 'that my Lord would marry his wench to [ ], and after Mr Lellos departure, putt hym in that house he is now in.' Percivall's charges against Coxden, 28 April 1607, PRO *SP 97/5*, f. 186.

21. PRO *SP 97/5*, ff. 188–9.

22. Glover to Cecil, 18 March 1607, PRO *SP 97/5*, f. 115.

23. Sanderson to Kitely, 17 and 18 January 1609, in Foster, pp. 259–50.

24. Sanderson to Kitely, 17/18 January 1609, in Foster, p. 260.

25. Kitely to Sanderson, 2 May 1609, in Foster, p. 264; corrected from BL Ms Lansdowne 241, f. 409v.

26. Barton died late in 1597, probably of dysentery, and was buried on Heybeliada (Halki), one of the Prince's Islands in the sea of Marmara; on the problems of dating and cause of death, see Foster, pp. 174–5, 296. In September 1999 I was unable to find Barton's gravestone there, but Caroline Finkel kindly found the gravestone, badly eroded, in the Crimean War Cemetery at Üsküdar (private correspondence, November 1999), where it was still decaying in July 2000. Photographs of the gravestone in its original site appear in Ahmet Refik, *Türkler*, pp. 11, 14.

27. Nicholas Leate in London to Sanderson in Pera, 22 December 1599, in Foster, p. 190.

28. See BL MS Cotton Nero B. xi, ff. 94–112.

29. Glover's uncle, Robert Glover, was burned for his beliefs at Coventry in 1555; see 'S. M. S.', 'The Mancetter Martyrs', p. 182

30. Lithgow, *Totall Discourse*, pp. 126–7.

7 Troublesome Travelling Churchmen

1. Sanderson at Pera to Nicholas Leate in London, March 1600, in Foster, p. 197.

2. See Wright, 'Jehovah's Blessing on the Eastern Trade', chapter 3 of *Religion and Empire*, pp. 57–83.

3. On Pocock's career, see Toomer, *Eastern Wisdome and Learning*, chapters 5 and 6.
4. Smith returned to take up a fellowship at Magdalen College, Oxford, and to write his *Remarks Upon the Manners, Religion and Government of the Turks* (1678). On his return, Covel was appointed preacher of Divinity at Cambridge, and later served two terms as Vice Chancellor of the University; extracts from his 'diary' were edited by Theodore Bent in *Early Voyages and Travels*. A Fellow of Exeter College, Oxford, Maundrell died before his *Journey from Aleppo to Jerusalem* (Oxford, 1703) could be published. Chishull was appointed chaplain to the Queen in 1711; his *Travels in Turkey and back to England* (1747) was published posthumously. Chishull's *Antiquitates Asiaticae* (1728) was one of the most controversial archaeological studies of its time.
5. See Pearson, *Biographical Sketch*. Pearson's study, based on the minute book of the Levant Company, leads him to conclude that 'it was not until 1624 that the factory at Aleppo, in cooperation it seems with some zealous friends at home, applied for a minister: and it was only in 1635 that a similar appeal was received from Smyrna,' p. 8. Records of earlier appointments, however, appear in the papers of the East India Company; see Stevens, ed., *Dawn of British Trade*, pp. 275–6, 281.
6. Capello to the Doge and Senate, 2 October 1599, *CSPV, 1592–1603*, #817.
7. George Dorrington to Sanderson, 11 August 1596, in Foster, p. 155.
8. Sanderson to Glover, 6 July 1608, in Foster, p. 252.
9. Sanderson to Colthurst, in Foster, p. 175 corrected and expanded from BL Lansdowne 241, f. 307v, where the letter is indicated as from 'Alexandretta this 23 May 1599'.
10. Stevens, ed., *Dawn of British Trade*, p. 281.
11. Purchas, 8: 486. I have been unable to find the original of this letter.
12. Pearson's candidate for this honour is Charles Robson, whose appointment of 22 December 1625 was backdated to 'the time of his arrival at Aleppo', which was before July of the previous year; *Biographical Sketch*, p. 54. Like Maye, Robson evidently began his chaplaincy in Aleppo before being formally appointed by the Company. In Robson's case there was also some doubt whether 'he had been admitted to the Ministry by the Orders of the Church of England', but a testimonial from Oxford seems to have been sufficient (ibid.): see Robson's *Newes from Aleppo* (1628).
13. If Biddulph's appointment began during Michaelmas 1598, then he was presumably taken on at a time when the ambassadorship itself was still being debated. In October of that year, John Chamberlain wrote to Dudley Carleton that 'John Wroth is to go ambassador to Turkey', 20 October 1598, *CSPD, 1598–1601*, p. 110. Wroth's appointment, however, was not approved by the Company merchants; see 'The differences betweene the Turkey merchants and Mr. Wroth', January 1599, PRO *SP 97/4* f. 9. At the time, Lello was already in Istanbul as a secretary to the Levant Company, but his appointment as ambassador not confirmed until the arrival of the *Hector*: 'It [the *Hector*] brings ... letters patent confirming the English Agent here as Ambassador of the Queen', Girolamo Capello to the Doge, 21 August 1599, *CSPV, 1592–1603*, #806.
14. Smith to Biddulph, cited in Stevens, ed., *Dawn of British Trade*, pp. 275–6.
15. Signature G in first editions of *The Travels* is incorrectly paginated; since correcting the error would throw all subsequent page numbers out, I have resorted to giving signature citations for this gathering.
16. See Said, *Orientalism*, p. 23, and Yeğenoğlu, *Colonial Fantasies*.

8   Journey to Aleppo

1. The villages in Lebanon visited by Biddulph have been identified by Yerasimos and can be found located on the maps provided in *Les Voyageurs*, see p. 480 and map 53.
2. For Fynes Moryson's vivid account of his brother's sickness, death and the danger from jackals after burial, see Moryson, *Itinerary*, 2: 61–7.
3. The Orthodox liturgy is still performed at 8.00 am every Sunday, while Catholic mass is celebrated at 3.00 pm by the local Capuchin community in the cave known as St Peter's Church – 'Senpiyer Kilisi' in Turkish – so named because Peter is said to have preached here and used the term 'Christians' for the first time.
4. Biddulph's comment that the people in question 'worship the Devill' clearly indicates that he has the Yezidis in mind, a sect of Kurdish origin who never embraced any form of Islam. Thomas Cartwright also confused the Kurds in general with the Yezidis in his Turcophobic *Preacher's Travels* (1611), writing: 'the Curdies...doe adore and worship the Divell, to the end he may not hurt them or their cattell' (pp. 20–1; reprinted in Purchas, 8: 487–8). Although his account was published after Biddulph's, Cartwright travelled in 1600. Among the papers in the British Library of the antiquarian Thomas Birch is the following transcription extracted from a lost original: 'Mr Edmund Dunch's Travels from February 1678/9 to July 1680. The sect among them [the Turks] that I saw most of, were the Izedee, or those of the Christian faith – I visited their priests, or fathers, who in countenance resemble Frankes more then others of that countrey, in a modest garb different from other people. They are very poor, live upon charity, and highly respected. I take them for a mighty good sort of men. They have pleasant countenances, and sung and danced bravely. They told us, that they were Christians, and detested Mahomet, but the Turks were strong, and they durst not declare themselves, as they did desire. Our table was often covered; every follower brought in his offering, beeing thin bread like pancakes just made for us, milk, leban [thick sour milk], wine, eggs, etc. This treatment was under tents at the bottom of a hill, to the top of which in the afternoon I climbed to see their cheife, who dwelt there in a convent. An old and very grave person he was; he sat still to receive us, I kissed his hand, and in respect to him, itt being an affront to refuse itt, I drank part of a draught of sour wine with him; but he spoake not a word, while I was there, and they say he never talkes. He was clad in a strange warm garment, peculiar to the holy men, and like the other preists, forcing[?] that this man upon his hat wore a cap hanging downe over his was fringed with silke —Mr. Frampton, once minister to the English in Aleppo, had been among these people formerly, and christened four of their children, as I have been told; thou little religion is to be found with them. They esteme any creature, that is blacke; and worship the devill, that he may doe them no hurt.' Birch added: 'Mem. See *Pococke's Travels*, Vol. ii. p. 1. pag. 102, 200, concerning a sect of religious persons among the Mahomentans there called Ja'seedes', BL Add Ms 4254, Birch papers, f. 107. Unfortunately it is not possible to know where Dunch met the Yezidis. Robert Frampton was chaplain in Aleppo 1655–66. These accounts are important since they indicate a continuing Yezidi presence west of the Euphrates during the seventeenth century. Following constant persecution by Sunni Muslims, other Kurds and Christians, the Yezidis had moved east to an area between Mardin, the Jebal Sinjar and Mosul by 1840 when they were visited by Austen Layard, the early Assyriologist: see *Nineveh and its Remains* (1849), 1: 270–325. Following Layard's account, the Yezidis came to be of considerable interest to generations of subsequent English travellers: for reports of visits to the Yezidi temple near Mosul, see W. A. and Edgar T. A. Wigram, *Cradle of Mankind* (1914), Lady Drower

(Ethel Stefana Stevens), *By Tigris and Euphrates* (1923), *Peacock Angel* (1941) and the more recent scholarly account by Edmonds, *Pilgrimage to Lalish* (1967). The Yezidis continue to be persecuted; most from the Mardin area of modern Turkey have migrated to Germany since the late 1970s, while those in and around Mosul were among the victims of Saddam Hussein's anti-Kurdish campaigns of the 1980s and were subject to the anti-Iraq bombing by NATO during the 1990s. Recent accounts of the sect can be found in Guest, *Survival Among the Kurds* (1993), McDowall, *A Modern History of the Kurds* (1997) and Fuccaro, *The Other Kurds* (1999).

9   Biddulph's Lessons from Aleppo

1. Eldred, 'The voyage of M. John Eldred to Trypolis in Syria by sea, and from thence by land and river to Babylon and Balsara, 1583', in Hakluyt, 3: 323.
2. Bruce Masters, 'Aleppo: The Ottoman Empire's Caravan City', in Eldem et al., eds., *Ottoman City*, pp. 17–78; these passages, pp. 26, 27.
3. Moryson, *Itinerary*, 2: 60.
4. Moryson, *Itinerary*, 2: 60–1.
5. Masters, 'Aleppo', p. 27.
6. Wragg, 'A description of a Voyage to Constantinople and Syria begun the 21. of March 1593', in Hakluyt, 4: 14.
7. By 'Chelfaline' Biddulph presumably means the 'Zulphaline' Christians from the border with Iran, who are also mentioned by William Lithgow, who writes that, in Cairo, 'a Traveller may ever happily finde all these sorts of Christianes, Italians, French, Greekes, Chelfaines, Georgians, Aethiopians, Jacobines, Syrians, Armenians, Nicolaitans, Abassines, Cypriots, Slavonians, captivat Maltezes, Sicilians, Albaneses, and high Hungarians, Ragusans, and their own Aegyptian Copties', *Totall Discourse*, p. 271.
8. See BL Lansdowne 241, ff. 394v–395v for petitions listing the Aleppo merchants.
9. See Matar, *Islam in Britain*, chapter 5, 'Eschatology and the Saracens', and, for the use of prophecy in pre-Reformation anti-Islamic propaganda, see Setton, *Western Hostility to Islam*.
10. In the United States, such beliefs survived well into the nineteenth century at least; see, for example, Bush's *Life of Mohammed* (1844), in which the Prophet fulfils Daniel 7: 8–26, while illustrating and confirming Revelations 9: 1–19: 'Commentators at the present day are almost universally agreed in regarding the fifth trumpet as symbolizing and predicting the appearance of the Arabian impostor, his spurious religion, and his Saracen followers' (p. 196); and see Gilman, *Saracens* (1895).
11. See *The Policy of the Turkish Empire* (1597), sigs. Bv–B2v.
12. Setton, *Western Hostility*, p. 4.
13. Biddulph, *Travels*, p. 49; for Luther, see Matar, *Islam in Britain*, p. 156.
14. See *The Policy*, sigs. E2–M2.
15. See Sanderson to Jeffrey Kerby, 22 January 1601: 'A ship cauled the Trogian, for accompt of Master Stapers and his sons, gone for Argier and so for Alexandria', in Foster, p. 214. Among Staper's other sons, Thomas, Rowland and Richard junior all died overseas, while Hewet arrived back in April 1607; Foster, pp. 18n, 236. According to Sanderson, the *Trojan* 'broke upon Tripoli Rocks' on her return journey in 1602; Foster, pp. 19, 128.
16. See Setton, *Western Hostility*, pp. 15–27, and Matar, *Islam in Britain*, pp. 153–5.

17. Biddulph's 'Syntana Fissa' suggests the Arabic '*Sitt al-Nisa*' or 'Lady of [all] women'. My thanks to Edmund Bosworth for this and subsequent help with Biddulph's vocabulary.
18. Biddulph's 'Eben Sacran' suggests Arabic *Ibn Sakran*.
19. Modern Turkish *Çiplak*.
20. Biddulph's phrase 'Cowsi Sepher' remains enigmatic. In Turkish, 'sıfır' means 'zero; nought, cipher', though Biddulph might be transcribing 'sefir' meaning 'Ambassador', or, less likely, 'sefer' meaning 'journey; voyage; campaign'. See Alderson and Iz, eds., *The Concise Oxford Turkish Dictionary* (1959). Edmund Bosworth has suggested that 'cowsi' recalls the Arabic *qawsi* or 'hair-like'.
21. See Nicolay, *Navigations*, p. 154.
22. Lithgow, *Total Discourse*, p. 180.
23. Masters, 'Aleppo', p. 22. And see Suraiya Faroqhi, 'Robbery on the Hajj Road and Political Allegiance in the Ottoman Empire (1560–1680)', in *Coping with the State*, pp. 179–96, esp. p. 184.
24. Masters, 'Aleppo', p. 30.
25. See Faroqhi et al., *An Economic and Social History of the Ottoman Empire*, pp. 416–17.
26. Freake to Sanderson, 30 November 1599, in Foster, p. 186.
27. Colthurst to Sanderson, 1 December 1599, in Foster, p. 188.
28. John Chamberlain to Dudley Carleton, 29 February 1600, *CPSD, 1598–1601*, p. 402.
29. See Griswold, *The Great Anatolian Rebellion*, pp. 86–8, 104–56; and Masters, 'Aleppo', pp. 29–31.
30. Masters, 'Aleppo', p. 30.
31. Masters, 'Aleppo', p. 31.
32. On Canbuladoğlu Ali Pasha's demands to the Sultan, and Ahmed's response, see Barkey, *Bandits and Bureaucrats*, pp. 189–91.
33. Glover wrote in December 1607: 'Newes is that Siampolat Ogli, Bassa of Aleppo, by Morat Bassa (who was sent generall against the Persians) hath had an overthrowe', in Foster, p. 244. After Ali's defeat, the Canbuladoğlu tribe split, part forming the Janbulad Druze's of Lebanon while the rest remained in the Jabal el-Kurd area between modern Syria and Turkey, where ballads celebrating Ali Pasha are still being sung; Masters, 'Aleppo', p. 31.
34. Contrast Chew's extraordinary claim: 'The excited enthusiasm with which Biddulph writes when he has to do, not with mere antiquities, but with the present state of affairs in the Levant is in itself a warrant of his reliability,' *Crescent*, p. 48.

10   Journey to Jerusalem

1. Richard Chiswell the younger (1673–1751), BL Add. Ms 10623, f. 29.
2. Ze'evi, *Ottoman Century*, p. 23; and see Singer, *Palestinian Peasants*.
3. Ze'evi, *Ottoman Century*, pp. 3–5.
4. See Cohen, *Economic Life in Ottoman Jerusalem*, and Ze'evi, *Ottoman Century*, chapter 2.
5. Ze'evi, *Ottoman Century*, p. 5.
6. Cohen, *Economic Life*, p. 4.
7. Ze'evi, *Ottoman Century*, p. 23.
8. Moryson, *Itinerary*, 2: 5.
9. Moryson, *Itinerary*, 2: 1.
10. See Thomas Freake to Sanderson, 21 March 1601, reporting on the date of their departure, in Foster, p. 215.

11. Sanderson's attitude toward Tient (also Tyant or Tyon) is understandable. On his return to Istanbul in 1599, part of Sanderson's commission as local treasurer of the Levant Company was to impose a duty on the expatriated English merchants, a job that made him instantly unpopular. One evening after supper, David Bourne and Tient attacked him: 'That devill Tient, behinde me, by maine force held me, whilst that doult Bourne with a stone stroke me' scarring his face, see Foster, pp. 197 and 18. Sanderson later vehemently denied seeking revenge on Bourne; see Foster, p. 31. On Tient's previous trip to Jerusalem, see George Dorrington to Sanderson, 23 June 1596, in Foster, p. 147, and Moryson, *Itinerary*, 2: 62. Abbott had been planning to travel to Jerusalem since at least October 1600, at which time Sanderson declined an invitation to join him. In January 1601, Sanderson briefly reconsidered, but in the event went by sea via Iskenderun setting out in May; see Foster, pp. 209, 214, 216, 218.

12. See Ze'evi, *Ottoman Century*, pp. 13–14.

13. Moryson, Itinerary, 2: 2.

14. On the mid-century scientific approach to study of the Holy Land, see David Howell's introduction to Maundrell's *Journey from Aleppo*, pp. xv–xxii. In his unpublished notebook, Greaves restricted himself to measuring non-biblical sites; he noted, for example, 'In Sultan Ahmet Church, Father to the present Grand Segnior Sultan Morat: The Breadth of it from N. to W. is 64 of my paces & 10 from W. to E. The great Cupola stands upon four very massy Pillars, to which at E. and W. at N. and S.', 'Observations' (c. 1638), BL Add. Ms 4243, ff. 50–86; this passage ff. 60–60v. Halifax has been attributed with the discovery of ancient Palmyra; see his 'Relation of two journies' at BL Add. Ms 6245; a version of the first journey was published by the Royal Society in the *Philosophical Transactions* for 1695. Another version, based on a different manuscript, was published in the *Journal of the Palestine Exploration Fund* (June, 1890) and reprinted the same year with notes by C. R. Conder.

15. To trace Biddulph's route, see Yerasimos, *Les Voyageurs*, p. 440 and maps 49, 53, 56, 60. In 1650 Thomas Fuller followed Biddulph's route from Aleppo to Jerusalem in his cartographical study *A Pisgah-Sight of Palestine*.

16. See, however, Ze'evi, who writes: 'In the eyes of Western guests they [*khans*] were very uncomfortable…Travellers were not given rooms or food', *Ottoman Century*, p. 13.

17. Following armed insurrection in Hama by the Muslim Brotherhood, an extremist Sunni organization opposed to Hafez Assad's regime, the president's brother Rifaat Assad bombarded and later bulldozed much of the old city. Estimates of those killed range from 5,000 to 24,000.

18. Sanderson, in Foster, p. 105.

19. Moryson, cites an Italian proverb to similar effect, *Itinerary*, 3: 452–3.

20. Kitely to Sanderson, 6 May 1609; BL Ms Lansdowne 241, f. 409v. In editing Sanderson's papers, Foster omitted the passage after the word 'Zante', commenting only, 'The writer goes on to accuse Biddulph of gross immorality and drunkeness' (p. 264).

11 Sir Henry Blount, 15 December 1602–9 October 1682

1. 'Manuscripts of Sir Harry Pope Blount by which he made out the Pedigree of the Blount Family,' BL Add Ms 36242, f. 119v.

2. A fifteenth-century copy of the original deeds establishing the estate from 1331 calls the manor 'Tydenhanger', BL Add Ms 36237, f. 1.

3. National Portrait Gallery, 536.

4. See Young and Emberton, *Sieges*, pp. 104–16.

5. Christopher Wase of Upper Holloway; not the writer.
6. A Catholic born in Antwerp, Huysmans was a favourite of Pepys and the court circle of Catherine of Braganza, whom he painted several times; see MacLeod and Marciari Alexander, *Painted Ladies*, pp. 89, 104–5.
7. Dethloff, 'Portraiture and Concepts of Beauty', p. 32.
8. National Portrait Gallery, 5491.
9. I have been unable to find an engraving said to have been made of Blount 'ad vivum' by D. Loggan c. 1679, mentioned in Granger, *Biographical History*, 4: 76.
10. Wood, *Athenae Oxoniensis*, 2: 534.
11. BL Add Ms 36242, f. 146.
12. Kippis, *Biographia Britannica*, 2: 378.
13. Evelyn, *Diary*, p. 399.
14. Aubrey, *Brief Lives*, p. 25.
15. BL Add Ms 36242, see f. 134v where he stipulates: 'Item I Grant & Committ the Guardianship of my son Ulisses & of all his Reall & Personall Estate to my Daughter Tyrrell untill he attaine the age of One & Twenty yeares if she so long live Charging her to breed him up as becomes my Son & her Brother. And my Will is that she maintaine him untill his Age of Eighteen yeares out of the Profitts of the said Copihold Tenements in London Colney.'
16. The will of Sir Thomas Pope Blount, d. 10 January 1638; BL Add Ms 36242, f. 77v.
17. Thomas Pope Blount died 7 August 1654; BL Add Ms 36242, f. 85v.
18. See Penrose, *Urbane Travellers*, p. 235, and the account of 'Tyttenhanger' in Tipping, *English Homes*, pp. 63–84.
19. Aubrey, *Brief Lives*, p. 26. Sir Alexander Croke provides the year of this deal and specifies that the buyer was Sir John Harpur; see Croke, *Genealogical History*, 2: 311.
20. BL Add Ms 36242, ff. 131v–132.
21. BL Add Ms 36242, f. 133.
22. 'A True Copy of the Family of Blount whose Christenings Marriages or Burials are found in the Register books of the church of ridge Hertfordshire, Extracted by me Harry Pope Blount, 1732', BL Add Ms. 36242, f. 245.
23. See BL Add Ms 36242, f. 244v: '1616. Lady Frances Wife of Sir Thomas Pope Blount Knt Buryd June 23. 14 Jac'. Croke erroneously dates her death as 1619, *Genealogical History*, family tree Number 17 between 2: 334 and 2: 335.
24. Harley, *Collection of Voyages*, 1: 512.
25. Warton, *Life of Sir Thomas Pope*, p. 206.
26. Douthwaite, *Gray's Inn*, p. 209–10. For the date of Blount's admission, see BL Harley Ms 1912, f. 13.
27. Croke, *Genealogical History*, 2: 311, citing Aubrey.
28. Blount's manuscript verses are to be found in BL Add Ms 25303, ff. 170v, 171, 179v, containing four amatory poems in the cavalier manner; BL Add Ms 33998, containing variant copies of two of the preceding; BL Sloane Ms 1446, containing one and adding two more.
29. Douthwaite, *Gray's Inn*, p. 238.
30. Anthony Wood thought that Blount was associated with publishing *Sixe Court Comedies* (1632) by John Lily, but these were produced by the stationer Edward Blount.
31. Howell's *Instructions* was first published in 1642. Rumsey was admitted to Gray's Inn in 1603 and served as Lent Reader in 1633, even as Henry Blount was preparing to leave England; Douthwaite, *Gray's Inn*, p. 70.
32. Blount, *Voyage*, p. 1. Blount might have accompanied James Howell, who made several journeys to these countries between 1622 and 1624 (Howell, *DNB*).

33. Kippis, *Biographia Britannica*, 2: 376–8.
34. Walkley, *New Catalogue*, p. 138.
35. Aubrey, *Brief Lives*, p. 25.
36. BL Add Ms 36242, f. 146.
37. 'Act for Probate of Wills', 8 April 1653, in Firth and Rait, eds., *Acts and Ordinances*, 2: 702.
38. 'In 1654, July 5, He sat with others in Westminster Hall for the Tryall of Don Pantabelou Sa the Portugal ambassadors brother', BL Add Ms 36242, f. 146.
39. 'Sir Henry Blount', www.usigs.org/library/blackwell/blountha.html lists daughters Hester, Eleanor, Charlotte and Philippa, while a daughter Frances (1648–99) is shown by the genealogical tree currently kept at Tittenhanger; my thanks to Pauline Grant for a copy.
40. Blount, *Oracles of Reason*, pp. 152, 155.
41. Gildon, *Miscellaneous Works of Charles Blount*, sigs. A4–A4v.

12   On Becoming a Passenger

1. Wyche to Coke, 28 December 1633, PRO *SP 97/15*, f. 228v.
2. Stanford Shaw, *History*, 1: 197. Nabbes, in his continuation of Knolles, dates this 7 May, *Generall Historie*, p. 18.
3. Freely, *Istanbul*, p. 226, presumably following Kâtip Çelebi. In his narrative account of the events based on von Hammer Purgstall, Edward S. Creasy put the death toll at over 100,000, see *History* (1961), p. 246–53.
4. Creasy, *History*, p. 251.
5. Shaw, *History*, 1: 198, citing Çelebi, *Fezleke* 2: 154. Thomas Nabbes, in his continuation of Knolles, *Generall Historie*, also gives the higher figure, suggesting Blount may have been his source: 'In this year [1633] a sudden fire breaking forth (the original whereof though diversly suspected, could have no clear discoverie) made such a gap in that part of the City of Constantinople, that it is left as it were of purpose unbuilt, to confirm the report which the Turkes give of it, that it consumed in a very short space seventy thousand houses' (p. 20).
6. On Murad's 1635 campaigns against the Savafids, see Murphey, *Ottoman Warfare*, pp. 75–6, and Shaw, *History*, 1: 182–3.
7. Nabbes's continuation of Knolles, *Generall Historie*, p. 21. Wyche's account of these events appears in his letter to Coke of 25 January 1634, PRO *SP 97/15*, f. 236.
8. On Wyche, who was not replaced by Sir Sackville Crowe until 1638, see Wood, *History of Levant Company*, pp. 88–9.
9. Blount's was hardly an original observation, but one repeated by generations of visitors since 1466, at least, when George Trapezuntios declared to Mehmed the Conqueror: 'The seat of the Roman Empire is Constantinople... Therefore you are the legitimate Emperor of the Romans... And he who is and remains Emperor of the Romans is also Emperor of the whole earth'; cited by Mansel, *Constantinople*, p. 1. Compare Jean de Thevenot: 'All who have seen *Constantinople*, agree in this, That it is the best situated City in the World; so that it would seem to be design'd by Nature, forbearing Rule and Command over the whole Earth' (*Travels*, 1687, 1: 19). The Irish soldier John Richards, who visited in the 1690s, observed: 'It would be but to little Purpose to delate my selfe in giving the Topographical discription of this most famous Citty, it haveing bin done allready by aboundance of Ingenious men of all nations. Yet something I will say because that it the most desired is of any other in the World att least nature may truly say that she has Impoverished her selfe to render it as it once was deservedly the mistres of the world... the climate is most

happy and the Aire so verry good, that the Inhabitants say themselves that were it not for the Plague they should live for ever' (BL Ms Stowe 462, ff. 33v–34).

10. Knolles, *Generall Historie*, sig. A3, and see 'The Authors induction to the Christian Reader, unto the Historie following', sigs. [A4–A6v].
11. Knolles, *Generall Historie*, sig. [A5v].
12. Moryson, *Itinerary*, 4: 371.
13. See Moryson, *Itinerary*, 4: 371, 379, 385, 387, 399, 406, 409.
14. Moryson, *Itinerary*, 4: 373.
15. Palmer, *Essay*, p. 4.
16. Palmer, *Essay*, p. 5.
17. Palmer, *Essay*, pp. 4–5.
18. In her recent study, Çirakman curiously misconstrues this passage, writing that 'the "Turkish way" for him is "absolutely barbarous"', *From the 'Terror of the World'*, p. 46.
19. *Ortelius his Epitome of the Theatre of the World* was issued in an augmented English edition in 1603; a complete *Theatrum* reissued in England in 1606, and an amplified edition in 1610. Mercator's *Atlas* was not issued in English until 1635.
20. My thanks to Barry Swabey of Plymouth for kindly sending me copies of the title-page and prize label in October 2001, since when the copy has passed into the hands of a private owner.
21. In 1634, England was also the leading trading partner with the Ottomans: see McGowan, *Economic Life*; he writes: 'Except for the disturbance of England's trade during the English civil wars, from which the Dutch drew some profit, the English were the undisputed leaders in the Levant trade between 1620 and 1683' (p. 21).
22. Blount's discussion is worth considering in terms of Gayatri Chakravorty Spivak's notions of 'worlding' and 'the ethical embrace'. See Raman, 'Back to the Future', and Spivak, 'Echo', in *Spivak Reader*.
23. Wyche to Coke, 28 December 1633, PRO *SP 97/15*, f. 228.
24. Wyche to Coke, 28 December 1633, PRO *SP 97/15*, ff. 237v–8.
25. On 4 August 1634, Francesco Zonca, the Venetian Secretary in England, wrote to the Doge and Senate concerning 'the present troubles of Poland through the movements of the Turk in that quarter', *CSPV, 1632–36*, #331, p. 254. My thanks to Dr Rhoads Murphey for confirmation that Blount could have had advance knowledge of the campaign only from 'sailors, ship captains, merchants or diplomats'. Personal communication, 5 June 2002.
26. Chew, *Crescent*, p. 43.
27. Palmer, *Essay*, sigs. A2–A2v.

13 The Sinews of Empire: Venice to Istanbul

1. Humphrey Conisby, BL Ms Cotton Nero B.xi, f. 14v.
2. See Brewer, *Sinews of Power*, though his model of the fiscal-military state differs from the Ottoman model.
3. Blount writes that Belgrade was 'wonne by Sultan Solyman the second, in the yeare 1525' (p. 9). The date is simply an error, but Blount presumably considered Beyazit I's son Suleiman to be the 'first', since he ruled in Thrace following his father's defeat by Timur. See Imber, *Ottoman Empire*, p. 17.
4. As it has done in contemporary Kurdish idiom as, for instance, in the song by Koma Agiri, 'Zindana Diyarbekir', sung by Fatma, *Fatma 1*, side A track 2.

5. Bayerle, *Pashas*, p. 5.
6. Bayerle, *Pashas*, p. 35.
7. Unlike the author of *A New Survey of The Turkish Empire* (1633), who writes: 'When I was present in the Turkish Army in an Expedition against the Persian, I saw a great Commanders head, with horse and servants, all three cut off, because that horse had been found grazing in another mans pasture unsatisfied for' (p. 35).
8. Personal communication, but see Calbi, *Approximate Bodies*.
9. See Matar, *Turks*, pp. 109–27.
10. Grimestone's dedication to Baudier, *History* (1635).
11. Baudier, *History*, p. 49.
12. Baudier, *History*, p. 57.
13. 'These Turks are goodly people of parson, and of a very faire complexion, but very villains in minde, for they are altogether Sodomites, and doe all things contrarie to a Christian,' William Davies, *True Relation* (1614), sig. B2v; discussed in Matar, *Turks*, p. 113.
14. Aubrey is recalling a satiric pamphlet, ascribed to Henry Neville, *The Parliament of Ladies*, which was published in May 1647 and contains the following: 'This day complaint was brought in against Sir *Henry Blunt* Knight, for publishing an heret-icall and dangerous Doctrine, viz. *That it is better to side with and resort to common Women then ladyes of Honour*: upon mature deliberation, thereupon the Ladyes with much indignation sent for him, who being come, and hearing his accusation read, was commanded to with draw during this debate, up standeth Lady *Foster* and offers to the consideration of the House, the dangerous effect of this opinion, what it might produce if it be suffered to spread among the people, to the utter decay of Trade, as also of the particular Committee of Rhenish wine, in the most parts Cheese-cakes, and filebubs, whereby the profit of this House will be greatly deminished. This speech was received with great applause of the whole House, and the said Sir *Henry Blunt* is called in the second time, who being commanded to kneele, refused, alleadging that the House was no lawfull judicature, but appealed to all the Commons of *England* and *Wales*; which suspended all proceedings therein for a time', p. 6.
15. 'Bir fincan kahvenin kırk yil hatiri vardır', see Metin Yurtbaşi, *Dictionary*, p. 219.
16. Rumsey, *Organon Salutis*, sig. a4.
17. Robinson, *Early English Coffee House*, p. 93.
18. See Holt, 'Pietro Della Valle'.
19. Comparing Ottoman and Italian architecture was a favourite sport among some travellers. Blount's contemporary, John Greaves, writing of the Aghia Sophia circa 1638, commented: 'Sta Sophia for the Grace and Beauty of the Church is not to be esteemed, within it is beyond expression. In the richness of the Pillars, in the Mosaic Work; to which that of St Marks in Venice is not comparable', BL Add. Ms 4243, f. 61v. The taste for Ottoman architecture, however, was evidently parti-san. Writing at the turn of the century, the Irish Catholic soldier-of-fortune John Richards observed: 'Of all the antient buildings with which this Citty was (no doubt of it) adorned, there dos not any thing remaine worth the takeing notice of Saint Sophia excepted. This once most glorious Temple, so much praised by the antients and so much talked of by our Modern Travellers dos not a little suffer by the extrava-gant Incomiums which they give it.' Richards prefers St Peter's which 'is not only longer, broader, and higher, but what is much more estimable is of a much more perfect Architecture. As to the Matterials Saint Sophia is Crusted on the Inside with Marble, which St Peters is not allover being not as yet finished, and eaven in this

respect it is much inferior to to [*sic*] St Marks of Venice Especially in the Pavement', BL Stowe Ms 462, ff. 35v, 36v–37.

14 Ottoman Egypt: African Empire in Ruins

1. According to Strachan, *Life and Adventures of Thomas Coryate*, p. 15.
2. Raymond, *Cairo*, p. 190.
3. Raymond, *Cairo*, pp. 219, 196, 236–7, 259.
4. On Cornelius Haga, see *The True Declaration of the arrival of Cornelius Haga*, (1613).
5. The current studbook issued for the Asil Club by W. George Olms, *Asil Arabians*, provides a documentary history of the breed. Of a written Ottoman register of Egyptian Arabians from the mid-seventeenth century I have found no further evidence.
6. Dent, *Horses*, p. 78.
7. Olms, *Asil Arabians*, p. 46.
8. Neville, *Parliament of Ladies*, p. 6.
9. Warton, *Life of Sir Thomas Pope*, p. 207.

15 The *Adventures* of 'Mr. T.S.' and Restoration England

1. Cited by Tal Shuval, 'Cezayir-i Garp', epigraph. Shuval's essay provides an excellent introduction to the problem facing historians of Ottoman Algeria as well as directions forward.
2. See R.D., *True Relation of the Adventures of Mr. R.D.* (1672) and *A True and Perfect Relation* (1671). Dryden may have had T.S.'s *Adventures* in mind while developing the comic subplot of his play *Don Sebastian* (1690); see Dryden, *Works*, 15: 391–2.
3. See, for example, Snader, *Caught Between Worlds*. Perhaps a confusion with Thomas Smith, the Oxford divine, who went as chaplain to Istanbul in 1668 with Daniel Harvey, and published his *Remarks* in 1678.
4. Pitt includes a list of titles in print, from which we learn little.
5. For Thomas Manley's publications, see George Fortescue, ed., *Catalogue*, 1: 887.
6. 'Though these passages may look like Merracles, yet I assure you they may be confirmed by several of our Nation (both Merchants and Travelers) who have been eye witnesses of it as well as my self'. R.D., *True Relation*, p. 3.
7. See Turner, *Libertines and Radicals*.
8. See Evans, 'Charles II's "Grand Tour"'.

16 Captive Agency

1. Said, *Orientalism*, p. 122.
2. I am not disputing David Armitage's important argument that the ideological origins of the British Empire are not be found in Anglo-Protestantism alone, since I am not dealing with the way a 'precise definition of Protestantism' resisted attempts to reveal 'justifications for migration and settlement', but rather with what he calls the 'common Christian justifications' that appear in literary and other cultural forms; *Ideological Origins*, pp. 98–9.
3. Colley, *Captives*, p. 98.
4. I borrow the term from Snader's *Caught Between Worlds*, which describes how these narratives, 'centered on the forced imposition of an allegedly inferior culture on the

representative of an allegedly superior culture,' treat captivity itself as a 'fundamental crisis of identity' from which emerge the 'variable patterns' of 'captive agency' and 'captive heroism', pp. 79–80.

5.   I borrow this term from Tal Shuval, who uses it to translate *ocak*: see 'Ottoman Algerian Elite'. Since I have no evidence or reason to believe that either Rowlie or T.S. is likely to appear in the lists of paid employees that Shuval uses to define the *ocak* as a class, I trust my use of 'military-administrative elite' in this context will not appear inappropriate.

6.   The legend that accompanies the portrait reads: 'Huius Eunuchi Fidei omnia Sacreta ASSAM WASCH: & gaza & mulieres prestantes Comissa Hic in Anglia natura in Civitate IARmouth quem Vocarunt turcae ASSAN AGA, in Anglia Samson Rowlii', Bodley Or. Ms 430, f. 47.

7.   See Matar, 'England and Mediterranean Captivity, 1577–1704', introduction to Vitkus, ed., *Piracy, Slavery*, pp. 1–52.

8.   See Skilliter, *William Harborne*, pp. 19–22 for discussion of a document concerning the voyage, which is most probably in the hand of John Hawkins, at PRO *SP 12/114*, ff. 84--5.

9.   Hakluyt, 3: 130.

10.   Sanderson, 'Autobiography', in *Travels*, ed. Foster, p. 12.

11.   Hakluyt, 3: 131. In October 1587, the Fugger correspondent in Istanbul wrote that Hassan Basha 'is the greatest corsair of them all now, and is to be entrusted with the control of all Barbary', *Fugger Newsletters*, p. 144.

12.   Skilliter, *Harborne*, p. 22.

13.   Shuval, 'Ottoman Algerian Elite', p. 325.

14.   Hakluyt, 3: 131.

17   For the Vainglory of Being a 'Traveller'

1.   Snader, *Caught Between Worlds*, p. 79.

18   Slavery in Algiers

1.   Hourani, *History of the Arab Peoples*, p. 229. I have also relied on Barnaby Rogerson's enormously useful *Traveller's History* (1998).

2.   See Lawless and Blake, *Tlemcen*, and Soucek, 'Rise of the Barbarossas'.

3.   *Algeria*, 1: 192.

4.   In *Forgotten Frontier*, Andrew C. Hess situates the battle 'near the Zawiya of Sidi-Musa, the lodge of a religious organization', p. 65. A long-term resident of Tlemcen, Alfred Bel disputed the site of the battle where Oruç died, claiming it was 'non loin de Mrnia, pres de la riviere Moulah (et non pas, comme on l'a dit, pres du Rio Salado – en arabe Oued Malah – entre Tlemcen et Oran)', *Tlemcen*, p. 26.

5.   Histories of Algeria regularly cut straight from here to the French occupation of 1830 with a few slighting comments about the Ottoman period. In six sentences, for example, Jean Grimaud moves directly from 'The greatest preoccupation of the Turks consisted of amassing wealth from piracy and exploiting the local population' to 'France came along to put an end to this state of affairs and to regenerate the country', *Monographie* (1929), pp. 91–2; my translation.

6.   Hourani, *History of the Arab Peoples*, p. 230, and see Shuval, 'Cezayir-i Garp'.

7.   *Algeria*, 1: 193.

8.   Nicolay, in Purchas, 6: 114.

9. For a contemporary account, see I.B., *Algiers Voyage* (1621).
10. Purchas, 6: 145–6.
11. Pepys, *Diary*, p. 33.
12. See *The Algerian Slaves Releasement* in Aston, ed., *A Century of Ballads*, pp. 221–4.
13. If T.S.'s *Adventures* are chronologically reliable, this would have been Youssouf Pacha; see Plantet, *Correspondance*, 1: 45.

19   On Tour with the Ottoman Army

1. Bayerle, *Pashas*, p. 126.
2. R.D., *True Relation*, p. 3.
3. *Algeria*, 1: 47.
4. See Pratt, *Imperial Eyes*.

20   Tlemcen: Life in a Desert City

1. Bel, *Tlemcen*, p. 25; my translation. For the date of construction of the Sahrij, see *Algeria*, 2: 110.
2. Bel, *Tlemcen*, p. 25; my translation.
3. 'Le poète compare Tlemcen, sous le gouvenmement turc, a la grenouille dans la gueule du serpent', cited by Bel, *Tlemcen*, p. 27.
4. Cour, *Catalogue des Manuscrits Arabes*, p. 7.
5. Interview, University of Tlemcen, 20 May 2003.
6. On such homosocial triangulations, see Sedgwick, *Between Men*.
7. The story of the providential statue also appears in R.D.'s *True Relation*, p. 6. My thanks to Nabil Matar for drawing my attention to this work.

Epilogue

1. Montagu, *Letters*, 1:330.
2. See Evans and Cheevers, *Relation* (1662).
3. See Cason, *Relation of the whole proceedings* (1647).
4. See Pepys, *Tangier Papers*, ed. Edwin Chappell.
5. For evidence of English women living in Izmir, see Anderson, *English Consul*, p. 6.
6. Sanderson to Glover, 20 February 1608, in Foster, pp. 247–8.
7. Forde, *Sermon* (1616), p. 75.
8. Sanderson to Martin Calthorpe, in Foster, p. 259.
9. Sanderson to Robert Barton, August 1606, in Foster, p. 232.
10. Sanderson to Glover, 18 August 1607, in Foster, p. 239. Foster speculates that the French book in question was 'The Pastoralles of Julietta (a translation from the French) which was registered at Stationers' Hall on 2 April, 1607 (Arber's *Transcripts*, vol. iii, p. 151)'. But Arber's entry reads: 'Entred for his copie [Master John Norton] under the hand of master whyte Warden. but not to be prynted without other sufficient Aucthorytie first obteined for yt A Booke called the *pastoralles of Julietta* translated out of Frenche into Englishe.' The book was eventually printed, but not until 1610, too late for Sanderson to be sending a copy to Lady Glover, and it was not translated by a woman: see Nicholas de Montreux, *Honours Academie* (1610), which was, however, entered to M. Lownes on 2 April 1607 and later reassigned to Thomas Creede, 11 November 1609: see *STC* entry 18053.

11. Gainsford, *Glory of England* (1618), p. 35.
12. Sanderson to Kitely, 17/18 January 1609, in Foster, p. 259.
13. Kitely to Sanderson, 6 May 1609, in Foster, p. 265.
14. Sanderson to Glover, 22 February 1611, in Foster, pp. 274–5.
15. Grimestone in Knolles, *Generall Historie*, p. 1313.
16. Elsewhere, Grimestone acknowledges receiving information from Glover; see Knolles, *Generall Historie*, pp. 1379, 1387.
17. Grimestone in Knolles, *Generall Historie*, p. 1313.
18. Forde, *Sermon*, p. 73.
19. Bulwer, *Anthropometamorphosis* (1653), pp. 546–7.
20. Montagu, *Letters*, 1: 310.

References

Abbreviations

CSPD   *Calendar of State Papers, Domestic Series*
CSPV   *Calendar of State Papers, Venetian Series*
DNB   *Dictionary of National Biography*
Foster   Sanderson, John, *The Travels of John Sanderson in the Levant, 1584–1602*. Ed. Sir William Foster. London: Hakluyt Society, 1931.
Hakluyt   Richard Hakluyt, *The Principal Navigations, Voyages, and Discoveries of the English Nation*. 1589. Rpt. 10 vols. London: Dent, 1913.
OED   *Oxford English Dictionary*
Purchas   Samuel Purchas, *Hakluytus Posthumus, or, Purchas His Pilgrimes, Contayning a History of the World in Sea Voyages and Lande Travells by Englishmen and others*. 1625. Rpt. 20 vols. Glasgow: MacLehose, 1905.
STC   *Short-Title Catalogue of Books Printed in England, Scotland, & Ireland and of English Books Printed Abroad, 1475–1640*. Ed. A.W. Pollard and G.R. Redgrave. Revised edition. 2 vols. London: Bibliographical Society, 1986.

Manuscripts

Beyazit Devlet Library, Istanbul
   Mustafa Safi, *Zubdetu't-tevarih*, Veliyyüddin Efendi Yazmalari, nr. 2428, ff. 32–4.
Bodleian Library, University of Oxford
   Or. Ms 430.
British Library, London
   BL Add Ms 4243
   BL Add Ms 4254
   BL Add Ms 6245
   BL Add Ms 7880
   BL Add Ms 10623
   BL Add Ms 17480
   BL Add Ms 25303
   BL Add Ms 32350
   BL Add Ms 32522
   BL Add Ms 33998
   BL Add Ms 36237
   BL Add Ms 36242
   BL Add Ms 36367
   BL Cotton Nero Ms B.xi
   BL Harley Ms 1912
   BL Lansdowne Ms 241
   BL OR Ms r4129
   BL Sloane Ms 1446
   BL Sloane Ms 2496

BL Stowe Ms 180
BL Stowe MS 462
Topkapi Palace Library, Istanbul
    TSK Revan 1304
Public Records Office, Kew
    State Papers 12, 75, 97, 105

Published works cited

Place of publication for early printed books is London, unless otherwise indicated. The lengthy titles of seventeenth-century publications have been shortened.

Abbott, G.F. *Turkey, Greece and the Great Powers: A Study in Friendship and Hate*. London: Robert Scott, 1906.

Alderson, A.D. and Iz, Fahir, eds. *The Concise Oxford Turkish Dictionary*. Oxford: Clarendon, 1959.

Algeria: Geographical Handbook Series. 2 vols. London: Naval Intelligence Division, 1943.

The Algerian Slaves Releasement, Or, The Unchangeable Boat-Swain. Rpt. in John Aston, ed. *A Century of Ballads*. London, Stock, 1887.

Anderson, Sonia. *An Englishman in Turkey: Paul Rycaut at Smyrna, 1667–1678*. Oxford: Clarendon, 1989.

Anon. 'Relics of the Past: Curious Musical Instrument of the Sixteenth Century'. *Illustrated London News* (20 October 1860): 380.

Aravamudan, Srinivas. 'Lady Mary Wortley Montagu in the Hammam: Masquerade, Womanliness, and Levantinization'. *ELR* 62:1 (Spring 1995): 69–104.

——. *Tropicopolitans: Colonialism and Agency, 1688–1804*. Durham, NC: Duke University Press, 1999.

Armitage, David. *The Ideological Origins of the British Empire*. Cambridge: Cambridge University Press, 2000.

Aubrey, John. *Aubrey's Brief Lives*. Ed. Oliver Lawson Dick. Boston: Godine, 1999.

Aydin, Kamil. *Images of Turkey in Western Literature*. Ankara: British Council, 1999.

B., I. *Algiers Voyage in a Journall or Briefe Reportary of all occurents hapning in the fleet of ships sent out by the King his most excellent Majestie, as well against the Pirates of Algiers, as others*. 1621.

Bak, Greg. 'Who Built the Organ for the Sultan?' *Journal of the British Institute of Organ Studies* 25 (2001): 135–43.

Barkey, Karen. *Bandits and Bureaucrats: The Ottoman Route to State Centralization*. Ithaca, NY: Cornell University Press, 1994.

Bartholemew, Georgievits. *The Ofspring of the House of Ottomanno, and Officers pertaining to the greate Turkes Court*. Trans. Hugh Goughe. 1570.

Bayerle, Gustav. *Pashas, Begs, and Efendis: A Historical Dictionary of Titles and Terms in the Ottoman Empire*. Istanbul: Isis Press, 1997.

Baudier, Michel. *The History of the Imperial Estate of the Grand Seigneurs: Their Habitations, Lives, Titles, Qualities, Exercises, Workes, Revenewes, Habit, Discent, Ceremonies, Magnificence, Judgements, Officers, Favorites, Religion, Power, Government, and Tyranny*. Trans. Edward Grimestone. 1635.

Beck, Brandon. *From the Rising of The Sun: English Images of the Ottoman Empire to 1715*. New York: Lang, 1987.

Bel, Alfred. *Tlemcen et ses Environs*. Oran: Fouque, 1907.

Bencherif, Osman. *The Image of Algeria in Anglo-American Writings 1785–1962*. Lanham, MD: University Press of America, 1997.

Bent, J. Theodore, ed. *Early Voyages and Travels in the Levant*. London: Hakluyt Society, 1893.

Bicknell, Stephan. *The History of the English Organ*. Cambridge: Cambridge University Press, 1996.

Biddulph, William. *The Travels of certaine Englishmen into Africa, Asia, Troy, Bithnia, Thracia, and to the Blacke Sea*. 1609.

Blanks, David, ed. *Images of the Other: Europe and the Muslim World Before 1700*. Cairo Papers in Social Science 19:2 (1997).

Blount, Charles. *The Oracles of Reason*. 1693.

——. *The Miscellaneous Works of Charles Blount, Esq*. Ed. Charles Gildon. 1695.

Blount, Henry. *A Voyage into the Levant*. 1636. Dutch translation, *Zee-En Land Voyagie Van den Ridder Hendrik Blunt, Na de Levant. Gedaan in het Jaar 1634*. Leyden: Pieter Van Der Aa, 1707. Rpt. in *Die Wijd-Beroemde Voyagien Der Engelsen In Twee Deelen*. 2 vols. Leyden: Pieter Van Der Aa, 1737.

Brewer, John. *The Sinews of Power: War, Money and the English State*. London: Unwin, 1989.

Brotton, Jerry. *Trading Territories: Mapping the Early Modern World*. London: Reaktion, 1998.

Bulwer, John. *Anthropometamorphosis: Man Transform'd: Or, The Articificiall Changling Historically presented*. 1650. Rpt. 1653.

Burian, Orhan. 'Interest of the English in Turkey as Reflected in English Literature of the Renaissance'. *Oriens* 5 (1952): 209–29.

Bush, George. *The Life of Mohammed; Founder of the Religion of Islam, and of the Empire of the Saracens*. New York: Harper, 1844.

Calbi, Maurizio. *Approximate Bodies: Aspects of the Figuration of Masculinity, Power and the Uncanny in Early Modern Drama and Anatomy*. Salerno: Oedipus, 2001.

Cartwright, Thomas. *The Preacher's Travels. Wherein is set downe a true Iournall, to the confines of the East Indies*. 1611.

Cason, Edmond. *A Relation of the whole proceedings concerning the Redemption of the Captives in Argier and Tunis*. 1647.

Chew, Samuel. *The Crescent and the Rose: Islam and England During the Renaissance*. New York: Oxford University Press, 1937.

Chishull, Edmund. *Travels in Turkey and back to England*. 1747.

——. *Antiquitates Asiaticae*. 1728.

Çirakman, Asli. *From the 'Terror of the World' to the 'Sick Man of Europe': European Images of Ottoman Empire and Society from the Sixteenth Century to the Nineteenth*. New York: Lang, 2002.

Clark, Andrew. *Register of the University of Oxford*. 3 vols. Oxford: Oxford Historical Society, 1888.

Clifford, James. *Routes: Travel and Translation in the Late Twentieth Century*. Cambridge, MA.: Harvard University Press, 1997.

Cocheril, Michel. 'The Dallams in Brittany'. *JBIOS* 6 (1982): 63–77.

Cohen, Amnon. *Economic Life in Ottoman Jerusalem*. Cambridge: Cambridge University Press, 1989.

Colley, Linda. *Captives: Britain, Empire and the World*. London: Cape, 2002.

Cook's Practical Guide to Algeria and Tunisia. London: Cook, 1908.

Cour, Auguste. *Catalogue des Manuscrits Arabes Conservés dans les Principales Bibliothèques Algériennes: Médersa de Tlemcen*. Algiers: Jourdan, 1907.

Creasy, Edward, S. *History of the Ottoman Turks*. 1878. Rpt. Beirut: Khayats, 1961.

Croft-Murray, Edward. *Decorative Painting in England, 1537–1837*. 2 vols. London: Country Life, 1962.

Croke, Sir Alexander. *Genealogical History of the Croke Family, Originally Named Le Blount*. 2 vols. Oxford: John Murray, 1823.

D., R. *A True Relation of the Adventures of Mr. R.D. an English Merchant, Taken by the Turks of Argeir in 1666*. 1672.

Davies, William. *A True Relation of the Travailes and most miserable Captivitie of William Davies, Barber-Surgion of London*. 1614.

Dent, Anthony. *Horses in Shakespeare's England*. London: J.A. Allen, 1987.

Dethloff, Diana. 'Portraiture and Concepts of Beauty in Restoration Painting'. In MacLeod and Alexander, *Painted Ladies*.

Douthwaite, William Ralph. *Gray's Inn: Its History and Associations*. London: Reeves and Turner, 1886.

Drower, Lady (Ethel Stefana Stevens). *By Tigris and Euphrates*. London: Hurst and Blackett, 1923.

——. *Peacock Angel: Being Some Account of Votaries of a Secret Cult and their Sanctuaries*. London: Murray, 1941.

Dryden, John. *The Works of John Dryden: Vol. XV*. Ed. Earl Miner et al. Los Angeles: University of California Press, 1976.

Edmonds, B.B. 'The Dallam Family'. *JBIOS* 3 (1979): 137–9.

Edmonds, C.J. *A Pilgrimage to Lalish*. London: Royal Asiatic Society, 1967.

Eldem, Edhem, Daniel Goffman and Bruce Masters, eds. *The Ottoman City Between East and West: Aleppo, Izmir, and Istanbul*. Cambridge: Cambridge University Press, 1999.

Epstein, Mordecai. *The Early History of the Levant Company*. London: Routledge, 1908.

Evans, David. 'Charles II's "Grand Tour": Restoration Panegyric and the Rhetoric of Travel Literature'. *Philological Quarterly* 72:1 (1993): 53–71.

Evans, Katherine and Sarah Cheevers. *This is a short Relation Of some of the Cruel Sufferings (For the Truths sake) of Katharine Evans & Sarah Chevers, In the Inquisition in the Isle of Malta*. 1662.

Evelyn, John. *The Diary of John Evelyn*. Ed. E.S. De Beer. London: Oxford University Press, 1959.

Faroqhi, Suraiya. *Coping with the State: Polticial Conflict and Crime in the Ottoman Empire, 1550–1720*. Istanbul: Isis, 1995.

——, Bruce McGowan, Donald Quataert, and Sevket Pamuk. *An Economic and Social History of the Ottoman Empire: Volume Two, 1600–1914*. Cambridge: Cambridge University Press, 1994.

Fatma. *Fatma 1*. Istanbul: Koçer Productions, 1999.

Firth, C.H. and R.S. Rait, eds., *Acts and Ordinances of the Interregnum, 1642–1660*. 3 vols. London: HMSO, 1911.

Forde, William. *A Sermon Preached at Constantinople, in the Vines of Perah, at the Funerall of the vertuous and admired Lady Anne Glover, sometime Wife to the Honourable Knight Sir Thomas Glover, and then Ambassadour Ordinary for his Majesty of Great Britaine, in the Port of the Great Turke*. 1616.

Fortescue, George, ed. *Catalogue of the Pamphlets, Books, Newspapers, and Manuscripts Relating to the Civil War, The Commonwealth, and Restoration, Collected by George Thomason, 1641–1661*. 2 vols. London: British Museum, 1908.

Foster, William, ed. *Early Travels in India, 1583–1619*. Rpt. Delhi: S. Chand, 1968.

Fox. *Mr. Harrie Cavendish his Journey to and from Constantinople 1589, By Fox, His Servant*. Ed. Alfred C. Wood. London: Royal Historical Society, 1940.

Freely, John. *Istanbul: The Imperial City*. 1996. Rpt. London: Penguin, 1998.

Fuccaro, Nelida. *The Other Kurds: The Yazidis of Modern Iraq*. London: I.B. Taurus, 1999.

The Fugger Newsletters, Second Series. Trans. L.S.R. Byrne. Ed. Victor von Klarwill. London: John Lane, 1926.

Fuller, Mary. 'English Turks and Resistant Travelers: Conversion to Islam and Homosocial Courtship'. In Kamps and Singh, eds., *Travel Knowledge*.

Fuller, Thomas, *A Pisgah-Sight of Palestine and the Confines Thereof, With The History of the Old and New Testaments acted thereon.* 1650.

Gainsford, Thomas. *The Glory of England, or a True Description of many excellent prerogatives and remarkable blessings, whereby She Triumpheth over all the Nations of the World.* 1618.

Gilman, Arthur. *The Saracens: From the Earliest Times to the Fall of Bagdad.* London: Unwin, 1895.

Goddard, Hugh. *A History of Christian-Muslim Relations.* Edinburgh: Edinburgh University Press, 2000.

Goffman, Daniel. *Izmir and the Levantine World, 1550–1650.* Seattle: University of Washington Press, 1990.

——. *Britons in the Ottoman Empire, 1642–1660.* Seattle: University of Washington Press, 1998.

Granger, James. *A Biographical History of England.* 4 vols. 2nd edn London: Davies, 1775.

Grimaud, Jean. *Monographie de la Commune de Pont-de-L'Isser.* Oran: Fouque, 1929.

Griswold, William, J. *The Great Anatolian Rebellion, 1000–1020/1591–1611.* Berlin: Klaus Schwarz, 1983.

Guest, John S. *Survival Among the Kurds: A History of the Yezidis.* London: Routledge, 1993.

Hakluyt, Richard. *The Principal Navigations, Traffiques, and Navigations of the English Nation.* 1589. Rpt. 8 vols. London: Dent, 1907.

Halifax, William. *A Relation of a Voyage to Tadmor, in 1691.* Ed. C.R. Conder. London: Harrison, 1890.

Hall, Joseph. *Quo Vadis? A Just Censure of Travell, as it is commonly undertaken by the Gentlemen of our Nation.* 1617.

Harley, Robert; Earl of Oxford. *Collection of Voyages and Travels.* 2 vols. 1745.

Hess, Andrew, C. *The Forgotten Frontier: A History of the Sixteenth-Century Ibero-African Frontier.* Chicago: University of Chicago Press, 1978.

Historical Manuscripts Commission 9: Calendar of the Manuscripts of the Most Honourable the Marquess of Salisbury, Preserved at Hatfield House, Hertfordshire. Part 19. London: HMSO, 1965.

Holt, Peter. 'Pietro Della Valle in Ottoman Egypt, 1615–21,' in Starkey and Starkey, eds. *Travellers in Egypt.*

Hourani, Albert. *A History of the Arab Peoples.* Cambridge, MA: Harvard University Press, 1991.

Howell, James. *Instructions and Directions for Forren Travell.* 1642. 2nd edn 1650.

Imber, Colin. *The Ottoman Empire.* London: Palgrave, 2002.

Jardine, Lisa. *Worldly Goods: A New History of the Renaissance.* London: Macmillan, 1996.

—— and Jerry Brotton. *Global Interests: Renaissance Art Between East and West.* London: Reaktion, 2000.

Kamps, Ivo and Jyotsna Singh, eds. *Travel Knowledge: European 'Discoveries' in the Early Modern Period.* London and New York: Palgrave, 2001.

Kelly, Laurence. *Istanbul: A Travellers' Companion.* New York: Atheneum, 1987.

Kimber, E. and R. Johnson. *The Baronetage of England.* 3 vols. London: Woodfall, 1771.

Kinzer, Stephen. *Crescent and Star: Turkey Between Two Worlds.* New York: Farrar Strauss, 2002.

Kippis, Andrew. *Biographia Britannica: Or, The Lives of the Most Eminent Persons Who have Flourished in Great Britain and Ireland.* 4 vols. 1780.

Knolles, Richard. *The Generall Historie of the Turkes, from The first beginning of that Nation to the rising of the Othoman Familie.* 1603. Rpt., the 'fift' edition, 1638.

Lawless, Richard, I. and Gerald H. Blake. *Tlemcen: Continuity and Change in an Algerian Islamic Town.* London: Bowker, 1976.

Layard, Austen. *Nineveh and its Remains: With an Account of a visit to the Chaldean Christians of Kurdistan, and the Yezidis, or Devil-Worshippers; and an Enquiry into the Manners and Arts of the Ancient Assyrians.* 3rd edn, 2 vols. London: Murray, 1849.

Lily, John. *Six Court Comedies.* 1632.

Lithgow, William. *The Totall Discourse of The Rare Adventures and Painefull Peregrinations.* 1632. Rpt. Glasgow: MacLehose, 1906.

MacLean, Gerald. 'Ottomanism before Orientalism: Bishop Henry King praises Henry Blount, Passenger in the Levant' In Kamps and Singh, eds., *Travel Knowledge.*

——. 'Performing East: English Captives in the Ottoman Maghreb'. *Actes du Ier Congrès International sur: Le Grande Bretagne et le Maghreb: Etat de Recherche et contacts culturels.* Zaghouane, Tunisia: Fondation Temimi, 2001.

MacLeod, Catherine and Julia Marciari Alexander. *Painted Ladies: Women at the Court of Charles II.* London: National Portrait Gallery, 2001.

Mansel, Philip. *Constantinople: City of the World's Desire, 1453–1924.* 1995. Rpt. Harmondsworth: Penguin, 1997.

Matar, Nabil. *Islam in Britain, 1558–1685.* Cambridge: Cambridge University Press, 1998.

——. *Turks, Moors, and Englishmen in the Age of Discovery.* New York: Columbia University Press, 1999.

——. 'England and Mediterranean Captivity, 1577–1704'. Introduction to Vitkus, ed., *Piracy, Slavery.*

Maundrell, Henry. *A Journey from Aleppo to Jerusalem at Easter A.D. 1697.* Oxford, 1703. Rpt. with Introduction by David Howell. Beirut: Khayats, 1963.

Mayes, Stanley. *An Organ for the Sultan.* London: Putnam, 1956. Turkish translation, Mehmet Halim Spatar. *Sultan' ın Orgu.* Istanbul: İletişim, 2000.

McDowall, David. *A Modern History of the Kurds.* London: I.B. Tauris, 1997.

McGowan, Bruce. *Economic Life in Ottoman Europe: Taxation, Trade and the Struggle for Land, 1600–1800.* Cambridge: Cambridge University Press, 1981.

Montagu, Lady Mary Wortley. *The Complete Letters of Lady Mary Wortley Montagu. Vol. I, 1708–1720.* Ed. Robert Halsband. Oxford: Clarendon Press, 1965.

Montreux, Nicholas de. *Honours Academie. Or the famous pastorall, of Julietta. With divers histories. Englished by R. T [ofte].* 1610.

Moryson, Fynes. *An Itinerary Containing His Ten Yeeres Travell.* 1617. Rpt. 4 vols. Glasgow: MacLehose, 1907.

Mundy, Peter. *The Travels of Peter Mundy, In Europe and Asia, 1608–1667.* Ed. Sir Richard Carnac Temple. Cambridge: Hakluyt Society, 1907.

Murphey, Rhoads. *Ottoman Warfare 1500–1700.* London: University College London, 1999.

Necipoğlu, Gülru. *Architecture, Ceremonial, and Power: The Topkapi Palace in the Fifteenth and Sixteenth Centuries.* Cambridge, MA.: MIT Press, 1991.

A New Survey of The Turkish Empire and Government, In A Brief History deduced to this present Time, and the Reign of the now Grand Seignior Mahomet the IV. The present and XIV. Emperor. With their Laws, Religion and Customs. 1633.

Neville, Henry. *The Parliament of Ladies. Or Divers remarkable passages of ladies in Spring-Garden; in Parliament Assembled.* 1647.

Newby, Eric. *On the Shores of the Mediterranean.* 1984. Rpt. London Picador, 1985.

Nicolay, Nicolas de. *The Navigations, Peregrinations, and Voyages, made into Turkie.* Lyon: G. Roville, 1568. English translation, Thomas Washington the Younger. 1585. German translation, with hand-coloured plates by Georg Mack, *Der Erst Theil. Von der Schiffart und Raisz in die Turckey und gegen Orient beschriben durch H.N. Nicolay.* Nürenberg: Conrad Saldoerffer, 1572.

Okeley, William. *Eben-Ezer: or, A Small Monument of Great Mercy.* 1675.

Olms, W. George. *Asil Arabians: The Noble Arabian Horses.* Fourth edn. Hildesheim, Zurich, & New York: Olms, 1993.

Ortelius, Abraham. *Abraham Ortelius his Epitome of the Theatre of the Worlde.* 1603.

Palmer, Thomas. *An Essay of Meanes how to make our Travailes, into forraine Countries, the more profitable and honorable.* 1606.

Pamuk, Orhan. *Benim Adım Kırmızı.* Istanbul: İletişim, 1998. Trans. Erdag M. Goknar, *My Name is Red.* New York: Knopf, 2001

Parker, John. *Books to Build an Empire: A Bibliographical History of English Overseas Interest to 1620.* Amsterdam: Israel, 1965.

Parker, Kenneth, ed. *Early Modern Tales of Orient.* London: Routledge, 1999.

Pearson, John. *A Biographical Sketch of the Chaplains to the Levant Company, Maintained at Constantinople, Aleppo and Smyrna, 1611–1706.* Cambridge: Deighton Bell, 1883.

Peirce, Leslie. *The Imperial Harem: Women and Sovereignty in the Ottoman Empire.* Ithaca, NY: Cornell University Press, 1993.

Penrose, Boise. *Urbane Travellers, 1591–1635.* Philadelphia: University of Pennsylvania Press, 1942.

Pepys, Samuel. *The Diary of Samuel Pepys: Volume 2, 1661.* Ed. Robert Latham and William Matthews. London: Bell, 1970.

——. *The Tangier Papers of Samuel Pepys.* Ed. Edwin Chappell. London: Navy Records Society, 1935.

Phelps Brown, Henry and Sheila V. Hopkins. *A Perspective of Wages and Prices.* London: Methuen, 1981.

Plantet, Eugene. *Correspondance des Deys d'Alger avec La Cour de France 1579–1833.* 2 vols. 1889. Rpt. Tunis: Bouslama, 1981.

The Policy of the Turkish Empire. The First Booke. 1597.

Pratt, Mary Louise. *Imperial Eyes: Travel Writing and Transculturation.* London: Routledge, 1992.

Raman, Shankar. 'Back to the Future: Forging History in Luis de Camoes's *Os Lusiadas'.* In Kamps and Singh, eds., *Travel Knowledge.*

Raymond, Andre. *Cairo.* Trans. Willard Wood. Cambridge MA: Harvard University Press, 2000.

Refik, Ahmet. *Türkler ve Kraliçe Elizabet (1200–1255).* Istanbul: Matbaaçılık ve Nesriyat, 1932.

[Rhodes, Henry]. *Catalogue of the Collection of Works of Art and Vertue, comprising pictures, books, prints, sculpture...formed by Henry Rhodes.* 1846. British Library Catalogue only.

Rimbault, Edward, F. *The Early English Organ Builders And Their Works, From the Fifteenth Century to the Period of the Great Rebellion.* London: Whittingham, 1864.

Robinson, Edward. *The Early English Coffee House.* 1893. Rpt. Christchurch, Hants.: Dolphin Press, 1972.

Rogerson, Barnaby. *A Traveller's History of North Africa.* Moreton-in-Marsh: Windrush, 1998.

Robson, Charles. *Newes from Aleppo.* 1628.

Rumsey, Walter. *Organon Salutis. An Instrument to Cleanse the Stomach, As also divers new Experiments of the Virtue of Tobacco and Coffee: How much they conduce to preserve humane health.* 1657.

Rycaut, Paul. *The Present State of the Ottoman Empire.* 1667.

S., S.M. 'The Mancetter Martyrs: The Glover Family'. *Notes and Queries,* 3rd Series. Vol. 1 (March 1862), p. 182.

S., T. *The Adventures of (Mr T.S.) An English Merchant, Taken Prisoner by the Turks of Argiers.* 1670. Dutch translation, *De Ongelukkiege Voyagie van Mr. T.S. Engels Koopman, Gedaan in den Jaare 1648.* Leyden: Pieter Van Der Aa, 1707. Rpt. in *Die Wijd-Beroemde Voyagien Der Engelsen In Twee Deelen.* 2 vols. Leyden: Pieter Van Der Aa, 1737.

Said, Edward W. *Orientalism: Western Conceptions of the Orient.* 1978. Rpt. Harmondsworth: Penguin, 1995.

Sandys, George. *A Relation of a Journey begun An. Dom: 1610. Foure Bookes.* 1615.

Sedgwick, Eve Kosofsky. *Between Men: English Literature and Male Homosexual Desire.* New York: Columbia University Press, 1985.

Setton, Kenneth, M. *Western Hostility to Islam and Prophecies of Turkish Doom.* Philadelphia: American Philosophical Society, 1999.

Shaw, Stanford. *History of the Ottoman Empire and Modern Turkey*. 2 vols. Cambridge: Cambridge University Press, 1977.

Shuval, Tal. 'The Ottoman Algerian Elite and its Ideology'. *International Journal of Middle East Studies* 32 (2000): 323–44.

——. 'Cezayir-i Garp: Bringing Algeria Back into Ottoman History'. *New Perspectives on Turkey* 22 (Spring 2000): 85–114.

Singer, Amy. *Palestinian Peasants and Ottoman Officials: Rural Administration around Sixteenth-Century Jerusalem*. Cambridge: Cambridge University Press, 1994.

Skilliter, Susan, A. 'Three Letters from the Ottoman 'Sultana' Safiye to Queen Elizabeth I'. In *Documents from Islamic Chanceries*. Ed. S.M. Stern. Oxford: Cassirer, 1965.

——. *William Harborne and the Trade with Turkey, 1578–1582*. London: British Academy, 1977.

Smith, Thomas. *Remarks Upon the Manners, Religion and Government of the Turks. Together with A Survey of the Seven churches of Asia*. 1678.

Snader, Joe. *Caught Between Worlds: British Captivity Narratives in Fact and Fiction*. Lexington: University of Kentucky Press, 2000.

Soranzo, Lozarro. *The Ottoman of Lazaro Soranzo. Wherein is delivered as well a full and perfect report of the might and power of Mahamet the third, Great Emperour of the Turkes now raigning*. Trans. Abraham Hartwell the Younger. 1603.

Spivak, Gayatri Chakravorty. *The Spivak Reader*. Ed. Donna Landry and Gerald MacLean. New York: Routledge, 1996.

Starkey, Paul and Janet Starkey, eds. *Travellers in Egypt*. London: I.B. Tauris, 1998.

Stevens, Henry, ed. *The Dawn of British Trade to the East Indies. As Recorded in the Court Minutes of the East India Company 1599–1603*. London: Henry Stevens and Son, 1886.

Strachan, Michael. *The Life and Adventures of Thomas Coryate*. London: Oxford University Press, 1962.

Sumner, G. 'The Origins of the Dallams in Lancashire'. *JBIOS* 8 (1984): 51–7.

Soucek, Svat. 'The Rise of the Barbarossas in North Africa'. *Archivum Ottomanicum* 3 (1971): 238–50.

Thevenot, Jean de. *The Travels of Monsieur de Thevenot Into the Levant. In Three Parts: Viz. Into I. Turkey II Persia III The East-Indies*. Trans. A. Lovell. 1687.

Timberlake, Henry. *A True and Strange Discourse of the Travailes of two English Pilgrimes*. 1603.

Tipping, H. Avery. *English Homes. Period IVB–Volume One: Late Stuart, 1649–1714*. London: Country Life, 1920.

Tonkin, Boyd. Column in *The Independent Magazine* (Saturday, 25 May 2002), p. 20.

Toomer, G.J. *Eastern Wisdome and Learning: The Study of Arabic in Seventeenth-Century England*. Oxford: Clarendon, 1996.

A True and Perfect Relation of the Happy Successe & Victory Obtained Against the Turks of Argiers at Bugia, By His Majesties Fleet in the Mediterranean, under the command of Sr. Edw[ard] Spragge. 1671.

The True Declaration of the arrival of Cornelius Haga, (with others that accompanied him) Ambassador for the generall States of the united Netherlands, at the great Citie of Constantinople. 1613.

Turner, James Grantham. *Libertines and Radicals in Early Modern London: Sexuality, Politics and Literary Culture, 1630–1685*. Cambridge: Cambridge University Press, 2002.

Vitkus, Daniel, J., ed. *Piracy, Slavery, and Redemption: Barbary Captivity Narratives from Early Modern England*. New York: Columbia University Press, 2001.

Walkley, Thomas. *A New Catalogue of The Dukes, Marquesses, Earls, Viscounts, Barons, of England, Scotland, and Ireland, with the times of their Creations*. 1658.

Warton, Thomas. *The Life of Sir Thomas Pope, Founder of Trinity College Oxford*. 1780.

Wigram, W.A. and Edgar, T.A. *The Cradle of Mankind: Life in Eastern Kurdistan*. London: Black, 1914.

Wood, Alfred, C. *A History of the Levant Company*. 1935. Rpr. London: Frank Cass, 1964.

Wood, Anthony. *Athenae Oxoniensis*. 2 vols. Oxford, 1692.

Woodhead, Christine. "The Present Terrour of the World'? Contemporary Views of the Ottoman Empire, c. 1600'. *History* 72 (1987): 20–37.

Wright, Louis, B. *Religion and Empire: The Alliance between Piety and Commerce in English Expansion, 1558–1625*. Chapel Hill, NC: University of North Carolinia Press, 1943.

Yeğenoğlu, Meyda. *Colonial Fantasies: Towards a Feminist Reading of Orientalism*. Cambridge: Cambridge University Press, 1998.

Yerasimos, Stephane. *Les Voyageurs Dans L'Empire Ottoman (XIVe–XVIe siècles): Bibliographie, Itinéraires et Inventaire des Lieux Habités*. Ankara: Société Turque d'Histoire, 1991.

Young, Peter and Wilfrid Emberton. *Sieges of the Great Civil War: 1642–1646*. London: Bell and Hyman, 1978.

Yurtbaşi, Metin. *A Dictionary of Turkish Proverbs*. Ankara: Özkan, 1993.

Ze'evi, Dror. *An Ottoman Century: The District of Jerusalem in the 1600s*. Albany, NY: SUNY Press, 1996.

Index

Abasa Pasha, Ottoman general 137
Abaza Mehmed Pasha, rebel leader 124
Abel Hamed, Prince 205
Abel Hamed Simon, Ottoman
    general 201, 207
Abbott, Edward 51, 101
Abbott, G.F. 6
Abdell Phat, Yezidi guide 83
Abdie, Anthonie 58
Abraham xii
Abu Hammu I, Ziyyanid sultan 213
adders 25, 31
Adriatic 74, 120, 142
Aeneas 71, 181
Africa 15, 51, 60, 130, 156, 182,
    195, 201, 204, 213, 214, 219
  origin of civilization 139
Ahmed I (1603–17) xvi, 99, 176, 223
akıncı, irregular Ottoman troops 145
Alcoran see Koran
Aldridge, Jonas 40
Aldridge, William 35, 40
Aleppo xiii, xvi, xvii, 23, 26, 27, 49, 51,
    56, 57, 63, 66–72, 74, 77, 78, 82–5,
    89–101, 103, 104, 108, 109, 114
Alexandria 83, 120, 125, 160,
    164, 166, 221
Algeria xiii, xvi, 179–84, 186,
    188, 192, 194, 195, 196, 200,
    201, 202, 206, 207, 215, 218
  French occupation 213
Algiers xvii, 14, 15, 17, 18, 74, 107,
    181, 182, 185, 186, 189, 191,
    192, 194, 195, 196, 199–203,
    205, 208, 215, 217, 218, 221
  King of (Youssouf Pasha?) 196–8
Ali Canbuladoğlu Pasha, Kurdish
    leader 98, 99
Almohad Empire 194, 212
Ambler, Eric 159
Ananias, house of, Damascus 105
Anatolia 25, 83, 124, 172, 195, 200
anchorite, of Zante 22
Angad 206, 214
An'nabk ('Nebecke') 104
Antioch (Antakya) 83

Appolonius 71
Arabic see languages
Arabian horses see horses
Arabs 84, 85, 86, 87, 92, 93, 94,
    96, 101, 107, 113, 158, 167,
    175, 200, 201, 205, 206, 207,
    208, 209, 217, 219
  cavalry 207, 208
archaeology 107, 202, 205
Aristotle 95
Arlestone, Derbyshire 119
Armenians 84, 94, 106, 137,
    173, 175
Armitage, David 241
Arrian 87
Asia 51, 126
Assad, Hafez 236
Assad, Rifaat 236
Assan Aga see Rowlie, Samson
Atlantic xvii, 12
Aubrey, John 118, 119, 121, 150, 152
Aydin, Kamil 226
'Azar' (Ras Asfour) 205, 206
Azoret Mouden 205

Bab Sharqi, Damascus 106
Bab Zuwayla, Cairo 161
Babylon 73
Bacon, Francis 120, 123, 130,
    134, 135, 140, 165, 176, 183
Baghdad 83, 170
Bak, Greg 226
Balkans xvi, 142, 143, 145, 146,
    154, 158, 171, 183
Barbarossa, Hayreddin xix, 194, 195
Barbarossa, Oruç xix, 194, 212
Barbary Coast 15
Barbour, Richmond xv
Barrett, William 84
Bartholemew, Georgievits 4
Barton, Edward 9, 33, 34, 61, 62,
    64, 83, 137, 153, 223
basilisks 207
Baudier, Michel 148, 149
Baylye (also 'Baylie' and 'Bayly') Mr 29,
    31, 39

beasts   24, 26, 31, 82, 86, 90, 106, 161,
    171, 196, 202, 203, 204, 205, 208, 209
Beck, Brandon   226
Bedford, Hertfordshire   119
'Bedtua' (Bettiwa?)   201, 214, 216
Bedwell, William   86
Behn, Aphra   xvi, 212
Bel, Alfred   212
Belen   82
Belgrade   120, 138, 143, 144, 145, 159
  eunuch of   174
'Bembouker', King of Fez   218
Benemsaib   212
Ben Osman Bucher   201, 202, 207–10
Bent, Theodore J.   6, 25
Bethlehem   110
Beyazit I (1389–1403)   187, 239
Bhabha, Homi   xviii
Bible   xiii, 7, 26, 49, 51, 54, 72,
    73, 78, 81, 83, 85, 91, 93,
    102, 103, 105, 108, 112, 126,
    140, 154, 168, 180, 187
  books cited:
    Acts   105
    Esdras   175
    Genesis   95
    Isaiah   105
    Jeremiah   175
    2.Kings   105
    Matthew   108
    Phil.   78
    Psalms   82, 85, 102, 113
    Revelations   85, 90, 91
    2.Samuel   85
    King James version   82
    Old Testament   78
Biddle, William, of Brasenose College,
    Oxford   51
Biddulph, Theophilus   230
Biddulph, William   xiii, xvi, xvii, 26,
    49, 125, 126, 127, 128, 129, 130,
    134, 142, 154, 175, 183, 221
  advises travellers   107
  appointed chaplain   56
  arrival in:
    Aleppo   68, 70
    Istanbul   75
  attitude to:
    Arabs   92
    Edward Barton   83
    Catholicism   86, 107, 108, 110
    Eastern Christians   94, 95

Thomas Glover   57–63
    Islam   85–7, 90
    Jerusalem   101
    Jews   92–4
    Kurds   83
    Henry Lello   61
    Maronites ('Nostranes')   79
    Ottomans   96, 97
    sexuality   88, 96, 111, 114
    Henry Timberlake   54, 110
  beard   52, 61–2, 92
  cites Nicolay   73, 75
  clothing   52
  conceals authorship   551
  defends Lello   57
  documentary style   73
  epistolary style,   77–8
  food   80, 83, 92, 103, 113, 147
  homesickness   72
  Orientalism   93
  satirized   61
  self-representation   52, 71, 73,
      78, 106
Bicknell, Stephan   226
birds   25, 161, 203, 204, 216
Biscay, Bay of   xvii, 188
Black Beauty   198
Black Sea   51, 76, 125, 156, 159, 166
Blacksmiths' Guild   3
Blake, William   114
Blount, Sir Harry Pope   121, 236
Blount, Sir Henry   xiii, xvi, xvii, 182,
      183, 184, 187, 197, 214
  attitude to:
    archaeology   155
    Christianity   146, 168
    food   147, 162
    gipsies   175
    horses   163
    Islam   167, 170
    Istanbul   156
    Jews   174
    Richard Knolles   127
    Fynes Moryson   128, 140
    sexuality   147, 149, 150,
        151, 168
  clothing   128, 155, 162, 171
  early travels   120, 135
  espionage   xvi, 126–9, 158, 159
  finances   119
  knighted   121, 141
  mottoes   117, 118

Blount, Sir Henry – *continued*
    poetry 120
    portraits 117
    self-representation 123, 128, 130,
        134, 135, 139, 140
Blount, Charles 121, 137, 168
Blount, Charles, Earl of Devonshire and
        Eighth Lord Mountjoy 128
Blount, Edward 237
Blount, Hester, Lady xvii, 117, 119,
        121, 168
Blount, Lady Frances (*née* Piggot) 119
Blount, Thomas 119, 121
Blount, Sir Thomas Pope 118, 237
Blount, Ulysses 71, 117, 118, 119,
        121, 150
Blount's Hall, Staffordshire 119
'Blouza' (Blaouza) 80
Blunt, Lady Anne 163
Blunt, Wilfrid Scawen 163
Bodin, Jean 165
Bodleian Library, Oxford xv, 67
Bon, Ottaviano 57, 58
Bond, James 158
Bonnington, John xvii
Bosnia 122, 143, 145
Bosphorus 34, 124
Bostan, Idris xii
Bostancı Basha, head gardener in charge
        of seraglio security 35
Bosworth, Edmund 234
'Bougia' (Bougie) 179
Boumelli 205
Brasenose College, Oxford 51
Breay, M.C. 227
Bristol 185
Britain xiv, 163
British Empire 134, 181, 183
British Library 6, 40, 83
British Museum 5
Brotton, Jerry xv
Buckett, Rowland 10, 39, 47
Buckingham Palace 134
Buda 145
buffalo 25
Bull, Cuthbert 29
Bull, Randolph 5
bulls 15
Bulwer, John 225
Burrell, John 108, 109
Burton, Jonathan xv
Bush, George 234

Bushell, Edward 59
Byron, Lord 137
Bythnia 51
Byzantium 75, 132
Byzantine mosaics 103

Cabala 174
Cable, Thomas 26
Cadiz, Bay of 189, 191
Caesar, Augustus 183
Caesar, Julius 154, 155, 164
Cairo xvi, 84, 120, 122, 130, 136, 138,
        139, 157, 158, 161, 162, 163, 164
Calbi, Maurizio 148
Calendars, ascetics 150
Calvin, John 36, 67
camels 126, 147, 155, 157, 207, 208
Canaan 51
'Canahaal', 'Canatudi' 210, 211
Cannosea 30
Cappadoccia xv
Cape St Vincent 188
Capello, Girolamo 34, 35, 40, 67
capitulations (ahidname) 9, 33, 185
captivity 184, 185, 191, 221
captive agency 183, 187, 194, 200
captivity narratives 180, 184, 191, 196
Carleton, Dudley 3
Casey, John 134
castration 185, 186
Catherine of Braganza 181
Catholicism, Roman Catholics 15,
        54, 55, 64, 67, 72, 74, 79–81, 101,
        102, 107, 108, 110, 111, 113, 114,
        135, 153, 173, 183
    Pope 49, 79
cattle 80, 94, 198, 208
Cecil, Sir Robert 58, 60, 228
Chamberlain, John 3
Chancie, Mr 14, 25
chaplains 66, 67, 70
Charles I (1625–49) 121, 141, 181
Charles II (1660–95) xv, 117, 181, 183
'Charrah' (Qara) 104
Cheevers, Sarah 221
'Chelfalines' (Zulphalines) 84, 94, 95,
        106, 234
'chequins' (also 'chickers', etc.) 8, 42,
        110, 228
Chester 117
Chew, Samuel xv, 138
chickens 210

China 5
Chios 26, 28, 29, 44, 57, 74, 75, 78, 156
  English consul 28
  women of 29
Chishull, Edmund 66, 231
Chiswell, Richard, the younger 100
Chorley, Lancashire 11
Christ 49, 61, 64, 74, 86, 88, 95, 100,
      107, 108, 110, 111
Christendom 26, 34, 131
Christianity and Christians xiii, xiv, 7,
      11, 27, 36, 38, 51, 54, 61, 63, 67, 68,
      69, 72, 73, 76, 78, 79, 80, 82, 83, 84,
      85, 87, 89, 90, 94, 95, 97, 100, 101,
      102, 111, 112, 113, 123, 125, 127,
      128, 129, 131, 132, 134, 135, 137,
      138, 139, 140, 143, 144, 146, 149,
      152, 159, 171, 172, 173, 174, 181,
      191, 221, 223, 224, 225
  apocalyptic history 85
  armies 135, 136, 137
  in Damascus 105
  prejudice 136
  primitive 205
  supernaturalism 123, 134, 183
  zealots 6
Cilicia 51
citationality 73, 85
Clark, Richard 120
clerical culture 73
clothing 25, 40, 42, 185, 214, 223, 225
coffee 118, 120, 151, 158, 162, 168
coffee-house culture 152, 162, 172
Coke, Sir Edward 124, 137
Colchester 76
Colley, Linda 184
Colombe, Marcel 179
Colthurst, Richard 67, 68, 69, 70, 85, 98
commerce 4, 33, 100, 133, 153, 157
Conisby, Humphrey 11, 39, 40, 142
Constantine 76
Constantinople *see* Istanbul
'Contera' *see* Quneitrah
Cooper, Sir Anthony Ashley 121
Cornishmen, interpreter in Istanbul 11,
      12, 36
  slave dealer in Algiers 196
Corpus Christi College, Oxford 66
Coryate, Thomas 5
'Cotifey' *see* Qutaifah
Counter-Reformation 85
Cour, Auguste 213

Covel, John 66, 231
Coxden, George 58, 59, 60, 231
Crabbet Park, Sussex 163
Crawford, Richard 185
Creasy, Edward 238
Crete 10, 75
Crimea 134
crocodiles 164
Cromwell, Oliver 117, 180, 181
Crooke, Andrew 122
crusades, crusaders 85, 100, 195
currants 17 *see also* Zante
'cutting cabin' 63–5
Cyclades 78, 113
Cyprus 10, 25, 78

Dallam, Lancashire xvii, 3, 10
Dallam, Robert 227
Dallam, Thomas xi, xiii, xv, xvi, xvii,
      51, 56, 62, 67, 71, 73, 82, 91, 110,
      112, 113, 125, 128, 150, 151, 152,
      171, 183, 191, 219
  and Mehmed III 3, 41–3
  and Thomas Glover 29–31
  and Henry Lello 34, 37, 39, 43, 45, 46
  attitude to:
    archaeology 24
    food 8, 14, 15, 18, 20, 21, 23,
        25, 28, 29
    religion 12, 13
    women 15, 20, 45
  clothing 8, 14, 40
  early life 3
  expenses 8
  manuscript 4, 5, 6
  musician 27
  narrative style 30
  organ destroyed 4, 223
  on Rhodes 26
  self-representation 9, 11
Dalmatia 120, 122, 128
Damascus xvi, 25, 51, 84, 97, 98,
      103, 104, 105, 106
Daniel, prophecy of 85, 86, 87, 91, 175
'Dansicke' (Gdansk) 64
Danube, river 136, 144, 151, 152, 174
Daraya 106
Dardanelles 29, 156
Dartmouth 12
Davenant, Sir William 120
David, King 72
Davies, William 239

Defoe, Daniel   xvi, 12, 180, 188, 189, 190
'deli' warriors   145
Delos   75
Derbyshire   119
Dervish   92
Descartes, René   71
Devon   12
devşirme   186
Diogenes   93
diplomacy   xiv, xvi, 3, 10, 24, 33, 36, 40,
    44, 51, 56, 58, 59, 125, 128, 152, 183,
    184, 184, 190, 200, 201, 202, 221
Diyarbakir   xv
Djerba   194
dogs   210
dolphins   14
donkeys   10, 126, 219
Donne, John   120
Dover   47
dragoman   10, 11, 12, 36, 41
Drower, Lady (Ethel Stefana Stevens)   233
Druses   82
Dryden, John   183
Dubrovnik   171
Dunch, Edmund   233
Dunkirk   23
'Dunkirkers'   *see* pirates
Dutch   9, 85, 159, 166, 182, 196, 201
  in Aleppo   96
  ambassador   *see* Haga, Sir Cornelius
  merchants   33

eagles   216
earthquakes   22, 74, 214, 218
East India Company   69
Eden (Ehden)   78
Edgehill, battle of (1642)   121
Edirne (Adrianople)   120, 125, 154,
    155, 156
  mosque   155
Egypt, Egyptians   84, 120, 122, 124,
    125, 138, 139, 156, 157, 158, 159,
    162, 164, 165, 183, 214
  priests   164
Eldred, John   57, 84, 230
Elias   82
Ellice, Robert   120
Ellice, Thomas   120
Elizabeth I (1558–1603)   xi, xv, xvi,
    3, 5, 6, 8, 9, 11, 33, 38, 39, 72, 75,
    120, 137, 153, 186
  death of   72

Elkin, John   51, 101
Elmswar Bidow Ben Hemmed   210
Elmswar Tapnez   206, 208, 209
Elvers, Anthony   185
'Emeer Useph'   80
England, English   xiii, xv, xviii,
    4, 8, 9, 13, 14, 15, 17, 20, 24,
    32, 40, 44, 45, 46, 53, 54, 56,
    57, 58, 59, 60, 61, 65, 66, 68,
    69, 70, 73, 74, 82, 85, 88, 91,
    97, 101, 109, 112, 113, 114,
    119, 120, 122, 132, 137, 150,
    152, 163, 165, 172, 179, 181,
    200, 211, 212, 221, 222,
    223, 224
  Church of   52, 67, 71, 72, 80, 82
    planned church in Istanbul   68,
      70, 71
  Civil War   121
  imperial ambitions   181, 182, 184
  merchants   9, 33, 98
    behaviour of   66, 70
  prostitute   114
  renegades   184
Englishness   xiii, xvi, 11, 27,
    34, 45, 53, 59, 77, 112, 130,
    170, 183, 204
  right to roam   14
  souvenir collecting   24
Enlightenment   123, 135, 165, 183
Erivan   124
eschatology   86
espionage   126–9, 140, 172
Evans, Katherine   221
Evelyn, John   118

Fatma, Kurdish singer   239
Fayyum   120
Felton, John   26
Fez   206
  King of   35   *see also* Bembouker
Finch, dragoman   11
Finkel, Caroline   231
fish   23, 161
Fleece Tavern   196
Flixton, Lancashire   xvii, 3
food   8, 15, 24, 25, 26, 36, 44,
    103, 192
Forde, William   49, 222, 224, 225
Foster, Sir William   223
Foxe, George   85
foxes   82, 204

Frampton, Robert, Bishop of
    Gloucester 66, 233
France, French 9, 33, 58, 59,
    78, 85, 120, 135, 123, 135,
    156, 164, 189, 213
  in Aleppo 96
  merchants 124
Franciscan monastery, Jerusalem 110
Franciscus Amyra, Maronite bishop 79
Freake, Thomas 98
Freely, John 226
fruit 25, 157, 161, 170, 202, 212
Fuller, Thomas 236

Gainsford, Thomas 223
Galata 35, 67, 125
Galilee 51, 108
Gallipoli 11, 29, 62, 75
Garibaldi Uprisings 5
Germany, Germans 3, 64
Gibraltar 14, 192
gifts, gift-giving xi, xv, 3, 6, 8–10,
    14, 15, 20, 23, 24, 28–30, 33–5,
    37, 38, 41, 43, 45, 151
Gildon, Charles 122
gipsies 137, 175
Giza 120, 157
Glover, Anne Lady (*née* Lamb) xviii, 49,
    57, 59, 222, 223
Glover, Robert 231
Glover, Sir Thomas 10, 11, 29, 30,
    31, 40, 56, 57, 58, 59, 60, 61, 62,
    64, 65, 69, 71, 75, 99, 113, 114,
    137, 153, 222, 223, 224
  accusations against 57–9, 62, 64,
    222, 223, 224
  accuses Henry Lello 59
  appointed ambassador 58
  defends himself 60
  knighted 56
  linguistic skills 64
  mother 64
  see also Sophia
goats 19, 80
Golan Heights 106, 107
  Hospital, Quneitrah 107
Gontaut-Biron, baron de Salignac 58
Gonzale, Mr 29
Grant, Pauline 237
Gravesend 3
Gray's Inn 120, 151
Greaves, John 102, 240

Greece, Greeks 10, 11, 22, 24,
    26, 29, 46, 63, 67, 84, 85, 96,
    106, 114, 131, 137, 138, 166,
    173, 175, 194, 225
  guide in Jerusalem 105
  Orthodox Church 20, 21, 63, 67,
    82, 110
Grimaud, Jean 242
Grimestone, Edward 148, 149, 224
Grimston, Sir Harbottle 148
Guicciardini 165
Gustavus Adolphus 136

Habbington, William 120
Hadjiat, Abdelhamid 213, 214
Haga, Sir Cornelius 159, 161, 240
Hagar 86
Hakluyt, Richard 4, 184, 185, 186, 195
Hakluyt Society 6
Halaç Rigla Reis, Ottoman general
    201, 208
Hale, Edward ('Ned') 10, 18, 19, 20,
    21, 39, 47
Haleç Sim Haly, Ottoman general
    201, 208
Halifax, William 102, 235
Hall, Bishop Joseph 55
Halley Hamez Reis, Ottoman
    general 200, 201, 202, 214,
    215, 217, 218, 219
Hama 104, 236
Hamburg 188
Hamore, Wiliam 185
'Hanadan' (Anadane) 83
Harborne, William 185, 186
Harley, Robert 119
Harran xv
Hartwell, Abraham, the younger
    5, 40
Harvey, Daniel 241
Harvie, John 10, 15, 24, 25, 27, 28,
    39, 47
Hassan Bassa, king of Algiers 185
'Hassia' (Hisyah) 104
'Hatcheeth' (Hadchit) 79
Haveland, Thomas 51
Hawarah 120
Hayes, Edwarde 26
Hellespont 75, 78
Henry, Prince 76
Heraclius 87
Herodotus 120, 164

Hertfordshire   117, 119, 121
Hess, Andrew C.   242
Heybeliada (Halki)   61, 231
Heycock's Ordinary   120
Holland, Hugh   60
Homer   75, 169
Homs   104
'Hora'   30
horses   34, 38, 82, 97, 103, 106,
    119, 126, 143, 145, 146, 147,
    148, 152, 157, 162, 163, 196,
    197, 198, 200, 206, 207, 215
  breeding   162, 163
  breeds:
    Arabian   158, 163, 165, 240
    Barbs   163
    British   163
    English thoroughbred   163
    Neapolitan   163
    Thessalian   163
Hourani, Albert   194, 195, 242
Howard, Henry   120
Howell, James   120, 134
Hungary   122, 137, 153
Huntington, Robert   66
Husein Pasha, Ottoman general   98
Huseyn Canbuladoğlu, Kurdish leader   98
Huysmans, Jacob   117, 118, 121
Hyde, Edward, later Lord Clarendon   120

Ibrahim Pasha, Governor of Aleppo   98
Illustrated London News   5
imperial envy   126, 131, 133, 182
India, Indians   77, 84
infanticide   95
innes   53   *see also* khans
Inns of Court   62
insects   204
Ireland   221
Isha Muker, Arab rebel   206, 208, 209
Ishmael   92
Isis   160, 164
Iskenderun   23, 25, 26, 46, 67, 68,
    70, 82, 84
Islam, Muslims   xiii, xiv, xv, xviii, 4,
    15, 75, 82, 85–92, 94, 97, 101, 102,
    103, 105, 107, 108, 110, 113, 123,
    131, 135, 136, 139, 148, 161, 164,
    166–9, 173, 174, 184, 185, 196,
    204, 214, 217, 218
  Sunni   83
Israel   73, 107

Istanbul   3, 4, 5, 6, 7, 8, 10, 11, 12, 14, 23,
    25, 26, 29, 30, 31, 32, 33, 39, 43, 45,
    46, 49, 51, 56, 57, 58, 59, 61, 62, 63,
    64, 65, 66, 67, 68, 69, 70, 71, 73, 74,
    75, 76, 77, 78, 83, 98, 113, 114, 120,
    123, 124, 125, 126, 128, 130, 131, 138,
    139, 141, 142, 152, 154, 156, 159, 161,
    170, 183, 185, 194, 222, 224, 225
  great fire of 1633   124
  Orthodox Patriarch of   83
Italy, Italians   15, 74, 77, 120, 135, 155,
    164, 173, 195
  in Aleppo   96
  consul in Cairo   157
  friars in Jerusalem   108
  merchants   108
  see also languages, Italian
Izmir   xix, 66, 67, 188

jackals   82
Jacob   71, 73, 78, 83
James I (1603–25)   58, 72, 118,
    149, 150, 163, 224, 225
Janissary corps   26, 61, 82, 98, 101,
    102, 103, 124, 128, 141, 143,
    145, 153, 154, 176, 195
Jardine, Lisa   xv
Jericho   51
Jerome   71
Jerusalem   xiii, xvi, 51, 52, 54, 61,
    78, 83, 90, 91, 100, 101, 102,
    103, 105, 110, 120, 183
  Holy Sepulchre   111
Jesuits   102, 107, 224
Job   104, 191
Jonah   26
Jones, Inigo   119, 120
Jonson, Ben   120
Joppa   120, 164
Joseph   63
Judaism, Jews   10, 27, 67, 68, 84–7,
    89, 92, 94, 95, 96, 101, 102, 105,
    113, 137, 139, 140, 146, 148, 154,
    158, 173–5, 195, 224
  in Jerusalem   100
Judea   51
Justinian   76

Kabylies of Bougie   194
Kapıcı, gatekeeper in seraglio   35, 37,
    41, 42
Kara Yazıcı, rebel leader   98

Kâtip Çelebi 124
Kelly, Laurence 226
Kendall, Herts 119
khans 103, 104, 128, 170
  Khan al-Gümrük, Aleppo 85
  Khan Haramain, Damascus 104
  'Khan of the Bridegroom',
    Qutaifah 104
  Mehmed Pasha Khan, Istanbul 125
King, Bishop Henry 120, 130, 131, 132,
    133, 134, 135, 138, 141, 169, 176, 183
King's College, Cambridge 6
Kinzer, Stephen xiii, xiv
Kirbie, Jeffrey (also 'Kerby') 51, 101,
    105, 111
Kitely, John 59, 60, 61, 62, 64, 65,
    114, 223
Knill, John 26
Knolles, Richard xiv, 5, 127, 129,
    137, 176, 190, 224
Konya 40
Koran 90, 167
Kurds 82, 83, 99

'Lacmine' 104
Lactantius 95
Lamb, Anne *see* Glover, Anne Lady
Lamb, M. of Padley 222
Lambert, Mr 31
Lancashire 3, 10, 11, 14, 45
Landry, Donna xv, xvii
language(s) 9, 15, 18, 30, 31, 43, 80,
    82, 92, 93, 129, 131, 133, 153,
    160, 166, 170, 172, 214
  Arabic 79, 80, 92, 94, 167
  Dutch 122
  English 31
  French 222
  German 122
  Greek 160, 222
  Italian 27, 67, 222
  Latin 72, 79, 80, 109, 121, 160, 168, 204
  Laz 166
  nautical jargon 12, 13
  Persian 92
  Syriac 79, 80, 81, 82
  Turkish 79, 80, 94
'Lavender, Theophilus' 52, 53, 54,
    55, 60, 61, 62, 70, 72, 74, 76, 113
  defends travel writing 53
law 89, 90, 97, 100, 120, 131, 144,
    152, 158, 170, 213, 216

Layard, Henry Austen 233
Lazarus 105, 111
Leate, Nicholas 224
Lebanon 95
Leggatt, John 122
Leicester 119
Lello, Sir Henry 3, 6, 7, 9, 10, 11, 12, 30,
    33–46, 56–62, 64, 67, 68, 75, 83, 98
  knighted 56, 59
  reluctant to leave 57
  in Venice 59
Lely, Sir Peter 117, 118
Leonidas 155
Levant Company 3, 5, 7, 8, 9,
    33, 34, 56, 57, 58, 62, 66–70,
    84, 89, 222, 231
Levni (Abdelcelil Çelebi) xvi
Lewis, Geoffrey xii
Lily, John 237
lions 202, 203, 204, 207
Lithgow, William 5, 17, 97
  praises Sir Thomas Glover 64
Livorno 195
lizards 25
Locke, Roger 120
London xiv, xvi, 3, 4, 5, 8, 10, 12, 13,
    14, 24, 26, 39, 56, 57, 58, 60, 64,
    66, 76, 84, 88, 98, 99, 103, 119,
    120, 121, 122, 138, 144, 149, 150,
    152, 162, 182, 188, 222, 224
  Tower of 76
London Colney, Hertfordshire 119
Lot's wife 219
Luther, John 85, 86, 87
Lycia xv
Lycurgus 96

Ma'arret en Nu'man ('Marrah') 103, 104
Macedonia 122
Maghreb 184, 185, 194, 213
Mainwaring, Sir William 117
Malta 23, 74, 164, 221
Mamelukes 84, 158, 161, 163, 164
Manley, Thomas 180, 182
Mansell, Sir Robert 195
maps, mapping 103, 122, 126,
    130, 182, 201
Markham, John 58
Marx, Karl xviii
mariners 7, 150, 189
  Turkish 166
Marlborough Downs 155

Marlowe, Christopher   19
Marmara Ereglisi   29
Maronites ('Nostranes')   79, 80, 81,
    84, 85, 94, 95, 106
Marseilles   24
Marston, Thomas   76
Martin, William   89
Masters, Bruce   234
Matar, Nabil   15, 85, 86, 185
Maundrell, Henry   66, 102, 231, 235
Maye, Mr   27, 28, 29, 67, 68, 69,
    70, 71
Mayes, Stanley   4, 10, 43
Mecca   92, 206
Mediterranean   xiii, xiv, xvi, xviii,
    3, 4, 7, 14, 17, 23, 150, 161, 180,
    182, 184, 185, 195
Mehmed II (1444–46, 1451–81)   75,
    132, 238
Mehmed III (1595–1603)   xi, xv, 3, 4,
    6, 7, 8, 9, 33, 35, 37, 38, 40–3, 45,
    88, 98, 124, 137
  character of   40
Meknes   213
Mercator   130
merchants   xiv, xvi, 6, 7, 10, 23, 34,
    39, 40, 58, 63, 75, 84, 85, 90,
    95, 100, 101, 103, 109, 125,
    142, 143, 144, 146, 174, 180,
    195, 219, 224
Merenids   194
Mesopotamia   51, 73
Middlesex   119
Mildenhall, John   10, 227
Milesius, Greek Orthodox Patriarch   83
Millward, John   76
Milos   75
Milton, John   107, 183
Moab   73
money   7, 8, 20, 21, 23, 26, 30, 35,
    43, 46, 57, 58, 63, 66, 70, 77, 86,
    103, 107, 109, 119, 125, 144, 163,
    183, 196, 201, 208, 219
Montagu, Lady Mary Wortley   154,
    221, 225
Moors   11, 15, 26, 84, 91, 92, 101,
    158, 167, 175, 200, 201, 209,
    210, 216, 219
Morgan, Nicholas   163
Morocco   181, 182, 194, 206
Moryson, Fynes   5, 82, 84, 101, 102,
    126, 128, 140

Moryson, Henry   82, 101
Mosul   83
Mount Hermon   54
Mount Houlahka   208
Mount Lebanon   78, 79, 80
Mount of Olives   111
Mount Scopos   xvii, 17, 18, 22
Mount Tabor   54, 108
Moyses Zim Kush, sultan   214, 215
Muhammad   76, 85, 86, 87, 90, 95,
    112, 166, 167, 168, 206
Muhammed Al-Nasir   161
mules   31
mummies   xvii, 157, 164, 165
Munday, Peter   228
Murad II (1421–51)   132
Murad III (1574–95)   xi, xvi, 9, 152,
    153, 195
Murad IV (1623–40)   123, 124, 125,
    138, 170, 176, 225
Murad Pasha, Ottoman general   145,
    146, 151, 152, 153
Murphey, Rhoades   238, 239
Mustapha, brother of Ahmed I   176
Mustapha Aga, black eunuch   xi
Mytilene, Lesbos   194

Nabbes, Thomas   125, 238
Naomi   73
Naples   165
National Portrait Gallery   118
'Nebecke' *see* An'nabk
Necipoğlu, Gülru   226
Neville, Henry   239
Newby, Eric   226
Newcastle   13
Nicolay, Nicholas de   29, 73, 75, 76,
    77, 96, 112, 195
Nile   xvii, 157, 164
Niş   120, 153
Norris, Richard   180, 182
North, Sir Dudley   12
North American Indians   97
'Nostranes'   *see* Maronites
novel   194

Okeley, William   188, 191
Oran   194, 196, 214
Orientalism   xv, 73, 93, 94, 113, 134,
    135, 165
Ortelius   130
Osman I (1288–1324)   132

Osman II (1618–22)   176
Osyris   160
Othello   xiii, xiv
Ottoman
  architecture   154
  army   xiv, 25, 67, 126, 135, 136, 137,
      138, 143, 145, 146, 147, 149, 150,
      154, 159, 166, 201, 202, 206
  cavalry   26
  cruelty   76, 96, 144, 145, 146, 216
  Empire   xiii, xiv, xviii, 3, 4, 7, 20, 25,
      45, 51, 84, 97, 98, 123, 125, 126,
      128, 129, 130, 131, 132, 134, 135,
      136, 137, 141, 142, 148, 149, 154,
      157, 164, 165, 169, 170, 171, 172,
      173, 174, 179, 182, 183, 184, 190,
      195, 200, 221
  hospitality   152, 159
  justice   96, 133, 135, 143, 144,
      146, 154, 158, 164, 165, 169,
      170, 175, 182, 219
  medicine   152
  navy   24, 84, 164, 166
  religion   86
  rule in Egypt   164
  sexuality   148
  tyranny   96
Oujda   209
oxen   208
Oxford   62, 121, 139, 149, 150, 168

Palermo   165
Palestine   51
Pallsgrave-Head Tavern, Strand   120
Palmer, Sir Thomas   55, 129, 141
Pamuk, Orhan   4
Paravan Pasha, Janissary guide   82
Parker, Kenneth   xv
Parsons, George   228
Parsons, Captain Richard   10, 13, 15,
      23, 24, 28, 30, 227
partridges   15
Patmos   156
Pausanias   75
Pearche, William   58
Pepys, Samuel   196, 221
Pera   36, 57, 59, 128, 222, 224
Percivall, Nathaniel (also Persivall)
      59, 76
Persia, Persians   77, 84, 88, 89, 94,
      138, 167, 173
  army   176

Pharaoh   64, 77
Philippoplis (Phillipi)   155
Phipps, C.B.   134
pigeons   82, 83
pigs   25
pilgrims   52, 54, 92, 100–2
Pindar, Sir Paul   11, 40, 224
piracy   13, 14, 23, 24, 189, 185, 189,
      194, 195
  casual   23, 24
Pisidia   51
Pitt, Moses   180, 182
plague   29, 163
Plato   71, 95, 169
Plutarch   96
Plymouth   13, 14
Pocock, Edward   66
Poland   63, 137, 138, 143, 145, 152,
      154, 166
The Policy of the Turkish Empire   87
polygamy   167, 168, 169
Pompey's Pillar, Bosphorus   76
Pope, Alexander   52, 221
Pope, Sir Thomas   119
Portugal   14
Portuguese ambassador   121
'Potarzeek' (Pazarcik)   154
Pratt, Mary Louise   210
presents   *see* gifts
prostitution   19, 20, 59, 66, 88, 150, 195
Protestantism, Protestants   xi, xiii,
      36, 51, 53, 54, 64, 67, 68, 70, 71,
      82, 85, 86, 88, 96, 101, 102, 106,
      107, 110, 111, 112, 135, 168, 189,
      191, 199, 224
  Anglo-Protestants   86, 90
  providence   32, 113, 135, 137, 138,
      183, 184, 187, 189, 191, 193, 198,
      199, 202, 219
  and racial difference   86
public sphere   152
Purchas, Samuel   5, 51, 137, 195, 199
Pyramids   xvii, 120, 154, 157, 164, 165
Pythagoras   71

quail   15
Quakers   221
quarantine   17, 74
Quneitrah ('Contera')   xvii, xix,
      106, 107
  museum   107
Qutaifah ('Cotifey')   104

R.D.   179, 180, 201, 202
Rainolds, William   185
Ragusa (Dubrovnik)   171
Raymond, André   161
Red Sea   51, 77, 164
Reformation   85
Renaissance   xv, 139, 148, 165, 168
renegades   11, 12, 15, 158, 172, 191,
       192, 195, 196, 200
Restoration, Stuart (1660)   117, 121,
       163, 179, 180, 181, 183, 184, 196
Rhodes   26, 27, 28, 36, 67, 78, 120,
       122, 158, 159, 160, 166
Rhodes, Henry   5
Richards, John   238
Ridge, Hertfordshire   119
Ridwan Bey   161, 162
Rimbault, Edward   5, 6
Roberts, A.   180, 182
Robinson, Edward   152
Robson, Charles   228, 232
Rogerson, Barnaby   242
Romania   99
Rome   67, 82, 86, 125
    Civil Wars   155
    Empire   173
    mosaics   103
Rose, Edward   82
Roseta   161
Rowlie, Francis   185
Rowlie, Samson   184–6
Royal Society   210
Rumsey, Walter   120, 151, 152
Rycaut, Paul   176, 184

Sabians   93
Saddam Hussein   233
Safi, Mustapha   xii, 4
Safiye, Valide Sultan   3, 8, 10, 34
Said, Edward   xv, xviii, 73, 123, 134, 135, 183
Salado, river   194, 242
Salah ed-Din   161
    tomb of   105
Salignac, Gontaut-Biron, baron de
       58, 59, 60, 67
Samaria   51
Samos   156
Sancto Seghezzi   161
Sanderson, John   8, 9, 10, 34, 56, 57,
       58, 59, 60, 61, 62, 64, 65, 66, 67,
       68, 69, 70, 71, 75, 92, 98, 99, 101,
       105, 111, 114, 185, 222, 223, 224

Sandys, Sir George   5, 17, 112, 120, 127, 229
Santones, religious beggars   173
Saqarra   157
Saracens   86, 87, 92
Sarah   86, 92
Sarajevo   143
Sarepta   82
Sava, river   144
Savafids   124   *see also* Persia, Persians
Saxons   155
scorpions   202, 203
Scotland   85, 160
Scriblerians   52
Scutari (Üsküdar)   124, 125
Selim I (1512–20)   84, 100, 194
Selim II (1566–74)   156
Sepley, W.   51
seraglio   *see* Topkapi Palace
Sergius   87
serpents   31, 164, 203, 204
sexuality   148, 149, 188
    corruption   148, 150
    heterosexuality   197
    homosexuality   147, 148, 150, 186
    libertinism   181
    misconduct   62, 64, 65, 66, 70
Shakespeare, William   xiii, xiv, xv, 120
sharks   192
Sharpe, Mr   31
'Sharry' (Bsharri)   80
Sheba   93
sheep   15, 19, 29, 80, 94, 205, 207, 208
sherbert   147, 151, 157, 162
Sherley, Thomas   230
ships
    Hector   xvii, 3, 4, 8, 9, 10, 11, 12, 13, 14,
       15, 17, 18, 23, 24, 25, 26, 27, 28, 29,
       31, 32, 33, 34, 35, 40, 45, 46, 67, 68,
       69, 70, 71, 91, 114, 228
    Sancta Maria   188
    Sir Robert   xvii
    Swallow   185
    Trojan   234
Shirley, James   120
Shuval, Tal   186, 241
Sicily   120, 164
Sidi Bou Medienne   214, 217
Sidon   82
silk   xiv, 23, 32, 37, 40, 82, 84
Sinan   126, 154, 156
Sipahis, Ottoman cavalry   124, 145,
       147, 171

Skilliter, Susan 226, 241
Skynner, Robert 120
slavery 7, 15, 44, 46, 53, 140, 158,
    165, 179, 181, 182, 184, 185,
    188, 189, 192, 196, 206
  sexual slavery 197, 198, 214
Smith, Sir Thomas, Governor of the
    Levant and East India
    Companies 56, 68, 70
Smith, Thomas, chaplain and scholar 66,
    210, 231, 241
Snader, Joe 192
snakes 25, 31
Socrates 122
Sodom and Gomorrah 196
sodomy 76, 148, 149, 150, 151, 195
Sophia, Thomas Glover's first wife
    62–5
Sophia, Bulgaria 120, 146, 153,
    154, 174, 225
Soranzo, Lozarro 5, 40
Spain, Spanish xvi, 3, 9, 15, 20,
    21, 97, 110, 120, 135, 191,
    192, 198, 201, 212
  renegades 201
  ships 191, 192
Spaletro (Split) 124, 142, 143
Spatar, Hehmet Halim 227
Spivak, Gayatri Chakravorty 239
Sporades 78
Spragge, Sir Edward 179
Squires, William Barclay 6
Stamp, Mr 33
Staffordshire 51
St Albans School 149
St Helena 76
St John the Baptist 104
St Mark's, Venice 240
St Mary's Church, Blaouza 80, 81
St Nicholas Church, Qara 104
St Paul 71, 74, 78, 105, 106, 130, 140
St Paul's Cathedral, London 62
St Peter 52, 64, 77
St Peter's Church, Antakya 232
St Peter's, Rome 240
St Sergius and St Theodorus Church,
    Qara 104
St Sophia's, Istanbul 76, 240
Stapers, James 89
Stapers, Richard 5, 89, 224
'Stefee' 208
Strachey, John 230

Strachey, William 57, 60
Suleiman I 100, 144
Suleymaniye Mosque, Istanbul 125
Surrey 119
Sweden 136
Swift, Jonathan 12, 52, 189
Syndefine, Derbyshire 119
'Syntana Fissa', a charitable prostitute
    92, 234
Syria, Syrians 51, 77, 78, 85, 98,
    103, 105, 107

T.S. xiii, xvii
  as ethnographer 196
  as horse 196
  as imperial agent 211
  as Ottoman 207, 214
  as pimp 181, 217
  self-representation 188, 193, 205
  sexually desirable 181, 196, 198
  as soldier 200, 205
  'Thomas Smith' 179
Tabriz 124
Tafna, river 205, 206
Taksim Square, Istanbul 225
Tangier 181, 221
Tarsus 26, 82
Tartars 84, 140, 167
Temesvar, Bey of 145
Tenerife 74
Tezrim 214, 218
Thames, river 88
Thebes 164
Thermopolyae 154, 155
Thessaly 122
Thevenot, Jean de 238
Thirty Years' War 135, 136, 137
Thrace 51, 122, 154, 155
Timariots 159, 166
Timberlake, Henry 5, 53, 54, 55, 81,
    89, 108, 109, 110, 113
  meets Biddulph 108
tin 8
Tipton, John 185
Tithurst, Hertfordshire 119
Tittenhanger Hall, St Albans xvii, 117,
    119, 121, 237
  rebuilt 119
Tlemcen xvii, 181, 194, 200, 201, 208,
    209, 212, 213, 214, 215, 216, 217, 218
  famed libraries 213
tobacco 24, 120, 151

Tonkin, Boyd   226
Topal Recep Pasha, Grand Vizier   124
Topkapi Palace   xvi, 3, 4, 7, 11, 31,
     32, 36, 39, 40, 42, 43, 44, 45,
     59, 76, 125, 223
trade   34, 125, 126, 128, 133, 134, 137,
     139, 142, 144, 201
   Venetian   146
Trapezuntios, George   238
travel
   advice for   18, 90, 92, 102, 107, 127,
      128, 136, 140
   contamination from   53, 54, 64,
      72, 74, 97, 183
   dangers of   74
   and education   181
   and espionage   129, 140, 158
   as performance   3, 7, 37, 71, 91,
      126, 128, 140, 151, 152, 159,
      185, 197–200, 223
   by sea   12, 17, 24, 74
   for wager   160
travel writing, 18, 55, 130, 132, 183
   autobiography   188
   citationality   73
   condemned   55
   defended   53, 55
   epistolary mode   77, 78
   fictional   179
   mendacity of   52
   picaresque   181, 199, 217
   popularity of   4
   professionalization of   5
   romance   180
   sales of   55
Trinity College, Oxford   119
Tripoli, Syria   78, 82
Troy   24, 51, 89, 156
Tunisia   194
turbans   155
Turkey, Turks   xvi, 10, 18, 27,
     28, 34, 84, 85, 86, 87, 89, 90,
     92, 93, 97, 113, 122, 123, 129,
     130, 132, 133, 135, 136, 137,
     139, 140, 141, 148, 154, 167,
     172, 182, 189, 190, 192
   music   172
   stereotypes   15
   women   63
   see also Ottomans, languages, Turkish
Tyon, Jasper (also 'Tient')   51, 101, 235
Tyre   82

Uluç Hassan   185
Ummayid Mosque, Damascus   105
United Nations   106
Urfa   xv, 98

Van   xv
Venice, Venetians   17, 34, 36, 40,
     47, 57, 58, 59, 67, 74, 108, 109,
     120, 122, 124, 138, 139, 141,
     142, 146, 154, 165, 171
   Doge and Senate   59, 67
   merchants   124
vermin   30, 31, 82
Vestal virgins   20
Victoria, Queen   134
Vienna   136, 144
Vitkus, Daniel   xv
vultures   216

Walker, Robert   117
Walsingham, Sir Francis   120
Walton, Isaac   120
Warrington, Lancashire   xvii, 3
Warton, Thomas   119, 168, 169
Wase, Christopher, of Upper
     Holloway   117, 236
Wase, Christopher, writer   236
Washington, Thomas   73, 75
watermelon   82, 83
Watson, Michael ('Myghell')   10, 18, 19,
     21, 39, 47
wealth   xi, xiv, 181, 185, 186, 188, 191,
     195, 206, 217, 218, 219
Webb, John   119
Wentworth, Lady   222
Westminster   119
Westminster Hall   121, 151
Whitehall   3, 8, 39, 120
Williams, Raymond   xviii
wolves   82, 205
women   xviii, 16, 17, 20, 21, 40,
     44, 45, 46, 53, 79, 82, 88, 111,
     113, 181, 217, 222
   of Chios   29
   expatriate   221
   harem   11
   Jewish   175
   Maghrebian   181
   Moorish   15
   Muslim   15
   Turkish   15, 147
Wood, Anthony   118, 127

Worcester, battle
  of (1651) 181
Worcester Cathedral 6
Wragg, Richard 84
Wright, Louis B. 227
Wroth, John 232
Wyche, Lady 225
Wyche, Sir Peter 124, 125, 128,
  137, 225
Wyseman, Mr 26

Yarmouth 26
Yedi Kale 76
Yerasimos, Stephane 4

Yezidis 83, 112, 232–3
Young, Robert 76

Zabulon, son of Jacob 82
Zante xvii, 10, 17, 18, 19, 22,
  23, 46, 68, 74, 94, 112, 113,
  114, 151, 221
  anchorite of 19
  currant trade 74
Zara (Zadar) 142
Zidi Dockra Moukadem 205
Zidi Hamed Hochbush 215
'Zinganaes' *see* gipsies
Ziyyanid Empire 212, 213